Last Chance Byway

LAST CHANCE BYWAY

The History of Nine Mile Canyon

Jerry D. Spangler and Donna Kemp Spangler

THE UNIVERSITY OF UTAH PRESS
Salt Lake City

Publication of this book is made possible in part by a generous grant from the Bill Barrett Corporation.

 The Defiance House Man colophon is a registered trademark of the University of Utah Press. It is based on a four-foot-tall Ancient Puebloan pictograph (late PIII) near Glen Canyon, Utah.

20 19 18 17 16   1 2 3 4 5

LIBRARY OF CONGRESS CATALOGING-IN-PUBLICATION DATA
Spangler, Jerry D.
  Last chance byway : the history of Nine Mile Canyon / Jerry D.
    Spangler and Donna Kemp Spangler.
      pages cm
    Includes bibliographical references and index.
    ISBN 978-1-60781-442-9 (paperback : alkline paper)
    ISBN 978-1-60781-443-6 (ebook)
  1. Nine Mile Canyon (Utah)—History. 2. Nine Mile Canyon
    (Utah)—Biography. I. Spangler, Jerry D. II. Title.
    F832.N55S62 2015 979.2′566—dc23
                                            2015015507

Printed and bound in Malaysia.

Contents

Acknowledgments

The history of Nine Mile Canyon is both colorful and mundane. It involved iconic individuals with names familiar to most everyone, and many more that are familiar to no one outside of their descendants. It is a story of wealth and greed and poverty and determination. There is humor and there is tragedy. Each thread, when woven with the others, creates a tapestry of the life and times of a remarkable place.

The history of the canyon has been written in bits and snippets over the years by historians far more qualified than we are. Bert Jenson's knowledge of the Nine Mile Canyon freight road and the Smith Wells watering hole is unsurpassed. Gary Weicks has tirelessly worked to reconstruct the U.S. military history of not only Nine Mile Canyon but the broader Uinta Basin region. The late Joel Frandsen was tireless in tracking down every tidbit of information on lawmen and outlaws in the region, giving depth and breadth to the entire outlaw legacy. Ed Geary, whose family roots run deep in this country, is a limitless well of knowledge. Each of these historians contributed immeasurably to the preparation of this book.

There were many others, all passionate about the history of Nine Mile Canyon, who shouldered our requests for information and photographs with politeness and even enthusiasm. They willingly offered commentary and perspective, people like Dennis Willis, Pam and Blaine Miller, Roy Webb, Jeff Rust, Ray and Deanne Matheny, and James A. Aton. But most of all, the history of the first settlers here could not have been written without Norma Dalton and her friends at the Nine Mile Canyon Settlers Association, who have worked tirelessly for the past decade to record the oral histories and legends that have been passed down through the generations. Whether fact or something a little less so, these stories contribute to the tapestry revealed in the following pages.

Last Chance Byway is the story not only of a place but of the people who lived here and the events that changed a sleepy place where at times cows might have outnumbered people by a thousand-to-one. It would become one of the most vibrant economic districts anywhere in rural Utah, only to have it all crash quickly and spectacularly. Most of this history occurred within a mere fifty years, from 1886 to 1936. So much of the history remains to be written.

All errors of fact are ours and ours alone. Unless otherwise noted, all place names used in the following pages are in the state of Utah.

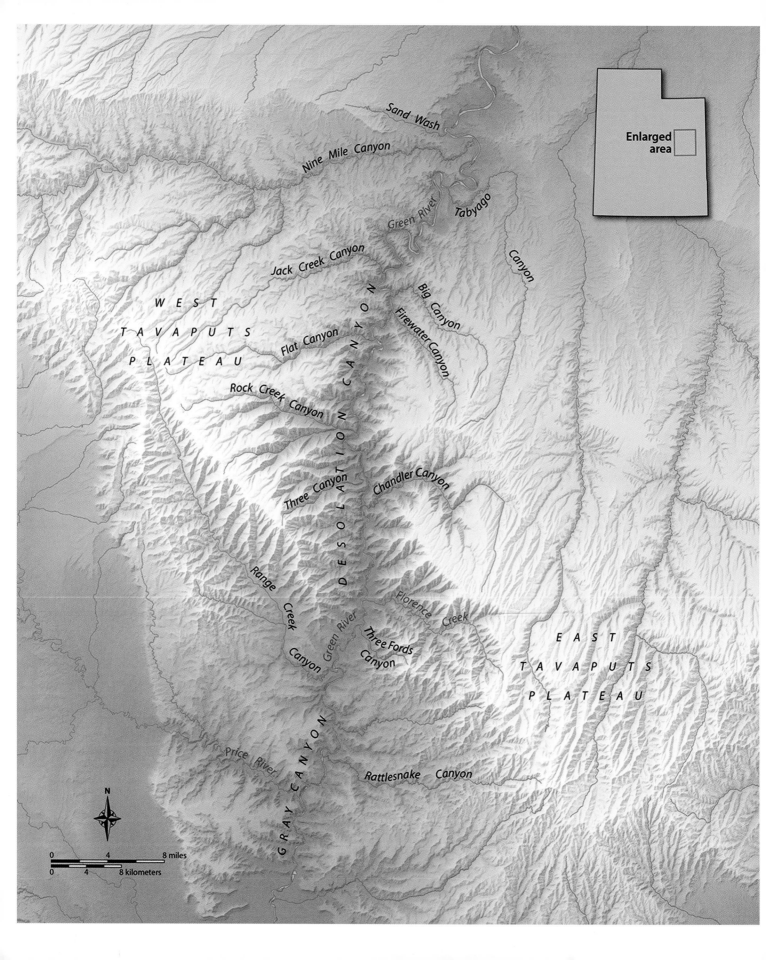

Enlarged area

Sand Wash

Nine Mile Canyon

Green River

Tabyago

Canyon

Jack Creek Canyon

WEST
TAVAPUTS
PLATEAU

Big Canyon

Firewater Canyon

DESOLATION CANYON

Flat Canyon

Rock Creek Canyon

Chandler Canyon

Three Canyon

Range

Creek

Florence

Creek

EAST
TAVAPUTS
PLATEAU

Green River

Three Fords
Canyon

Canyon

GRAY CANYON

Price River

Rattlesnake Canyon

N

0   4   8 miles
0   4   8 kilometers

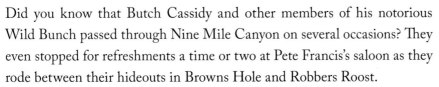

The Conundrum of Nine Mile

Country worthless, though imposing.
—Jack Sumner, 1869

Did you know that Butch Cassidy and other members of his notorious Wild Bunch passed through Nine Mile Canyon on several occasions? They even stopped for refreshments a time or two at Pete Francis's saloon as they rode between their hideouts in Browns Hole and Robbers Roost.

The few remaining old-timers in these parts repeat those tales with a twinkle in their eyes and a wry sense of certainty. It has to be true. They heard it from a mother or a father or a distant cousin who, more often than not, heard the account from someone else. But did it really happen?

Separating fact from fiction is nigh impossible when it comes to the brief but colorful history of Nine Mile Canyon. There are precious few written materials that pertain specifically to the earliest settlement of the canyon. Sure, there are a handful of early newspaper accounts, most of them related to freighting on the Nine Mile Road. And there are the personal papers of cattle baron Preston Nutter, although most of these were penned long after the canyon's raucous reputation had faded into the obscurity of semirespectability. And the earliest land records are almost nonexistent, since all of the first settlers were squatters without legal claim to the ranches they pioneered.

Who were these intrepid first Euro-American settlers of Nine Mile Canyon? When did they arrive here and how did they come by this oasis in a desert wilderness? And why did most of them pull up stakes and move on to greener pastures after a mere generation? There are no simple answers to those questions, although we will in the following pages offer a glimpse into the lives and personalities of the many figures who are woven into the historic fabric of Nine Mile Canyon. There were individuals

Opposite: Map of Tavaputs Plateau region with major drainages referenced in this volume.

Scenic view of Nine Mile Canyon alfalfa fields that dominate the canyon floodplain today. Alfalfa, also referred to as lucerne, is not native here but was brought into the canyon in the 1880s or 1890s by ranchers as more efficient forage for cattle. Photo by Ray Boren.

who were either famous or infamous, depending on your perspective, people like Robert Leroy Parker and Gunplay Maxwell, Sam Gilson and Preston Nutter. Many others passed their lives without the attendant notoriety of their contemporaries, whose important contributions have been largely ignored or forgotten, people like Cotton Rich, William Brock, and Shadrach Lunt.

The Euro-American history of Nine Mile Canyon is complex, and it cannot be told in traditional, linear fashion. Events surrounding the freighters on the Nine Mile Road occurred simultaneously with the emergence of cattle empires and the lawless element that preyed upon them. The story of Gilsonite cannot be told without the machinations of the Denver and Rio Grande Railroad and the economic transformation the railheads brought to Price. The story of Preston Nutter cannot be understood without the complexities of homesteading laws that allowed the dozens of small ranches to flower the landscape around, and sometimes inside, his sprawling empire. Amazingly, most of the events described hereafter occurred between 1886 and 1936—a span of only fifty years, to historians a mere blink of an eye. These stories understandably overlap from chapter to chapter, and some repetition we found to be unavoidable.

By all accounts, Nine Mile Canyon was one of the last places to be settled in the state of Utah, and it was one of only a handful where settlement occurred outside the patterns established by the Mormon Church—patterns which dictated uniform, orderly city blocks neatly arranged around a center of communal worship.[1] Nine Mile Canyon never had a townsite, a permanent community center, or a branch of the Mormon Church, which, as Edward Geary notes, "must make it almost unique among Utah communities."[2] Instead, Nine Mile Canyon evolved as a hodgepodge of scattered ranches and saloons with scarcely any central gathering place, although there were post offices and voting precincts, places that carried monikers like Brock, Harper, and Minnie-Maud.

Whatever the appellation, Nine Mile was unquestionably a rowdy place crowded with freighters, cattlemen, innkeepers, barkeeps, soldiers, blacksmiths, outlaws, charlatans, hooligans, and sodbusters battling the twin demons of floods and drought to coax their reluctant crops from the soil. It was an eclectic social quilt of Mormon families, many with roots in the Price and Vernal areas, and non-Mormons who found refuge here from the religious and economic elements that characterized most other Utah communities at that time.

From the mid-1880s through the 1910s, Nine Mile Canyon was one of the most colorful and economically vibrant districts in the entire state, by some accounts "The Lifeline of the Uintah Basin."[3] By the 1920s, the halcyon days of Nine Mile Canyon were over, and only a handful of the toughest—a more accurate description might be *stubborn*—ranchers remained behind to tend their herds and alfalfa fields.

Of course, the Euro-Americans who arrived here in the late 1800s were not the first to lay claim to the canyon. Hunters and gatherers—nomadic clans who followed the ripening of seeds and the movement of game—had passed through Nine Mile Canyon for thousands of years, during what archaeologists call the Archaic period. By about A.D. 600 (perhaps even a few centuries before) small groups of farmers began to settle in the canyon,

The subtle beauty of wildflowers in Nine Mile Canyon. Photo by Ray Boren.

Ancient cliff ruins in Nine Mile Canyon are reminders of the ancient Fremont culture—farmers and foragers who lived here for a millennium before abandoning the canyon about A.D. 1300. Photo by Jerry D. Spangler.

growing their maize and squash along the creek, and also gathering nuts and seeds and hunting game in the higher elevations above the canyon bottom. These are referred to today as Fremont farmer-foragers, and by about A.D. 1000 there were lots of Fremont people living here—perhaps more than any other time before or since. But by A.D. 1250, their crops had been devastated by repeated and persistent droughts, and most of the Fremont abandoned Nine Mile Canyon, leaving behind thousands of rock art images as a haunting testament to their sojourn here. In their wake came the ancestors of the modern Ute Indians—themselves gatherers of seeds and hunters of bighorn sheep, elk, and deer.[4]

But this is the story of the last to arrive: the cowboys and farmers, the outlaws and lawmen, the businessmen, opportunists, and speculators. Most of the characters, at least the most colorful ones, were never permanent residents here, and some never lived here at all. But their impact on the history of the canyon was profound nonetheless. In fact, only a few families put down roots here, and of those that did, few stayed all that long. It was and still is a tough place to make a living, made tougher by boom-and-bust cycles of beef prices and the all-too-predictable droughts that could turn grasslands into wastelands. Only three ranching families actually live in Nine Mile Canyon today, and none spends the entire winter there. Nine Mile Canyon is, on most days, still a lonely place but for the rumble of trucks servicing the natural gas wells on the plateau above, and the occasional tourist marveling at the rock art galleries.

Nine Mile Canyon is but a small part of what geographers refer to as the West Tavaputs Plateau, named for a Uintah Ute chief of the 1870s.[5] The highest reaches of the plateau at 10,000 feet elevation are blanketed in lush forests of aspen and Engelmann spruce interspersed with thick grasses and sage, a virtual Eden for elk and mule deer, as well as the predators who feed on them. The high plateau dips, sometimes gently, sometimes precipitously, northward toward the Uinta Basin.[6] The Green River and its spectacularly wild Desolation Canyon form the eastern boundary of the West Tavaputs Plateau, and the seemingly impenetrable escarpment of the Book Cliffs—those towering stone walls visible to every motorist traveling on U.S. 6 between Price and Grand Junction—defines the southern periphery. The west side merges into the high divide of the Wasatch Plateau where some streams flow east toward the Green River and others flow west into the Great Basin. Nine Mile Canyon and the myriad side drainages that feed into it are nestled along the northern edge of the West Tavaputs Plateau, bordered by the Badland Cliffs on the north.

Ancient Fremont rock art is especially common in Nine Mile Canyon, enough so that it is referred to as "The World's Longest Art Gallery." Archaeologists estimate there are more than one hundred thousand individual images pecked and painted on the canyon walls. Photo by Ray Boren.

The high West Tavaputs Plateau marks the southern edge of the Uinta Basin, which is visible in the distance. The plateau highlands are rich in deer, elk, bear, and other wildlife. Photo by Jerry D. Spangler.

Chief Tavaputs, a Ute leader of the 1800s, is the namesake for the Tavaputs Plateau—a vast area hundreds of square miles on both the east and west sides of the Green River. Used by permission, Utah State Historical Society, all rights reserved.

The West Tavaputs Plateau is a fearsome land: part cathedral, part inferno, all of it formidable and defiant.[7] It has invariably been described as dreary, desolate, and even frightening in its isolation. "Country worthless, though imposing," is how Jack Sumner, a diarist on John Wesley Powell's 1869 Colorado River Exploring Expedition, first described it.[8] It is mostly arid but for a few isolated springs known to every weather-beaten cattle rancher who, without exception, exudes worshipful respect for the awesome powers that created such a daunting landscape.

By and large, the West Tavaputs Plateau has defied human attempts to tame it. As such it remains one of the last great wildernesses in North America, brushed only by a cadre of river adventurers floating the Green River along the eastern boundary and weekend motorists who traverse the Nine Mile Canyon Road, now paved, that skirts its northern periphery.

It takes a special breed to venture into the heart of these wilds, fearless but cautious and prepared for the worst demons imaginable. Men like Major John Wesley Powell, the intrepid, one-armed Civil War veteran who, despite his own ambitious claims, was probably not the first white man to descend the Green River through Desolation Canyon. But his was a journey that inspired a public romance with this wild, unknown region and those who dared challenge the forces of nature. Frederick Dellenbaugh, who was only seventeen years old at the time he accompanied Powell's 1871 expedition down the Green and Colorado Rivers, captured the romanticism of that era, writing of the fearsome challenges of those rivers:

> [It was]...a match of human skill and muscle against rocks and cataracts, shut in from the outer world, always face to face with the Shadow of Death. It was to be a duel to the finish between the mysterious torrents on one side and a little group of valiant men on the other. Never had plumed knight of old a more dreadful antagonist. Like the Sleeping Beauty, this strange Problem lay in the midst of an enchanted land guarded by the wizard of Aridity and those wonderful water-gods Erosion and Corrasion [*sic*], waiting for the knight errant brave, who should break the spell and vanquish the demon to his lair.[9]

Most of the West Tavaputs Plateau remains wilderness. But these days, this landscape seems far less impregnable than it did in 1871, or even in 1971, as developers push forward with new technologies that have opened portions of the plateau to natural gas drilling. Roads now snake their way into remote areas of the high plateau to service the wells, and bright electrical lights from the twenty-four-hour-a-day pumping of natural gas illuminate the night sky. The splendid isolation that inspired the 1871 explorers is slowly eroding.

The human history of Nine Mile Canyon and the surrounding West Tavaputs Plateau cannot be unfolded without an appreciation of this remarkable landscape. To river-runners splashing their way down the Green River, the Tavaputs Plateau is a swirl of sandstone bathed in the gold hues of rising and setting sun, marked only by occasional glimpses of bashful bighorns or the whispery flight of passing waterfowl. To motorists paying homage to the thousands of ancient rock art images in Nine Mile Canyon, it is a ribbon of alfalfa fields guarded by canyon walls studded

Green River at the mouth of Nine Mile Canyon. The green flatlands are part of what was once Preston Nutter's "lower" ranch. Photo by Jerry D. Spangler.

John Wesley Powell would have passed the mouth of Nine Mile Canyon on his initial expedition in 1869, and his crew passed again in 1871. There is no indication any of them stopped here or even knew of its existence. Photo courtesy of the U.S. Geological Survey Photographic Library.

with the dark green hues of pinyon and juniper. To cattle ranchers, it is a tapestry of canyons and alpine meadows rich in livestock fodder, to sportsmen a paradise for herds of trophy deer and elk.[10] To archaeologists, it is an untapped library of ancient secrets.

The West Tavaputs Plateau, with its crown jewels Nine Mile Canyon, Range Creek, and Desolation Canyon, is all of that and more. It is a massive landscape stretching as far as the eye can see—hundreds of square miles of plateaus, canyons, cliffs, mesas, hoodoos, spires, arches, alcoves, and other Gothic formations that overwhelm the senses. On one extreme, there are the lush alpine meadows at 10,000 feet elevation, briskly cool in the summer and buried by deep snows in the winter. On the other extreme, the furnace-like deserts at about 4,500 feet seem to resist the encroachment of plants and animals alike. In between are vast expanses of formidable canyon terrain carpeted with hardy evergreens, and, in a few cases, flowing water that nurtures life in all its glorious shades.

Water is and always has been the lifeblood of this desert region. Where there is water, there are also plants and animals of economic importance

to humans. It is not surprising, then, that humans would choose to live in proximity to those resources needed for daily sustenance. Nine Mile Creek was and remains an important source of water that has influenced every economic twist of fate that has defined the Euro-American history of this canyon, whether it was habitat for beaver, or quenching the thirst of draft animals making the arduous journey between Price and Fort Duchesne, or the watering of alfalfa fields that provided essential winter feed for the cattle.

Once nearly eradicated by overhunting and diseases carried by domestic sheep, wild bighorns are now common throughout the West Tavaputs Plateau. Photo courtesy of the Colorado Plateau Archaeological Alliance.

Puzzles and Paradoxes

Nine Mile Creek in the fall. The creek was probably much bigger in the days before farmers began diverting it for irrigation in the 1880s. Photo by Ray Boren.

So much of the history of Nine Mile Canyon remains shrouded in tales that can neither be proven nor debunked, all of which creates a frustrating puzzle for those trying to piece together the canyon's history. For example, one popular account has it that the wagon road through Gate Canyon, the major side drainage midway down Nine Mile that afforded the easiest travel route to and from the Uinta Basin, once passed below a massive arch. The constant rumble of freight traffic and stage coaches would sometimes dislodge small rocks that would fall on the wagons passing through "the gate." In about 1905, the arch was determined to be at risk of imminent collapse, and Newt Stewart was hired to blow it up.[11]

But did that really happen? Descendants of the original Nine Mile settlers hold to the Newt Stewart version as gospel truth. And like holy pilgrims, the true believers can and will take you to the exact spot where the deed happened.

But a different version survives among Ute tribal members living in the Uinta Basin. By their account, it was U.S. Army troops from Fort Duchesne who brought artillery into Gate Canyon and set about destroying the arch in a training exercise. They can even show you where errant cannon balls slammed into the cliff walls, scarring the vertical cliff faces with deep, unnatural bowls. Understandably, the Utes have no abiding reverence for what the military did to their sacred land.[12]

We may never know the exact sequence of events that led to the destruction of the arch, or whether it even happened. There are no surviving photographs of the arch, and there is no mention in the few historic documents of any arch in Gate Canyon. In fact, the only written account of any kind is the one found in a roadside guide written eighty years after the fact, drawn from Stewart family recollections of the incident.

It seems odd that no one would have mentioned the arch during the decades before its alleged demise in 1905. A road passing below a natural

The location where old-timers say the original Gate Canyon arch was located. Photo by Jerry D. Spangler.

Ute legend has it the scars on the cliff face here were reportedly made by artillery fire as troops from Fort Duchesne blew up the arch. Photo by Jerry D. Spangler.

arch would have, indeed should have, evoked awe and wonder among diarists of the day. Thousands of people would have passed through the arch before 1905, but apparently not a word was written about it.

Maybe the Gate Canyon arch was exactly as represented in legend and lore. And if that is true, then sadly a geologic wonder was destroyed. Later on, Newt Stewart said it was a "shame" the arch was destroyed. "I don't know how long that arch had been there, but considering what it took to blow it down, if it had been there for 5,000 years, it would have stood for another 5,000."[13]

Perhaps the most perplexing conundrum here is the incongruously named canyon itself. It is not nine miles long, as the name implies. Rather it is forty-five miles from the mouth to the point it splits into two major branches, and then another twenty miles or more to the headwaters. So how did the canyon get its rather paradoxical name? There are plenty of local folk tales, even more assertions of fact that cannot be substantiated. According to *Utah Place Names: A Comprehensive Guide to the Origins of Geographic Names*, the canyon was so named because it is nine miles long—a spurious claim indeed.[14]

Another legend has it that W. A. Miles settled the canyon with his wife and seven daughters, hence the "nine Miles."[15] And while the Miles family is intertwined with the history of the region, the drainage was known as "Nine Mile" years before the Miles family arrived here. Most accounts today, repeated authoritatively through scores of Internet postings about the canyon, attribute the name to Captain Francis Marion Bishop, a cartographer on Major John Wesley Powell's Colorado River Exploring Expedition of 1871 (the Internet postings frequently and erroneously attribute Bishop's participation to the 1869 expedition).[16] According to the official Bureau of Land Management website for the canyon, Bishop "used a nine-mile transect for mapping the canyon," and hence he is responsible for the canyon's name.[17]

The only problem with this story is that neither of Powell's expeditions in 1869 and 1871 stopped anywhere near Nine Mile Canyon, and Bishop certainly did not conduct a "nine-mile transect" there.[18] And though the journals of the expedition participants make mention of a Nine Mile Creek—the first references anywhere to a creek by that name—the stream they were referring to is known today as Rock Creek, located deep in the heart of Desolation Canyon about forty miles to the south.[19]

So if today's Nine Mile Creek is not the Nine Mile Creek of the 1871 Powell expeditions, what was its name at that time? Some historians believe Nine Mile Creek could be the Euwinty River referred to in the 1825 journals of William Ashley, although others dismiss this idea.[20] Ashley clearly made a distinction between the Tewinty River, which became known as the Uintah River to trappers, and the Euwinty River quite some distance to the south (more on this in chapter 2).

Fur trappers certainly knew about the creek, but what did they call it? Famed trapper Warren Angus Ferris in 1836 reconstructed a map of the

The name Nine Mile Canyon is credited to Francis Marion Bishop, a cartographer on the second Powell expedition who reportedly made a nine-mile triangulation here in 1871. But this never happened. Used by permission, Utah State Historical Society, all rights reserved.

An 1836 map of the Uinta Basin created by fur trapper Warren Angus Ferris. The Duchesne River depicted here is in the approximate location of Nine Mile Creek today. Image from *My Life in the Rocky Mountains*, courtesy of L. Tom Perry Special Collections, Harold B. Lee Library, Brigham Young University.

Uinta Basin and noted the presence of a stream far to the south of the Uintah River—in the approximate location of Nine Mile Creek—but he called it the Duchesne River. Historian Dale Morgan pondered: "Is it possible the name migrated north?"[21]

This notion is not that far-fetched. In 1845, famed explorer John C. Fremont published a map of the Uinta Basin, pinpointing the location of Fort Uinta at the "forks" where the Uintah River and Whiterocks River join. Well to the south of Fort Uinta he depicts two other major "forks" draining to the Green River, one called "Duchesne Fork" and the other called "Red Fork." Since neither of the forks that carry those names today drain into the Green River directly, could it be that Fremont (and Ferris before him) were referring to something altogether different? Perhaps it was Nine Mile Creek?[22]

By 1866, a General Land Office map of the area shows two different streams labeled White River, one on the east side of the Green River (it is still called the White River today) and the other on the west side in the

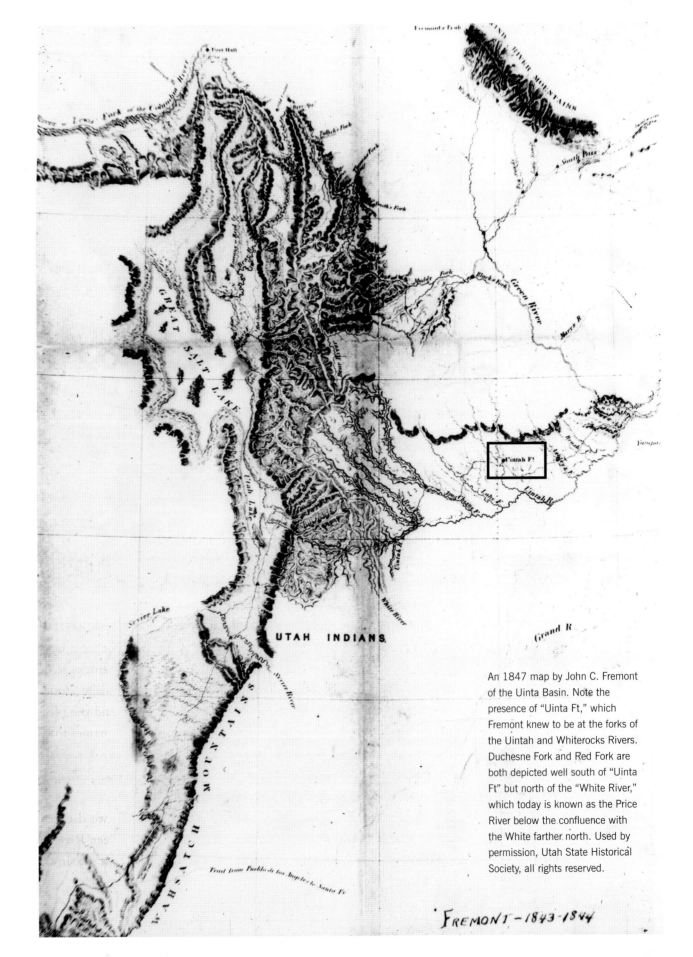

An 1847 map by John C. Fremont of the Uinta Basin. Note the presence of "Uinta Ft," which Fremont knew to be at the forks of the Uintah and Whiterocks Rivers. Duchesne Fork and Red Fork are both depicted well south of "Uinta Ft" but north of the "White River," which today is known as the Price River below the confluence with the White farther north. Used by permission, Utah State Historical Society, all rights reserved.

This 1879 General Land Office map by C. Roeser is the earliest map to use the name 9 Mile Cr. for the upper, south fork of Minnie Maud Creek. Image courtesy of Special Collections, Marriott Library, University of Utah.

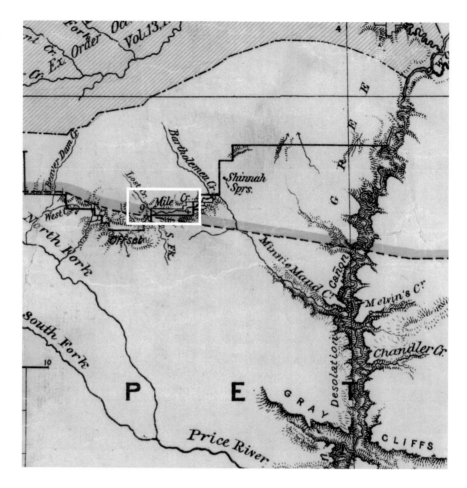

The origins of the name Minnie Maud are likewise clouded in local lore.[29] Geary cites local accounts that the name might have an aboriginal origin that is sometimes spelled "Minniemaud," but there is no citation for the source of that information.[30] Another account has it that the canyon was named for two twin sisters, Minnie and Maud Hall, born in Escalante, Utah, in 1893, and who moved to the canyon the following year, although this also occurred seventeen years after the creek first carried the Minnie Maud name.[31]

Another popular account suggests that Major Powell named the creek for two relatives, Minnie and Maud, and there appears to be some support for this particular legend, albeit with some revisions. A review of records at *FamilySearch.org* found that Major Powell's brother, William Bramwell "Bram" Powell, married Wilhelmina "Minnie" Paul Bengelstraeter. Together, they had a daughter, Maud, born August 22, 1867, in Peru,

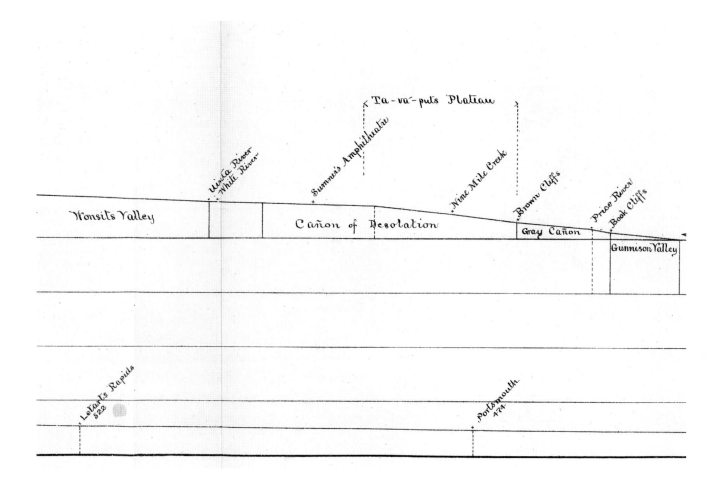

The profile map of Desolation Canyon included in Powell's *Arid Lands* report of 1879 depicts Nine Mile Creek about forty miles to the south of today's Nine Mile Creek, at what is now known as Rock Creek.

Illinois. No reference was found in the database that Maud went by Minnie Maud, but according to Maud's biographer, Karen A. Shaffer, her actual given name was Minnie Maud, though she later dropped the Minnie once her professional career blossomed.[32]

Donald Worster's authoritative biography of Major Powell states that Maud was a child prodigy on the violin, debuting with the New York Philharmonic Society at the age of sixteen. She formed her own Maud Powell String Quartet and played the leading concert halls of Europe.[33] She would have been about nine or ten years old and first emerging as an acclaimed child violinist in Illinois when the creek in eastern Utah came to bear her name.

Major Powell's fondness for his accomplished niece apparently continued in the decades that followed, even though fame spirited Maud away to London and the Major off to Washington, D.C., where he later directed the

Almon Harris Thompson, the brother-in-law to John Wesley Powell, conducted stream tests on Minnie Maud Creek in 1877. The stream carried that name through at least 1947. Used by permission, Utah State Historical Society, all rights reserved.

Bureau of Ethnology and the U.S. Geological Survey. When Bram Powell moved to Washington, D.C., to become superintendent of public schools, Maud was a frequent visitor to her uncle's house on M Street where she entertained Washington's scientific and political elite with her musical virtuosity.[34] If the Minnie Maud name can be attributed to Major Powell's favorite niece, then Powell must have had some influence over the creation of the 1876 General Land Office map, released two years before his own map. Powell's use of the name Nine Mile Valley in 1878 for the upper south fork of Minnie Maud Creek is the only map reference by that name. Beginning in 1879, this fork was known as Nine Mile Creek or 9 Mile Creek.[35]

The fact Powell used the name Minnie Maud Creek implies that Powell recognized a distinction between Minnie Maud Creek on the north and Nine Mile Creek (today's Rock Creek) on the south, although the latter is not mentioned in the *Arid Lands Report*. It can also be inferred that today's Nine Mile Canyon, explored and tested for its water potential in 1877, was unnamed at the time of the Colorado River Exploring Expeditions of 1869 and 1871, and that it was probably unknown to the participants at that time, thereby requiring a new appellation wherein Powell honored his niece (she was also Thompson's niece, and we should not rule out the possibility that Thompson, not Powell, named it). It would also support the contention that Rock Creek today is and was the Nine Mile Creek of the 1871 Colorado River Exploring Expedition.

So how did Minnie Maud Creek become Nine Mile Creek? Therein is a riddle that escapes easy solution. Official government maps continue to use the name Minnie Maud Creek through at least 1947, and many locals with deep roots in the canyon still use that name.[36] But the name Nine Mile Creek was being used in the popular media by at least 1890 for the entire drainage, when the *Deseret News* referred to two names for the stream, "Minnie Maud, or Nine Mile Creek."[37]

It is certainly possible that the name Nine Mile Creek, which had been reserved for only the upper south fork, became popular because the freight road, which had been established by 1886, followed this fork, and maybe travelers found it impossible to know where this fork ended and Minnie Maud began.

What is clear is the name Nine Mile Creek and Minnie Maud Creek were used interchangeably throughout the history of this region, even though official government maps consistently used the Minnie Maud Creek label until fairly recent times. Even as the canyon became known as Nine Mile Canyon, the creek was still Minnie Maud Creek. Today, both the creek and the canyon are referred to as Nine Mile, with the Minnie Maud name reserved only for the northern tributary.

And therein is another mystery. From 1879 through 1911, the north fork now known as Minnie Maud was labeled on the maps of the day as Bartholomew Creek. Who was Bartholomew? We haven't a clue.

Maud Powell was the beloved niece of John Wesley Powell, as well as niece to Almon Thompson, who was married to Powell's sister, Emma. Her biographer indicates she was born Minnie Maud Powell, but dropped the Minnie once she became a famous musician. Photo courtesy of Karen A. Shaffer, Maud Powell Society, Brevard, North Carolina.

Beaver Fever

William Ashley and the Discovery of Nine Mile Canyon

This place [Fort Robidoux] is equal to any I ever saw for wickedness and idleness. The French and Spaniards are...as wicked men, I think, as ever lived.
—CHRISTIAN MISSIONARY JOSEPH WILLIAMS, 1842

It is impossible to know with certainty who were the first Euro-Americans to leave their boot prints in Nine Mile Canyon. It might have been Spanish and Mexican traders out of New Mexico in search of more efficient trade routes, and Nine Mile Canyon certainly was a good route if you wanted to go north to the Uinta Mountains from New Mexico. But the Spanish were probably more interested in a shorter east-west route to their garrisons in California, not one leading farther north.

And there is no evidence, apocryphal or otherwise, that Spanish exploration ever took them through Nine Mile Canyon, unlike the Uinta Basin where legends of Spanish gold mines abound and there are reports of Spanish-era artifacts and inscriptions. One exception could be what Mildred Dillman, the grand dame of Nine Mile Canyon history, referred to as "Spanish carvings...found in the old Fort on the Miles ranch," although she did not explain why she believed them to be "Spanish."[1]

The initial trade route chosen by the Spanish was through the Uinta Basin, about fifty miles to the north of Nine Mile Canyon. The Spanish *entrada* is commonly attributed to Fathers Francisco Atanasio Domínguez and Silvestre Velez de Escalante, who in 1776 made an epic journey north through western Colorado and then west through the Uinta Basin and eventually to Utah Lake, then south into the St. George area.[2] The expedition, which had been dispatched to find a northern route from New

Nine Mile Canyon wildflowers.
Photo by Ray Boren.

Scenic view of Nine Mile Canyon. Photo by Ray Boren.

Mexico to Monterrey, California, was ultimately a failure, but it remains a remarkable story of human survival in an unknown land.

Although written accounts are indeed rare, Spanish traders, and perhaps missionaries, returned to the Utah Lake area, presumably using the northerly Uinta Basin route pioneered by Domínguez and Escalante, throughout the early 1800s. Accounts of trading in horses and slaves are common enough to indicate the Spanish knew the region by at least 1805,[3] and permanent trade with the Utah Utes had been established by 1813, although this trade was technically illegal at that time.[4] Historian Floyd O'Neil cited historic Spanish documents to "show that there was a very considerable traffic between the Yutes and the Spaniards during the years 1776 and 1830."[5] Any of these early forays could have led to the discovery of Nine Mile Canyon.

The northerly route through the Uinta Basin eventually proved much too long, and subsequent Spanish expeditions commonly chose more direct

"Old Fort" above the Miles Ranch where "Spanish carvings" were once noted. No such carvings were observed here when the site was redocumented by archaeologists in 1989. Photo by Jerry D. Spangler.

Caleb Rhoades, pictured here with his wife, Sidse, was among the very first settlers of Price in 1878, and by 1879 he was in Nine Mile Canyon. Photo courtesy of the Bernie Rhoades Family.

Opposite: Map indicating the location of major nineteenth-century trade and fur trapper routes and trading posts (1776 to 1850).

routes through central Utah, collectively referred to as the Old Spanish Trail, which twisted their way through the San Rafael Swell and bypassed the Utah Lake area altogether.[6] According to popular accounts, however, the Spanish were operating gold mines in the Uinta Mountains as late as the 1870s. Thomas Rhoades, and later his son Caleb, generated considerable public interest with claims that Ute Chief Wakara had shown the elder Rhoades deposits of lost Spanish gold in the Uinta Mountains.[7] The legend of the Lost Rhoades Mines remains a colorful fixture of Utah folklore. Most serious scholars believe any claims of secret Spanish gold are imaginative. But one fact is inescapable even to skeptics: there are Spanish artifacts in the region. Respected historian John D. Barton indicated he had personally observed Spanish-made bridle bits, spurs, and cannon balls that had been found in the Uinta Basin.[8]

Almost every area in Utah has folklore about Spanish gold cached away for safekeeping. Sometimes the story is twisted a bit to be Aztec gold hidden from the Spanish. But the stories all have a recurrent theme: vast treasures of gold awaiting discovery by a seeker worthy enough to decipher the clues. Interestingly, the Nine Mile area has no such legends of lost mines or hidden Spanish gold or treasure maps.

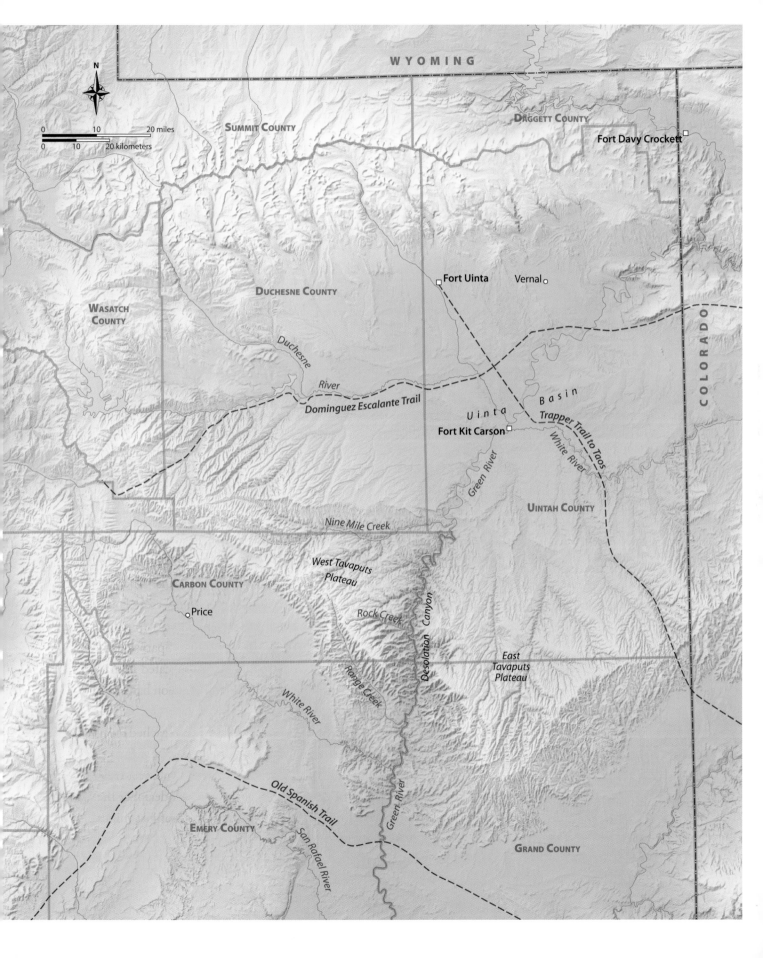

WYOMING

N

0   10   20 miles
0   10   20 kilometers

SUMMIT COUNTY

DAGGETT COUNTY

Fort Davy Crockett

DUCHESNE COUNTY

Fort Uinta   Vernal

WASATCH
COUNTY

Duchesne

River
Dominguez Escalante Trail

U i n t a   B a s i n

Trapper Trail to Taos

Fort Kit Carson

Green River

White River

COLORADO

Nine Mile Creek

UINTAH COUNTY

West Tavaputs
Plateau

CARBON COUNTY

Price

Rock Creek

Desolation Canyon

East
Tavaputs
Plateau

Range Creek

White River

Green River

Old Spanish Trail

EMERY COUNTY

San Rafael River

GRAND COUNTY

The 1879 "Rhoades" inscription found at the mouth of Pinnacle Canyon, a tributary to Nine Mile Canyon. This is probably Caleb Rhoades. Photo by Jerry D. Spangler.

But it does have Caleb Rhoades. At the mouth of Pinnacle Canyon, a southern tributary to Nine Mile Canyon, is a faded inscription that reads "Rhoades 1879"—the year after Caleb Rhoades and the extended Powell family arrived in what would become Price.

The Quest for Beaver

The first Euro-Americans to gaze on Nine Mile Canyon were probably fur trappers in pursuit of beaver pelts coveted by haberdashers the world over. Why our confidence in this statement when there is precious little archaeological or historic evidence for it? Quite simply, our reasoning is based on two lines of evidence: (1) Nine Mile Creek has a beaver population today and it most certainly had beaver almost two centuries ago when the fur trade flourished, and (2) the Uinta Basin, only a short distance north of Nine Mile Canyon, was teeming with fur trappers by the mid-1820s, enough of them to warrant the construction of trading posts. As the beaver-rich environs of the Uinta Mountains, Wasatch Plateau, and Wind River Mountains became more and more crowded with trappers, and the beaver became less and less plentiful there, the West Tavaputs Plateau to the south of the Uinta Basin trading posts would have become more attractive. Nine Mile Creek might not have been rich in beaver, but it had beaver nonetheless.

When this happened is not known with certainty, but the fur trade had certainly become well established in the Uinta Basin by 1825, and it does not stretch the imagination that trappers and traders would have explored

Beaver, such as this one swimming in the Green River near the mouth of Nine Mile Canyon, were probably never plentiful in Nine Mile Creek and other streams in the area, but they were most certainly present here. Photo by Dan Miller.

Many believe the inscription above dated "1818" near the mouth of Sheep Canyon is the oldest in Nine Mile Canyon, but it is actually a hoax. In 1931, the "1818" inscription actually read "1918" (left). Top photo by Jerry Spangler; photo at left courtesy of the Peabody Museum of Archaeology and Ethnology, Harvard University, PM 971-21-10/100162.1.6 (digital file #98470001).

every nook and cranny within hundreds of miles of any trading post at that time.[9] Polly Schaafsma mentions an 1819 inscription in Nine Mile Canyon, and, "according to the Nutters, this is the date when the first French Trappers appeared in the area." The location of the inscription was not given, and no such dated inscription has since been located.[10]

Another inscription commonly attributed to the trappers is "J.F. 1818" at the mouth of Sheep Canyon, a southern tributary in upper Nine Mile Canyon. But a 1931 photograph in the possession of the Peabody Museum at Harvard University clearly indicates the original inscription read 1918 and that the "9" was later modified into an "8"—in other words the early 1800s date is a hoax.

Monument to Utah fur trappers and explorers Etienne Provost, John C. Fremont, and others at *This Is the Place State Park* in Salt Lake City. Photo by Jerry D. Spangler.

The Euro-American fur trade in the Rocky Mountains began in about 1811 or 1812 when American trappers with John Jacob Astor's company explored an unknown region south of the Missouri River drainage. There is no indication they ventured into the Uinta Basin or anywhere near Nine Mile Canyon at that time. Rather, historical documents place the opening of the Uinta Basin fur trade at about 1824. That year, French-Canadian trapper Etienne Provost, at the time with the American Fur Company, led a party of trappers from Taos into the Green River region while traveling to the Great Salt Lake.[11] Also in 1824, Antoine Robidoux, a trapper from St. Louis, wrote the *Missouri Intelligencer* that he also had led a trapping party from Taos to the Green River. It is possible Robidoux and Provost traveled together from New Mexico to the Uinta Basin in 1824, and that Robidoux split off from Provost to explore the Green River region.[12]

William Hubbard, also of Missouri, led a third party into the Uinta Basin in 1824, indicating in a brief account in the *Missouri Intelligencer* that he "accidentally fell in with five other Americans, among whom was Mr. Rubideau."[13] Somewhere in the region, Antoine Robidoux's party was attacked by Arapaho Indians, who killed two trappers and confiscated furs and mules. Sometime after the attack, Robidoux met up with about twenty-five of Provost's men and traveled with them to Taos in what is today New Mexico.[14]

Floating the Green

A central figure in the Uinta Basin fur trade—and the first character that might have been directly tied to the history of Nine Mile Canyon—was famed fur trader William Ashley, who entered the region in the spring of 1825 to supply trappers at an annual rendezvous, a "trappers' flea market" of sorts. A rendezvous always featured plenty of horse racing, gambling, liquor, and other vices, but in reality it was a means whereby Ashley could acquire furs from Native Americans and "free" trappers not affiliated with trading companies. It also meant the trappers need not transport their furs all the way to St. Louis or Taos—the two fur trading hubs of the day. They could remain in the mountains and have more time to trap beaver. Ashley was the quintessential "middle man" who bought the pelts "wholesale" and then transported them to market, all at a hefty markup.

William Ashley was indeed a remarkable figure in the history of the West. He spent most of his adult life in the then-frontier town of St. Louis, where he garnered a reputation for "energy, ambition, and imagination as well as political savvy." Ashley was elected Missouri lieutenant governor in 1820, and the following year he and Andrew Henry partnered up in a trapping business on the upper Missouri River. But by 1823 the venture failed. So Ashley did what many failed businessmen do even today: he ran for public office. He lost the race for governor of Missouri by only a few votes. Broke from the costs of the campaign, he headed west in the fall of 1824, a desperate forty-six-year-old giving it one more chance.[15]

On April 22, 1825, while camped along the Green River north of Green River, Wyoming, Ashley split his company into four parties, sending three of them overland. Ashley's group, consisting of seven trappers, was

Ashley Falls, named for William H. Ashley, as it appeared in 1871. Photo courtesy of the U.S. Geological Survey Photographic Library, J. K. Hillers Collection.

determined to travel south into the Uinta Basin by floating the Green River.[16] This river had been known to the Spanish as the San Buenaventura, and to the trappers it was the Seeds-ke-dee, a Crow name meaning prairie hen. The Spanish also called it Rio Verde, and William Ashley, who had earlier referred to it as the Seeds-ke-dee, on June 7, 1825, made the first written reference to "Green River," a name it still carries today.[17]

Ashley fashioned two crude boats of cottonwood poles that were then wrapped with buffalo hides. Lacking resin or tar, the seams were waterproofed with buffalo tallow. Near the northern foothills of the Uinta Mountains, Ashley cached most of the knives, cloth, powder, traps, and other supplies needed for the rendezvous; the balance was carried on the boats for the purpose of trading for horses. The boats were overweight, and a portion of the trade goods were subsequently cached near the mouth of Henrys Fork just before entering the rapids below Flaming Gorge.[18]

According to the recollections of trapper James Beckwourth, Ashley's attempt to float the Green River was an epic adventure filled with peril, particularly for Ashley who could not swim.[19] At one spot, now named Ashley Falls, Ashley painted his name and the date "1825" on a rock face with vermilion paint. This signature was noted by John Sumner during John Wesley Powell's 1869 Colorado River Exploring Expedition[20] and again in 1871 when Walter Clement Powell, a participant in Powell's second expedition, added the inscription "Colorado River Exp. 1871" just below the Ashley inscription.[21] Frederick Dellenbaugh, another 1871 participant, wrote: "The letters were in black, just under slight projection and were surprisingly distinct considering the 46 years of exposure."[22]

Upon emerging from Split Mountain, Ashley's party encountered French trappers from Taos belonging to the company of Etienne Provost and Francois Leclerc. Ashley cached additional quantities of his trading goods just below the confluence of Ashley Creek. A short time later, on May 20, 1825, the water-saturated buffalo-hide boats were abandoned, and on May 21, Ashley's party reached the mouth of the Uintah River (called the Tewinty River by the Utes at that time), where he cached the remainder of his trade goods.[23] At this point, Ashley dispatched three trappers to procure game for his return trip. Ashley and the remaining three trappers hollowed out a cottonwood tree into a crude dugout canoe and continued down the Green River in hopes of finding Utes from whom they could purchase horses. On about May 27, 1825, the Ashley party camped near the mouth of another river, called the Euwinty River, where they encountered Utes willing to trade two horses.[24]

Historians still debate long and hard as to how far Ashley actually floated on the Green River and what was the Euwinty River where he stopped. Some historians believe Ashley abandoned the canoes at the mouth of Nine Mile Creek before returning overland to the Uinta Basin.[25] John D. Barton makes the case Ashley traveled only as far as the confluence of the White River.[26] James M. Aton believes Ashley never made it as far as Nine Mile Creek, but rather stopped about eighteen miles below Willow Creek "somewhere above the mouth" of Nine Mile Canyon.[27]

If the Euwinty River was indeed Nine Mile Creek, then Ashley might have been the first to write about the canyon itself. On June 1, 1825, Ashley wrote that he rode twenty-four miles up the Euwinty River where he camped for the night to await the arrival of French trappers with whom he planned to trade for more horses.[28] If the Euwinty River was Nine Mile Creek, then twenty-four miles would have put him somewhere near the mouth of Gate Canyon—a major transportation route out of Nine Mile Canyon north to the Uinta Basin.

The 1825 rendezvous was a smashing success. Ashley returned to St. Louis in the fall of 1825 with roughly nine thousand pounds of beaver pelts, which rescued him from bankruptcy. He then entered into a successful partnership with (or sold out to) the most renowned American trapper of the day, Jedediah Smith, while Ashley himself diverted his attentions to Missouri politics. In 1831 he was elected to the U.S. House of Representatives, and he won reelection twice. In 1836, he again lost the governor's race. He died two years later, a wealthy man.[29]

By the time of Ashley's arrival in 1825, the Uinta Basin had become crowded with competing groups of fur trappers. In the summer of that year, British-owned Hudson's Bay Company employees were in the Uinta Basin region trapping beaver, resulting in numerous conflicts with American trappers out of St. Louis. But only Provost, licensed out of Taos, was in the region legally, inasmuch as the Uinta Basin was entirely south of the forty-second parallel and thus in Mexican territory. Provost returned to the Uinta Basin to trap until 1828, becoming the dominant personality of the Uinta Basin fur trade at that time. Other trappers, including Jedediah Smith, were in the region, although there are few written accounts of their observations.[30]

At about this same time, other trappers had been exploring the Green River country south of the Uinta Basin where the discovery of Nine Mile Creek would have been inevitable. Dale Morgan, who edited Ashley's journal, noted that the lower Green River area near modern-day Green River, Utah, was well known to Taos trappers by 1824 and early 1825, and "had

Figure 2.12. Denis Julien inscription at the mouth of Hell Roaring Canyon on the lower Green River. Some believe the image depicted here is a boat. Photo by Jerry D. Spangler.

Ashley descended the river that far, he might have found traces of these trapping operations."[31]

The trappers probably eyed the Green River as a transportation corridor early on in the fur trade, and Ashley might not even have been the first to attempt to float the river. Fur trappers, many of whom cut their teeth on the upper Missouri River where boats were commonly used to transport pelts and supplies, would certainly have looked to exploit navigable portions of the Green River. During his own adventurous sojourn down the Green River in 1825, Ashley's journal reflects that he had met four French trappers at Ashley Creek who had "descended the river in a canoe but finding it so very dangerous and destitute of game returned…they give a lamentable account of their voyage—they had to live on the skins of beaver which they had caught in the neighborhood."[32] These trappers could have been referring to Desolation Canyon since there is no indication that they were referring to the same canyons through which Ashley had already passed.

Another account, printed in 1858, indicates that trappers Louis Ambrois and Jose Jessum had tried to float the Green River in canoes in 1831, but they were forced to abandon the expedition and climb canyon walls to safety.[33] Perhaps the most intriguing evidence of boats on the Green River is an inscription that reads "D. Julien 1836, 3 mai," located at the mouth of Hell Roaring Canyon on the lower Green River. This inscription is accompanied by a motif that some have interpreted as a sailboat, suggesting Julien used the Green River to transport his supplies and beaver skins by boat.[34]

Denis Julien was a renowned trapper in the Uinta Basin region, a French Canadian by way of St. Louis.[35] He arrived in the Uinta Basin in 1828, bringing with him a penchant for leaving his name on the cliff walls. At least nine Denis Julien inscriptions have been identified, including the 1836 Hell Roaring depiction. Another May 1836 Julien inscription is located in the heart of Cataract Canyon—a fiercely dangerous section of rapids on the Colorado River. The location of the inscription is such that it could only have been reached by someone in a boat.[36] Julien apparently survived the cacophonous rapids of Cataract Canyon because there is also an 1838 Julien inscription in the Echo Park area of the Green River and an 1844 Julien inscription in the Devils Park area of Arches National Park.[37] Another possible Julien inscription dated "February 13, '33" is located in Sand Wash—just north and east of Nine Mile Canyon.[38]

It does not stretch the imagination to surmise that Denis Julien, and probably other trappers, were intimately familiar with the entire stretch of the Green River through Desolation Canyon, and they would have discovered and explored all of the streams that flowed into the river from east and west. Nine Mile Creek most certainly would have been discovered and explored at this time.

The Trading Posts

The scores of trappers arriving to make their fortune led inevitably to the construction of several trading posts in the Uinta Basin. And those trading posts became social hubs where dozens of trappers and their Indian wives and children, as well as a motley assortment of misfits, would congregate, especially during the winter months. These larger groups required a constant supply of fresh meat, which would have taken the hunters farther and farther afield to find game. Nine Mile Canyon, which is winter habitat for deer and elk today, was probably within the range of those hunters.

The first trading post in the region was built in 1828 at the confluence of the Whiterocks and Uintah Rivers about fifty miles north of Nine Mile Canyon. This post was apparently a joint venture between William Reed and Denis Julien. Accompanying the trappers were James Reed, an eleven- or twelve-year-old nephew of William Reed, and Auguste Pierre "Sambo" Archambeaux, a teenager at the time who would eventually acquire considerable fame through the years as a trapper and guide. Gale Rhoades quoted from an account in which James Reed stated, "I came out West with my uncle, William Reed, when he set up the trading post, I was about 12 years old, I guess, and we come all the way from Kentucky."[39] The post was operated until 1832, when Antoine Robidoux purchased it. Julien and Archambeaux remained at the fort, apparently in Robidoux's employ.[40]

Antoine Robidoux, along with two brothers, had first entered the Uinta Basin in 1824 by way of Taos. He established his first trading post, called Fort Uncompahgre, on the Gunnison River in western Colorado in 1828. Antoine Robidoux trapped throughout the Uinta Basin and Uinta Mountains while his brother Louis remained on the Gunnison River to manage the trading post there.[41]

Antoine Robidoux inscription in Westwater Canyon on the East Tavaputs Plateau. The inscription has befuddled researchers because of the 1837 date and the stated intent to establish a trading post at that time when he had already established a post years before. Photo by Steven J. Manning.

Antoine Robidoux portrait, assumed to have been made in about 1843, or about the same time he was still operating Fort Uinta. Palace of the Governors Photo Archives (NMHM/DCA), Negative No. 007803.

In 1830, Antoine was encountered on the Malad River in southern Idaho, where he told John Work, a Hudson Bay trapper, that he intended to spend the winter on the White or Green River. Barton states that Robidoux purchased the Reed Trading Post in 1832, apparently constructing a new post called Fort Uinta on the east side of the spring. However, there is considerable disagreement as to when and where Robidoux established Fort Uinta.[42] Some scholars place the establishment in 1831 or 1832,[43] whereas others have argued the fort was not constructed until 1837.[44]

Much of the disagreement is centered on a historic inscription in Westwater Canyon in the East Tavaputs Plateau that indicates *"Antoine Robidoux passe ici le 13 Novembre 1837 pour etablire maison traitte a la Rv. vert ou wiyte."* Directly translated, the inscription reads "Antoine Robidoux passed here on November 13, 1837, to establish a house of trade on the river Green or White." However, journals of various trappers and traders indicate that Robidoux had already established a trading post, invariably referred to as Fort Uinta or Fort Robidoux, by 1831 or 1832.

The historical record also implies the existence of two Robidoux trading posts, one called Fort Robidoux at the confluence of the White and Green Rivers, and a second, called Fort Uinta, at the confluence of the Uinta and Whiterocks Rivers. Charles Kelly believed Robidoux intended to establish a trading post at the mouth of the White River, but "this intention was never carried out, since Gen. Fremont and others visited Fort Uinta in the old location as late as 1844."[45] The record is unclear as to whether Robidoux actually built two separate trading posts in the Uinta Basin or whether references to Fort Uinta and Fort Robidoux are one and the same.[46] John Barton offers a convincing argument for the establishment of Fort Uinta in late 1831 or early 1832; he also argued that Robidoux started construction of a second fort, Fort Robidoux, in 1837, but abandoned the project.[47] It is also interesting to note that the early maps of the American West continued to depict Fort Robidoux at the mouth of the White River on the Green River even into the early 1900s.

The Robidoux inscription in Westwater Canyon and the many other trapper inscriptions scattered throughout the East Tavaputs Plateau are important to the history of Nine Mile Canyon because of what they infer. Trappers could easily have traveled the route south out of the Uinta Basin, through Nine Mile Canyon, then along the base of the Book Cliffs to the river crossing at Green River, Utah. But they apparently chose, based on their inscriptions left along the way, a more direct but more difficult, higher-elevation route through Willow Creek and Westwater Creek on the East Tavaputs Plateau to transport their supplies and pelts back and forth from Taos.

Robidoux typically employed about twenty trappers who, along with Native American women, made the fort the center of business activities in the Uinta Basin. Called "engages," these trappers were under contract to bring their pelts to Robidoux for a predetermined price. This contrasted with practices of free trappers who sold their skins at the annual rendezvous to the highest bidder.[48]

Fort Uinta also conducted a brisk trade with free trappers, Native Americans, and travelers. Among those visiting Fort Uinta were icons of western history like Kit Carson, Miles Goodyear, Hubert Howe Bancroft, Marcus Whitman, and John C. Fremont. In a very real sense, the trappers organized themselves into small, highly mobile communities much like hunters and gatherers of previous generations.

Warren Angus Ferris, a wide-ranging trapper who might have been the first to make a map of the Uinta Basin—and perhaps the first to depict Nine Mile Creek on any map[49]—wrote in 1834:

> Our camp presented eight earthen lodges, and two constructed of poles covered with cane grass, which grows in dense patches to the height of eight or ten feet, along the river. They were all completely sheltered from the wind by the surrounding trees. Within, the bottoms were covered with reeds, upon which our blankets and robes were spread, leaving a small place in the center for our fire.... Our little village numbers 22 men, nine women and 20 children; and a different language is spoken in every lodge, the women being of different nations, and the children invariably learn their mother's tongue before any other. There were 10 distinct dialects spoken in our camp, each of which was the native idiom of one or more of us, though French was the language predominant among the men, and Flat-head among the women; yet there were both males and females who understood neither.[50]

Descriptions of trapper lifeways at the Uinta Basin trading posts were offered by several travelers through the region, many of whom stopped at Fort Uinta (or Fort Robidoux) for supplies and guides. In October 1842, A. L. Lovejoy and Marcus Whitman visited "Fort Wintey."[51] Also in 1842, Methodist missionary Joseph Williams described a visit to Fort Robidoux as

> very disagreeable to me on account of the drunkenness and swearing, and the debauchery of the men among the Indian women. They would buy and sell the squaws to one another.... This place is equal to any I ever saw for wickedness and idleness. The French and Spaniards are all Roman Catholics, but are as wicked men, I think, as ever lived.[52]

Rufus B. Sage, who accompanied Williams on the 1842 trip, recalled:

> Among the visitors at the Fort were several old trappers who had passed fifteen or twenty years in the Rocky Mountains and neighboring

Explorer John C. Fremont arrived in the Uinta Basin in 1843 by way of "Duchesne Fork," which might have been Nine Mile Creek. Photo courtesy of Wyoming State Archives, Department of State Parks and Cultural Resources (Negative No. 27657).

countries. They were what might with propriety be termed "hard cases." The interval of their stay was occupied in gambling, horse racing and other like amusements. Bets were freely made upon everything involving the least doubt, sometimes to the amount of five hundred or one thousand dollars—the stakes consisting of beaver, horses, traps, etc.[53]

John C. Fremont, who might have also explored Nine Mile Canyon in late May 1844, wrote on June 3 that they had reached "Uintah Fort, a trading post, belonging to Mr. A. Roubideau, on the principal fork of the Uintah River."[54] With the help of guides from the fort, the expedition crossed the river. Fremont described these guides as

a motley garrison of Canadian and Spanish engages and hunters with the usual number of Indian women. We obtained a small supply of sugar and coffee, with some dried meat and a cow, which was a very acceptable change from the pinole on which we had subsisted for some weeks past. I strengthened my party at this place by the addition of Auguste Archambeau, an excellent voyager and hunter belonging to the class of Carson and Godey.[55]

The success of Fort Uinta was contingent upon Robidoux's ability to transport furs and hides to the Taos trading hub in Mexican territory and to return with trade goods, especially alcohol. In 1842, Rufus Sage traveled in Robidoux's trading caravan to New Mexico and indicated it consisted of eight mules, each loaded with 250 pounds of furs. Travelling about thirty-five to forty miles a day, the caravan reached Taos in about fourteen days.[56]

Others ventured into the region in an attempt to compete with Robidoux. Some were American trappers based out of Taos, whereas others were British trappers with the Hudson's Bay Company, and yet others were Americans based out of St. Louis. The focus of most of these efforts appears to have been at the confluence of the Green and White Rivers.

In the fall of 1833, Kit Carson and Stephen Louis Lee traveled north from Taos with the intent of establishing a trading post at the confluence of the Green and White Rivers—the same location indicated in the 1837 Robidoux inscription and just north of the mouth of Nine Mile Canyon.

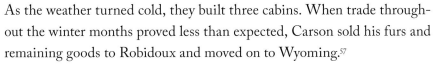

Fort Kit Carson as it appeared in 1871 when the Colorado River Exploring Expedition camped here. Photo courtesy of the U.S. Geological Survey Photographic Library, J. K. Hillers Collection.

Christopher "Kit" Carson was one of many notable explorers in the Nine Mile region. His makeshift trading post at the mouth of the White River was about thirty-three miles north of the mouth of Nine Mile Canyon. Used by permission, Utah State Historical Society, all rights reserved.

As the weather turned cold, they built three cabins. When trade throughout the winter months proved less than expected, Carson sold his furs and remaining goods to Robidoux and moved on to Wyoming.[57]

The cabins built by Kit Carson came to be known as Fort Kit Carson, even though the trading post operated only one winter. This site was known and utilized by subsequent trappers as a winter residence. Warren Angus Ferris reported its existence on his early map of the West,[58] and he was apparently camped at the site of Fort Kit Carson in 1834 when a second party of trappers from Taos joined the encampment. By November 23, 1834, Ferris and other trappers had been joined by twenty to thirty Utes, including Chief Conmarrowap and his wife, transforming Fort Kit Carson into a bustling winter camp—and quite possibly the largest community anywhere near Nine Mile Canyon at the time.[59]

On July 15, 1871, the Colorado River Exploring Expedition camped at the mouth of the White River, where historian Charles Kelly, editor of the Walter Clement Powell journal, states that Kit Carson had spent the winter of 1832–1833. At this location, Clem Powell noted the presence of an "almost new" cabin wherein members of the expedition slept.[60] This cabin could have been remains of Fort Kit Carson, although it is unlikely the cabin would appear "almost new" after three decades of abandonment.

This 1849 signature in Nine Mile Canyon is probably not indicative of the date it was made. Photo courtesy of the Colorado Plateau Archaeological Alliance.

This period of enhanced competition undoubtedly resulted in forays by trappers into less optimal beaver country, such as Nine Mile Canyon. Mildred Dillman noted the presence of an 1839 date at the mouth of Dry Canyon, a tributary of Nine Mile Canyon, but this inscription has not been reidentified. As previously mentioned, she also indicated "Spanish carvings" on the Miles ranch, which she attributed to Antoine Robidoux's trappers.[61]

By 1840, the fur trade had diminished into irrelevance. The last rendezvous was held in about 1842, and many fur trappers later became guides for the government explorers mapping the uncharted western territories and the waves of immigrants bound for Oregon and California. Some apparently turned to slave trading and horse stealing. Antoine Robidoux was apparently not averse to the slave trade or other mistreatments of the local Native Americans. In 1844, Fort Uinta was attacked and burned to the ground; Robidoux's Fort Uncompahgre in Colorado was also burned.[62] The razing of Fort Uinta may have afforded Robidoux a convenient excuse to abandon his increasingly unprofitable business enterprises. In any event, the burning of the fort marked the end of the fur trapper era in the Uinta Basin.

Robidoux apparently returned to Missouri and later enlisted as a guide and interpreter for the U.S. Army during the Mexican-American War of 1846 to 1848. He was wounded at the battle of San Pasqual and never fully recovered. He returned to Missouri blind and destitute. Congress awarded him a small pension in 1856 for his war services. He died in 1860 at the age of sixty-five.[63] He left behind a region devoid of beaver and an indigenous population seething with hatred for Euro-Americans.

It is probable that guides, hunters, prospectors, and others happened through Nine Mile Canyon in the years that followed the burning of Fort

This inscription near the mouth of Cottonwood Canyon is the oldest documented so far in Nine Mile Canyon that passes muster. It might be that of Stephen Groesbeck, a Utah pioneer who settled in Springville. Photo courtesy of the Colorado Plateau Archaeological Alliance.

Uinta. There is one signature of "Warren Sulser 1849" in middle Nine Mile Canyon, but this is suspect. The signature is in black axle grease—and there was no road through the canyon at that time and hence no wagons in need of axle grease.[64]

It would be more than twenty years before someone else left a mark here—an 1867 inscription that includes the depiction of a rider leading a string of pack horses or mules and the name "S. Groesbeck."[65] Using the Ancestry.com database, we believe this might have been Stephen B. Groesbeck, born in about 1827 in New York. Stephen and his wife, Mary, were living in Illinois by 1857, and by 1860 the family was living in Nebraska Territory, part of a western migration by early Mormon pioneers that found the family settling in Utah County.[66] If Stephen Groesbeck indeed left his inscription in Nine Mile Canyon in 1867, he would have been about forty years old at the time. And the inscription would mark the beginning of an entirely different chapter in the history of Nine Mile Canyon: immigrants in search of land, not pelts.

Portrait of Stephen B. Groesbeck. Photo from the Nicholas Groesbeck Morgan Collection, courtesy of Karen G. Morgan.

3

A "Worthless Mineral"

Sam Gilson and the Gilsonite Rush

Most if not all of the complaints made against Latter-day Saints are signed by one S. H. Gilson, who is understood to be the head of the dirty department of the crusade.
    —DESERET NEWS, 1885

The inscription on a gnarly tree trunk in Horse Canyon—"Sam Gilson, 1878, by God"—is now weathered beyond recognition, which is not all that surprising after more than 130 years exposed to the elements. Yet it remains a fading testament to one of Utah's greatest forgotten legends, a man who altered forever the history of Nine Mile Canyon, while leaving his name etched on several chapters of Utah's most colorful periods.[1]

Never heard of Sam Gilson? To some, he was an extraordinary lawman when the West was still wild. He was an inventor and a visionary—a Renaissance man for his day. To others he was but a scoundrel and

In 1878, Sam Gilson carved his name into this tree trunk near the mouth of Horse Canyon, perhaps while herding horses north to the Uinta Basin. It is illegible today. Photo by Jerry D. Spangler.

Opposite: Map of locations related to Sam Gilson.

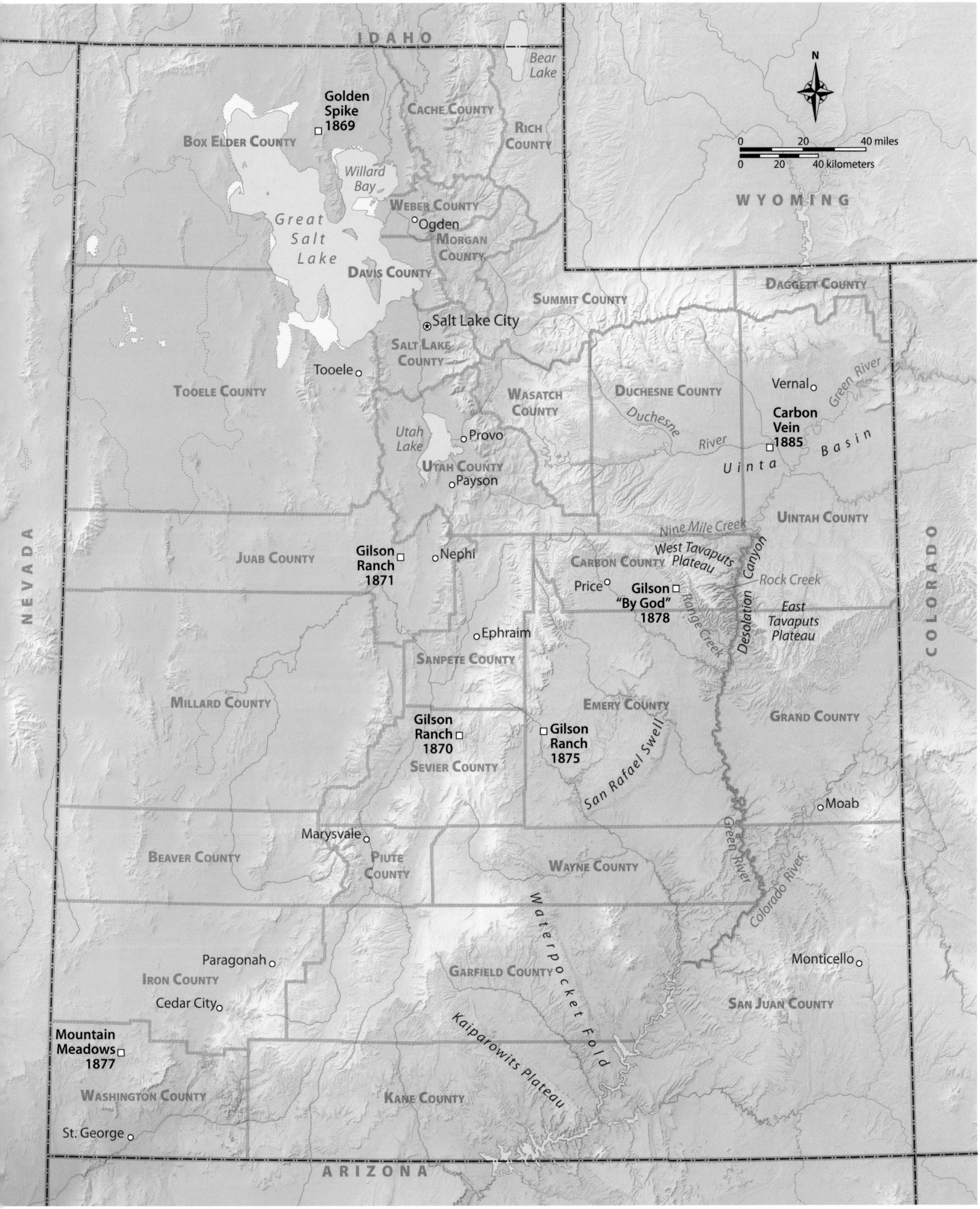

IDAHO

N

WYOMING

0   20   40 miles
0   20   40 kilometers

BOX ELDER COUNTY

Golden Spike 1869

Bear Lake

CACHE COUNTY

RICH COUNTY

Willard Bay

Great Salt Lake

WEBER COUNTY

Ogden

MORGAN COUNTY

DAVIS COUNTY

SUMMIT COUNTY

DAGGETT COUNTY

⊛ Salt Lake City

SALT LAKE COUNTY

DUCHESNE COUNTY

Vernal

Green River

Tooele

TOOELE COUNTY

WASATCH COUNTY

Duchesne

Carbon Vein 1885

River

Utah Lake

Provo

U i n t a   B a s i n

UTAH COUNTY

Payson

Nine Mile Creek

UINTAH COUNTY

Gilson Ranch 1871

Nephi

CARBON COUNTY

West Tavaputs Plateau

Rock Creek

NEVADA

JUAB COUNTY

Price

Gilson "By God" 1878

Desolation Canyon

East Tavaputs Plateau

COLORADO

Ephraim

Range Creek

SANPETE COUNTY

MILLARD COUNTY

EMERY COUNTY

GRAND COUNTY

Gilson Ranch 1870

□ **Gilson Ranch 1875**

San Rafael Swell

SEVIER COUNTY

Green River

Moab

Marysvale

BEAVER COUNTY

PIUTE COUNTY

WAYNE COUNTY

Colorado River

Waterpocket Fold

Paragonah

GARFIELD COUNTY

Monticello

IRON COUNTY

SAN JUAN COUNTY

Cedar City

Mountain Meadows 1877

Kaiparowits Plateau

WASHINGTON COUNTY

KANE COUNTY

St. George

ARIZONA

Scenic fall in Nine Mile
Canyon. Photo by Ray Boren.

Wildflowers in Nine Mile
Canyon. Photo by Ray Boren.

opportunist. As is usually the case, the truth probably lies somewhere in between. But the story of Sam Gilson is remarkable nonetheless.

By 1878, the year he inscribed his name on the tree trunk, Samuel Henry Gilson was still largely unknown in the Territory of Utah, one of thousands of adventure-seekers who had come West in search of fortune. One account has it that he was an Indian scout and that he rode for the Pony Express in Nevada,[2] another has it that he and his brother, James W. Gilson, merely supplied horses to the Pony Express[3]—one of the most adventurous but brief periods of the American West from 1860 to 1861. Yet another account is that Sam Gilson both supplied the horses and rode for the Pony Express,[4] although at age twenty-four or twenty-five he would have been among the oldest of the riders. In the years that followed, he became a rancher, a husband, and a father to twelve children.[5]

By his own account, Samuel H. Gilson was born in 1836 in Illinois to a family with the earliest roots in the Americas. He claimed his clan arrived in 1612 and that family blood had been spilled in every American conflict since that time. In 1853, at the age of seventeen, he left his home in Plainfield, Illinois, and crossed the Great Plains to California, taking jobs in towns that had sprung up in the wake of the California Gold Rush of 1849. He also claimed to have been "known" in almost every corner of Nevada.[6] Another account has it that he initially settled in Austin, Nevada, and married Alice Larkin Richardson, who was a Missourian and descendant of Daniel Boone. He went into the cattle and mercantile business with his brother, first in Lander County and then White Pine County in Nevada, later moving on to Utah, first to Juab County, then to Castle Valley, and after that to Salt Lake City.[7]

When he first arrived in Utah is not entirely clear. One account says he attended the laying of the cornerstone of the Salt Lake Temple in 1853. If he indeed was there, he was probably passing through the city on his inaugural trip west to the California gold fields. Thirteen years later he was said to have been present at Promontory, Utah, on May 10, 1869, when the driving of the Golden Spike commemorated the completion of the first transcontinental railroad.[8] By 1870, he had established "Mountain Ranch" in Salina Canyon, and another ranch west of Nephi, where his family resided.[9] At some point, Gilson made a business out of rounding up wild horses near his Juab County ranch and trailing them east across the Wasatch Plateau

Samuel H. Gilson. Used by permission, Uintah County Library Regional History Center,

In his early life, Gilson was said to have been present at the driving of the Golden Spike at Promontory, Utah. If so, he could be in the mass of people celebrating the event. Photo courtesy of Special Collections, Marriott Library, University of Utah.

to the Book Cliffs, then north across the Tavaputs Plateau to the Uinta Basin and finally to the Union Pacific railheads in Wyoming.[10] The shortest route to the railheads would have been through Nine Mile Canyon—largely unknown at the time—and it is probable that Gilson knew the Nine Mile route as early as 1876, based on an inscription discovered in 2012.

In 1878, he inscribed "Sam Gilson, 1878, by God" on a tree about ten miles southeast of Nine Mile Canyon. What was he doing in eastern Utah in 1878? He had a lifelong interest in prospecting and it's possible he was investigating the exposed coal seams in Horse Canyon. Or he could have been trailing horses to railheads in Wyoming, although Horse Canyon is not exactly "on the way" to Wyoming.[11] Or if he lived a spell in Price, as Bender claims, the inscription could have been carved onto the juniper tree during any number of activities associated with his ranching or mining ventures (Gilson is not listed among the earliest settlers of Price, who first arrived here in 1878). Woodard believed that Horse Canyon was so named because of Gilson's 1878 attempt to herd horses to the Uinta Basin but that he took a wrong turn into Horse Canyon. He also wrote that Gilson returned to Horse Canyon that same year to investigate the coal seams and that he built two coke ovens there,[12] although this initial foray into coal mining failed.[13] A later attempt at Kenilworth was more successful.[14]

There is no explicit claim that Gilson fought in the Civil War from 1861 to 1864, but his sympathies were with the South, something that decades later would haunt his unsuccessful bid for public office and prompt a lengthy treatise of explanation as to his true moral character.[15]

> When the Civil War broke out I kicked against the government of the United States. Fifteen million people made the same kick as I did. I made the kick honestly as many others did. I was raised to believe that slavery was right. I believed the South did what she should have done when she fought for her rights.[16]

His apologetic defense of society's right to fight for its sacred beliefs seems a bit self-serving if not downright hypocritical. He certainly did not extend that same tolerance to the Mormons living in Utah in the latter half of the nineteenth century.

Marshal S. H. Gilson

Any anonymity Sam Gilson may have enjoyed as a rancher and would-be prospector had evaporated by 1884, just as the U.S. government's campaign against Mormon polygamy entered a new era of aggressive enforcement by the U.S. Justice Department. That year, U.S. Attorney W. H. Dickson hired Gilson as part of an elite detective force assigned to enforce the Edmunds Act, an effort by Congress to root out and prosecute high-ranking Mormon officials who were married to more than one woman.[17] One account has it that Gilson was the first such detective so hired.[18] From that time on, Sam Gilson was known in most newspaper reports as "Marshal S. H. Gilson."[19]

It is not known why Gilson joined the Marshal's Service but it appears he had some prior experience as a lawman. In an 1885 *Deseret News* editorial attacking Gilson,[20] the Mormon Church–owned newspaper compared the 1885 antipolygamy crusade to an earlier campaign in 1871 by U.S. Justice McKean. The *Deseret News* asserted that Gilson "occupied a similar post during the former anti-Mormon assault, when the most villainous attempts were made to swear away the lives and liberties of President Brigham Young and others." There are no newspaper accounts from 1871 that mention Sam Gilson specifically, who would have been thirty-one years old at that time. But in the May 8, 1872, edition there is a passing reference to a "Sam Gillson, ex-bailiff of the late illegal grand jury" who had been arrested at that time for threatening to kill a man named John Thomas.[21]

Woodard states Gilson had become a deputy U.S. marshal, working under Marshals William Nelson and M. T. Patrick, by at least 1871, or about the same time he would have been starting his ranch sixteen miles west of Nephi. He cites an account where an accused murderer, William A. Hickman, heard that Deputy Gilson was looking for him, and that Hickman went to the Gilson ranch to learn his intentions. The two had dinner together, after which Hickman wrote, "I found Gilson to be a man that had much experience in his life in this line and was well posted on the crimes of Utah."[22]

Another account has it that Gilson was the U.S. marshal who presided over the execution of John D. Lee of Mountain Meadows infamy in 1877,[23] but credible historical documents all list the U.S. marshal presiding over the event as William Nelson. But Gilson might indeed have been in the Marshal's Service at that time and could have been present at the Mountain Meadows execution site. It would have been his character to be in attendance at any grand event marking a historic occasion. His 1913 obituary in the *Deseret News* mentions that he was a deputy under "Colonel William Nelson" in the "early history of Utah," but it offered no other details.[24]

Woodard states that Sam Gilson in 1875 established cattle ranches at Oak Springs and Quigempah (later referred to as the Ireland Ranches) in what is today known as Castle Valley,[25] whereas his obituary in the *Deseret News* claims it was Gilson and his brother, James, who were the early pioneers of Emery County. According to another account, Gilson was a

cowhand who, in 1875, helped John Bennion move two thousand head of cattle from Tooele County through Salina Canyon to Castle Valley.[26]

Israel Bennion, a young lad at the time, recalled Gilson's eccentric nature. Wrote Israel's son, Gilson was a "black-bearded giant" who "scorned hardship and traveled without food or bedroll. At night he pulled his saddle blanket over his shoulders and slept on the ground." And he liked his meat rare. When needed, he would shoot a young calf, throw a slab of meat briefly onto the fire, and eat it, ashes and all, "with blood dripping down both sides of his magnificent beard."[27]

If the 1875 date is correct for Gilson's own ranches in Castle Valley, Gilson might have been more than a simple cowhand hired to move the Bennion herds. His own cattle might have been part of the larger herd (and it could explain why he felt entitled to kill a calf and eat it during the cattle drive). The 1875 date would also make Sam Gilson the first to establish a ranch in Castle Valley in what is today Emery County.[28] If he did establish a ranch here at this early date, his family probably did not accompany him, since two of Gilson's daughters, Harriet and Pancha Kate, were

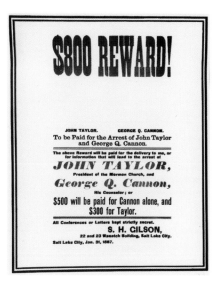

Sam Gilson's wanted poster seeking the arrest of LDS Church leaders George Q. Cannon and John Taylor. Courtesy of Special Collections, Marriot Library, University of Utah.

Deputy U.S. Marshal Sam Gilson was particularly good at his job in arresting polygamists, many of whom were imprisoned at the Utah State Penitentiary in Sugar House. George Q. Cannon, a major target of Gilson's campaign, is center frame. Courtesy of Special Collections, Marriott Library, University of Utah.

born in Nephi in 1877 and 1879, respectively. By 1880, the Gilson family was living in the Salina Canyon area;[29] among their neighbors at that time were James Hamilton, William Hamilton, and Andrew Jackson "Daddy" Russell—all of whom would later become the first permanent settlers of Nine Mile Canyon.

Gilson again donned the marshal's badge sometime in 1884, the same year he moved his family to Salt Lake City, and he quickly rose to become the unofficial commander of the detective squad and the focal point of dozens of news articles, most of them unflattering. The *Deseret News*, in particular, targeted Gilson as the instigator of Mormon persecution. Perhaps because of his many years living among the Mormons, Sam Gilson was very good at what he did. Within a short time of being named deputy U.S. marshal he had obtained enough evidence to indict ten prominent Utahns, including one of the church's twelve apostles and the editor of the *Deseret News*[30]—something that undoubtedly led to the newspaper's persistent editorial campaign against him. In one account, the *Deseret News* wrote, "Gilson assumed the role of grand ringmaster" in a raid upon a Gardo House where he alleged Mormon leaders John Taylor and George Q. Cannon were hiding.[31]

This room, it was alleged, had a secret chamber in which it was claimed someone was hidden. Beds, wardrobes and furniture of various kinds were shifted but no indication of anything unusual was noticed. Gilson then tried to tear the carpet up in one corner, but soon changed his mind. He then sounded the walls in various places and wanted to know why the room was irregular in form, evidently not having the sense enough to see that it conformed with the outside of the building in shape. He then wanted to know if there was a fireplace not used. He said he had been told there was a revolving fireplace which afforded a means of excretion.[32]

The church-owned paper smugly reported that the marshals "then returned as they started out—empty handed."[33] There were several deputy U.S. marshals working throughout the territory at the time, several of whom are named in various newspaper articles, some in more flattering terms than others. But by most accounts in the *Deseret News* it was Marshal S. H. Gilson who evoked the most disdain among the Mormon faithful. In one editorial, the *Deseret News* wrote, "Most if not all of the complaints made against Latter-day Saints are signed by one S. H. Gilson, who is understood to be the head of the dirty department of the crusade."[34] Sam Gilson is mentioned by name more than a dozen times in the *Deseret News* from 1884 to 1887, often with colorful adjectives such as "irrepressible" and "notorious" and in one instance "d----d scoundrel."[35]

There is no question that the Mormon Church, with its leaders and assets besieged by the federal government, dished out sarcasm and vitriol to judges and lawmen and politicos it deemed to be enemies. That Sam Gilson would be named so often in these attacks suggests that he was an enthusiastic enforcer of the Edmunds Act, enough so that he came to personify the campaign against the Mormons. His success as a detective might well have been rooted in the fact he had lived among the Mormons for more than a decade and undoubtedly knew the nuances of Mormon society and how they hid their polygamist practices from the "gentiles." This stood in contrast to the other marshals and prosecutors who "were in effect in an alien land, far from their friends and families, and wholly ostracized from the tight-knit Mormon majority."[36]

Gilson's high profile set him up for accusations that he had defrauded a widow,[37] that he was a political opportunist,[38] and that he and other marshals were selectively prosecuting Mormons for the same practices common among the gentiles.[39] Opined the *Deseret News*:

> Would it not be a good idea to have a detail to watch the Hotel de Flint and every other house of the kind in town, spot the respectable male gentiles, married and single, who go in and out, and when an arrest is made, subpoena every prostitute in the house, and let Mr. Dickson ask them if they had sexual intercourse with the arrested party.[40]

Deputy Gilson continued to wear his official badge through at least early 1887 when he was at the forefront of raids in Salt Lake City to arrest prominent Mormon polygamists.[41] But his marshal duties appear to have been a part-time job. As discussed later in this chapter, Sam Gilson was already in the Gilsonite business in the Uinta Basin throughout his tenure as a lawman.

Based on the limited evidence on hand, Sam Gilson was a non-Mormon living among the Mormons in a world far different than his homeland in Illinois or the gold fields of California. In his later responses to blistering newspaper attacks, he maintained that his life-long love of democracy made it impossible to abide the Utah theocracy where individual rights were subservient to the will of the church. It is not at all surprising that he would throw in with the Liberal Party comprised of non-Mormons seeking to "reform" Utah politics. Wrote Gilson,

> We claimed that the laws of the country must be obeyed; that no theocracy should or would be planted on the American continent; that the power of the Mormon Church must be abolished; free government must be established in Utah; that the ballot box must be pure and represent the will of the people; church and state must be separated, and entire freedom of speech and press must prevail. We simply demanded what our Constitution guaranteed.[42]

All of this might seem irrelevant to a history of Nine Mile Canyon. There were no polygamists hiding out in the canyon, as far as anyone knows from the written record.[43] It was what happened while Sam Gilson was still a deputy U.S. marshal and ostensibly tracking down evildoers that would forever change the history of the canyon. And what he did in 1886 more than hints at the prospect that Gilson was a quintessential opportunist, perhaps even exploiting insider knowledge of a soon-to-be-built U.S. government freight road from Price through Nine Mile Canyon to Fort Duchesne in the Uinta Basin—information that would transform Gilson from "notorious" lawman into a well-heeled businessman in no short order. It is within the realm of possibility that Gilson even advised the army on where the new route should be built. He, better than most, knew the Nine Mile country.

Prospector Sam

By many popular accounts, Sam Gilson discovered a bright, shiny mineral hydrocarbon which came to bear his own name—Gilsonite. Now Gilson no more discovered Gilsonite than Christopher Columbus discovered America or Brigham Young discovered the Great Salt Lake. But the mineral bears his name even today, a testament to Sam Gilson's unbridled hucksterism and self-promotion. As one story goes, Gilson, sometime between 1882 and 1884, "observing an anthill, became curious about the black shiny material that the ants were carrying. Following the ant's trail, he discovered a vein buried under a few inches of wind-blown sand."[44] Another story has it that a groundhog kicked up some of the mineral that caught Gilson's eye. Gilson's daughter, Alice Eggleston, said both stories are true.[45]

Truth told, folks had known about Gilsonite for ages. Ancient Americans in the Uinta Basin melted it into a tar-like substance to patch baskets a millennium ago or more, and in its natural state it could be fashioned into prehistoric jewelry items. Gilson wasn't even the first white man to toy with the substance. The material was reportedly examined by the Columbia School of Mines in 1865.[46] Another account attributed to 1869 has it that John Kelly, the blacksmith at the Ute reservation, had asked the Utes to bring him some coal. They returned with Gilsonite. When it was burned, it melted, turning extremely hot and smoky "as it melted and ran flaming from the forge, nearly burning down the blacksmith shop."[47]

The mineral had also come to the attention of geologists accompanying Ferdinand Hayden's landmark U.S. government surveys of the Western

territories in 1876.[48] At that time, the mineral was not recognized as something new, but was commonly referred to as "asphalt" or "asphaltum," and
there was little interest in the substance.[49] It wasn't until 1885 that Professor
William P. Blake of Provo (by way of New Haven, Connecticut) recognized the substance as a new mineral and assigned it the name Uintahite.[50]

Bender states that Uinta Basin cattlemen had given Gilson several bags
of the substance in 1885, reportedly found in the Fort Duchesne area, and
that he took the mineral home with him and began experimenting with it.
Gilson's wife later remembered that she "was not exactly overjoyed with
her husband's discovery, since he filled practically every pot and pan in the
house with the messy stuff in order to carry out his experiments."[51]

At least some of the experiments were successful. Three patents were
awarded to Gilson in 1887, and another in 1889, for things ranging from
chewing gum to insulation for wires to a new paint used on the piles at
Saltair, at the time the preeminent Utah resort on the shores of the Great
Salt Lake.[52]

The 1885 date suggested for Gilson's initial interest in Gilsonite is
intriguing because of a recent discovery in Nine Mile Canyon. On a cliff
wall behind Balanced Rock is the inscription "SH Gilson," the date 1885,
and another name, "Bert Seaboldt," the man who would become Gilson's

business partner in Gilsonite speculations. And the date would infer that their conspiracy to control Gilsonite claims—and the potential need for a freight route to haul the ore through Nine Mile Canyon—were rooted in events the year before they filed their first claims.

In 1885, any practical use of Gilsonite faced an insurmountable problem: there was no way to get it out of the Uinta Basin for processing and refinement. And then there was the problem that the richest deposits known at that time were all located on Ute tribal lands and off limits to prospectors, in theory at least. It was at that time, for all intents and purposes, "a worthless mineral."[53]

Gilsonite is a mineral somewhere between crude oil on one extreme and coal on the other. It is shiny, black, light weight, and converts easily to a rubbery liquid. The weathered surface resembles coal, whereas a fractured surface is shiny like obsidian. In Utah, which has more deposits than anywhere else in the world, it occurs in veins from three inches wide to almost eighteen feet wide. They are most commonly associated with oil shale deposits in the upper Green River Formation and the lower Uinta Formation of ancient Lake Uinta—Tertiary-age deposits 57 to 36 million years old.[54]

Left: Gilson and Seaboldt filed their first Gilsonite claims in early 1886. This 1885 inscription in Nine Mile Canyon suggests they were laying the groundwork for their Gilsonite operation a year or so before that. Photo by Jody Patterson.

Right: The original Nine Mile Road passed next to the cliff above this formation, known as Pig Rock or Balanced Rock, not below it as it does today. The Gilson-Seaboldt inscription is located next to the original road bed. Photo by Ray Boren.

No one knows who developed the first commercial use for Gilsonite or what it was. Maybe Sam Gilson was the first. Initially, Gilsonite was used in varnishes and paints for horse-drawn carriages, was mixed half-and-half with liquid asphalt for road-building materials, and also mixed with rubber compounds to make buggy and coach tires.[55] When demand for one purpose waned, another use would emerge.

The sequence of events that led to the Gilsonite boom of the late 1880s is confusing and the historical accounts are not always consistent. Bender states that Sam Gilson made yet another trip to the Uinta Basin in 1886, where he was shown an ore deposit now referred to as the Carbon Vein. But he also states the first seven claims—the Carbon No. 1 to Carbon No. 7 Claims—were filed in Salt Lake City on January 9, 1886,[56] which would have left Gilson only nine days to make the horseback trip through Nine Mile Canyon to the Uinta Basin and back in time to file the claims.[57]

Bender also states that it was about 1886 when Gilson went into partnership with Bert Seaboldt, who became equally enthusiastic about the mineral's potential, but the Nine Mile Canyon inscription suggests their relationship was in place at least a year before that. Seaboldt was "assistant to the chief engineer and was manager of construction for the Denver and Rio Grande Western Railway between 1882 and 1890,"[58] although Seaboldt's name is not mentioned once in Robert Athearn's seminal history of the railroad.[59] According to Bender's account, Seaboldt knew about Gilsonite prior to 1886, due to an earlier visit to Pardon Dodds, former head of the Ute agency in the Uinta Basin, where he met a fellow named George Basor.

> Basor showed Seaboldt several pieces of the black stuff and then took him to the Carbon Vein, which may have been a mistake on Basor's part. Seaboldt learned that Basor had done no assessment work on his claim and had not recorded it, since it was on the Uintah Reservation, so he jumped the claim and posted his own notices.[60]

Also in 1886, Seaboldt sent Gilson to the Smithsonian Institution in Washington, D.C., with a sample of the ore to determine exactly what it was. The scientists there declared it a 99.6 percent pure hydrocarbon or bitumen.[61]

The Gilson-Seaboldt partnership occurred at the same time there was considerable unrest in the Uinta Basin, with white settlers fearful of increased Ute hostilities and the Utes increasingly angry over encroachment on tribal lands by prospectors and cattlemen. In late summer 1886, the U.S. Army began construction of Fort Duchesne in hopes that a military presence would prevent open hostilities by deterring white trespassing and potential Ute reprisals, and to keep the peace between three different Ute bands forced to live together (see chapter 4 related to the Nine Mile Road).[62]

In 1885 and 1886, as Sam Gilson was laying groundwork for his business enterprise, he was still a deputy U.S. marshal earning a mere pittance to track down Mormon polygamists.[63] How he found the time—or the money—to investigate ore deposits, make a trip to Washington, D.C., file and pay for claims, and then promote the mineral that bears his name is not entirely clear. Kretchman claims the moneyman behind the endeavor was St. Louis mining engineer Charles O. Baxter, who became president of the company that bought out Seaboldt and Gilson a few years later.[64]

By all appearances, the venture was gathering momentum in 1886. But the partners had a major problem: the seven Carbon Vein claims were all on Ute tribal lands. And in 1887, Seaboldt went to Congress to "attempt the impossible," to convince Congress to remove the Gilsonite lands from the reservation.[65] He carried with him $25,000 contributed by two unnamed associates[66] that apparently made the impossible possible (this is discussed in greater detail in chapter 4). In 1888, Congress removed 7,040 acres from the Uintah Reservation—it became known as "The Strip"—with the richest Gilsonite deposits.[67]

At the same time Seaboldt was in Washington, D.C., Gilson and Baxter were busy filing additional claims throughout the Uinta Basin.[68] And in 1888, Gilson and Seaboldt organized the Gilsonite Manufacturing Company, shipping three thousand tons of ore to the railhead at Price that first year of operations. At $80 a ton at the railhead, the fledging enterprise had grossed $240,000 in its first year.[69] Most of that was profit. Miners were paid $4 a day, and a good miner could bag about two tons a day. The cost of shipping the ore by wagon ran about $10 to $12 per ton.[70]

Why Sam Gilson and Bert Seaboldt began acquiring any and all claims as early as 1886 is not clear. Had Gilson's experiments rendered new uses that would make extraction profitable? Maybe, but there was still the problem of getting the ore out of the ground and to the railhead for shipment to eastern markets. It was otherwise worthless—unless Sam Gilson knew something that other prospectors and speculators did not: the U.S. government was set to solve the transportation dilemma at no cost to the speculators.

Gilson was, at that time, a deputy U.S. marshal in the employ of the U.S. attorney for Utah. The U.S. Justice Department was closely aligned with the U.S. military, which had remained in Utah since the 1850s to keep a watchful eye on the pesky Mormons who were always rumored to be in revolt against the United States. Fort Douglas was perched on the bench high above Salt Lake City where the Mormon Temple was within easy striking range of cannonballs. Federal troops were occasionally summoned to assist the U.S. marshals in their law enforcement duties, and the U.S. Army made reciprocal requests of the Justice Department.[71] In the mid-1880s, the U.S. Army hatched a plan to build a freight road from the Denver and Rio Grande railhead at Price through Nine Mile Canyon to a newly planned post, to be called Fort Duchesne, about ninety miles to the north.

It is not unreasonable to surmise that Gilson knew of the planned transportation route and what it would mean to the development of the Gilsonite veins. And there must have been some confidence that Seaboldt's "lobbying" of Congress to have the tribal lands removed from the reservation would be successful. By the time the freight road opened in fall of 1886, Gilson and Seaboldt had already locked up all the richest Gilsonite claims known at that time.

There is no evidence that Sam Gilson ever seriously hoisted a pick and shovel himself. Gilsonite mining in the 1880s and 1890s was hard work. According to Kretchman,

> Early-day mining was in most mines a strictly one-man operation. Not only did he pick out the ore, but usually sacked it too. The veins were dug out on a rising slope so that the ore rolled back down the slope as it was dislodged. When a sufficient amount had been dug out, the miner would place a large burlap bag, capable of holding 200 pounds of Gilsonite, between his legs and scoop the Gilsonite into the bag with his hands. In the wider veins he used a short-handed shovel in one hand, and held the sack in the other. A rope and pulley hoisted the filled bags to the surface, with a team of horses providing the power. Naturally, this limited the depth to which mining operations could be carried on efficiently. At the turn of the century the maximum depth was only about 100 feet.[72]

Gilson and Seaboldt may have been the most ardent boosters of Gilsonite and its potential, but they got out of the business almost as quickly as they got into it. The Gilsonite Manufacturing Company sold out to the Gilson Asphaltum Company of St. Louis in September 1889 for a reported $150,000 (or $185,000 according to a different account). The new

company's president was C. O. Baxter, who Kretchman says was in cahoots with Gilson and Seaboldt in buying up the lion's share of Gilsonite claims in 1886 and 1887. The Gilson Asphaltum Company was a front for none other than Adolphus Busch, the beer-brewing magnate whose Budweiser brand continues to this day.[73]

Seaboldt, according to one story he related years later, gave some Gilsonite varnish to C. E. Soest, a long-time friend who was at the time vice-president of Anheuser-Busch Brewing Company. Soest's boss, Adolphus, was impressed with the "perfect" varnish and took the varnish to a friend who owned a varnish company. Coincidentally, in walked C. O. Baxter, who was in the "picture frame business" and was making his regular varnish purchase. Busch dispatched Baxter to investigate the Gilsonite deposits, and later Busch's counsel, Charles Nagel, was sent to negotiate the sale of the Gilsonite claims to a company with Baxter as president.[74] The only problem with this story, of course, is that Baxter already knew the Gilsonite deposits well—he, Gilson, and Seaboldt had been filing on claims since 1886, and Baxter was probably the moneyman behind Gilson and Seaboldt.

Left: Early Gilsonite miners preferred deposits on a slope like this one where the bags of ore could be rolled downhill to be loaded onto a wagon. Courtesy of Special Collections, Marriott Library, University of Utah.

Right: Beer magnate Adolphus Busch would come to control most of the Gilsonite deposits over the next two decades. Gilsonite turned out to be a failure as a varnish for Busch's beer barrels, but it had many other profitable uses. Library of Congress (cph.3c21004).

Busch became interested in the varnish as a cheaper alternative to the Italian materials used at that time to line beer barrels. "The experiment was a costly and disappointing failure, however, for the Gilsonite coating flaked off and ruined the beer."[75]

But there were other profitable uses for Gilsonite, and the Busch family maintained ownership of the company for the next eleven years. The company retained Seaboldt as its superintendent of mines, and some other employees were kept on, but Sam Gilson was not one of them, even though the new company bore his name. It is reported that when the new

St. Louis owners met in Price for their initial board meeting, Gilson jokingly offered them one silver dollar if they would keep his name on the company. The motion carried and the company was officially incorporated as the Gilson Asphaltum Company, with "Gilsonite" as its patented trademark.[76] The mining of the "worthless mineral" would continue quite profitably for the next half century, but apparently it did so without Sam Gilson.

But Sam had been bitten by the mining bug, and flush with profits from the sale of his interests in the company, he apparently "prospected" for gold, copper, and silver, among other minerals. He is said to have started the first coal mine at what is today Kenilworth,[77] and he was credited with "the naming of more minerals discovered in Utah than any other man."[78] In 1888, the same year he started the Gilsonite Manufacturing Company, he was granted a Desert Land Patent for his Emery County ranch.[79]

Activist and Renaissance Man

In the spring of 1904, at the age of sixty-eight, Sam Gilson's name shows up in newspaper accounts related to a massive strike by 120 Italian immigrant coal workers in Price. Gilson himself penned articles for the newspapers decrying local officials' treatment of the miners and accusing the coal company, judge, county attorney, and sheriff of corruption. In return, establishment newspapers vilified him. Gilson's spirited defense of the strikers eventually became personal. At one point, Gilson gave a tongue-lashing to local lawmen, spiked with colorful language, at which point Gilson was arrested and charged with "abusive language" and "disturbing the peace." Sheriff Wilcox, the subject the Gilson tirade, told one newspaper he intended "to kill Gilson in his tracks" if Gilson had made a move to strike him. The account quoted Wilcox, "What does he (Gilson) know about conditions at the strikers' camp or anywhere else in the county, when he has been loafing around Price for two years?"[80]

Sam Gilson in his later years. Used by permission, Utah State Historical Society, all rights reserved.

Why Sam Gilson became a labor activist is not clearly stated in the extensive coverage of the events surrounding the strike. But he did have coal-mining interests in the county, and the target of the strike—the Utah Fuel Company—would have been a primary competitor. And they were not small, speculative holdings. According to one newspaper account,

SAMUEL H. GILSON'S FLYING MACHINE

Sam Gilson's flying machine as illustrated in the *Salt Lake Tribune*. Image scanned from Utah Digital Newspapers.

Gilson and a partner controlled thirty thousand acres of coal-rich land north of Price, with outright ownership of five thousand acres. Gilson guaranteed production of ten thousand tons of coal a day. The only impediment was the refusal of the Rio Grande Western to extend a branch line eight miles to the mines.[81] The railroad, of course, was also in the coal business, and they were not about to help a competitor.

Another possibility is that Gilson passionately believed in the rights of the downtrodden, in particular immigrants. His spirited defense of the Italians, which included such noble statements as "the pauper had the same rights before the law as the millionaire," and "strikers should not be persecuted because they saw fit to quit the employ of the coal company,"[82] harkened to statements he made ten years earlier about the rights of immigrants to revolt against their oppressors—remarks that got him labeled a traitor. At the time, Gilson responded: "If it is treason then I am a traitor; if it is anarchism then I am an anarchist; if it is in violation of the laws, they may make the most of it. I can assure you I am sane."[83]

Gilson's eloquent defense of his beliefs and actions eventually garnered respect from friends and adversaries alike. The *Ogden Standard*, which had earlier in 1894 vilified Gilson as crazy and seditious, later described him as "a man of independent means, a miner and a citizen of recognized stability, moderation and prudence."[84] The *Deseret News*, which had repeatedly

Gilson family plot at Mount Olivet cemetery in Salt Lake City. Sam's grave is unmarked. Photo by Jerry D. Spangler.

attacked him during the 1880s as a scoundrel, had not a bad word to say about him upon his death on December 3, 1913, not even mentioning his role in the crackdown on Mormon polygamists in the 1880s.[85]

By all accounts Sam Gilson was a remarkable businessman, quick to file claims and astute as to when to sell his interests. He was a brilliant inventor and knew the patent system well. Which makes his biggest financial blunder all the more remarkable: he failed to file patents on his inventions related to the airplane. Utah newspapers in the early 1900s are filled with news stories of Gilson's "flying machine" and "air ship," and photographs of the contraptions in flight are oddities of history. According to Gilson's widow, he had been building model airplanes since the 1860s, and he predicted that someday a man would eat breakfast in San Francisco and dinner in New York. The Wright brothers even visited Gilson at his Salt Lake home. But he messed up on the patent paperwork and "cost the Gilson family a fortune."[86]

Sam Gilson was without doubt an indelible part of the fabric that makes up Utah's rich history. And his role in the history of Nine Mile Canyon cannot be understated, even if he never lived there, perhaps rarely passed through it. The only hard evidence we have that he was ever there are three inscriptions, the 1885 inscription discussed above, an 1876 inscription found at the east edge of the mouth of Argyle Canyon, and another inscription that reads "SH Gilson 1910"—a date scratched onto the canyon wall just three years before his death at age seventy-seven.[87] But Sam Gilson was responsible in large part for Nine Mile Canyon becoming one of the state's most important economic thoroughfares of that era.

He died in 1913 and is buried in the family plot at Mount Olivet Cemetery in Salt Lake City. There is no headstone marking his grave. His partner in the Gilsonite boom, Bert Seaboldt, apparently died in anonymity.[88]

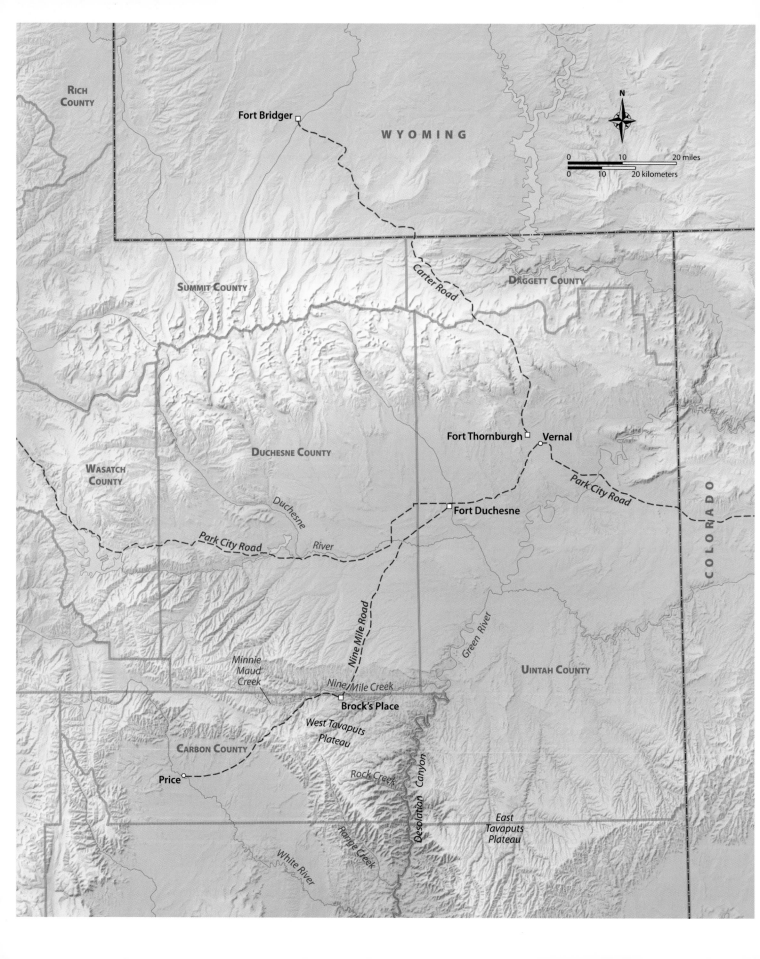

Soldiers, Schemers, and a Road to Riches

I have seen quite a few travel this road, to different mines, the Fort, Ashley and surrounding country.
—An unnamed Fort Duchesne soldier, 1887

The official reasoning for the Nine Mile Road, repeated in newspaper articles and historical accounts, was to transport supplies to Fort Duchesne and to the Indian agencies. Supplying the military post and agencies was a U.S. government responsibility, and as such the U.S. Army constructed the road for that legitimate purpose. And under that scenario, the freight would be traveling in only one direction, from the Denver and Rio Grande railheads at Price through Nine Mile Canyon to the Uinta Basin.

But the legitimacy of the new road, constructed by the military at taxpayer expense, obscures a more subtle reality, one where certain individuals

Opposite: Map of military roads and installations.

Scenic view of upper Nine Mile Canyon. Photo by Jerry D. Spangler.

Wildflowers in bloom in lower Nine Mile Canyon. Photo by Jerry D. Spangler.

eventually got very, very wealthy. In fact, the road was probably never intended to be a one-way transport of supplies to the Uinta Basin.

To appreciate why the road was built in the first place requires a consideration of the larger political and economic forces at play at the time. And, as the popular twentieth-century axiom advises, if you "follow the money" you come to suspect the Nine Mile Road was not only a route to deliver supplies to soldiers. It was also a critical component to a scheme by mineral speculators, perhaps in conspiracy with the Denver and Rio Grande Railroad,[1] to wrest control of lucrative military freight contracts from the rival Union Pacific, while at the same time securing a monopoly on the seemingly inexhaustible Gilsonite deposits just waiting for a means to transport them to market.

It is unclear why Nine Mile Canyon was ultimately chosen by the military, given a wagon route—the Carter Road—already existed. This route led north out of the Uinta Basin through the Uinta Mountains to the Union Pacific railheads near Fort Bridger, Wyoming. The northerly route had higher elevations that could become snowbound, but it was already

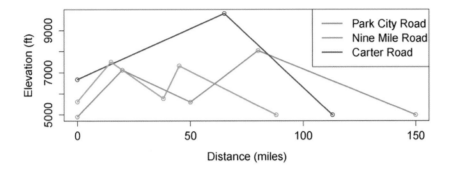

Chart comparing elevations and distances by traveling the Nine Mile Road versus the Carter Road and Park City Road.

functional.[2] So also was a longer, westerly route connecting the Uinta Basin to Park City, Utah. A southerly route through Nine Mile Canyon, although somewhat shorter, would seem redundant. And as all would come to discover in the years that followed, it also presented its own unique logistical challenges to timely freight deliveries, from freak blizzards to flash floods, either of which could make the road impassable for weeks on end. In effect, the military exchanged one set of problems for another equally onerous set of obstacles to timely freight deliveries.

Origins of a Road

Deciphering when the road into Nine Mile Canyon was first constructed, and who constructed it, is an exercise in futility. It was probably built sometime before the 1886 date traditionally assigned to the road, but how much sooner? And why would it have been needed prior to 1886?

Current evidence suggests that road building by U.S. Army troops in 1886 amounted only to improvements to an existing road to make it passable to freighters traveling to and from Fort Duchesne.[3] One local legend has it that the premilitary road extended into Nine Mile Canyon only about thirty-two miles, at which point it cut north up Trail Canyon and then east across a broad, flat bench area before continuing north to the Uinta Basin, thereby avoiding the steep, twisting route through Gate Canyon that would bedevil freighters in later years. Yet another tradition holds that early Price settler John A. Powell assisted the army in locating the route through Nine Mile and Gate Canyons, which has been interpreted by some to mean there was no road before that time.[4]

Local legend has it that John A. Powell guided the U.S. Army into Nine Mile Canyon in 1886, identifying the route through Gate Canyon. He is depicted here with his second of three wives. He had a ranch in Nine Mile Canyon with his third wife, and a sister and a daughter had ranches there with their families. Photo used by permission, Utah State Historical Society, all rights reserved.

This inscription can be read as February 9, 1886, or September 2, 1886, either of which is plausible for a military reconnaissance into Nine Mile Canyon. Photo by Jody Patterson.

Based on an inscription, "2.9.86," left by a B Company soldier (Sixth Infantry, Fort Douglas) on a cliff wall, the early military exploration of Nine Mile Canyon, assisted by Powell, might have occurred in February 1886 when there was considerable unrest among the Uinta Basin Utes that could have prompted the dispatch of troops from Fort Douglas.[5] But archaeologist Jody Patterson, who recently redocumented the site, points to standard U.S. Army protocols that clearly specify the day comes first, followed by the month and then year. If the inscription was made by someone steeped in army tradition, the date could be read September 2, 1886.[6]

William Miller states the initial construction of the Nine Mile Road began in 1885,[7] whereas Gary Weicks, making excellent use of military documents and newspaper accounts, suggests it could have been as early as 1883 when the Denver and Rio Grande railhead, called Price Station, was first established. This 1883 date is consistent with local histories, which claim the famous Rock House at the mouth of Harmon Canyon was constructed by the Dennis Winn family in 1883.[8] And it would seem likely some type of wagon road existed at that time to supply the needs of the Winn family and the few others who might have been living there at that time.[9]

Weicks makes a convincing case that a rough road used by light wagons was certainly in place by the time soldiers arrived in the fall of 1886.[10]

The famous "Rock House" reportedly built by the Dennis Winn family in 1883, or three years before the army "constructed" a road through the canyon. Photo courtesy of Jerry D. Spangler.

On September 10, Lieutenant J. C. Parker, along with four soldiers and an "interpreter" (Company F, Twenty-First Infantry, Fort Duchesne), stocked with ten days' provisions, were ordered to report on the condition of the settler road and the repairs that would be necessary to make it suitable for army freighting.[11] Six days later, Major Edward Bush and sixty-two infantry soldiers (Companies B and G, Sixth Infantry, Fort Douglas), along with provisions for three weeks, one hundred rounds of ammunition per man, four saddle horses, five four-mule wagons, and construction equipment, were ordered into Nine Mile Canyon to "put the road in as good a condition as practicable."[12]

The date of the September 10 order is intriguing because it came eighteen days after troops had already arrived at the site of Fort Duchesne, only to find few or no supplies to build a fort. Troops would not have begun work on the Nine Mile Road until sometime after September 16. Yet the Salt Lake Tribune reported on October 8, 1886, that the Fort Douglas troops had just returned from completing "a first-class roadway from Price's Station to Fort Duchesne."[13]

These dates and the rapidity with which the military completed its road construction suggest there was already some kind of road in Nine Mile Canyon, and the military's efforts were directed at making it passable to

Captain Stephen Perry Jocelyn was one of the first army commanders to work on the Nine Mile Road in 1886. Used by permission, Utah State Historical Society, all rights reserved.

the heavier freight wagons. The Salt Lake Tribune reported on September 18, 1886, that the troops had been focused on leveling two bad grades, making two sharp curves passable, and widening narrow dugways[14]—hardly work that constituted a new road. Whatever Major Bush accomplished was apparently not enough. Scarcely a month later, Captain Stephen Jocelyn (Company B, Twenty-First Infantry, Fort Duchesne) was ordered to re-examine the road to assess how it might better handle heavy freight.[15]

The fledgling fort was at the time suffering from a woeful lack of timber to build barracks and even tents to house the men at the onset of a brutal Uinta Basin winter. Messengers were dispatched to the military supply station at Price Station and to Fort Douglas in December of that year, but these efforts produced little relief.[16] If supplies were being delivered to the fort in 1886, they were simply not enough. Most of the soldiers passed the winter of 1886–1887 huddled in tents.

Why a road would have been built prior to 1886 is more of a mystery. As we discuss in chapter 5, those living in the Price area were tied by blood and economics to communities in Juab County and Utah County to the west. Those living in the Uinta Basin at that time were more tied to the Heber City area in Wasatch County, and there was already a wagon route to Park City. It might well have been that prices for basic frontier commodities were so much less expensive at the railheads in Price that eager entrepreneurs had jumped on the opportunity long before the military arrived at the same conclusion. There might have been irregular shipments by that route as early as 1883, although the population of the Uinta Basin was small at that time and demand would have been minimal.

Fort Thornburgh and the Carter Road

The origins of the Nine Mile Road are actually rooted in events that occurred several years before soldiers set to making the route passable. Mormon colonists had traditionally viewed the establishment of military posts as an unequivocal threat to their freedoms and sovereignty. But the outbreak of hostilities in 1879 with Utes at the White River Agency in Colorado, and the subsequent removal of Yampa and Uncompahgre Utes to the Uinta Basin reservation, prompted Euro-American families residing there to request military protection (there were only 100 to 150 of them at the time).[17] The War Department agreed that a military fort would be needed to protect white settlers and to ensure the Utes remained on the Utah reservations.[18]

In 1881, Brigadier General George Crook, commander of the Department of the Platte, dispatched Captain H. S. Hawkins and almost two hundred soldiers (Companies D, F, G and H, Sixth Infantry, Fort Douglas), along with seventy-five freight wagons and seventy-five pack mules, to the Uinta Basin to establish a military post at the new Ouray Agency near the confluence of the White, Duchesne, and Green Rivers;[19] the fort was to be named in honor of Major Thomas Thornburgh, who was killed in the 1879 Ute revolt in Colorado, commonly called the Meeker War. Other troops were dispatched from Fort Fred Steele in Wyoming (Companies C and E, Fourth Infantry) to help with improvements to the Park City Road. By August 1881, the soldiers had set up camp across from the Ouray Agency at the confluence of the Green and Duchesne Rivers.[20]

The Utes were openly hostile to a military fort so near their homes, and the Department of Interior asked the secretary of war to move the military post to a less provocative location. As a result, Fort Thornburgh was established that fall some thirty-five miles away at the mouth of Ashley Creek Canyon. Fort Thornburgh was intended to be an elaborate thirty-two-structure facility to have been completed during the fall of 1881 at a cost of $84,000. But the absence of any congressional appropriations in 1881 required the soldiers to pass a frigid Uinta Basin winter in tents. Again in 1882, there was no appropriation. In 1883, Congress appropriated a mere $1,500, enough to construct eight adobe buildings.[21] In October of that year, Fort Thornburgh commander Major E. G. Bush announced he was moving his troops to Fort Douglas in Salt Lake City to pass the winter.[22] The fort was abandoned for good on July 22, 1884, the army having relented to local opposition from settlers—all of them squatters—who claimed the Fort Thornburgh site as their own land.[23]

To accept the military's reasoning that the later Nine Mile Canyon supply route was shorter and not as steep is to ignore certain realities of the time. Military freight contracts were highly coveted, and anyone who won a freighting contract could become wealthy. Those contracts were not about who could deliver supplies cheaper and more efficiently, but rather they were about cronyism.

General George Crook, commander of forces in the western territories and a decorated Union general during the Civil War, directed the construction of Fort Thornburgh and later Fort Duchesne. By some accounts, he chose the actual location of Fort Duchesne. Image from Harper's Weekly, October 15, 1864.

Judge William Carter was one of the wealthiest and most politically influential figures in southwestern Wyoming. He forged the Carter Road over the Uinta Mountains into the Uinta Basin at his own expense and was awarded the military freight contract. Photo courtesy of Wyoming State Archives, Department of State Parks and Cultural Resources (Neg. No. 1588).

Judge William Carter was one such opportunist. He was a life-long friend of General William S. Harney, a politically powerful army man and war hero who used his influence to have Carter appointed to Fort Bridger, Wyoming, as a "sutler"—a civilian trader who managed the purchase and sale of merchandise for the military. Fort Bridger is located near the Union Pacific railhead, and the railhead itself is sometimes referred to as Carter Station. Judge Carter became very wealthy through this arrangement with the army, and he parlayed his wealth into political influence, becoming the most prominent citizen of the Green River country in Wyoming. He had a reputation as a southern gentleman, a gracious host, and, to the military men at least, a man of honesty and integrity. He was appointed a judge even though he was not a lawyer and not even schooled in the law, a practice that was not unusual at the time.[24]

When the military in 1880 announced its plan to build Fort Thornburgh in the Uinta Basin, Judge Carter knew he was in an optimal position to supply the post. But a lot of other folks in Colorado and Utah wanted the contract, too, and competition was fierce. Carter financed the construction of a road through the Uinta Mountains, confident that he would get the military contract at the end of the day. He did.[25]

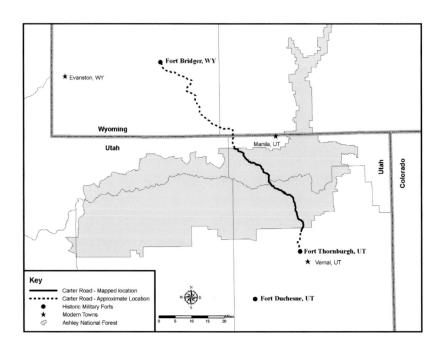

Map indicating the location of the Carter Road in relation to Fort Thornburgh, Fort Duchesne, and Fort Bridger. Image courtesy of USDA Forest Service, Ashley National Forest.

The Carter Road was completed in the fall of 1881, but not before Judge Carter fell ill at one of the construction camps.[26] He died shortly thereafter at his home in Fort Bridger, and his son, Willie Carter, took over the contract.[27] Freight traffic was hampered by mud, rain, and snow, and in the summer of 1882 four companies of infantry were sent to improve the road and to construct a telegraph line from Fort Thornburgh to Fort Bridger.[28]

Fort Thornburgh was abandoned in 1884 and the military shipments ceased. But the road had already become a major economic lifeline to the Uinta Basin, a route whereby gold, silver, and copper ore were shipped north and in return the Uinta Basin settlers could readily obtain supplies from Carter Station. A second wagon route from the Uinta Basin to Park City was also operational at that time.[29] And by all accounts, the Carter Road and the Park City Road continued to serve military needs long after the Nine Mile Road was built. The Carter Road remained a valuable transportation route into and out of the Uinta Basin through at least 1926, when it was replaced by a new highway.[30]

If the Carter Road and Park City Road were already in place and functional, why would the War Department in 1886 choose to construct an entirely new route through Nine Mile Canyon from Price Station to the newly established Fort Duchesne? If you follow the money it seems to lead to Bert Seaboldt, the Denver and Rio Grande Railroad executive and first big-time speculator, along with Sam Gilson, to lock up claims to Gilsonite deposits almost a year before the Nine Mile Road was actually completed. It is probably not coincidence, given Seaboldt's connection to the Denver and Rio Grande Railroad, that the valuable Gilsonite ores would be destined for Price instead of north to the rival Union Pacific rail stations.

There is no paper trail indicating the military was in cahoots with Seaboldt and the Denver and Rio Grande. But the timing of the events seems more than coincidental (see chapter 3). Adding to this suspicion is a reference by Herbert Kretchman that the dominant Gilsonite concern of the day—the Gilson Asphaltum Company, which bought out Gilson and Seaboldt in 1889—also had the lucrative contracts to haul the military freight from Price to Fort Duchesne.[31] The rates charged to the military were twice as much as those paid to haul Gilsonite on the return trip.

Fort Damn Shame

The forced removal of White River and Uncompahgre Utes of Colorado to the Uinta Basin did not set well with the Uintah Utes of Utah, the latter of whom had played no part in the events that prompted the removal. When interband warfare broke out during the winter of 1885–1886, J. D. C. Atkins, commissioner of the Bureau of Indian Affairs, recommended the establishment of a new fort near the Uintah Reservation "to discipline and control" the Utes. Later in 1886, Crook selected a site for a new fort, to be called Fort Duchesne, about three miles above the confluence of the Duchesne and Uintah Rivers midway between the Whiterocks and Ouray agencies. At about the same time, the military decided to construct a supply route through Nine Mile Canyon, eschewing the northern route built in 1881 through the Uinta Mountains.

The official reasoning was the Nine Mile route was preferred because it was shorter and had maximum elevations 2,000 feet lower than those in the Uinta Mountains. This is true to a point. The actual length of the Carter Road is not known with certainty (the portion of that route in Wyoming has not been identified). One possible route to Carter Station would have been 91 miles from Fort Thornburgh, or 113 miles from Fort Duchesne. The Nine Mile Road from Price Station to Fort Duchesne was 86 or 88 miles (accounts vary as to the exact length).[32] The difference would have been about a day and a half more for wagon travel on the Carter Road under ideal conditions.

The elevation climbs on the Carter Road were 3,220 feet coming from Fort Bridger and 4,270 coming from Fort Duchesne. On the Nine Mile Road, there were climbs of 3,425 feet going to Fort Duchesne and 4,060 feet returning to Price—a negligible difference in terms of the burden on the mules pulling the wagons. But the real difference was the maximum elevation, where the Nine Mile Road held an advantage: The maximum elevation on the Carter Road was almost 9,900 feet, whereas it was only about 7,500 feet on the Nine Mile Road—a significant difference of 2,400 feet. In theory, the lower elevation on the Nine Mile Road should have resulted in less snow and a shorter winter season.

On August 20 (or August 23), 1886 four companies of the Twenty-First Infantry under the command of General Crook from Fort Fred Steele in Wyoming and Fort Sidney in Nebraska, arrived to begin construction of Fort Duchesne, such as they could with limited supplies. Troops B and E of the Ninth Cavalry, under the command of Major Frederick Benteen out of Fort McKinney, arrived about two days later.[33] Troops B and E were African American soldiers, referred to by the Utes and other Native Americans as "buffalo soldiers." This detachment served on the Uinta frontier for the next twelve years, earning high praise and respect from the civilians who used the Nine Mile Road.[34]

The name Frederick Benteen might sound familiar to western history buffs. Benteen was famous—or infamous, depending on your point of view—for his role in the Battle of Little Bighorn in 1876, where Lt. Colonel George Armstrong Custer met his demise at the hands of Sioux and Cheyenne warriors. Custer's mistake was dividing his Seventh Cavalry

Major Frederick Benteen. War Department photograph by D. F. Barry, courtesy of the National Park Service.

into three attack forces, which made each of them vulnerable to the overwhelming enemy forces. Custer's command was annihilated, whereas the commands of Captain Benteen and his superior officer, Major Marcus Reno, were pinned down and suffered horrific losses. A military inquest into Reno's conduct cleared him of wrongdoing, but Custer apologists to this day blame both Reno and Benteen for not doing enough to come to Custer's aid at Little Bighorn.

Benteen's command of the Ninth Cavalry buffalo soldiers might be interpreted as a professional slap at the outspoken career soldier.[35] Benteen (as well as Custer) had earlier refused commissions with African American units, reflecting the bigotry common in the day.[36] His command of buffalo soldiers at Fort Duchesne probably had less to do with changing personal attitudes toward African Americans and more to do with the cloud that hung over his military career after Little Bighorn. Quite simply, he was not in a position to dictate the terms of his service. According to historian Will Bagley, Benteen expressed open contempt for the soldiers under his command and for his white neighbors. "Some think I came here to fight Indians," he said, "but I came here to fight Mormons."[37]

Benteen, who was indisputably fearless under fire, eventually survived the withering criticism of his role at Little Bighorn and was later promoted to the rank of major. And in 1886 he was given command of Fort Duchesne—a military outpost that had yet to be built. When he arrived, wrote historian Harold Schindler, "Benteen found no lumber, no nails, no plans. To say that he was furious and frustrated would be putting it mildly."[38] Schindler asserts that necessary supplies were simply unavailable and delayed, and when they did arrive the prices were inflated.[39] The Nine Mile Road was completed by late September or early October 1886, but sufficient freight traffic had not yet begun to arrive by that route.[40] Forty military wagons drawn by teams of six mules and loaded with supplies had arrived by way of the Carter Road within two or three weeks of the soldier's arrival,[41] but it wasn't enough and the troops faced the bitter prospect of spending the winter in tents.

Why adequate supplies had not already been delivered by way of the Carter Road or even the Park City Road probably irritated Benteen to no end. Always one to make known his feelings, he railed at the incompetence

Fort Duchesne, Utah, established 1887

Fort Duchesne commander Major Frederick Benteen is back row on right. The soldier on the far left is identified as "Wittich." Next to him is Lieutenant Truitt, who commanded one contingent of Fort Duchesne soldiers building the telegraph line, and next to him is Lieutenant Henry Styler, who commanded another contingent working on the telegraph. Captain Stephen Jocelyn, who directed much of the road improvements, is kneeling on the far right. Mrs. Benteen is seated on the right and her niece is next to her. Note the tents in the background that served as quarters during the first winter at Fort Duchesne. Used by permission, Utah State Historical Society, all rights reserved.

Once supplies began rolling into Fort Duchesne the military constructed permanent barracks, parade grounds, and officers' quarters. This drawing of early Fort Duchesne offers a general layout of the fort. Used by permission, Utah State Historical Society, all rights reserved.

of the military supply system.[42] Much of Benteen's indignation seems to have been directed at J. S. Winston, who held the largest freight contract.[43]

Winter months are brutal in the Uinta Basin even with modern conveniences, but they must have been downright miserable to the dispirited soldiers forced to live in tents. And with winter settling in, Benteen's fortunes

Frederick Benteen (lower row, second from right) with other officers at Fort Douglas, presumably in early 1887 at the time of his court martial. Courtesy of Special Collections, Marriott Library, University of Utah.

turned from bad to worse. Always fond of whiskey, Benteen spent more and more time at the Post Trader's store, where alcohol was not in short supply. He was frequently intoxicated, and in one instance he fell drunkenly into the mud and had to be helped to his tent by a junior officer. On another occasion, he berated a visiting sheriff as a "God damned Mormon." And then there was the time he urinated on the walls of a tent; inside were the wives of two junior officers.[44]

About that same time, in late 1886, General Crook sent an investigator to determine why it was taking so long to get Fort Duchesne up and running. The official report laid the blame squarely on Benteen's shoulders, alleging he was "frequently unfit for duty through excessive use of intoxicating liquors."[45] Benteen was relieved of his command, and on March 5, 1887, he was arrested and taken to Fort Douglas to face a court martial. The famed Civil War veteran and Indian fighter was found guilty of three counts of drunkenness and one count of conduct unbecoming an officer,

and was sentenced to be dismissed from the army. The sentence was later commuted by President Grover Cleveland to suspension of rank and duty for one year at half pay.[46]

Benteen was long gone from Fort Duchesne by the time the Nine Mile Road began delivering a steady stream of supplies to the fort in 1887—twenty thousand tons of military freight the first year alone.[47] But Nine Mile Canyon would have been one of the last things the grizzled frontier soldier would see in his professional career. He was transported to his court martial through Nine Mile Canyon to Price and then by rail to Fort Douglas in Salt Lake City.[48]

The buffalo soldiers of the Ninth Cavalry continued to serve with honor and distinction on the Utah frontier through 1901, earning high praise and respect from their Mormon neighbors. When regiments of the Ninth Cavalry departed for Cuba to fight alongside Teddy Roosevelt at San Juan Hill, Price residents lined the streets to cheer. African American soldiers and white civilians lunched together and played baseball together, and in the evening the town treated the soldiers to songs and entertainment.[49] The buffalo soldiers would return to Fort Duchesne, but the last of them departed in 1901, reassigned to serve in the Philippines.

Making Connection

The Uinta Basin winter of 1886–1887 must have been miserable for the Fort Duchesne troops quartered in tents. And the misery was heightened by the isolation from the outside world. In a letter to his wife, Captain Jocelyn wrote:

> [T]he worst of the condition of things, at present, is the lack of proper mail facilities and telegraphic communication. I consider that to be largely the fault of Colonel Benteen, the K.O. In his place, I should send semi-weekly couriers to Price until a regular mail route is established and in running order, but he does not deem it necessary. Nor have we any immediate hope of a telegraph. The one constructed at great expense from Bridger to Thornburgh was sold at auction upon the abandonment of the latter post for $49.[50]

There is no doubt that Benteen was aware that the lack of consistent communication with Fort Douglas was hampering his ability to acquire needed supplies. By the time soldiers took the initial steps to construct a

Stone building at the edge of the Nine Mile Road on what used to be the William Brock Place. It is believed to have been constructed by the military in about 1887 as part of its telegraph relay station here. Photo by Ray Boren.

telegraph line to Price Station, in late March 1887, Benteen had already been relieved of his command and escorted to Fort Douglas.

The construction of a telegraph line, undertaken mostly by soldiers at Fort Duchesne, was a massive effort involving scores of soldiers working nonstop for five months. In March 1887, soldiers carefully measured eighty-six miles of the route to determine exactly how many wooden poles would be needed for the telegraph line and where they would be placed. And then troops from Company F were dispatched to cut the poles. In late April, Lieutenant Henry Styler and his entire command of Company B (Twenty-First Infantry, Fort Duchesne) began the actual construction, starting at Price Station and working their way through Soldier Canyon, Whitmore Park, and into Nine Mile Canyon.[51]

By July 1887, only forty-nine miles of telegraph line had been completed, which would have placed the troops near Gate Canyon. Lieutenant Truitt and Company K (Twenty-First Infantry, Fort Duchesne) were then dispatched to relieve Company B, complete the telegraph line to Fort Duchesne, stretch the wire on the already completed portion, and inspect the poles and cables for defects. At least "a couple" of relay stations were built in Nine Mile Canyon.[52] (One was clearly at Brock's ranch near the mouth of Gate Canyon, and according to local lore the other was located at the Ed

This crumbling stone building, also on the Brock Place, is believed to be one of two constructed by the military in about 1887 as part of its telegraph relay station. Photo by Ray Boren.

Lee Ranch near the mouth of Argyle Canyon.) The soldiers had completed the tasks and returned to Fort Duchesne by the end of August 1887.[53]

At some point that year, the soldiers were back in the field replacing telegraph poles. As Henry Fiack, one of the first soldiers at Fort Duchesne, recounted, "A bunch of young Ute braves promptly cut it [telegraph] down and made firewood out of the poles, with the net result that the cavalry herded them to the fort, where they were confined to the guardhouse for a time, on a very wholesome diet of bread and water."[54] In August 1890, every other wooden pole was replaced with metal poles that still dot the landscape along the modern Nine Mile Road.[55]

The Nine Mile Road was a far cry from the road it is today. It was narrow, rutted, and required constant maintenance, a task that fell squarely on the military. In September 1887, only a month after troops had returned from constructing the telegraph line, more than seventy troops from Company A and K (Sixth Infantry, Fort Douglas), under the command

A metal telegraph pole in Nine Mile Canyon, one of dozens that still dot the landscape along the Nine Mile Road. The metal poles were erected in 1890 after the wooden poles were cut down. Photo by Jerry D. Spangler.

of Captain William Badger and Captain Charles Penny, were again working on the road. Company K was ordered back to Fort Douglas at the end of October, but Company A would continue working on the road until late November.[56] At the same time, in October 1887, all available troops of Company B (Twenty-First Infantry, Fort Duchesne) spent thirty days working on the northern section of the road.[57]

Clearly, Major Bush should be credited for the first phase of military road construction in 1886. But 1887 was the heyday of the military construction efforts, on both the road and the telegraph line. There were hundreds of U.S. Army personnel, some from Fort Douglas and others from Fort Duchesne, working in the canyon. Maintenance of the road would require their attention for years to come.

As we discuss in chapter 5, the improvement of the Nine Mile military road precipitated a rush of farmers and ranchers who sought to capitalize on the freighting business. And this was clearly underway by 1887. One soldier, identified only as "One of the Boys," writing in the Salt Lake Tribune in late 1887, observed, "I have seen quite a few travel this road, to different mines, the Fort, Ashley and surrounding country."[58] The freight trade increased dramatically in 1888, when three thousand tons of Gilsonite ore were first shipped from the Uinta Basin to Price. And that says nothing of the military freight and the supplies being shipped to civilians in Vernal and Ashley. Within a short time, tens of thousands of tons of freight were being moved back and forth between the Uinta Basin communities and Price every year.

A twice-weekly stage route was established in 1888 and it became a daily service in 1889.[59] The stage service provided regular mail service to Fort Duchesne. Prior to that time, mail had arrived (unpredictably) at the fort by way of the Carter Road through the Uinta Mountains. Dillman states that early Nine Mile resident Frank Alger, who owned a ranch just east of Harmon Canyon, operated a stage line from Price to Myton, although she does not explicitly state he started the stage line. But she did ride it. "To ride on the stage with its swinging seat of buckskin over that was an experience not to be duplicated in many places of the world and, thank heaven, not very often."[60]

The military assigned soldiers to Brock's Place (or Brock's Station) at the mouth of Gate Canyon to operate the telegraph line and protect the military's interests on the Nine Mile Road, and there are stone buildings along the road that were reportedly constructed for that purpose (one has a sign indicating U.S. Army but this was probably erected long afterwards to satisfy tourist curiosity). If any of the soldiers assigned here were African Americans of the Ninth Cavalry it was not mentioned in the various newspaper accounts of the day. In fact, soldiers of any kind are not mentioned at all in the comings and goings at Brock's Place, and their bivouac here might have been occasional and brief.

By Hook or Crook

There is no dispute that the military was seriously engaged in road building, especially in 1887. But the route itself proved to be not much better than the Carter Road. In January 1888, all contact with Fort Duchesne was severed for a four-week period, the Nine Mile Road being choked with impassably deep snows, average temperatures of minus 24 degrees, and broken telegraph lines.[61] In other words, the complaints offered about the Nine Mile Road were no different than those expressed earlier about the Carter Road.

But the military was hell-bent on constructing a new road from Price Station. But when did the military first become aware of the route? The military is never known for quick decisions in such matters, and even slower to implement them. Who brought it to their attention?

It might well have been Sam Gilson, who had been visiting the Uinta Basin to investigate the strange mineral that now bears his name. Gilson would have certainly known about any premilitary route through Nine Mile Canyon. He probably knew the canyon was an ideal transportation corridor as early as the 1870s when he was trailing horses from the Price area north to Wyoming. And as we discussed in chapter 3, he was well connected to the commanders at Fort Douglas. His partner in Gilsonite speculation was Bert Seaboldt, who was connected to the Denver and Rio Grande Railroad, which had a huge financial stake in wresting military freight contracts from its bitter rival, the Union Pacific.

Any interest Gilson might have had in the Nine Mile Road was undoubtedly rooted in his investment in Gilsonite. In theory, Gilson could have shipped the Gilsonite north on the Carter Road, which was still well traveled in 1886. But the reality is that Gilsonite was never shipped on that route, and in fact was never harvested until after the Nine Mile Road had been opened.

Is it coincidence that Gilsonite mining emerged in 1887 just as the military completed the road improvements? Probably not. Just as Judge Carter had constructed the Carter Road with the certainty he would get the military contracts, Gilson and Seaboldt were investing heavily in Gilsonite claims at least nine months before the first army troops were dispatched to improve the Nine Mile Canyon route. Gilson and Seaboldt seem to have been certain that the "worthless mineral" was about to become very valuable, thanks to the military.

There is no evidence that military commanders at Fort Douglas were bribed by Gilson and Seaboldt to choose the new route to benefit the speculators or the Denver and Rio Grande Railroad. But it would not have been beyond the pale of Gilson and Seaboldt to do so. Their scheme had tentacles that reached deep into the U.S. Congress, which in 1888 removed 7,040 acres with the richest Gilsonite deposits from the Uintah Reservation and made them available to speculators. Of course, the legislation included a clause that recognized all claims filed on the tribal lands prior to the removal—claims that had all been bought up by Gilson, Seaboldt, and their close associates as early as January 1886.

It is often asserted that the speculators used unsavory means to get the Gilsonite deposits removed from the reservation.[62] And they probably did.

Bert Seaboldt, who lobbied Congress directly in 1887 and 1888, carried with him $25,000 in cash to Washington, D.C. That amount of cash in 1887 is the equivalent of almost $610,000 in 2012 dollars—certainly a lot more than was needed for mere travel expenses at that time.[63] Was it a bribe to congressmen and other federal officials? Call it a cost of doing business in that day and age.

But who was actually behind the $25,000? As we discussed in chapter 3, Gilson and Seaboldt filed their first claims on Gilsonite—a supposedly worthless mineral—on January 9, 1886, or nine months before construction had actually begun on the Nine Mile Road. Neither man was rich at that time. Gilson was at the time a deputy U.S. marshal with a meager income.[64] Bert Seaboldt was "assistant to the chief engineer and was manager of construction for the Denver and Rio Grande Western Railway between 1882 and 1890."[65] The moneyman behind them has long been assumed to be Charles O. Baxter, who became president of the company that bought out Gilson and Seaboldt in 1889. That company, the Gilson Asphaltum Company, was owned by famed beer-maker Adolphus Busch. Given Gilson and Seaboldt owned their company, the Gilsonite Manufacturing Company, for only one year, it does not stretch the imagination to surmise that Gilson and Seaboldt were actually front men for what Baxter and Busch intended all along: a monopoly on Gilsonite.

There is no question the enterprise was immediately successful. Some 3,000 tons of ore were shipped to the railhead at Price the first year of operations in 1887. At $80 a ton at the railhead, the fledging enterprise would have grossed $240,000 in its first year,[66] or $5.9 million in 2012 dollars.[67]

Kretchman suggests the first Gilsonite shipments occurred in the fall of 1887, which if true meant Gilson and Seaboldt were illegally poaching Gilsonite ores before Congress had removed the lands from the Ute reservation.[68] Bender hints at this, noting Seaboldt had built a "tent city" at the site of the Carbon Vein and removed about a thousand pounds of ore for "testing." He was warned by Indian Agent T. A. Byrnes that he was trespassing on Ute lands, which "was very likely not news to Seaboldt."[69] If he was trespassing, then the event would have occurred in 1886 or 1887 before the claims were removed from the reservation in 1888. The Nine Mile Road would have been passable to Gilsonite freighters by late 1886 and certainly

Colonel T. A. Byrnes, the Indian agent, and Lieutenant (Henry) Styler upon arrival at the site of Fort Duchesne in 1886. The Native American at the far right was identified as General Crook's scout. In 1887, Styler commanded a contingent of Twenty-First Infantry from Fort Duchesne that began work on the telegraph line between Fort Duchesne and Price Station. About that same time, Byrnes caught Bert Seaboldt poaching Gilsonite ores on tribal lands. U.S. Signal Corps photo courtesy of the National Archives and Record Administration.

by 1887. Of interest here is the reference that folks were already traveling the route in 1887 on their way to "mines."[70] Although this could be a reference to the small gold and silver mines in the Uinta Mountains, more likely it was a reference to the Gilsonite mines.

Whether intentional or not, the Gilsonite industry was subsidized by the government. U.S. Army troops continued to repair and maintain the Nine Mile Road through August 1891, and work on the telegraph line continued through at least April 1892.[71] By late November of 1892, the army had all but abandoned Fort Duchesne, leaving behind only a two-troop garrison, and "the responsibility of maintaining the heavily used road now shifted to the primary users, including the well-funded Gilsonite interests, Carbon County, and individual freighting outfits."[72] No mention is made of who took over operation of the telegraph line, but by 1900 it was, according to census records, being run by civilian operators.

Squatters, Freighters, and Barkeeps

On the Nine Mile Road from 1886 to 1901

If ever there was a case of justifiable homicide, that was one.
—William Brock, 1889

In the first half of the 2000s, the Bill Barrett Corporation discovered vast natural gas reserves on the plateaus high above Nine Mile Canyon. In short order, the canyon corridor was transformed from a sleepy, quiet backwater with occasional ranch traffic into a major transportation route with thousands of trucks of all sizes and shapes transporting drilling gear, water, and supplies. Those who loved the quiet decried the industrialization of the canyon. But in many respects, the transformation mirrored what had happened more than a century before, when a quiet canyon paradise occupied by a few reclusive ranchers was quickly and radically altered by the discovery of and a need to transport a different kind of hydrocarbon—Gilsonite.

From 1886 through the early years of the 1900s, Nine Mile Canyon was one of the busiest economic corridors in the state of Utah, its narrow dirt road choked by scores of freighters moving back and forth between the Uinta Basin and the Denver and Rio Grande railheads at Price. And because of the road, the population of Nine Mile Canyon eventually surged to its highest level—more than one hundred souls at one point—in Euro-American history. There were hotels, saloons, blacksmith shops, and general stores selling all sorts of wares from wagon parts to jelly beans.[1]

The story of life along the Nine Mile Road is remarkable in its own right, replete with accounts of danger, murder, and political intrigue. Some of the colorful characters involved are famous and others are infamous, while most are largely forgotten, the only remaining evidence of their sojourn being the names and initials they scrawled on the canyon walls.[2]

A native inhabitant of Nine Mile Canyon. Photo by Ray Boren.

The remnants of the saloons and hotels have mostly disappeared, collapsed from decades of neglect and decay, or in some instances destroyed by thoughtless individuals. Only a handful of the early ranch structures remain. One of the oldest standing historical structures in the canyon—a saloon where two men met violent deaths—was finally dismantled and hauled away in 2011.[3] In effect, little remains of the hustle and bustle and raucous flavor that characterized life on the Nine Mile Road in the nineteenth century.

The First Arrivals

Archaeologists have long maintained that Nine Mile Canyon was, in all likelihood, a major transportation corridor throughout prehistoric times,

Opposite: Twilight comes to Nine Mile Canyon. Photo by Ray Boren.

Left: This 1881 inscription in upper Nine Mile Canyon is one of the oldest in the canyon. It probably predates the Nine Mile Road by two or three years. Photo courtesy of the Colorado Plateau Archaeological Alliance.

Right: Once the wagon road was established, passersby commonly left their names and dates in black axle grease—something every teamster carried to ensure the wagon wheels were well lubricated. There are hundreds of axle-grease signatures in the canyon. Photo courtesy of the Colorado Plateau Archaeological Alliance.

offering the most direct access between the Uinta Basin and the San Rafael Swell.[4] And for the same reason it is assumed the canyon would have been well known to the fur trappers of the 1820s, 1830s, and 1840s, some of whom undoubtedly ventured south and west from trapper enclaves in the Uinta Basin to explore the beaver potential of the Wasatch Plateau and Tavaputs Plateau (see chapter 2).

Exactly when white settlers put down roots in Nine Mile Canyon is not clear. Geary says it "seems doubtful" there was a permanent Euro-American presence here before the construction of the freight road in 1886.[5] However, Dillman maintains the first ranchers arrived here "long before 1880," but she offers no names or dates.[6] A major cattle trail passed near the upper reaches of the canyon by the 1860s, and in all likelihood cattle herds tended by restless cowboys had wandered into the area by at least the 1870s.[7]

Also in the 1860s, the U.S. Army might have pioneered a route that follows what is essentially U.S. Highway 6 through what is today Price and Green River that would have passed within a few miles of Nine Mile Canyon. An 1878 map depicts the route of Captain Henry R. Selden at this location.[8] In 1860, Selden was ordered to march his troops from Camp Floyd west of Utah Lake to New Mexico to protect immigrant travel and commerce there. Fort Selden in New Mexico would later be named for him.

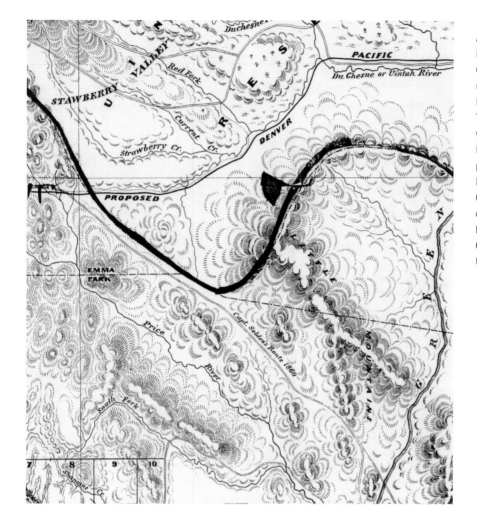

An 1878 map of Utah indicating a route followed by Captain Henry R. Selden, who moved his troops from Camp Floyd to New Mexico in 1860. This route conforms closely with the current route of U.S. Highway 6 and would have passed within a few miles of Nine Mile Canyon (Nine Mile Canyon might be the unnamed drainage just below the thick black line). Courtesy of Special Collections, Marriott Library, University of Utah.

But passing cowboys and soldiers hardly constituted a permanent presence in Nine Mile Canyon, or in the Price River Valley, for that matter. Watt lists the first settlers of the Price area as Abraham Powell and Caleb Rhoades,[9] who arrived in 1877, followed by their kinfolk the following year.[10] By 1879, some of these first Price residents, among them Frederic Empor Grames and Caleb Rhoades, had also ventured deep into Nine Mile Canyon where they left their names etched on the canyon walls.

It is not surprising there would be no mention of a road or trail through the canyon to the Uinta Basin at that time, as there would have been little need for one—all of the new arrivals at that time were connected by blood and economics to the Mormon settlements sixty miles to the west in Utah County and Juab County.

F. E. Grames is Frederic Empor Grames, related by marriage to the John and Abraham Powell families. He was among the first settlers of Price in 1878. He later sold his business interests in Price and established a ranch in upper Nine Mile Canyon. Photo by Jerry D. Spangler.

There is no documentation as to how the first settlers came to find Nine Mile Canyon, but William Miller suggests it could have been the result of Mormon military campaigns against the Utes. The Black Hawk War of 1865 to 1872 was a tumultuous time in Utah with episodic violence and reprisals on both sides. Roughly seventy Mormon settlements were abandoned and families forced to coalesce into larger groups, and a number of protective forts were constructed. Mormon settlers also organized into militias that pursued the Indians through unfamiliar territory. In doing so they discovered areas previously unknown that were suitable for settlement.[11]

The earliest written descriptions of what is known today as Nine Mile Creek were those offered by A. H. Thompson, brother-in-law of famed explorer John Wesley Powell, who visited here in 1877 and briefly described the creek in Powell's *Report on the Lands of the Arid Region*.[12] Government surveyors might have been in the area a year or two earlier, as evidenced by the depiction of the canyon on maps as early as 1876. The canyon itself was apparently surveyed by Deputy U.S. Surveyor Augustus Ferron, who visited in 1878 (see chapter 1).[13] Ferron's map indicated the presence of one ranch belonging to "Alford Lunt,"[14] located in upper Nine Mile Canyon near where Minnie Maud and Nine Mile Creeks converge.

Alfred Lunt was from Nephi in Juab County, as were the Whitmore brothers, who started a ranch at about this same time in the Sunnyside Canyon area (at the time it was called Whitmore Canyon), with a summer range in Whitmore Park in upper Nine Mile Canyon. One unsubstantiated source indicates that George and James Whitmore arrived in 1879.[15] Given the proximity of the two ranches, the fact that both were from well-to-do families in Nephi,[16] and their near-simultaneous arrival here, it can be surmised they were well acquainted with each other before setting up their ranches (the ranches might even have started out as a cooperative venture).[17]

Miller believes the Lunt ranch in Nine Mile was a livestock grazing operation and not a permanent residence. Alfred Lunt continued to live in Nephi and all his children were born there during the time he had the ranch in Nine Mile Canyon.[18] It seems unlikely, however, that Ferron would have noted the presence of the Lunt ranch if there had not been permanent structures. Miller's search of patent records revealed Alfred Lunt never owned title to the lands where his ranch was located, nor did the Lunt family ever file for a land claim in the area. Alfred's ranch was gone by 1900 when the area was claimed by several immigrant families from the Salina Canyon area.[19]

The title of "first settler" of Nine Mile Canyon is commonly bestowed on Shadrach (or Shedrach) Lunt,[20] known to all as "Shed," who was a younger brother to Alfred. Dillman described Shed as "a wonderful man…kind and at peace with the world," who was perhaps the first to graze cattle in the canyon.[21] He also had a reputation as somewhat of a hermit, preferring to live on the outermost fringes of the Wild West with no neighbors and lots of uncontested elbow room.[22]

Like so many Nine Mile Canyon legends, this characterization of Shed Lunt has been greatly embellished over the years. Far from being a hermit, he also maintained a home in Nephi where he probably passed the winter months. He was married to Ann Pitt and he fathered at least seven children between 1873 and 1896. And ranching was apparently good to the Lunt family as they built a fine two-story brick home—a minimansion by pioneer standards of the day—in Nephi where Shed and Ann raised their children.

Shadrach Lunt was born in Birmingham, England, in 1851 and, as was common for converts to the Mormon faith at that time, he immigrated with his family, first to Salt Lake City and then to Nephi. He was five years old when his family left England. His brother Alfred was five years older and a sister, Elizabeth, was two years older; he had another brother, Nephi, who was four years younger and just a baby at the time.[23]

Over a sixty-year career as a cattleman, Shed would leave his mark on the history of not only Nine Mile Canyon, but also on Desolation Canyon, where one feature, Lunt's Horse Pasture, bears his name today. Green River historian James M. Aton believes Shed settled in Nine Mile Canyon in 1877,[24] which would have been the same year that Abraham Powell and Caleb Rhoades first arrived in the Price area. This is supported by Lunt family historian Myrna Rasmussen, who indicated the Lunt brothers wintered their herds in the Price area in the winter of 1876–1877, and in the summer of 1877 they pushed the herds into Nine Mile Canyon. The brothers had 2,500 cattle at one unspecified point in time.[25] Dillman indicates Shed built his ranch at the site of what would become known as Brock's Place, which later became the Preston Nutter Ranch.[26]

In the summers, Shed trailed his cattle south onto the West Tavaputs Plateau, where he eventually discovered Desolation Canyon—a land not yet occupied by cattle or cowboys. He is credited with blasting a trail from the top of the plateau down Steer Ridge Canyon, a trail still used by ranchers more than a century later. Perhaps as early as 1879, he built a small ranch at the mouth of Rock Creek in the heart of Desolation Canyon, where he lived for more than twenty years before selling out in the early 1900s.[27] In 1889, he was driving cattle through Nine Mile with Frank Foote, also from Nephi, when the latter was killed in a saloon brawl. Later in life Shed was a watchman for Preston Nutter on the same West Tavaputs summer range where he had been the first cowboy.[28] According to the family, cattle rustling became such a problem in the early 1890s that the brothers in 1895 rounded up what remained of their cows and sold out.[29]

There are few physical reminders today of the Lunt family in Nine Mile Canyon. There is an old log cabin at Rock Creek reportedly built by Shadrach Lunt sometime after 1887.[30] And there is a message scrawled in black pigment in middle Nine Mile Canyon near the lower Rich Ranch that reads, "For coughs and colds, go to Dock Lunt, Nephi"—a primitive billboard, of sorts, certainly intended to garner the attention of passersby on the Nine Mile Road.[31]

Local legend has it that Shadrach Lunt was somewhat of a hermit during his tenure in Nine Mile Canyon, but that might be exaggerated. He had a wife and at least seven children, all living in Nephi. And apparently he did well for himself in the cattle business, as evidenced by the minimansion he built in Nephi. Photo by Jerry D. Spangler.

The Whitmore Empire

The Whitmore brothers—James and George—were iconic figures in the early settlement of central Utah, although their contributions warrant only passing references in the various recent histories of the region. They were both well-respected businessmen and well heeled, with the capital to influence local politics and commerce. They established a ranch at or near Sunnyside, Utah, on the south slopes of the Book Cliffs in 1879 or

Scrawled in axle grease, the "billboard" reads: "For coughs & colds go to Dock Lunt, Nephi." Photo courtesy of the Colorado Plateau Archaeological Alliance.

thereabouts, and legend has it they were running more than ten thousand head of cattle within a year or two of their arrival.

But where did they come from? Both were Texas-born, both immigrated to Utah with their Mormon convert parents at very young ages, and both arrived in the Price area by way of Nephi. As we discuss in the chapter on the canyon's outlaw legacy (see chapter 6), the Whitmore brothers also had a long-running blood feud with an outlaw named Joe Walker, who believed the Whitmore brothers had absconded with his inheritance—a cattle herd entrusted to the Whitmores' father, who once had a large livestock operation on the Arizona Strip east of St. George. Is there any reason to believe Joe Walker?

The official histories of the Grand Canyon–Parashant National Monument and Pipe Springs National Monument indicate that Dr. James Whitmore, a Mormon convert from a small town near Dallas, Texas, was the first rancher at Pipe Springs, in 1863.[32] Dr. Whitmore was a highly successful rancher with eleven thousand sheep, five hundred head of cattle, and one thousand grapevines. With his ranch foreman, Robert McIntyre, he staked out corrals, built a dugout, fenced off ten acres, and planted apples and grapes. Both men were killed in 1866 by a Navajo raiding party.[33]

Joe Walker also claimed to be a Texan by birth. According to old-timers interviewed by Pearl Baker, Walker's father had died shortly after his son's

birth, leaving his wife without the means to continue operating their Texas ranch. Joe Walker's mother entrusted the Walker cattle herd to a relative named Dr. Whitmore, who had immigrated to Utah. After Dr. Whitmore was killed, the surviving Whitmore sons denied knowledge of the arrangement. Walker's persistent theft of their cattle was viewed by Walker as taking back what was rightfully his.

This was Joe's story—the Whitmores flatly denied either the relationship or the claim, and refused to have anything to do with Walker.

The Whitmore Ranch near present-day Sunnyside was established in 1879 by George and James Whitmore. Photo courtesy of the L. Tom Perry Special Collections, Harold B. Lee Library, Brigham Young University.

He had no resources of either money or influence and, like most of his class at the time, knew little of and believed less in legal action. He was bitter, although people who knew him best liked him, and thought he was justified in his outlawry.[34]

By Walker's accounts, the Whitmore brothers kept the Walker herds for themselves, using the cattle to become the largest cattle ranch in Nine Mile Canyon in the 1880s and 1890s.

But the Whitmore brothers were all quite young at the time of their own father's death, certainly too young to have wronged Joe Walker. If there is any kernel of truth to the Walker story, it is just as reasonable to surmise the surviving Whitmore children never knew about any Texas relatives.

According to various genealogical records, the elder James Whitmore was born in Tennessee in about 1825.[35] Various histories indicate he married Mary Elizabeth Carter at Waxahachie, Texas, in 1853, but a closer review of Texas marriage records indicates Mary Elizabeth's name at the time was Elizabeth Flaherty, a widow when they married on February 23, 1853.[36]

A history compiled by the Whitmore family indicates Elizabeth was the daughter of Richard Carter, a wealthy and prominent man in Texas at that time. She married Flaherty in about 1850 and they started their own four-hundred-acre ranch. Soon thereafter, her husband died of yellow fever while taking the herds to market in Louisiana.[37]

She then met and married James Montgomery "Doc" Whitmore—a local druggist who had helped her with medicines for her sick cattle—in 1853. In 1856, they joined with neighbors to heckle Mormon missionaries who had arrived in the area, but instead they were converted by the preaching, as were James's brother and sister. Elizabeth was disowned by her father, and the Whitmore family was ostracized by their friends and neighbors.[38]

According to Mormon immigration records, the Whitmore clan—comprised of James Montgomery Whitmore and wife, Elizabeth Carter Flaherty, both thirty years old at the time; and their three small children, three-year-old George Carter, one-year-old James Montgomery, and infant Joseph—immigrated to Utah from Texas in 1857 as part of the Homer Duncan Company of Mormon converts, which left Texas in May

1857 and arrived in Salt Lake in September of that year. Also accompanying them were Franklin Perry Whitmore, twenty-two, James's brother, and Mary Louise Whitmore, nineteen, who was James's sister.[39] The family history indicates they left their Texas ranch unsold and the crops standing in the field because no one would buy from Mormons. The Whitmores drove 1,300 head of cattle with them to Salt Lake City.[40]

The Whitmore family was still living in Salt Lake at the time of the 1860 census. By 1861 they were "called" by church leaders to go to St. George as part of the "Cotton Mission." James Whitmore brought four hundred head of Texas longhorns with him to St. George and then secured a certificate for 160 acres around Pipe Springs, Arizona, in 1863. He was clearly the largest cattle operator on the Arizona Strip at that time.[41]

Before he was killed at Pipe Springs at age thirty-nine, James and Elizabeth Whitmore had eight children. The oldest, George Carter, would have been twelve at the time of his father's death, his brother James, ten. George and James figure prominently in the subsequent history of the Nine Mile region and in the eventual death of Joe Walker at the hands of a posse (see chapter 6).

The Whitmore family did not come to Nine Mile country directly after the Navajo raid that left Mary Elizabeth a widow with young children. One account has it that George first moved to Nephi in 1872 at the ripe age of eighteen, and that he soon became a leading entrepreneur.[42] It is not known if his mother or brothers joined him at this time, but within a few years most of the Whitmore clan was living in Nephi. By 1879, George and James were involved in the cattle business in the Nine Mile area in a big way.

By one account, soon after their arrival they were running fifteen thousand head of cattle and controlled the entire West Tavaputs Plateau north of the Price River. They had two ranch headquarters, one along the Price River near Price and the other in Whitmore Canyon, now known as Sunnyside. At one time, they hired as many as thirty cowboys and ranch hands.[43] Their summer range was known as Whitmore Park—the high country in upper Nine Mile Canyon.

The various historical accounts differ somewhat from the family history, which states that mother Elizabeth in 1883 "purchased" a ranch in Carbon County, which her sons operated.[44] This is unlikely since her sons had been running herds there since 1879, and there would have been no need

George Whitmore was one of the most preeminent businessmen in central Utah, and was even sought after to be a gubernatorial candidate. This portrait hangs in the Whitmore Mansion, now a bed and breakfast, in Nephi. Photo by Jerry D. Spangler.

James Whitmore, with his brother George, ran a cattle operation in upper Nine Mile Canyon that was reported to have ten to fifteen thousand head—the largest of its kind anywhere in the region. He later established the first bank in Price. Photo courtesy of the L. Tom Perry Special Collections, Harold B. Lee Library, Brigham Young University.

to purchase a ranch since it was public domain. But Elizabeth might have provided the breed stock and perhaps capital whereby her sons were soon running ten to fifteen thousand head of cattle in the Nine Mile Canyon area. The family history states that Elizabeth—by then remarried to John Albert Casey— returned to Salt Lake City driving her substantial cattle herds ahead of her.[45] It is unlikely that the increasingly urbanized Salt Lake Valley could have accommodated any large cattle herds at that time, and she might have looked to move the livestock to her sons' Carbon County ranch instead. Elizabeth, who remained in Salt Lake City until her death in 1892, was a frequent visitor to her sons' ranch, traveling by train to Price and then by wagon to Sunnyside.[46]

There is no dispute that her sons were successful in business. By 1885, George had started the First National Bank of Nephi, which led to three other banks in Payson, Fountain Green, and Fillmore (his brother James also started the First National Bank in Price in 1901). George also speculated in land and had large holdings in Nevada and Utah, mostly in Carbon County. He was elected to the Utah Senate and later in life he turned down a request to run for governor because of poor health.[47]

By all accounts the Whitmore brothers were wealthy, although it is unknown exactly how this wealth was derived, whether it was family money or returns on their own business ventures or some combination of both. The amount of the family wealth must have been enormous. The

George Carter Whitmore Mansion in Nephi is a reminder of the family fortune (the spectacular Queen Anne Victorian mansion is now on the National Register of Historic Places).

When George and James first pushed their herds into the Nine Mile area in 1879, the brothers would have been twenty-five and twenty-three years old, respectively. For the next two decades, they were among the most politically powerful families in the region, rivaling even the influence of the Pleasant Valley Coal Company when it came to Carbon County affairs. They were even credited in one account with the firing of a local sheriff for failing to stem the rustling of their cattle herds.[48] From the 1880s through 1890s, the Whitmore name was not just prominent in the local histories, it was prominent everywhere. But by the early 1900s, the Whitmore family name was mentioned far less often, and by the 1920s it was mentioned hardly at all. George died in 1917 and James died in 1920, leaving behind vast fortunes to their heirs.

View of Whitmore Park in upper Nine Mile Canyon, named for the Whitmore brothers of Nephi who ran massive herds here. Photo by Ray Boren.

The wealth of the Whitmore family can be surmised by the opulence of the Whitmore Mansion in Nephi, built by George Whitmore. It is now on the National Register of Historic Places. Photo by Jerry D. Spangler.

James Beckstead claims the demise of the Whitmore cattle empire can be attributed to the railroad and mining interests that "besieged them."[49] One local legend has it the next generation of Whitmores had grown weary of Utah and its stifling social scene, and that they and their inheritances moved on to sunnier climes in Southern California, at the time emerging as a destination for the rich and famous. Some family members indeed moved on to California; George died in 1917 while visiting family in Pasadena. By other accounts, the Whitmore family retained its financial interests in Carbon County, including its cattle ranches, well into the 1930s and perhaps much later.[50]

Another cattle operation that arrived in Nine Mile Canyon in 1879 was the Argyle family. Hyrum and Ben Argyle, sons of original Mormon handcart pioneers had been running cattle in the Diamond Fork area of Spanish Fork Canyon in the 1870s. But their herds had become too large and the range too crowded. Ben Argyle went in search of new rangelands and stumbled upon Nine Mile Canyon in 1879, and by that fall they had moved their herds into the canyon. They remained with the cattle throughout the frigid winter of 1879–1880. The major northern tributary of Nine Mile Canyon is called Argyle Canyon to this day.[51] It is not specified how many cattle they were running, nor is there any mention of the Whitmore and Lunt herds that were already in the canyon at that time.

The Whitmore and Argyle brothers were not the only large cattle operators to eye the potential of the rangelands of the West Tavaputs Plateau. In 1885, Benjamin Van Dusen, James Dart, and Augustus Ferron—the latter was the same who had mapped Nine Mile Canyon in 1878—organized the Range Valley Cattle Company and claimed all of the Range Creek drainage and much of the high country above.[52] They ran about 2,500 head of cattle in the same general area as the Whitmore brothers. There are no references to conflicts between the Whitmores and the Range Valley partners, and the expansive West Tavaputs Plateau might have been big enough for both operations to coexist.

Beckstead, citing interviews with Whitmore Cattle Company employee Clarence Pilling, indicates another rancher also arrived in the area in 1879, a Lord Elliot, purportedly of British royalty but a royal who had nonetheless been banished by his family. He established a ranch just south of Sunnyside where he built a "beautiful mansion," at least by Utah standards at that time. He was reportedly a tall, quiet fellow who wore a pearl-handled Colt revolver on each hip. The ranch was quite profitable.[53]

In the 1890s, Lord Elliot apparently brought thousands of sheep into the Tavaputs Plateau country. This did not set well with the Whitmores and, according to Pilling, there was at least one donnybrook at a local spring where thirty or so Whitmore cowboys mixed it up with a similar number of Lord Elliot employees.[54] Lord Elliot left the country as mysteriously as he had arrived.

> At the turn of the century Lord Elliot had withstood drought, range wars and takeover attempts by the Rio Grande Railroad. However, when his beloved wife died suddenly, he was never the same. Soon after he sold his sheep and cattle…[and] simply walked out, leaving his possessions, mounted his horse, and rode off, never to be heard from again.[55]

It is unknown what, if any, role Lord Elliot might have played in the history of Nine Mile Canyon. He probably knew of Nine Mile Canyon, might even have run his livestock there. What is clear is that by the early 1900s there was a new cattle king on the Carbon County landscape, and he controlled most of the West Tavaputs country once claimed by the

Whitmores and the Range Valley Cattle Company. His name was Preston Nutter.

We do not know if there were others in the Nine Mile country in the 1870s. But when the Lunt brothers arrived in 1877 or 1878, and the Whitmore brothers, the Argyle brothers, and Lord Elliot moved their herds into the area in 1879, Nine Mile Canyon would have been largely uninhabited and unclaimed—ripe for any ambitious young rancher seeking his own spread. The canyon and the surrounding plateaus were all public domain, federal land that had not been claimed by formal title or deed.

A Cash Windfall

The quiet anonymity Nine Mile Canyon might have had in the 1870s was shattered by the mid-1880s when the canyon became the preferred route for shipping military supplies to Fort Duchesne (see chapter 4). At least by 1887, most everyone in the Price and Uinta Basin areas would have been familiar with the route, maybe even traveled it. And it did not take long for a few enterprising families to lay claim to their own ranches along the canyon bottom.

There were two ways to make good money in Nine Mile Canyon at that time: you could haul the freight or you could provide goods and services to those who did. Historian Ed Geary, whose grandfather was a freighter in the canyon, suggests there were on average about fifty trips each direction each week. With an average round trip lasting two weeks, a hundred or more teamsters would have been on the road in any given week. Geary said a good freighter could make as much as ninety dollars a week, although freighters had to factor in the vagaries of weather that could make trips much longer, and there were also the costs of maintaining the teams and equipment.[56]

Freighting was a lucrative business that forever changed the economic landscape of Price and Nine Mile Canyon. In 1887, the *Salt Lake Tribune* reported that a contract to haul 2 million pounds of government supplies had been let at a rate of $1.12 per hundred pounds (this was about a third of the price the military had been paying to ship freight from the Union Pacific railhead at Carter Station). According to Geary's math, an average freight outfit could haul up to 9,000 pounds. The government contract alone would require 220 trips for a two-wagon outfit, 3,300 man hours to complete the contract, and a payoff of $22,400.[57] Even divided among scores of teamsters, if there were that many in 1887, that was good money in the 1880s. "Indeed, it [freighting] was probably the chief factor in establishing Price as a commercial center for the region."[58]

For the freighters, the emergence of Gilsonite mining in the Uinta Basin was a second windfall. Not only could they be paid for hauling military supplies north to Fort Duchesne and the Indian agencies, but they would be paid a second time for hauling the Gilsonite ore to Price on the return trip. The cost of shipping the ore by wagon ran about $10 to $12 per ton, or about half of what they were paid to haul government freight.[59] If Geary's calculations are correct that a freighter could carry up to four and a half tons each way, a single two-week round trip could gross about $135—a tidy sum of money in the 1880s, even if some of that was skimmed by middle-men contractors who arranged the trips.[60] This $135 ballpark figure is the equivalent of $3,300 in 2012 dollars.[61]

The Gilsonite industry also opened the freighting business to more competition. Whereas one-way traffic from Price was tilted in favor of Price-area freighters, the two-way traffic also meant that Uinta Basin farmers who had horses and wagons could also get in on the action.

With that much money at stake, it is not at all surprising that different entities would attempt to control the freight business. Geary states that the Indian agencies, to control costs, eventually had their own wagons and teamsters to haul government supplies. Businesses in Price and Vernal would secure contracts with the government and the Gilson Asphaltum Company and then subcontract with individual freighters, taking their own cut along the way.[62]

Kretchman, however, says the Gilson Asphaltum Company had secured the contract to haul government freight north to the Uinta Basin,[63] which meant the company would have had a monopoly on the lucrative freighting business in both directions. Watt indicates the Gilson Asphaltum Company opened its freight store in Price in 1887, but it had competition by 1888 when the Emery County Mercantile opened. In 1890, the Price Trading Company was founded to capitalize on the burgeoning trade.[64] Among the partners in that enterprise was John Montgomery Whitmore,

younger brother of George and James, at the time cattle barons in the Nine Mile country.

These "stores" effectively functioned as intermediaries in the Nine Mile freighting business, securing contracts with the U.S. government and with the Gilsonite mines in the Uinta Basin to ship materials in both directions at fixed rates. In all likelihood, the individual freighters probably never got rich. And the work could be grueling. Two areas proved particularly troublesome to the freighters. One was the pass over Soldier Creek Canyon just

The freighting business led directly to a burgeoning business district in Price, which acted as subcontractors with the Gilsonite mines and the military. The Price Trading Company was one of many early establishments here. Photo courtesy of L. Tom Perry Special Collections, Harold B. Lee Library, Brigham Young University.

The Price Co-operative Mercantile Institution was one of the early commercial establishments in Price. Used by permission, Utah State Historical Society, all rights reserved.

north of Wellington, where deep snows were a common occurrence in the winter months, and the other was Gate Canyon, which was susceptible to flash floods. During the rainy seasons, there was the problem of mud. It was not uncommon that a round trip of two weeks under good conditions could be double that time with bad weather. But the work was steady and there was plenty of demand—so much that not enough freighters could be found to handle all the shipments.[65]

Price was well established by 1886 when the military arrived to work on the Nine Mile Road, although the community must have left a lot to be desired. Captain Stephen Jocelyn of Fort Duchesne observed in late 1886, "This is a nasty little alkali hamlet of a dozen houses or so."[66] The discovery of harvestable coal at Pleasant Valley in 1875 and the arrival of the Denver and Rio Grande Railroad in 1883 had resulted in a small but thriving community. By 1885, there were 355 people living in Price.[67] If it can be estimated that half the population were adults and only half of those were men, there would have been only about 60 men who *could* have gotten into freighting at that time. Then subtract the shopkeepers and businessmen and those already working for the railroad, and the pool of potential teamsters dwindles substantially. Yet in 1887, the first year supplies were shipped on the Nine Mile Road, some twenty thousand tons of military freight were shipped from Price to the Uinta Basin.[68]

At four and a half tons per load, there would have been almost 4,500 trips through the canyon that first year. Even if the freighters could make 20 trips a year—an ambitious target that would have been contingent upon weather—there would have been a need for at least 225 teamsters in 1887. And the amounts being shipped in both directions would increase exponentially in the years ahead. Little wonder that "almost everyone in Price and Wellington owned a wagon to haul goods between Price and the Uinta Basin, and many Emery County farmers engaged in freighting as well."[69]

Freighting provided much-needed cash for small-time family farmers barely hanging on. As Arthur E. Gibson wrote, "Most of our farmers and early settlers were...also freighters. Money was not as plentiful in those days as it is today, and any farmer who had either two, four or six good horses and a couple of wagons would be ready at most any time to make a trip on the freight road."[70]

By most accounts, a trip each direction would take six or seven days, which meant that freighters were making about twelve to fourteen miles a day. It also meant that camping along the route—lands in this area were still public domain—was a routine part of doing business. The location of these camps is not known with certainty, but it can be surmised by the clusters of axle-grease signatures left by freighters on the canyon walls, places like the Johnston Ranch (now the Cottonwood Glen Picnic Area) and Brock's Place (now the Nutter Ranch). Leaving your name on a cliff is probably not something you did while traveling and trying to make good time, but rather after a long day on the road at an evening camp.

Not surprisingly, several enterprising families saw an opportunity to capitalize on the freight traffic, offering the weary teamsters more creature comforts. In much the same way that truck stops spring up along modern interstate highways, a series of "ranches" had sprung up along the route shortly after 1886, offering for a price feed and water for the draft animals, hot meals, intoxicating liquors, a bed to sleep in, and by some popular accounts, companionship.[71]

Brock's Place, with a stage stop and telegraph relay station, was the largest of the establishments haunted by the freighters. In 1889, Brock had nine rooms, as well as a saloon.[72] By 1901, when Pete Francis operated the joint, there were twenty rooms and a saloon. There was a hotel at Edwin Lee's place, a saloon at John Eagan's place, and a dry goods store at Frank Alger's place.

There were also "bootleg" establishments called whiskey ranches, and Nine Mile was known to have several of them. One such whiskey ranch was operated by Lucius Benton in the Whitmore Park area. There is little doubt that Benton was selling hard liquor to the soldiers working on road improvements, but Benton, who was present in the area by at least 1887,[73] swore under oath, "Don't keep a boarding house; have tobacco and whiskey for my own use. Have no license to sell whiskey; don't sell it." But two soldiers also told the court that they had left camp to "go there to get some whiskey."[74]

Almost nothing is known of Lucius Benton except for a September 1887 article in the *Provo Daily Enquirer* where Benton was the star witness in a criminal case against two soldiers, Hyrum R. Paulk and Valentine Young, who were accused of killing and butchering a cow belonging to George Whitmore. Benton said he was out looking for horses when he heard voices. Creeping through the brush, he watched as the men skinned the cow about five hundred yards from his cabin. He later confronted the soldiers as each was carrying a hindquarter of freshly butchered beef back to the camp. "Well boys, you've got one, have you?" he said.[75]

Benton sought out George Dummer, who was at that time living in a cabin built for the Whitmore ranch hands tending livestock in Whitmore Park. Dummer recovered the cowhide with Whitmore's distinctive X

Axle-grease signature in Gate Canyon dating to October 1886—or within a month of the time the road was improved to handle freight traffic. Photo by Jerry D. Spangler.

brand and he gave it to Benton, who buried it for safekeeping. The two men then sought out William Turner (perhaps Sheriff J. W. Turner), who also visited the kill site with Dummer and Benton.[76]

Turner, Benton, and Dummer later visited the soldiers' camp. Dummer testified that he saw soldiers bringing fresh beef out of the tent of the commanding officer, Captain Penny. Benton identified the two suspects to Captain Penny, and Turner testified he saw the cooks preparing to cook fresh beef steaks, but "when they saw me they dodged away with it."[77]

What seemed like an open-and-shut case was not, however. The soldiers closed ranks around their comrades. The defendants testified they had been hunting rabbits above Benton's cabin, not shooting George Whitmore's cow. Other soldiers testified the defendants were in their quarters and answering to roll call at the time of the incident. Others testified that no beef was served in the camp, but there was venison provided by an officer. And witnesses said there was no blood on the defendants' uniforms. Both men were acquitted.[78]

As mentioned earlier, Geary believes it is "doubtful" that settlers came into Nine Mile Canyon before the road was completed in the fall of 1886.[79] But once the road was built there was a veritable population boom. Who came first and when they came is difficult to reconstruct (the 1890 U.S. Census records were all destroyed in a fire). They all laid claim to prime parcels of land along the canyon bottom, but none of them filed legal claims, or if they did they never fulfilled the federal requirements to secure actual title to the lands.

In 1890, the primary means to acquire title to the lands was the Desert Land Entry Act, passed in 1877 to "encourage and promote the economic development of the arid and semiarid public lands of the Western United States. Through the Act, individuals could apply for a desert-land entry to reclaim, irrigate, and cultivate arid and semiarid public lands."[80] William Miller indicates only three entries were ever filed for Nine Mile Canyon, but he does not indicate who they were or when they were filed. None of these claims were ever patented. The only homestead claims were patented well after 1900.[81] In other words, during the raucous heyday of Nine Mile Canyon, no one was there legally.

Vice and Violence

Freighting on the Nine Mile Road was a tough profession that was populated by tough men willing to undergo privations on a lonely road with only the passage of fellow freighters for fleeting companionship. There were also the drifters and opportunists, some of them quite unsavory, who wandered in and out of the canyon.[82] It was therefore not surprising that enterprising individuals would cater to the coarser wants of the teamsters by providing certain amenities, primarily strong drink and games of chance. And liquor was in no short supply at "Brock's Place"—a veritable hub of social activity in Nine Mile Canyon from about 1887 to 1902. Like many a frontier oasis of that era, Brock's Place became a haven for vice and occasional violence.

Brock's Place is so named after William Brock, a storekeeper, saloon owner, and postmaster whose "place is said to be pretty tough."[83] Brock had apparently acquired squatters' rights from Shadrach Lunt, but exactly when this occurred is not known but it was probably in late 1887. On July

5, 1887, Lieutenant Truitt and Company K soldiers at Fort Duchesne were given marching orders to proceed to "Lunt's Ranch."[84] But by January 1888, Sergeant P. J. Bolton, writing in the *Salt Lake Tribune*, reported that William Brock had built a hotel and stables, and that the military had established a telegraph office there staffed by soldiers.[85]

How many people actually lived at Brock's Place at any one time is not known. The few newspaper accounts of the day indicate there were numerous people living there: hired hands working for Brock, a blacksmith, soldiers assigned to the telegraph office, and probably others. There were also women there. One of these might have been Sally Edith Brinkerhoff, who met William Brock there and married him in 1890.[86]

William Brock's tenure of the ranch came to an abrupt end in 1889 when he killed a man named Frank Foote in a dispute in the saloon where Brock was serving drinks. According to a detailed newspaper account of the preliminary hearing,[87] Brock was in the saloon with several freighters and local residents, among them Shadrach Lunt, Thomas Mitchell, John Eagan, and John Alger, all of whom were later called as witnesses.[88] Also present were a mail carrier named Workman and a man named Whitman. According to Mitchell's account, Frank Foote, a man named Bunt, and another named Mr. Cole rode up to the saloon on horseback about eleven a.m.; Foote was armed with a .44-caliber Colt pistol that he wore open for all to see. Foote ordered up a drink but apparently did not want to pay for it. Rather, he demanded to wrestle Brock for it. Mitchell indicates that Brock "threw" Foote and claimed the drink for himself. Foote called Brock a liar and a "wrangle" ensued during which Foote swung wildly at Brock with a hundred-pound scale with metal hooks. Foote reportedly yelled at Brock, "Goddamned you. If you don't set 'em up I will do you up."[89] Brock then warned, "You have made two or three plays already, but you don't want to keep it up, for I am as well heeled as you are."[90]

The witnesses said that Foote reached for his pistol and as he pulled it from his holster, Mitchell grabbed Foote's hand and pushed the gun back in the holster with a warning not to do something crazy. As Foote and Mitchell were wrestling over the gun, Brock fired a shot into the saloon wall, sending the witnesses scrambling for the door. Brock and Foote were standing about six feet apart.

Mitchell testified at a preliminary hearing that "Brock had his gun on the counter and was looking at Foote. I cried out, 'For God's sake, don't shoot.' Brock looked at me and then his pistol went off and Foote fell."[91] The second shot struck Foote in the forehead, taking off the back of his head.

There are differing accounts of what happened next. One account has it that Brock turned his pistol over to either John Eagan or John Cole, and soon thereafter Brock and Mitchell rode to Fort Duchesne so Brock could turn himself in to the authorities.[92] Another has it that Brock was disarmed by the witnesses, but that Brock somehow eluded them and secured two pistols and a rifle and escaped to Fort Duchesne, where he then turned himself in to authorities.[93]

It is not surprising that Brock would flee. Brock was in a pickle on several fronts. Foote's gun was still in its holster when he was killed, and the term "murder" was freely applied in the newspaper accounts of the day. Foote was characterized as "an honest, upright man,"[94] and he was well connected. Foote's father, who attended the inquest, was a judge in Nephi, and the Foote family was highly regarded there. And Frank Foote was a Mormon, married about a year with a wife and young baby at home, and any trial would undoubtedly involve a Mormon jury; Brock was not Mormon. Brock openly worried about being lynched by local cowboys who might seek retribution for killing their friend.[95]

William Brock and his wife, Sally Edith Brinkerhoff. This is supposedly their wedding photo taken in August 1890 one month before he was acquitted on murder charges. Brock sold his interest in the saloon and hotel to pay for his defense. Photo courtesy of Dianne Brock.

William Brock signature in Nine Mile Canyon. The complete signature appears to read "Eat at Brocks." Brock opened the first commercial establishment in the canyon in late 1887. Photo by Dianne Brock.

The old "saloon" where William Brock reportedly killed Frank Foote, and later Dave Russell killed Pete Francis. The structure seems a bit small to have accommodated all of the witnesses to the shooting. This structure was dismantled in 2011. Photo by Jerry D. Spangler.

John Alger, who was listed as a resident of Brock's Place, was not exactly displeased that Frank Foote was gone. He told the court that Foote was the leader of "a gang of cowboys" and that he "had run all the bluffs around there he was going to."

Brock was taken to jail in Provo by Emery County sheriff Loveless, where he hired Arthur Brown of Salt Lake as his defense attorney. He also gave an interview to the *Daily Enquirer*, the Provo newspaper of record at the time, retelling the events and adding "if ever there was a case of justifiable homicide, that was one."[96] The court did not see it that way and Brock was formally bound over to stand trial on murder charges.

The subsequent trial in September 1890 in Provo was a media circus attended by all the major newspapers of the day. The *Salt Lake Tribune* offered the most detailed account of the trial, devoting an entire page to the most colorful testimony. Shadrach Lunt, John Alger, John Eagan, and Thomas Mitchell all testified at length. The prosecutor paraded character

The old blacksmith shop built by William Brock next to the saloon. Photo by Ray Boren.

witnesses who testified to the good moral character of the deceased. The defense rebutted with a story of Frank Foote pulling a gun on a train baggage-man who had tried to get Foote to pay a fare for his dog. The hooked scales thrown by Foote were introduced into evidence.[97]

At the end of the testimony, the judge instructed the jury not to consider first-degree murder or second-degree murder, but instead the charge to be considered was reduced to manslaughter. The jury returned a "not guilty" verdict after only fifteen minutes of deliberation.[98]

William Brock would have been about thirty-one years old at the time of Foote's killing, and by his own account he had been in Utah about twelve years.[99] Diane Brock, who has researched the Brock family history, indicated that he was born in 1858 in Oswego, New York, but no one knows how or why he came to Utah. In 1886, he sold a homestead near Jensen in the Uinta Basin, which might have provided the stake to buy out Shadrach Lunt. And that same year he registered a cattle brand at

Whiterocks, also in the Uinta Basin. Sometime in 1889, the same year as the Foote killing, he filed mining claims in Sunnyside Canyon.[100]

There is no indication Brock ever went back to Nine Mile Canyon after the trial, and the operation of Brock's Place was turned over to Pete Francis. Dianne Brock indicated that William Brock signed over title to Francis on July 14, 1890, for an unspecified sum to pay for his defense.[101] By 1897, Brock was a foreman for a Gilsonite mining operation in the Uinta Basin.[102] By the early 1900s, he was operating a ranch near Green River, Utah, apparently spending considerable time searching for a treasure widely rumored to have been hidden in a cave by George "Flat Nosed" Curry of Wild Bunch notoriety.[103] Curry had been killed by a posse earlier in 1900 on the banks of the Green River at the mouth of the canyon that bears his name today.[104]

Brock's Place would continue to carry his name for the next two decades after he left the canyon.

An interesting side note is a reference in the *Deseret News* that William Brock also had a collection of ancient pots and baskets that he had collected, perhaps from the ancient Fremont ruins in Nine Mile Canyon. This collection was of considerable interest to travelers on the Nine Mile Road.[105]

Not much is known of Pete Francis, other than he lived at the ranch with his wife and two young children. They probably assumed control of the ranch in 1889 when Brock fled the canyon, but Pete could have been in Brock's employ much earlier than that. There are only a few references to Pete Francis in the historical record prior to 1901 when Francis was himself killed in a saloon brawl.

The period from 1889 to 1901 would have been a heyday for Brock's Place, with a steady stream of freighters along the road, lots of cattle on the ranges, and plenty of drifters of questionable repute.[106] It could well be that Pete Francis was a questionable character himself. According to one 1897 newspaper account, a lawman named Ren Wilkins ventured into Nine Mile Canyon to serve arrest warrants on Pete Francis and none other than Gunplay Maxwell, who had been accused by George Whitmore of stealing sixty-seven head of livestock. Whitmore accompanied Wilkins as far as Brock's Place but refused to go into the cabin with Wilkins to serve the arrest warrants.[107]

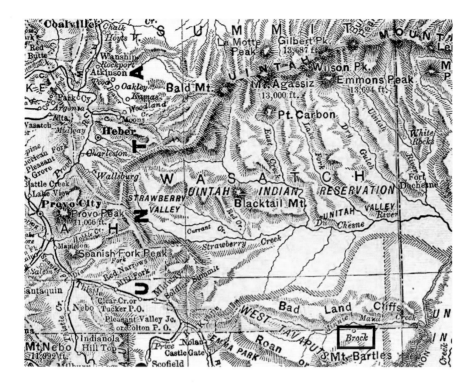

Wilkins was admitted to the cabin by a Mrs. Maxwell and there he found Gunplay seated next to a window with revolvers on each hip and two Winchester rifles lying ready on the table. The two men engaged in pleasant conversation and eventually reached an agreement. Maxwell would accompany Wilkins to Price, but only if he could remain fully armed "to protect himself against Whitmore and his men, who he believed desired to kill him." Mrs. Maxwell strongly objected to the arrangement with the statement, "Why you damned coward, they'll get you in jail and keep you there."[108]

About that time, Pete Francis walked into the cabin and expressed his own willingness to accompany Wilkins to Price under the same conditions. Around midnight, all retired for the evening in anticipation of the long ride to Price the next day. During the middle of the night, Gunplay Maxwell fled to parts unknown. Francis offered to keep his part of the bargain, but "as it was considered doubtful if a case could be made against him he was not taken. Officer Wilkins accordingly returned empty handed."[109] A year later, Maxwell would be arrested during a botched holdup of a Springville bank.

The newspaper account observed that Pete Francis's two children were living there at the time, but no mention was made of Francis's wife, Alice. It is possible the Mrs. Maxwell referred to in the account was actually Alice Francis. But it might indeed have been Ada Slaugh (Mrs. Maxwell) who was tending house there. A later newspaper account from 1901 indicates that Pete Francis was, by that time, divorced from his wife, who was living in Salt Lake City with his two sons.[110]

Whether Francis was an outlaw himself or just friendly with them cannot be determined from the available historical record, although it is claimed that Francis's saloon was a favorite watering hole for outlaws on their way to and from Browns Hole and Robbers Roost.[111] In 1901, the *Salt Lake Herald* trumpeted the erroneous report that famed Wild Bunch cohort Elza Lay had been killed in Mexico, and made a passing reference that Butch Cassidy had been seen at Pete Francis's place just four days before Francis was himself killed. The source of the information was an informant to Deputy U.S. Marshal Joe Bush, a veteran of the outlaw wars of the 1890s.[112]

Pete Francis's life ended violently on October 7, 1901. By one account, he was sitting on a cot near the bar when Dave Russell, a stage driver who owned a ranch in upper Nine Mile Canyon, walked into the saloon. Witnesses said Francis jumped up from the cot and reached for a gun, remarking, "I guess I'll just kill that damned Mormon stage driver right now." Russell pulled his own gun and fired two shots, one of which struck Francis in the left eye and the other in the center of the forehead, killing him instantly.[113]

A more detailed account in the *Eastern Utah Advocate* indicates there was longstanding bad blood between the two men. Charles "Rowdy Dowdy" Banning, who appears to be the source of the story, was at the time a jack-of-all-trades hired to do odd jobs around the ranch, and that evening he was working behind the bar, serving liquor to freighters. There were four other men playing poker at the time: Jim Engfield, Joe Gurr, George Stewart, and a stranger called "Tex." The stage from Price, being driven by Russell, arrived between seven and eight p.m. It was the end of Russell's leg of the stage route, and he right away sidled up to the bar and ordered four drinks. Francis accused Russell of not paying for the drinks, but Banning assured Francis that he had paid. Francis struck Russell twice on the face and hurled curses at him until he left.[114]

A short time later, Francis and Banning turned down the lights to retire for the night when there was a noise at the door. Francis was sitting on the edge of a cot when Banning opened the door. Russell then entered with an unnamed companion and two shots were fired, both of which struck Francis in the face, "as though made at target practice."[115] Russell then sought out his friend, early Nine Mile rancher Hank Stewart, to ride with him to Price to turn himself in to authorities.[116]

A later account of the preliminary hearing indicated the killing had occurred during an evening of "drunken revelry," and that Russell's life had been threatened. Witnesses were listed as William Smith, Joseph Gurr, and Charles "Rowdy Dowdy" Banning. Russell was ordered by a Price judge to stand trial on the charge of first-degree murder.[117] Newspaper accounts after that point are sparse. One account in the *Deseret News* indicates Russell had been incarcerated in the Utah State Penitentiary for "safe keeping" pending his trial.[118] A one-paragraph story in the *Eastern Utah Advocate* less than a week later indicated Russell was acquitted by a jury after less than three hours of deliberation, a result that "had been expected and created no great surprise."[119]

It might not have happened exactly as was reported in the newspapers of the day. Norma Dalton, who was raised in Nine Mile Canyon, remembers her father, Thorald Rich, once showed her how Dave Russell had leaned in through an open window and shot Francis in the head as he slept. Her father also related a story that Dave Russell and a companion named Smith, both teenagers at the time, were infuriated that Pete Francis had cheated them at cards. Bolstered by strong drink, "they drew straws to see which would put an end to that cheater. Dave lost the draw."[120]

In the aftermath of the shooting, newspaper reports indicated that Francis left behind a widow and two children. But the *Eastern Utah Advocate* later clarified that Pete was divorced and that his ex-wife had arrived in Price two days after the killing from her residence in Salt Lake. It also indicates the couple had two sons, ages ten and eleven, which means the two boys would have been born shortly after Francis took over the ranch from William Brock in 1889 (they may have been among the first white children to have been born there). One newspaper account lists the value of the Francis estate at $9,400,[121] and another at $4,000, which included the ranch, a mercantile business and "some livestock."[122] The livestock apparently included sheep, something that might have put Pete Francis crossways with hard-bitten cowboys opposed to the influx of flocks at that time.[123] There is no mention of the twenty-room hotel that Francis had built there.

The value of the Francis estate is relevant because it hints at what followed next. Alice Francis apparently had no interest in returning to Nine Mile Canyon to operate a saloon and hotel. But there was someone on the sidelines waiting for the chance to acquire the ranch. By some accounts, Mrs. Francis leased the ranch to cattle baron Preston Nutter in 1901,[124] or within a matter of weeks of her ex-husband's death. By other accounts, Nutter bought the ranch outright in 1902, immediately closing down the saloon and converting the hotel into a bunkhouse for his cowboys.[125] Brock's Place would soon become the headquarters of Nutter's far-flung ranching operation, hailed by some as the largest in the West at the time. And no longer would it be a haven for drunken brawls, gambling, and vice.

Of course, the problem with shutting down Brock's Place was that it never stopped the demand for the services such places provided. There were dozens of saloons in Helper and Price, Fort Duchesne and Vernal. But they could not satisfy the wants of the lonely freighters six or seven days between watering holes. And public attitudes toward intoxicating spirits, as well as female companionship for hire, were much more tolerant in those days. The Mormon Church might have had prohibitions against tobacco and strong drink, but Mormon freighters often viewed these as mere suggestions once they were on the road.

Helper and Price already had a plethora of saloons that offered a complete menu of vices, not only to freighters but to coal miners and weary railroad passengers. Brock opened his saloon in 1888 catering to cowboys and freighters, and that same year another saloon opened at Bridge (later Myton) at the end of the Nine Mile Road where it crossed the Duchesne River, which catered to freighters and soldiers. In other words, a freighter could have a drink or two or three at either end of the weeklong trip, as well as halfway through during a well-timed stopover at Brock's Place. And any earnings they might have made hauling freight might easily have been lost in a game of poker at any one of the stops.

Preston Nutter wanted nothing to do with drinking and gambling. So in 1902, Nutter's neighbor on the west, John Eagan, constructed his own saloon about three miles up canyon from Brock's Place. He intended to build a hotel there, as well, but it was never completed.[126] Also stepping into the commercial vacuum created by the closure of Brock's Place was Frank Alger, whose ranch about five miles west of Brock's Place became the focal point of social activities with its general store. And there was a post office and hotel at the Edwin Lee ranch. There is no indication Alger or Lee sold alcohol or provided the other vices sought by the freighters.[127]

Local histories have stated the post office was moved to Frank Alger's place after Brock's Place was shut down, and the post office name was changed from Brock to Harper in 1905, or about three years later. This is erroneous on two counts. The post office was moved to Edwin Lee's place near the mouth of Argyle Canyon, not the Frank Alger place, and this actually happened in early 1900, or almost two years before Pete Francis was killed.[128] Alger was already operating a general store at his place that catered to canyon residents and freighters. This suggests that Frank Alger

In 1902, John Eagan constructed a saloon about three miles up canyon from Brock's Place. The hotel he had planned was never completed. Photo courtesy of the Colorado Plateau Archaeological Alliance.

and Edwin Lee were already competing with Pete Francis for the lucrative trade along the Nine Mile Road, and that Edwin Lee had already wrested the post office contract away from Pete Francis. It could well have been that traffic was substantial enough by 1900 that it warranted two hotels and two social centers. By 1910 the Harper Precinct boasted a population of 130 souls[129] and traffic on the road was still bustling.

A small log building next to the Nine Mile Road at the Preston Nutter Ranch is reported to have been the saloon where Frank Foote and Pete Francis met their demise. There was a sign—not nearly old enough to be authentic—that indicates this was a saloon. But the small structure does not seem large enough to have accommodated all the witnesses said to have been present at the shootings. There is no indication of any attached buildings where there were rooms to rent—it was said to have had nine rooms under Brock's management and twenty rooms under Pete Francis. We may never know for sure. The old hotel burned to the ground in 1936, and the "saloon" was dismantled in 2011, ostensibly to be reconstructed as a tourist attraction farther up canyon. The large side canyon just north of the Nutter Ranch is today known as Pete's Canyon.

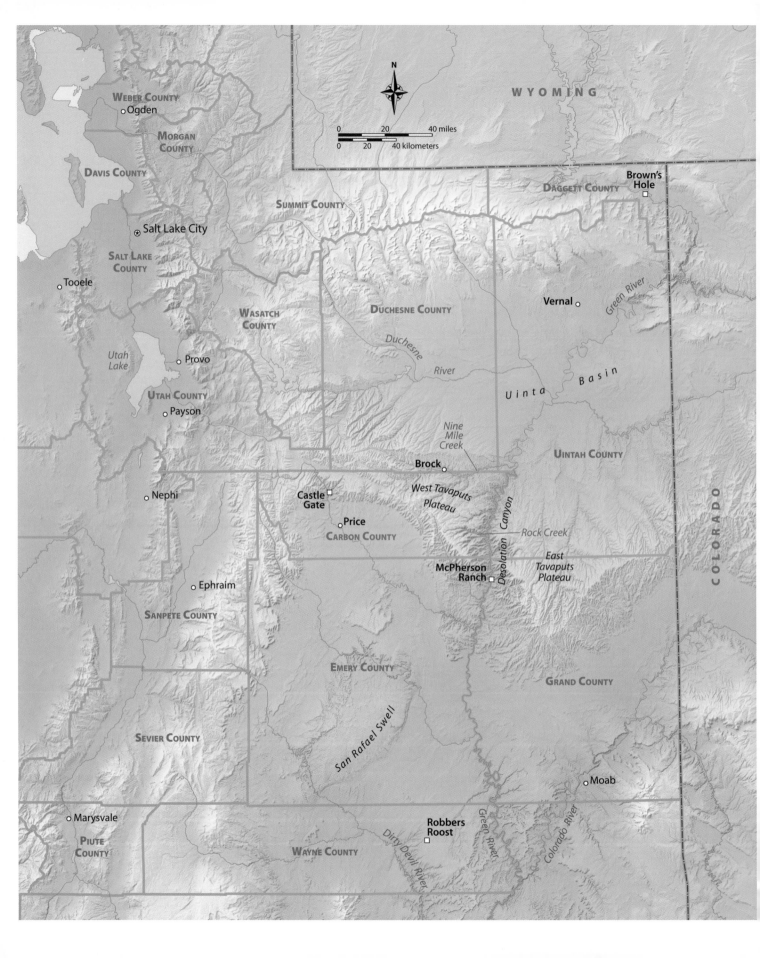

Hellfire and Gunplay
Law and Lawlessness in Eastern Utah

You ain't a bad man; you're just a petty-larceny horse thief. I'll give you five seconds to get going; otherwise there'll be a funeral in Vernal and you will be riding at the head of the procession.
—Butch Cassidy to Gunplay Maxwell, 1897

The era of the Robin Hood outlaws of the American West ended more than a century ago, but the tales of daring bandits and their hair-raising escapes from determined lawmen continue to evoke fascination and fable. Names like Robert "Butch Cassidy" Parker, Willard "Matt Warner" Christensen, Harvey "Kid Curry" Logan, and Harry "Sundance Kid" Longabaugh are as legendary now as when they haunted the trails of eastern Utah in the 1890s. Indeed, there is a fiercely devoted cadre of enthusiasts—researchers, writers, and Old West buffs—who spend much of their lives and personal fortunes tracking down every detail of the famed Wild Bunch, and then arguing incessantly over those details.

The purpose of this particular story is not to rehash the history of Butch Cassidy and his Wild Bunch cohorts, but to place Nine Mile Canyon into the historical context—the outlaw era of 1890 to 1909. From the dozens and dozens of sources available to us, we chose to draw primarily from three sources: *The Wild Bunch at Robbers Roost*, by Pearl Baker, who grew up at Robbers Roost, the one-time impregnable hideout used by scores of outlaws, including the Wild Bunch. She interviewed many old-timers who remembered the events and individuals described. We also chose *The Outlaw Trail*, by famed Utah historian Charles Kelly, who mixes interviews and official records into one of the most colorful tales ever told. And we especially liked *Butch Cassidy: A Biography*, by Richard Patterson, who is convincingly skeptical of various claims and is a counterbalance to the hero worship prevalent among many Wild Bunch enthusiasts.[1]

Cactus in bloom. Photo by Ray Boren.

Opposite: Map of outlaw hideouts in eastern Utah.

View of Devil's Canyon, a northern tributary of Nine Mile Canyon and a reported lair of outlaws during the lawless 1890s. Photo by Jerry D. Spangler.

For clarity in the following discussion, and to help those readers uninitiated in the nuances of outlaw history, we offer a brief background to the places and persons that figure prominently in the episodes of the 1890s:

- The Hideouts: There were two primary refuges used by outlaws of that era. One was in Browns Hole (called Browns Park today), located on the shared borders of Utah, Wyoming, and Colorado. During the 1890s, there was little or no cooperation between the lawmen of the three states, and outlaws could escape arrest by simply crossing over the state line in one direction or another as needed. But that was rarely necessary. The haven was rumored to be heavily guarded, and lawmen simply avoided Browns Hole at all costs. The second hideout was Robbers Roost near the San Rafael Swell of central Utah, between the Dirty Devil River and the Horseshoe Canyon drainages. Getting to the Roost involved intimate knowledge of a labyrinth of narrow, easily

Famous portrait of members of the Wild Bunch, taken in 1901 at a photo studio in Texas before Butch and Sundance fled to South America. Depicted here: (front row) Harry A. Longabaugh, Ben Kilpatrick, Robert Leroy Parker; (back row) Will Carver and Harvey Logan.

guarded canyons. And if a sheriff's posse dared venture that far, they could find themselves facing more than a hundred armed outlaws and misfits. Lawmen simply avoided the Roost.

- The Gangs: There are two major gangs mentioned in the histories. The Hole-in-the-Wall Gang was the predecessor of the Wild Bunch and was based in Wyoming. It does not play much into the history of eastern Utah other than this collection of rustlers and thieves included Butch Cassidy. From this gang Cassidy recruited the best and the brightest as the core of his more ambitious and sophisticated crew which was dubbed the Wild Bunch, with Butch as the undisputed leader. The Wild Bunch moved frequently back and forth between Browns Hole and Robbers Roost. There are references to the "Robbers Roost Gang," although most historians would probably agree that it was not a single gang but a hodgepodge of outlaws who came together through opportunity and circumstance.

- The Legend: After his incarceration for horse theft, Butch Cassidy swore off petty theft and cattle rustling for much grander schemes: robbing trains, payrolls, mining companies, and banks. And there was popular support for the Wild Bunch escapades. To the poverty-stricken farmers and small-time ranchers, the exploits were seen as stealing from the rich who were getting richer at their expense, and tales are recounted in many of the histories of the outlaws finding safe haven with sympathetic honest folk

The Wild Bunch in Nine Mile

So how does Nine Mile Canyon fit into this story? We found that the role of Nine Mile Canyon in the outlaw history of eastern Utah is, in fact, very poorly documented. There are tales repeated as fact that outlaws used the canyon as they passed to and from their lairs in Browns Hole and Robbers Roost. And one tale—not well corroborated in the written histories—is that Butch Cassidy had planned a daring holdup of the military payroll bound for Fort Duchesne as the wagons passed through a narrow portion of Gate Canyon a few miles north of Nine Mile Canyon, but that the robbery was aborted when the outlaws saw the payroll was heavily guarded by soldiers.

In fact, there are few reliable reports that Butch Cassidy or his cohorts were ever in Nine Mile Canyon. On April 21, 1897, Butch Cassidy and Elza Lay, with perhaps Joe Walker and Bub Meeks guarding their flanks on the getaway, pulled off the most spectacular robbery in Utah history to that time, robbing the Pleasant Valley Coal Company payroll at Castle Gate just west of Price and escaping with $9,860 in cash, gold, and silver.[2] Their lengthy escape *south* to Robbers Roost is well documented by historians, and there is no reason to doubt it happened as described at that time. But there is one other intriguing newspaper reference that offers an alternative twist on the escape.

On the night after the robbery, unknown individuals took eight horses from a corral at the Bracken and Lee Ranch in Nine Mile Canyon (the Edwin Lee ranch at the mouth of Argyle Canyon), and left behind in their place eight horses that had been ridden hard. The next day, the agent at the Whiterocks Indian Agency to the north of Nine Mile Canyon was robbed of cash and a fresh mount, and the bandits promptly escaped into Browns Hole where the law dared not go.[3] The implication of this reference, of course, is that outlaws riding hell-bent-for-leather to Robbers Roost were a clever diversion, and that the posse had followed riders into the Swell while Cassidy and the cash quietly slipped north through Nine Mile Canyon to the Wild Bunch refuge in Browns Hole.

A second reference to the Wild Bunch here came in 1901 when the *Salt Lake Herald* reported—erroneously—that famed Wild Bunch cohort Elza Lay had been killed in Mexico. The account made a passing reference that Butch Cassidy had been seen at Pete Francis's saloon on the Nine Mile Road just four days before Francis was himself killed. The source of the information was an informant to Deputy U.S. Marshal Joe Bush, a veteran of the outlaw wars of the 1890s.[4]

Nine Mile Canyon is rarely mentioned by the outlaws themselves or by the writers who have chronicled their history. The canyon was clearly known to the outlaws, but there were three things about the canyon that made it an unlikely choice as a primary transportation route between the two outlaw hideouts: (1) the route was crowded with freighters, stage coaches, and ranchers, and there was certainly risk they could be recognized and that someone would turn them in for the bounty placed on their heads; (2) an actual wagon road would have made it easier for a posse to pursue them, when their signature escape was, in fact, long rides through the most wild lands imaginable where lawmen feared threats of ambush at every blind turn; and (3) there was a telegraph line through Nine Mile Canyon between Price and Fort Duchesne, with relay stations along the route, that would have made it far too easy to warn lawmen at either end that wanted bandits were headed that direction.[5]

To understand the history of Nine Mile Canyon in the 1890s is to appreciate the general lawlessness of eastern Utah where the line between cattle ranching and cattle rustling shifted with convenience. There was "honest" rustling where unbranded mavericks and maybe a few not-so-wild calves were rounded up and branded. And then there was the wholesale theft of hundreds of head of cattle from the large cattle operators, who might not come to miss the livestock until it came time to move the herds to the rail heads.[6] Kelly makes the case that "almost every small rancher in southern Utah was a rustler on the side."[7] Certainly, most, if not all, of the famed Wild Bunch and probably most of the others who took up residence at Robbers Roost and Browns Hole started out as cattle rustlers. Needless to say, the outlaws of that era were top-notch cowboys whose skills with horses and ropes were legendary. Butch Cassidy was a fine cowboy himself who did a short stint in the Wyoming State Penitentiary for stealing horses, the only time he was ever convicted of a crime.[8]

By most accounts, it was Elza Lay who was Butch's best friend and right-hand man in the Wild Bunch days, not Harry "Sundance Kid" Longabaugh as portrayed in the movies. Lay was arrested in New Mexico, spent several years in prison before being pardoned, and later died an old man in Los Angeles. He seems to be one of just a few members of the Wild Bunch to escape a violent death. Used by permission, Uintah County Library Regional History Center, all rights reserved.

Upon his release in January 1896, Butch was no longer content to rustle a few cows and horses here and there. He returned to his old haunts in Browns Hole and by the late summer of 1896 he had organized a gang collectively referred to as "The Wild Bunch," with charter members Elza Lay and Bub Meeks, the latter of whom had been rustling Preston Nutter's cattle in the Uinta Mountain area the year before.[9] Their first robbery was August 13, 1896, in Montpelier, Idaho. Within a short period of time, the gang had taken up residence at Robbers Roost, probably in early 1897. Butch Cassidy was always the undisputed leader of the Wild Bunch, and Elza Lay was his best friend and right-hand man. Together, they executed a rash of bold robberies: coal companies, payrolls, trains, and banks. Virtually every heist during that era was laid at the foot of the Wild Bunch.

On this point an important distinction should be made. Robbers Roost was teeming with outlaws, consorts, and sympathizers, by some accounts more than a hundred at any given time. And not every outlaw was a member of the Wild Bunch. Rather, the Wild Bunch was quite exclusive, with Butch and Elza hand-picking their collaborators. Membership was apparently fluid, with the roster of criminals changing with each escapade. And Wild Bunch members might even put together their own crew without Butch Cassidy if the occasion presented itself. Not everyone who wanted into the Wild Bunch was accepted into the ranks, and not all of the "Roosters" were looked upon favorably within the Robbers Roost community.

The exploits of the Wild Bunch garnered considerable public attention. The governors of the western states offered large rewards, and the establishment press called for officials to put an end to the lawlessness. But there was public sympathy for the outlaws from the small-time farmers and ranchers in the sparsely populated hinterlands. In 1897 when the Wild Bunch took up residency in Robbers Roost, the nation was in the fourth year of a crippling economic depression fueled by the Panic of 1893. Cash and credit were in short supply, families everywhere were going bankrupt, and poverty was rampant. There was a pervasive attitude at the time that the bankers, mine owners, and railroad tycoons were getting richer at the expense of the poor. Matt Warner, one of the most famous and feared outlaws of his day, and a close personal friend of Butch Cassidy from the Browns Hole days, wrote in his autobiography,

Like lots of cowboy outlaws in them days Butch and me liked to give lots of our money to the poor, the needy and the deserving. In this way we made sort of Robin Hoods of ourselves in our own eyes, gained a lot of popularity and protection from the public, and squared ourselves in our own estimation.[10]

Joe Walker's Vendetta

Although references to outlaws in Nine Mile Canyon are sparse, that is not to say the canyon does not have a colorful outlaw history. Two prominent outlaws of that era laid claim to the Nine Mile country: Joe Walker, who terrorized the Whitmore Brothers and their herds in upper Nine Mile Canyon, and Clarence Lewis "Gunplay" Maxwell, who purportedly had a ranch in Nine Mile Canyon and came to despise Walker for crowding his own territory and thereby making it tougher for Maxwell to pilfer the Whitmore herds for himself. Both men had notorious outlaw careers and both died violently at the hands of lawmen. The stories of the two outlaws with the closest ties to Nine Mile Canyon are intertwined.

Joe Walker was an on-and-off-again member of the Wild Bunch, while C. L. "Gunplay" Maxwell ached to be invited to join but was never accepted into the gang. Pearl Baker says Walker was thirty-five or forty when he first arrived in the Robbers Roost country in the early 1890s, which probably made him an elder statesman among the Roosters. She claims he came to the area to take back what was rightfully his—an inheritance stolen by the Whitmore brothers (see chapter 5).[11]

Kelly places Walker's arrival in the area in 1891, but he gives a different account. He indicates Walker had married one of the Whitmore "girls" over the objections of her brothers, presumably George and James,[12] and that the two brothers had done everything in their power to make life miserable for the Texas cowboy.[13] Whichever account is closer to reality, there is no dispute that Walker had a personal vendetta against the Whitmores, rustling their horses and cattle mercilessly—and for the most part not preying on the other small ranchers operating in the area. As Pearl Baker observed,

During these years, Joe managed to make a "whelty" around to Price now and then to keep the Whitmores apprised of his continuing and

This image could be an early photo of the outlaw Joe Walker, or it might be someone else named Joe Walker who was photographed about the same time. Photo courtesy of L. Tom Perry Special Collections, Harold B. Lee Library, Brigham Young University.

predatory interest in their affairs. They had splendid horses, although it wasn't that so much as it was the nuisance value of his depredations that was so satisfying to Joe and so unnerving to the Whitmores.[14]

By Baker's account, some ranchers might have been sympathetic to Walker, but in Price the Whitmores were wealthy and respectable, and Walker soon earned the enmity of the leading citizens there. In the summer of 1895, Walker and some friends shot up the town, which was not that unusual in the day. But because it was Walker it made headlines in the local paper, "and from that day on he was a marked man."[15]

In March 1897, Walker stole three of the Whitmore's finest horses and the Whitmores swore out a warrant for Walker's arrest. The posse members are listed as Sheriff Azuriah Tuttle, J. M. Whitmore, M. C. Wilson, J. M. Thomas, and C. L. Maxwell (the latter is the same outlaw that Walker already knew well). According to Kelly, Maxwell had offered to guide the posse because Walker had trespassed on his own rustling territory, Nine Mile Canyon. The posse caught up with Walker at Mexican Bend in the San Rafael Swell and a shootout ensued. Kelly's account has it the sheriff was wounded and Maxwell had his rifle shot out of his hands.[16]

Baker's account offers a different twist. She maintains that Walker and Maxwell had stolen two of the Whitmores' top saddle horses and made their getaway into the San Rafael Swell. But the two men argued and split up, with Walker going on south with the stolen horses and Maxwell returning to Price. But Maxwell meant to get even with Walker and went straight away to the Whitmores to let them know where their horses were, which led to the shootout with the posse at Mexican Bend with Sheriff Tuttle.[17] Her account omits any mention of Maxwell at the shootout.

In either case, Walker escaped, and a few weeks later, Walker was helping Butch Cassidy and Elza Lay to rob the Pleasant Valley Coal Company payroll in Castle Gate (Baker's account has it that Walker cut the telegraph lines to facilitate the escape).[18] It was about this time that the governor of Utah, Heber Wells, placed a $500 bounty on Walker's head.[19]

By the following spring, in 1898, Walker was back in Nine Mile Canyon rustling more Whitmore cattle. The Whitmore ranch foreman, Billy McGuire, and a younger Whitmore named Bud gave chase and caught up with Walker as he was driving the stolen herd through Price River Canyon. But Walker surprised McGuire and gave him a severe beating. "Joe turned to Bud and asked him if he cared for a helping of the same. Bud assured him that he didn't, and as Joe didn't recognize him as one of the hated Whitmores, he let the two go and went on about his business."[20]

The beating of McGuire was the ultimate indignity to the Whitmores, and a posse was quickly assembled to give chase. The accounts of what happened next vary, but there is agreement that the posse included U.S. Deputy Marshal Joe Bush, Sheriff C. W. Allred and eight deputies, among them McGuire, two members of the Whitmore family, and an ex-Texas Ranger named Jack Watson (more on him in chapter 7). They rode down the Price River to its mouth, then crossed the river and moved north in the direction of the Jim McPherson ranch at Florence Creek, a known haven for outlaws on the run. On May 18, 1889, under the cover of darkness and just before dawn, the posse crept around the outlaw camp where they saw four men sleeping in bedrolls.[21]

According to Kelly's account, based on an interview with a member of the posse, a warning was shouted for the men to surrender and two of the outlaws immediately raised their hands. The other two opened fire, and when they had run out of bullets they tried to run. They were both killed in a hail of gunfire.[22] But Baker's account, which is more often repeated as fact, has it that Walker was shot dead while still in his bedroll, that he never even reached for the pistol under his pillow.[23]

One of the dead men was immediately identified as Joe Walker—the Whitmores would certainly have recognized him immediately. The second man was identified at that time as none other than Butch Cassidy, and one of the captured men as Elza Lay, which turned out to be false on both counts. The two dead bodies were hauled to Price, put on public display and then quickly buried, but doubts soon surfaced about the identification of the second dead rustler. Those who knew Butch Cassidy said it wasn't him. The two outlaws who had surrendered—two minor rustlers named Mizoo Schultz and Sang Thompson—identified the dead man as John Herron (or Herring), also a minor cattle rustler and fellow Rooster. Schultz and Thompson were later released for lack of evidence that they had any involvement in the rustling of the Whitmore livestock.

A story told by Kelly and repeated by Patterson has it that Butch Cassidy happened to be traveling through Price on his way to Robbers

Sheriff Azuriah Tuttle was wounded in a shootout with outlaw Joe Walker in the San Rafael Swell while trying to recover horses stolen from the Whitmore brothers. Photo courtesy of the Tuttle family.

Roost when he learned he had been "killed" in a shootout with the posse, and that his body had been placed on public display. As a practical joke, he convinced a friend to hide him in a wagonload of straw and drive down the Price main street so Butch could observe the festivities.[24] Butch's sister related that Butch told her "it would be a good idea to attend his own funeral just once in his lifetime."[25]

Dianne Brock, who has family roots to the earliest settlement of Nine Mile Canyon, says the story is indeed true. According to family stories passed down from generation to generation, Butch's "friend" who gave him the ride through downtown Price was Jim Sprouse, a long-time freighter on the Nine Mile Road. Sprouse was Dianne's great-grandfather.[26]

The killing of Joe Walker—coupled with a widely heralded compact between the governors of Utah, Wyoming, and Colorado to rid the region of the Wild Bunch once and for all—might have been a wake-up for Butch Cassidy and the other core members of the Wild Bunch to abandon their comfortable refuges in Browns Hole and Robbers Roost.[27] By late 1898 or early 1899, Butch Cassidy, Elza Lay, and others of the Wild Bunch had relocated to New Mexico, and it seemed Utah was finally rid of the Wild Bunch, although the gang would continue to terrorize railroads and banks in Wyoming, Nevada, and Montana over the next two years.

Bad Luck Maxwell

Even without the Wild Bunch, Robbers Roost and its cadre of hustlers, misfits, and two-bit crooks continued to be a thorn in the side of authorities, who could never seem to muster the courage to displace them once and for all. One of these small-timers was C. L. "Gunplay" Maxwell, one of the more colorful patrons of Robbers Roost and one of twelve notorious outlaws on whom Utah governor Wells had placed a $500 bounty. He tried for years to be accepted into the Wild Bunch, but he was always seen as a pretender who never quite measured up to the Wild Bunch standards. This could have been due to the fact that he was cursed with perpetual stupidity or bad luck, or both. That aside, Maxwell survived longer than most outlaws of that era. And with the Wild Bunch out of the tabloid spotlight, Maxwell, with his media-ready nickname, later became a darling of the tabloid press, especially in 1908 and 1909.

Maxwell is reported to have been raised in a middle-class Boston suburb, then fled west after killing a man in a saloon brawl, probably in the late 1880s. In about 1888 or 1889, Maxwell, using the name James Otis Bliss, took up with Ada Slaugh of Vernal, and a daughter, Myrtle Bliss, was born July 22, 1892.[28]

Ada Slaugh is a bit mysterious herself. She was certainly posing as Mrs. Maxwell by at least 1889 and they had a child together, but by 1894 she was engaged to Charles Hirsch, who died that year in a Gilsonite mining explosion. In 1895, she wrote letters to Hirsch's family indicating she was "lonely tonight" and desired to visit them.[29] Her involvement with Hirsch might have been prompted by an extended period of loneliness when Maxwell, arrested in 1893, was serving time in the Wyoming State Penitentiary for grand larceny under the name Richard Carr.[30] Upon his release in about 1895, she was again Mrs. Maxwell. When Maxwell was later sent to the Utah State Penitentiary following a botched 1898 robbery, she again "married" someone else, only to resume her role as Mrs. Maxwell upon his release. After Maxwell's death, she married another Robbers Roost outlaw, Pete Logan, also known as Pete Nelson. It seems she could not abide being alone.

Maxwell's real name is a matter of conjecture. His name on Wyoming prison records was Richard Carr, a known alias for James Bliss, which is thought by many Old West historians to be Maxwell's real name.[31] Newspaper accounts list Maxwell's alias as "L. C. Bliss"[32] or "Richard Bliss."[33] Kelly says he was also using the name "John Carter."[34] In the years just before his death, he was going by the name "W. H. Seaman."[35] Patterson believes Maxwell could have come to know Butch Cassidy while both were inmates at the Wyoming State Penitentiary.[36]

In 1909, after his death, the *Deseret News* reported that Gunplay Maxwell's true name was Carr, that he was a member of the Hole-in-the-Wall Gang in Wyoming but had double-crossed his outlaw friends, who returned the favor by having him arrested and jailed for stealing a horse that was intended as payment to the gang's attorney.[37] The *Salt Lake Herald* and *Carbon County News* gave Maxwell's real name as Dick Carr,[38] which is consistent with the name of the Wyoming inmate serving time with Butch Cassidy. If Maxwell had indeed double-crossed members of the Hole-in-the-Wall Gang, as the *Deseret News* reported, this could explain why Butch

Wyoming State Penitentiary mug shot of Richard Carr, believed to be C. L. "Gunplay" Maxwell. He might have met fellow inmate Butch Cassidy at that time. Photo courtesy of Wyoming State Archives, Department of State Parks and Cultural Resources (Penitentiary Negative No. 136).

Cassidy never trusted Maxwell in the years that followed, no matter how eager Maxwell was to join the Wild Bunch.

In 1902, when Maxwell applied for commutation of an eighteen-year prison sentence, he swore his true name was James Otis Bliss.[39] It is also quite possible that none of the aliases hint at who Maxwell really was. Ada Slaugh, his first wife (and maybe one of two women with that title at the time of his death), when asked what his true name was, replied,

It was not Maxwell, it was not Seaman, it was not Bliss, the stories that he was the son of a prominent family in Massachusetts [are] not true. He was adopted by that family when he was a kid. Bliss is not his name, neither is his name Maxwell or Seaman. He was not born in America.[40]

Outlaw historians agree C. L. Maxwell operated out of a ranch in Nine Mile Canyon in the early 1890s, although the location is a bit cloudy. Kelly has it that Maxwell's ranch was near the Preston Nutter Ranch, which he indicated was formerly the Bracken and Lee Ranch.[41] But the Bracken and Lee Ranch was much farther up canyon, just above the mouth of Argyle Canyon. The Preston Nutter Ranch was, at that time, the Pete Francis hotel and saloon—a known hangout for Gunplay Maxwell and other unsavory characters. Maxwell and Francis were certainly well acquainted and possibly "business" associates, but there is no indication Maxwell had his own ranch there.

A March 1897 photograph taken inside the Oasis Saloon in Price depicts Maxwell, Pete Francis (see chapter 5), and two others playing poker. Later that same month, C. L. Maxwell and Ada Slaugh moved in with Pete Francis at the Nine Mile roadhouse.[42] And the threesome were still living there in July of that year when Provo lawman Ren Wilkins ventured into Nine Mile Canyon to serve arrest warrants on Pete Francis and Gunplay Maxwell, who had both been accused by George Whitmore of stealing sixty-seven head of livestock.[43] There he found Gunplay seated next to a window with revolvers on each hip and two Winchester rifles lying ready on the table. Maxwell escaped during the night, and Wilkins saw no real advantage in hauling Pete Francis to jail, and he left empty-handed.[44]

Francis and Maxwell were reportedly behind a plot in April 1897 to rob an army payroll and Indian annuities valued at $30,000 to $60,000 as it passed through Nine Mile Canyon. Maxwell was in charge of selecting the location of the holdup (tradition holds that it was in Gate Canyon) and Francis would provide information on when the payroll would be transferred and how the guards would be deployed. Butch Cassidy and his gang would assist in the actual robbery.[45] The robbers' plans leaked and the military increased the guard on the payroll, causing the bandits to abort the holdup.[46]

There is not a lot of historical record to support the idea that Francis and Maxwell were about to rob the military payroll. But there is some. A few weeks after the payroll robbery was aborted, Butch Cassidy, Elza Lay, and Joe Walker robbed the Pleasant Valley Coal Company and made a daring escape into the Robbers Roost country. Erma Armstrong, citing an unspecified newspaper account, quoted the paymaster of the Pleasant Valley Coal Company as saying the bandits who robbed the coal company were "the same band of marauders" who had been lurking around Price a few weeks before.

> When Col. Randlett, going to Fort Duchesne, alighted from the train carrying an immense sum of money...(he stepped from the car into an army ambulance surrounded by a company of armed soldiers of the Ninth Calvary...as the thugs slunk off to their favorite saloon and with regret watched the cloud of dust arise from the retreating cavalry in the midst of which was much United States cash.[47]

Historian Ronald Coleman indicates that Captain Wright and Troop F of Ninth Cavalry had been dispatched to protect the railroad depot in Price, and another detachment was sent to Helper to guard the station there. A reported $30,000 annuity destined for Ute Indians in the Uinta Basin was off-loaded in Price under the watchful eyes of forty soldiers, who guarded Indian agent Captain G. A. Cornish and the money on the long trip to Fort Duchesne through Nine Mile Canyon.[48]

The idea this plot can be laid at the feet of the Wild Bunch seems rather fanciful. It is unlikely that Butch Cassidy would have agreed to participate in any robbery that he had not carefully planned himself, much less one that was organized by Gunplay Maxwell. By some accounts, it was Butch

C. L. "Gunplay" Maxwell playing poker in Price in about 1897. From left to right: Chub Milburn, Mark Braffet, Maxwell, and Pete Francis, owner of the saloon at Brock's Place in Nine Mile Canyon. Photo is credited in earlier publications to both the Vern Jeffers Collection and Erma Armstrong.

himself who tipped the military to the robbery plans by Maxwell and Pete Francis because he knew he would be blamed for it (and robbing money meant for poor Indians was probably not in keeping with Butch's standards of robbing from the rich).

From Bad to Worse

As described by Pearl Baker, Maxwell had not fared so well as an outlaw, so he apparently decided to join the other side in hunting them down—perhaps in retaliation for being rejected by Butch Cassidy. In April 1897, at a County Commission meeting, Carbon County sheriff Gus Donant put forward Maxwell's name for confirmation as a sheriff's deputy. Not only did the commission not ratify the appointment, but the commissioners demanded Donant's resignation for willfully failing to perform his duty "to the detriment of the best citizens and taxpayers, and to the disgrace of the county."[49] The commission appointed C. W. Allred to replace him. April would have been about the same month Maxwell and Francis were planning to rob the military payroll.

The exact date of the commission meeting is not indicated, but it is relevant. Baker says it was "just days" before Butch Cassidy and Elza Lay robbed the Pleasant Valley Coal Company payroll and made their spectacular getaway with the help of Joe Walker and Bub Meeks,[50] and Patterson gives the date as sometime in the first week of April.[51] Although the petition to fire Donant came from James L. Smith, manager of the coal company, Baker believed the pressure to fire Donant had actually come from the politically powerful Whitmore brothers, who were exasperated that Donant was less than enthusiastic about apprehending Joe Walker, who had been rustling their herds with impunity.[52]

Kelly noted that Donant was still the sheriff on duty at the time of the Castle Gate holdup two weeks after the commission meeting and that he "ran around in circles, lost several hours, and when he at last got underway, started off in the wrong direction."[53] Patterson's reading of the minutes led him to believe that James L. Smith had a premonition of trouble brewing and that Donant was not doing enough to protect the company from "desperados" that had infiltrated the country.[54]

If Donant had been fired and a replacement already named, why was Donant still the sheriff at the time of the Wild Bunch raid at Castle Gate? And why would the coal company demand his resignation if nothing had yet happened to lead anyone to believe Butch Cassidy was prowling in the area? A more likely scenario is that Smith presented his petition to the commission sometime after the Castle Gate robbery and after Donant and his posse had failed to bring in any of the perpetrators of the deed. It is possible that Donant, in a last-ditch effort to save his job, attempted to hire an outlaw, Maxwell, with intimate knowledge of Robbers Roost who could guide the posse into the lair. That the Whitmores had a hand in the dismissal cannot be ruled out.

Donant's firing undoubtedly ended Maxwell's hopes of becoming a lawman, if he ever really intended to become one. Rustling was the one thing that Maxwell was good at. One account has it that Maxwell, sometime shortly after his arrival at Robbers Roost in 1895, along with Jack Cottrell and Bill Tomlinson, kidnapped a local rancher and then set about stealing the family's entire herd, five hundred head at a time, until there were none left.[55]

Maxwell might have had a local connection to get rid of the pilfered beef. Maxwell's brother reportedly moved to Price and opened a butcher shop, which provided an easier way to dispose of stolen livestock.[56] Later newspaper accounts indicate Gunplay had earlier operated his own butcher shop in Thermopolis, Wyoming, in the same manner to dispose of stolen beef.[57]

After July 1897, Maxwell then drifted north to Vernal and then on to Wyoming, always with Ada close by. In May 1898 he apparently botched a bank robbery in the Ashley Valley. It was about that time he earned the moniker "Gunplay" through a magazine article that observed, "He had several run-ins with Butch Cassidy, and came out each time with his feathers, his disposition, and his prestige ruffled."[58]

Maxwell has been described as "a thin man of medium height, aquiline features, and a dark pencil-thin mustache."[59] By most accounts Maxwell was a surly, taciturn, and violent man, but one who was often unable to back up his bravado. Kelly and Baker both take apparent glee in describing Maxwell's misfortunes, from picking a fight with a smaller Gilsonite miner who promptly took away Maxwell's guns and stomped him mercilessly,[60] to getting pistol-whipped with his own guns by some tough cowboys who did not take kindly to Maxwell shooting at their feet.[61]

Butch Cassidy, the undisputed leader of the Wild Bunch, didn't like Maxwell, and Maxwell might have returned the sentiment, although he ached to be accepted into the Wild Bunch. One story, attributed to 1897, has it that Maxwell rode to Vernal to view legal proceedings against some cattle rustler friends, camping just outside of town. As it happened, Butch Cassidy was also in Vernal. With typical Maxwell bravado, he sent word to Cassidy to leave town or suffer the consequences.

> So Butch rode out to the camp, and Maxwell rode to meet him, both men with guns drawn. When they were neck-and-neck, Butch spoke: "This town ain't big enough for both of us Gunplay. You ain't a bad man; you're just a petty-larceny horse thief. I'll give you five seconds to get going; otherwise there'll be a funeral in Vernal and you will be riding at the head of the procession." Maxwell hesitated only two fifths of the allotted time, then turned his horse and galloped back to Nine Mile.[62]

Regardless of whether or not that incident occurred, it illustrates a common theme in the historical accounts: Maxwell was repeatedly stung by Cassidy's disrespect, and the snub only fueled Maxwell's desire to prove the famous outlaw wrong. In no time, Maxwell was forming his own gang comprised of Robbers Roost regulars to pull off a robbery that, at first appearances, had all the earmarks of a Wild Bunch job. Everything, that is, except the careful planning and attention to detail. In the summer of 1898, Maxwell and an accomplice, a man identified only as Porter, decided to rob a Provo bank.[63] The plans were changed to rob the Springville bank instead, but the revised plans were never communicated to the outlaw who was waiting with the relay horses in Provo Canyon—which is nowhere near Springville. Maxwell and Porter made their escape in a horse-and-buggy—a slow means of escape that allowed the posse to catch them in the foothills above Hobble Creek. Porter fired on the posse, which returned fire and killed Porter. Maxwell surrendered and was later convicted and sentenced to eighteen years in the Utah State Penitentiary.[64]

A little more than a year later, in December 1899, his wife, Ada, married Thaddeus H. Watson and moved to Vernal with her new husband and her daughter, Myrtle.[65]

Less than five years into his stint, Maxwell's sentence was commuted and he was released. Newspaper accounts indicate that Maxwell was released because he had saved the life of a prison guard who was being savagely beaten during an attempted mass prison break in 1902.[66] Another account has it that Maxwell appealed the conviction because the number of jurors was eight instead of twelve, and he had not been indicted by a grand jury.[67] Yet another account says he was pardoned, at least in part based on letters of support from Sheriff Tuttle and James M. Whitmore.[68]

A fellow inmate found it ironic that Maxwell would be pardoned for good behavior when Maxwell had been planning his own escape since his arrival, and even spent a year in solitary confinement when guards discovered he had fashioned a makeshift pistol.[69] After his release, Maxwell drifted to mining boomtowns in Nevada, may have hired on as a gunman to protect mining payrolls, and was implicated "in at least a dozen holdups, two jewelry robberies, one stage robbery, and has passed several hundred dollars' worth of worthless checks, escaping prosecution in nearly every instance and conviction in every case."[70]

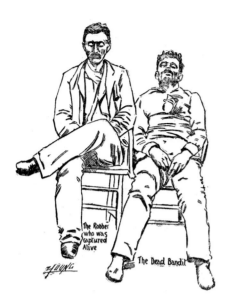

Artist's sketch of the arrested Maxwell (left) and his dead partner, a man named Porter. Used by permission, Utah State Historical Society, all rights reserved.

The Demise of Gunplay

Sometime after his release from prison in November 1903 he moved back to Scofield, working as a guard for the coal company during the frequent labor strikes, and even donned a badge as a county deputy sheriff. And at some point, he was joined by Ada Slaugh, who had again resumed her role as Mrs. Maxwell, and they bought a house next to the Wilson Hotel. By 1907, Maxwell was in Nevada and Ada had sold their house in Price and moved to Salt Lake City, where she went to work at the Clift House Hotel.[71]

Maxwell had returned to his old haunts in Carbon County by September 1907 when he was drunk in a Helper saloon and picking a fight with a railroad fireman, L. C. Reidel, and another railroad man, Paddy Mack. In the ensuing brawl, Mack was pistol whipped and Reidel was critically wounded, but not before getting off some shots of his own. Maxwell was hit in the shoulder and arm.[72] The incident provoked considerable outrage in Price and Helper, and there was even talk of lynching Maxwell.[73]

Exactly what Maxwell was doing in Helper is not clearly stated in the newspaper accounts. But it can be surmised that he was again working as a gunman and enforcer for Utah Fuel Company, the successor to the Pleasant Valley Coal Company and the largest and most politically powerful company in Carbon County. Days after the incident, Maxwell was observed strolling around Salt Lake City, his arm in a sling, alongside his long-time friend, M. P. Braffet, who was at that time the general counsel for Utah Fuel and one of the men who posted Maxwell's bond.[74]

Reporters caught up with Maxwell later while he was eating at a local restaurant. When asked to give his side of the story he replied, "You fellows seem to be able to write enough without my talking, so I will shut up and let you." When pressed further about what was inaccurate, he replied, "It's all untrue, and when the time comes you'll find out all you want to know, all right?"[75] The account went on to describe Maxwell as looking anything but a famous gunman. "He's tall and thin, stoop-shouldered, has dark hair and sharp black eyes. Last night as he looked out from under the rim of his big black hat he appeared disappointingly docile and meek."[76]

With the tide of public sentiment clearly on the side of his victims, Maxwell left Utah and returned to Nevada, and by some accounts made a side trip to San Francisco. In early 1908, using the name W. C. Seaman, he "married" Bessie Hume, a wealthy widow from San Francisco.[77] When

W. C. and Bessie Seaman arrived in Salt Lake City in February to cele-
brate their honeymoon, Bessie caused quite a stir when newspapers accused
her of the shocking sin of smoking in a café, something tolerated among
women in Paris and New York but not in Salt Lake City.[78]

Things were quiet until Maxwell got into a tussle with an old acquain-
tance, John Foote, in the Wilson Hotel and drew his guns, sending patrons
scrambling for the door. That incident brought newspapermen running
for an interview. When reporters began to question whether Bessie Hume
was really as wealthy as had been reported, Maxwell turned up his waist-
coat, "and displayed a string of jewels that would make a pawn shop window look like a bunch of broken bottles. The sparklers, which really looked
like diamonds, were arranged with picturesque disorder across Maxwell's
shirt."[79] Gunplay and Bessie apparently moved to Ogden, and there is little written about him in the following year. Reidel recovered from his
wounds, and Maxwell avoided conviction, perhaps with the intervention of
his friends at the Utah Fuel Company.

In 1904, upon his release from prison, Maxwell was hired by the Utah Fuel Company as a guard during the coal strike. He is the man near the far left frame with a rifle. The man to his left is Mark P. Braffet, Maxwell's long-time friend and personal attorney, who at the time of this photo was the attorney for the Utah Fuel Company. Photo used with permission of the Utah State Historical Society, all rights reserved.

In late August of 1909, Maxwell was again in Price, and according to newspaper accounts he had hatched schemes to rob a bank in Green River and a paymaster for the Independent Coal and Coke Company in Kenilworth. But lawmen were tipped off and the targets were heavily guarded, and Maxwell found himself under surveillance. When he attempted to draw his gun on Sheriff Ed Johnstone, the lawman put two bullets into Maxwell's chest, killing him.[80] One account relates Johnstone drew his own gun and killed Maxwell only after Maxwell had fired first and missed from only ten feet away.[81] Other stories contend that Johnstone lured Maxwell out of the Oasis Saloon and shot him in the back.[82]

At a formal inquest, at which Johnstone was cleared of any wrongdoing, it was revealed that Maxwell held a grudge against Johnstone, and had made threats against him because he had "spoiled" his schemes.[83] It was also discovered Maxwell was an opium addict; there were needle tracks from his wrists to his shoulder, and a hypodermic needle and opium gum were found on his person.[84]

Johnstone, whom the press dubbed "Shoot 'em Up Ed," was initially praised for bringing to an end the notorious life of Gunplay Maxwell. "Scores of citizens crowded about Deputy Sheriff Edward Johnstone when the verdict of justifiable homicide was rendered, and the thanks of the whole community have been tendered to the man who relieved the state of the presence of Maxwell."[85] A Salt Lake banker reportedly offered Johnstone $1,000 for the gun used to kill Maxwell, and the Utah Fuel Company—Maxwell's former employer—offered Johnstone a $500 reward check. Johnstone refused both offers.[86] The governor of Utah, William Spry, later awarded him a diamond ring and pearl-inlaid handcuffs and guns for his service to the state.[87]

Ada Maxwell saw things differently, calling the shooting "murder, cold-blooded murder," adding that "he was no angel, but he was not as bad as he had been painted."[88] Bessie Seaman never spoke to reporters. When Maxwell's body was searched, officers found $500 in pawn tickets for her jewelry.[89]

Any fame Johnstone might have enjoyed dissipated quickly. Seen as a lackey for the coal company, he was vilified by pro-union elements and slanderous stories were repeated over and again. In 1912, Johnstone was carrying a payroll when he thought two men were trying to rob him. He shot and killed one of them and wounded the other. It turned out they were seventeen-year-old boys. He was accused of murder, convicted of manslaughter, and served six months at the Utah State Penitentiary.[90]

He went back to being a lawman upon his release, but while on a case in California in 1919, he contracted pneumonia and was hospitalized in Alameda. Delirious and consumed by the urgency to complete his mission, he wandered out of the hospital. He was found unconscious in the street and died a short time later.

His enemies reported that he had "become a down and outer, destitute of all possessions and friends, until he had died in a California gutter."[91] It wasn't true, but it reflected the enmity of the day between unions and the coal companies.

Ada Slaugh subsequently married Pete Logan, also known as Pete Nelson, a part-time "Robbers Rooster" and reportedly Maxwell's partner in the botched robbery of the Springville bank. Pete later went to work for Preston Nutter, and both Pete and his new bride, Ada, lived in Nine Mile Canyon for many years. Ada is buried in Prescott, Arizona.[92]

Newspaper accounts of the death of the famed gunman seem to agree that his body was hauled to Salt Lake City for burial. But in the Price Cemetery, there is a headstone with the name C. L. "Gunplay" Maxwell, a marker shared with three other bad men, including Joe Walker. Was the one-time scourge of Price actually buried in Price? Old West historian Joel Frandsen had been researching that conundrum, and prior to his death in 2014, he found that the person buried in the Price Cemetery is John Carter, one of Gunplay's many aliases. But he also found a death certificate that shows he was buried in Salt Lake City under the name "Chas. L. Maxwell alias of Wm. H. Seaman," which was Gunplay's alias at the time he was killed in the shootout with Sheriff Johnstone. The cemetery records indicated he had died of gunshot wounds and was buried under the name William H. Seaman.[93]

Sheriff Ed "Shoot 'em up" Johnstone, the man who killed C. L. Maxwell in a gunfight in downtown Price. Photo courtesy of Joel Frandsen.

An Outlaw Creed

Walker and Maxwell were most certainly not the only outlaws who took up residency in Nine Mile Canyon, but the names of the others, probably living here under aliases, have been lost through the passage of time. It was

Tombstone marking the final resting place of four "outlaws" in the Price Cemetery. But C. L. "Gunplay" Maxwell is not one of them. He is buried in an unmarked grave in Salt Lake City. Photo by Jerry D. Spangler.

especially common for cattle rustlers to hire on with legitimate ranchers as a cover while on the run or while planning their next caper. The ranchers didn't mind the outlaw presence, or at least they turned a blind eye to it. The most infamous of these was Jim McPherson, whose ranch deep in Desolation Canyon could offer up meals, fresh mounts, and respite from the posses—something the law could never quite prove.

Ranchers probably had faith in an outlaw creed that outlaws would not steal from their employers, which wasn't always true but it worked from time to time. Who better to recognize the wily ways of rustlers than rustlers themselves? Some ranchers had an open door policy to the outlaws. There are no specific references to outlaws in the employ of the Whitmore brothers, the largest ranch operation in the Nine Mile area in the 1890s, but they might have hired some shady characters from time to time—intentionally or not.

Nine Mile Canyon has a number of outlaw stories. A cabin on a high point overlooking the mouth of Daddy Canyon is referred to today as the "Outlaw Cabin," which was reportedly a "temporary shelter for the outlaws as they came through here on their way to Robbers Roost."[94] And outlaw treasure is reportedly buried at a "rock house" at the head of Devils Canyon.[95]

Stories are still shared among the old-timers about various attempts to rob the Nine Mile stagecoach (most often the story takes place in Gate Canyon). One account credits Gett Alger with foiling a robbery attempt when he was driving the stage to Myton. Another account, related by descendants of the Lee Lisonbee family, claims Lee was driving the stage when it was held up by the Wild Bunch. Lee's wife, a passenger, hid the military payroll under her baby's soiled diapers, and the loot and passengers all made it safely to Fort Duchesne.[96]

A lot of the outlaw stories are centered on Preston Nutter. In 1902, Preston Nutter moved his ranching headquarters into Nine Mile Canyon, eventually becoming the largest private cattle rancher in the state of Utah at that time (see chapter 7). Nutter had earlier run his massive herds on the east side of the Green River in the Hill Creek country of the East Tavaputs Plateau and to the north in the Strawberry Valley. In 1892, Nutter reportedly caught Gunplay Maxwell rustling his cattle.

According to the account offered by Nutter's daughter, Virginia Nutter Price, Nutter hauled Maxwell to Vernal to file charges, but "before he

Left: Jim McPherson had a remote ranch at Florence Creek deep in the heart of Desolation Canyon. The ranch was a known "safe haven" for outlaws on the run. Here he poses with his horse "Eagle," which according to family legend he acquired from outlaw Joe Walker. Photo courtesy of Special Collections, Marriott Library, University of Utah.

Bottom left: Thorald Rich visiting an outlaw "stone cabin" on a high point with a view to the mouth of Daddy Canyon. Photo courtesy of Norma Dalton.

Bottom right: Another stone cabin that locals attribute to outlaws hiding out in Nine Mile Canyon, this one at the head of Devil's Canyon. Photo courtesy of Norma Dalton.

could be brought to trial on the rustling charge he was killed escaping from a bank holdup."[97] This clearly did not happen. Maxwell survived another nineteen years after that incident. By the time Nutter moved his headquarters to Nine Mile Canyon, Maxwell was serving the last months of a sentence in the Utah State Penitentiary for the botched Springville bank robbery.

George Fasselin, whose family roots run deep into the history of Nine Mile Canyon and the Tavaputs Plateau, says it was common knowledge among the smaller ranchers in Nine Mile that Nutter employed a crew of unsavory individuals of questionable morals, probably rustlers, to protect his massive herds. These individuals were not housed at the Nutter Ranch headquarters at the mouth of Gate Canyon with the regular cowboys, but at a camp farther downstream at the mouth of Prickly Pear Canyon, where the stone foundations of their cabins are still visible. Fasselin said these cowboys were referred to as "the undesirables."[98] Nutter's daughter echoed this sentiment, writing, "Like a lot of other ranchers, Nutter often found it more practical to hire the outlaws to work as cowhands during their cooling off periods. Most of them were cowboys at one time or another and made top hands, but what was more important their code prevented them from rustling from an employer."[99]

Hiring outlaws as insurance against rustlers was a time-honored tradition, although a risky one if the law suspected the rancher was part of the gang. Utah lawmen were always suspicious of rancher Jim McPherson, whose remote ranch deep in Desolation Canyon at Florence Creek was a known haven for outlaws. And it was conveniently located about midway between hideouts at Browns Hole and Robbers Roost.

In 1898, Butch Cassidy and Elza Lay, having left Robbers Roost behind, were working as cowboys at the WS Ranch in New Mexico. When Elza was arrested in connection with a nearby robbery there, Butch asked the rancher, William French, to post his bond. Lawmen were skeptical when the rancher expressed surprise that the famous outlaws, who had hired on under aliases, were part of his ranch crew, praising them as top-notch cowboys.[100]

Nine Mile Canyon cattle baron Preston Nutter would have found the story somewhat familiar. On one occasion, Pearl Baker relates that George "Flat Nose" Curry, one of the most famous members of the Wild Bunch,

One of several stone foundations near the mouth of Prickly Pear Canyon reported to have been used by the "Undesirables"—outlaws hired by Preston Nutter to watch his herds during cooling off periods. Photo by Jerry D. Spangler.

Another residence of the "Undesirables," also near the mouth of Prickly Pear Canyon. Photo by Jerry D. Spangler.

and Charley Lee from Torrey, were arrested for stealing a single black cow in the San Rafael Swell and then selling it. Both men were hauled into court (Pearl Baker does not indicate which court or when this occurred). None other than Preston Nutter posted Curry's bond. Nutter showed up in court but Curry did not. The judge demanded that Nutter produce the outlaw or forfeit bail. In the meantime, Lee was convicted and sent to prison.

Curry showed up sometime later and turned himself in, at which time the judge threw out the case against him.[101]

The story, if true, illustrates that Nutter recognized that good relations with the outlaws was simply a cost of doing business. And it appears he was very well acquainted with the Wild Bunch, perhaps even hiring them as cowboys on his far-flung rangelands, whether on the West Tavaputs Plateau, in the Strawberry Valley of the Uinta Basin, or on the Arizona Strip. And Curry, at least, had enough respect for Nutter that he did not leave the cattleman on the hook for his bail. Butch Cassidy had long since moved on to South America by the time Nutter set up his headquarters in Nine Mile Canyon in 1902. But "undesirables" were always welcome at the Nutter Ranch.

The Cattle King
The Myth and Legacy of Preston Nutter

Of the many legendary characters who weave in and out of the history of Nine Mile Canyon, few have attained the near-mythical status of Preston Nutter—the rags-to-riches cattle baron who, by some accounts, rivaled the great cattle kings of Texas and Wyoming. Unlike the ruthlessness of his contemporaries, as the story goes, he was unbendingly tough when need be but honorable and charitable amid his fortune. But as is the case with any good legend, the story of Preston Nutter is peppered with truth and salted with fiction.

Newspapermen and biographers invariably use modifiers like "cattle baron" or "cattle king" to describe Preston Nutter, almost to the point they seemed to be part of his name. Preston Nutter, the "Last Great Cattle King."[1] Preston Nutter, "one of the best-known cattle barons on the Utah scene."[2] Most of these accounts detail cattle purchases and sales, and occasionally his legal squabbles. Some accounts assert Nutter had herds of as many as a hundred thousand head of cattle ranging between his spread on the Arizona Strip and his headquarters in Nine Mile Canyon—claims that were probably grossly exaggerated. According to old-timers, his herds were so large that he had no idea how many cattle he actually owned,[3] something that is also unlikely given his meticulous attention to business details. Another account claims that at one time Nutter owned more land and ran more cattle than any other rancher in the West.[4]

So who was Preston Nutter? The *Salt Lake Telegram* described him succinctly in his 1936 obituary as "one of the last links between the old west and the new, over six feet tall, white haired, gray eyed, straight as a lodgepole pine and physically hard as the saddle leather on which he rode." On those points there is no disagreement. Rather, the fiction emerges in the

Portrait of a young Preston Nutter. Photo used by permission, Utah State Historical Society, all rights reserved.

Right: The Nutter Ranch in Range Creek Canyon. Photo by Ray Boren.

Below: Nutter Ranch in Nine Mile Canyon. Photo courtesy of the Colorado Plateau Archaeological Alliance.

minor details of his story, some of which are irrelevant to the bigger picture. For example, many accounts state that Nutter would only ride his trusted mule. Truth of the matter is Nutter rode horses and mules alike, but he insisted the latter were smarter animals that would recognize their limitations. Other accounts state that he spent most of his life in the saddle, riding back and forth between his spreads on the Arizona Strip and in Nine Mile Canyon. A review of his diaries, now at Special Collections at the Marriott Library at the University of Utah, indicate he spent far more time riding a train than he ever did on a horse or mule, and that most of his energy, especially in the latter half of his life, was focused on the mundane tasks of managing a large business.[5]

More relevant to this story are the minor details that shed light on the character of Preston Nutter. And some of those details reflect inexplicable lapses in judgment, a willingness to bend the truth to suit his interests, and a fierce determination to drive his opponents into the ground by any means necessary if they dared to challenge him. As the adage goes, no one gets rich without stepping on people to get there. And Preston Nutter was unquestionably rich.

Perhaps the most prevalent myth is that Preston Nutter protected his operations by filing lawsuits rather than by hired guns, and only once did he ever lose in the courtroom. While it is true that Nutter spent a lot of time in court, he was more often than not a defendant in the legal actions, and he lost quite frequently. And for that matter, if attorneys could not do the job he was not above hiring ruthless range "detectives" to protect his herds by whatever means necessary.

Most of what is known about Preston Nutter comes from two sources: a brief (and immensely flattering) biography written by his daughter, Virginia Nutter Price, which was published in the *Utah Historical Quarterly* almost thirty years after Nutter's death; and a biographic summary written by Roy Webb, who catalogued the vast Preston Nutter Corporation Collection when it was donated to Special Collections at the Marriott Library at the University of Utah. Two other major accounts, one in *Cowboying: A Tough Job in a Hard Land*, by James Beckstead, and a brief article in the *Outlaw Trail Journal*, by Janet Taylor, for the most part repeat the same information with a few additional juicy details.

To better understand the man behind the myth, we also examined Preston Nutter's journals and business files, and we poured over more than a hundred newspaper accounts of Nutter and his business dealings. What we found was an extremely complex figure. On one hand he was generous to the community, he gave liberally to distant family members in need, he was humble about his wealth, he was given to romantic impulse, and he was known far and wide as being fair. On the other hand, he could be ruthless in his determination not only to win but to crush his opponents. He could be deceitful, he solicited perjured testimony and might even have lied to the court himself, he did not pay his taxes, he crippled other ranchers by blocking their access to water, and he could be petty over small sums of money.

Gold Fever and the Man Eater

Preston Nutter was perhaps destined to be a rancher. He was born in 1850 in what is today Clarksburg, West Virginia, to Christopher Nutter and Catherine Pugh Nutter. By most accounts, his father was a landowner and breeder of fine horses,[6] although one account has it that his father was a cattleman.[7] In 1859 his father died suddenly, followed soon thereafter by his mother. According to family records, Preston (and presumably his brothers and sisters) was sent to live with an aunt and uncle who were strict Methodists. Webb indicates he ran away from home after a few months,[8] whereas Nutter's daughter indicates he ran away "after a miserable two years with relatives he disliked."[9] He worked a spell as a store clerk and a cabin boy on the Mississippi River. By 1863 he had saved enough money to buy his first horse, which he branded with a "63"—a brand that would mark Nutter's horses and mules the rest of his life.[10] It was also the same year that Nutter, a mere lad of thirteen, signed on with a government supply wagon train headed west—a land of unlimited opportunity that stood in sharp contrast to his Civil War–racked homeland.

There are scant written records related to Preston Nutter in the years following, and most of what is known has been handed down through family histories. Webb indicates he drifted to Idaho and Nevada, where he acquired a mining claim that he eventually sold for $5,000.[11] He used the proceeds to finance two years at a San Francisco business college, although the name of the school is not known, nor the years he attended. His daughter indicates he tended horses at the famed Cliff House while going to school. The next date mentioned is 1871 (or 1873) when Nutter was back in Idaho prospecting for gold. Word reached the camp in 1873 of a rich strike in the San Juan Mountains of Colorado, and as prospectors are wont to do, Nutter and a friend named Montgomery packed their bags and headed south into Utah on their way to southeastern Colorado.

Even if Preston Nutter had not become a legend in the cattle business, he would have been a historical footnote for what happened during the winter of 1873–1874. Upon his arrival in the Provo area in November 1873,

Nutter met twenty other would-be prospectors from Bingham Canyon west of Salt Lake who were also headed to the Colorado gold fields. Plans were made to join forces for the overland trip to Colorado. A trip that late in the year was risky, but gold fever was rampant and all were eager to get on their way—especially one Alferd G. Packer.[12] According to Nutter's daughter, Packer professed an intimate knowledge of the Colorado country and persuaded the group to hire him as a guide, although the group came to quickly realize he was a "whining fraud" and that he had been lost since the group departed from Provo.[13] But Preston Nutter's own courtroom testimony in Packer's later murder trial indicates Packer was merely one of the would-be prospectors on the ill-fated expedition, that Packer was "helping a man by the name of McGrew with his team, and thus was paying his expenses to the San Juan country."[14]

The expedition was poorly provisioned, and by the time they arrived near what is today Gunnison, Colorado, they were low on supplies and winter storms were threatening. While traveling across the Uncompahgre Reservation they met the famous Ute chief Ouray and his wife, Chipeta. Chief Ouray advised that any attempt to venture into the snowbound San Juan Mountains was foolhardy, inviting the group to instead spend the winter near his own encampment until the snows had melted. Packer was insistent that Ouray was after what little money the group had left and campaigned for the group to continue on to the Los Pinos Agency still forty miles distant. The group set up a winter camp with Ouray, but several members grew restless and determined to make it to Los Pinos. Five men—Mike Burke, Oliver D. Lutzenheizer, George Driver, and Isaac and Tom Walker—set off with all the supplies they could carry on their backs.[15] About a week later, in mid-February 1874, six more members of the winter camp set out on a different trail: Shannon Wilson Bell, James Humphreys, Frank "Butcher" Miller, George "California" Noon, Israel Swan, and Alferd Packer. Preston Nutter was among the ten men who remained with Chief Ouray through the rest of the winter.

The events of what happened in the Colorado mountains that winter have evoked ghoulish fascination ever since.[16] Of the second group, only Alferd Packer made it to Los Pinos, "looking fat and flourishing…and had money jingling in his pockets."[17] Packer's details about what happened amid the winter blizzards and starvation changed repeatedly, although

Preston Nutter was the prosecution's star witness against Alferd Packer, pictured here, who became one of the most notorious figures in Colorado history when he killed and ate five companions in the San Juan Mountains. Courtesy, History Colorado (Scan #10026096).

the one constant that emerged in the sensational newspaper headlines of the day was that Packer confessed to having eaten the flesh of his dead companions. Packer insisted he had killed Bell in self-defense and only after Bell had killed the others and was coming for him. He said he had only eaten human flesh after succumbing to the madness of isolation and starvation.

Preston Nutter arrived at Los Pinos on April 16, 1874, and was immediately summoned to meet with the agency commander, Major Adams. In the room was Alferd Packer, who "seemed excited; shook hands and said he never expected to see me again. Said he did not know where the rest of the party were, that he had frozen his feet and they left him and went south."[18] Other members of the Ouray winter camp soon arrived and "it was intimated that Packer wished to make a confession and we gathered into Adams' office to hear it."[19] Packer was arrested and agreed to lead authorities to the bodies. Preston Nutter went along to make positive identifications.[20]

Packer professed ignorance of the countryside and led the search party in circles, claiming he was lost. According to Nutter's courtroom testimony, "We had a controversy, and I told Packer I was satisfied that he had killed the men and he ought to be hung." Later, in May or June of 1874, the remains of the bodies were found by a search party sponsored by *Harpers Weekly Magazine*, and Nutter was again called to identify the victims—a fact that made him the star witness in Packer's subsequent 1883 murder trial. Packer was found guilty and sentenced to be executed. The sentence was later overturned by the Colorado Supreme Court and a second trial on lesser manslaughter charges warranted Nutter's return to the courtroom in 1886. Packer was again convicted and sentenced to prison. Packer was paroled in 1901 at the age of sixty-one, worked a short stint as a night watchman at the *Denver Post*, wandered about the West, and died in 1907. Packer's last words were: "I am innocent of the charges."[21]

Preston Nutter, by family accounts, shunned the media spotlight his entire life, but he probably could not deny the powerful influence of the press. The Alferd Packer incident and national press coverage that followed had made the young man—Nutter was only twenty-four when the victims' bodies were discovered—well known in the local mining communities. And he may have parlayed that fame into a successful business venture: hauling freight to the mining camps. According to the family accounts, he actually did little or no prospecting in the Colorado gold fields, but instead recognized he could make more money as a freighter, and he used his remaining capital to buy ox teams, horses, mules, and wagons.[22] Webb indicates that by 1876 he had acquired a string of mules and pack saddles which he used to haul freight to the mines around Lake City, Colorado.[23]

It is not clear where Nutter got the capital to start the freighting venture and whether or not he had partners as he did in many of his other ventures, but the business was apparently quite profitable, and Nutter himself must have been well regarded in the community. As most successful businessmen of the day, he joined the local Masonic Lodge (he continued to provide support to his home lodge later in life). In 1880, at the age of thirty, he was elected to the Colorado Legislature as a Democrat, serving a single term that undoubtedly brought him into contact with wealthy and powerful businessmen in Colorado. At that time, he owned property in Lake City valued at $1,900.[24] Nutter was an astute and forward-thinking businessman, and he recognized that traditional horse-and-wagon freighting would be crippled once the approaching Denver & Rio Grande Railroad arrived at the mining communities.

Birth of an Empire

At about the same time he was elected to the Colorado Legislature, Nutter began laying the groundwork to fulfill a lifelong dream. He wanted to be a cattleman. Webb indicates Nutter began buying cattle and holding them on his lands near Montrose in 1883.[25] Nutter's daughter points to an 1881 receipt showing a transfer of $6,100 to a bank in Manti, Utah, for a cattle purchase as the beginning of Nutter's cattle enterprise.[26] The size of that transfer indicates Nutter intended to get into the business in a very big way. The price Nutter paid per head is not known, but cattle prices in the early 1880s were depressed, and $6,100 could have been enough to purchase as many as a thousand head.[27]

Where did he intend to range that many cattle? By all accounts, Nutter had been keeping his herds on the lands he owned near Montrose.[28] But this area was crowded with prospectors and merchants and probably other cattlemen. And the intrusion of such a large herd would not have been viewed favorably, nor was it likely that Nutter owned enough private land to accommodate such a large number. If he was running his herds on the vast Uncompahgre Reservation, where he counted Chief Ouray among his friends, it was an inopportune time to do so. In late 1879, Indian Agent Nathaniel Meeker was killed during an uprising by White River Utes far to the north of the Uncompahgre country. The revolt was quickly crushed

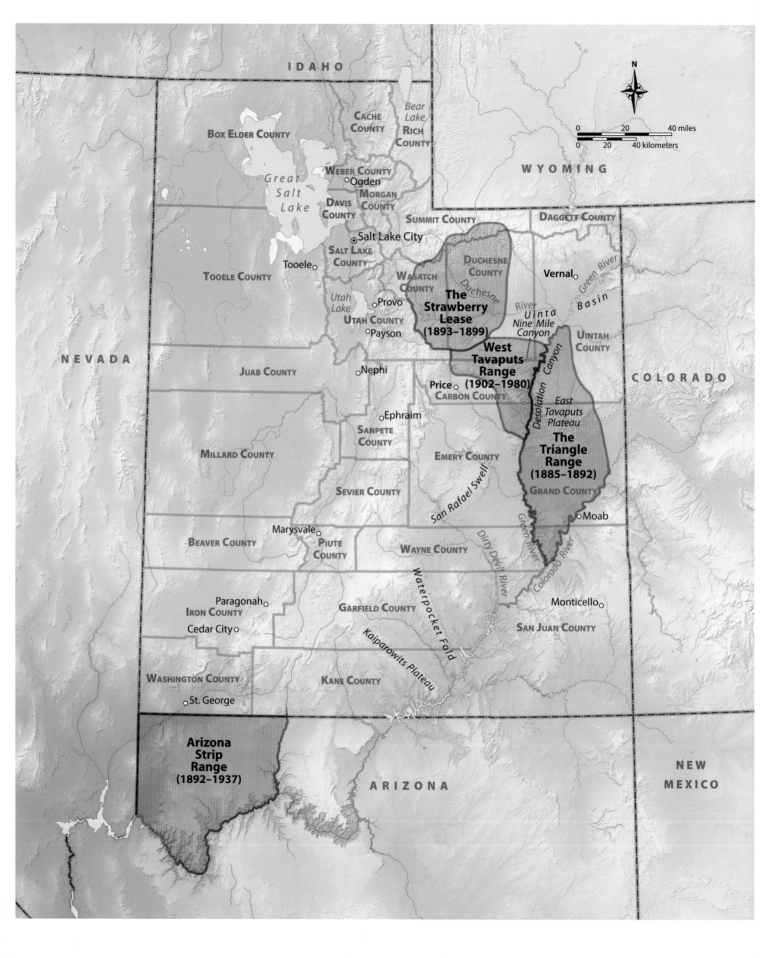

by the military, and in the twisted logic of the times the White River Utes and the Uncompahgre Utes, who had played no part in the uprising, were forced from their homes in Colorado.[29] By 1882, all Uncompahgre Utes had been relocated to the deserts of northeastern Utah and the Uncompahgre Reservation was opened to homesteaders—sodbusters who resisted the free-range policies of the ranchers. In short, the rangelands of the Uncompahgre country were closing down just as Nutter began purchasing large numbers of cattle.

The scope of Nutter's initial foray into cattle ranching—the period between 1881 and 1885—remains unknown and undocumented. But it was sometime during this period that Nutter sold his freighting business and moved to Grand Junction.[30] By inference, this would have been no earlier than 1883 when he gave up his legislative seat representing the Lake City area. Most accounts agree that sometime in 1885 he moved his herds to the largely unclaimed ranges in eastern Utah known as "The Triangle," an area ten-by-thirty miles in size centered on Thompson Springs along present-day Interstate 70 east of the Green River. The Triangle included the southern Book Cliffs, the high rangelands of the East Tavaputs Plateau, and the largely barren deserts north of Moab. Nutter's daughter indicated he was seeking a range large enough to "eventually" run between fifteen and twenty thousand head of cattle.[31] More importantly, there was a railhead at Thompson Springs to facilitate the shipment of livestock.

Nutter's daughter indicated that he "acquired" the Triangle range, but the meaning of this word is obscure. Federal land at that time was open range and the grass was free for the taking, which could lead to confrontation between the cattlemen over "first rights." Nutter's only competition of any size in the area was the Webster City Cattle Company—an outfit with which Nutter had running legal battles during the 1890s.[32]

The railheads at Thompson Springs proved most fortuitous to Nutter's operation, and the railroad helped cement Nutter's legend as a canny cow man. The winter of 1886–1887 was exceptionally harsh, with blizzards blanketing available forage in deep snows. Cattle died by the thousands. Instead of spreading the herd, as was the custom in the day, Nutter bunched the animals at Thompson Springs and shipped in hay to feed them through the winter. As noted by Virginia Nutter Price, "There is every indication that it paid off because his losses were small and receipts

Opposite: Map indicating the four cattle ranges used by Preston Nutter.

show him buying more cattle throughout the entire bleak winter."[33] There were plenty of livestock available for purchase as the harsh weather, coupled with poor cattle prices, had devastated family farms throughout the region and the small ranchers were selling out.[34] In 1888, he went into partnership with two other ranchers, Ed Sands and Tom Wheeler, creating the Grand Cattle Company. He bought them out the following year.[35]

As discussed in chapter 4, the establishment of Fort Duchesne in the Uinta Basin in the fall of 1886 resulted in increased demand for beef both for military personnel and for the Indian Agency, and in about 1888 Nutter secured the government contract to supply the military outpost with beef.[36] He also expanded deeper into the East Tavaputs Plateau, specifically into the area known as Hill Creek. Exactly how many cattle he was running in the Triangle at this time is speculative. Taylor indicates the number was "at least 5,000." The number certainly fluctuated as herds were bought and sold. Nutter's own journal entry for June 13, 1887, indicates he had between 1,275 and 1,300 head.[37] It was also about this time that Nutter and his cowboys first began pushing cattle into Desolation Canyon and across the river into Range Valley, known today as Range Creek Canyon (the earliest mention of Nutter in Range Valley is an 1886 reference to Cherry Meadows, where Nutter later established an outlier ranch that became part of his Nine Mile Canyon operation in the early 1900s).[38]

Thievery and Retribution

It would have been during his days running cattle on the Hill Creek region that Nutter first became acquainted with the outlaw elements who roamed unfettered in eastern Utah and western Colorado. Nutter's daughter relates a story attributed to 1892 of Nutter catching Gunplay Maxwell red-handed rustling his cattle in the White River area near Hill Creek and that he hauled the famous outlaw to Vernal to press charges. But, she says, Gunplay got out of jail before the trial and was killed robbing a bank before he could be tried on the rustling charge—something that clearly never happened (see chapter 6).[39]

Henry Rhodes Meeks Jr., better known as Bub Meeks, a founding member of the Wild Bunch, also had a penchant for rustling Nutter's herds.[40] And in one instance, Nutter bailed out of jail none other than

George "Flat Nose" Curry, one of the most notorious members of the Wild Bunch.[41] His obituary claims "he knew well and was respected by Butch Cassidy and others notorious in western annals."[42]

Virginia Nutter Price maintains, and there is no reason to doubt her, that Nutter commonly hired outlaws on the lam during their "cooling off" periods. The outlaw code of the day supposedly prevented the outlaws from stealing from an employer, but this has probably been greatly exaggerated. For example, one of Nutter's top hands was Pete Nelson, a well-known Robbers Roost rustler married to Ada Slaugh, the widow of Gunplay Maxwell (see chapter 6). Pete's son, going by the name Lee Sage, later wrote a colorful autobiography wherein his father, spurred by the nagging of his stepmother, had been pilfering the herds of his employer, a renowned cattle baron. Although Sage changed the names of everyone involved, the cast of characters is unmistakably Pete Nelson, Ada Slaugh, and Preston Nutter.[43]

But Nutter's was a large spread, up to fifty miles or more to a side, and the larger the cattle operation the more likely the theft of some livestock would go unnoticed. And rustling was a persistent problem whether or not he hired outlaws as cowhands. Arrests seem to have been rare, or at least rarely noted in newspaper accounts. In 1897, Charles Atwood's arrest for rustling Nutter's cattle in the Strawberry Valley was noted by journalists, but there are few other specific references to rustlers.[44]

On this point, we feel obliged to dispel a common myth about Preston Nutter. The traditional histories have lionized Nutter as one who was different from the cattle barons of Wyoming and Texas in that he did not resort to violence to deter the rustling of his herds or the encroachment onto his range by sheepherders, but rather preferred to use the court system. He indeed loved to litigate, but he was also not above hiring tough men to do very nasty deeds. In 1896, Nutter, through his friend Sheriff Cyrus "Doc" Shores of Montrose, Colorado, hired one of Shore's deputies, John A. "Jack" Watson, as a "detective" to put an end to the rustling. But Watson was not just any detective. He was an ex-Texas Ranger, a violent drunk who was in and out of jail, an on-again-off-again outlaw, a former deputy, and, by his own accounts, a stone-cold killer.[45]

According to a Watson biography, the scarred and grizzled enforcer looked every part an outlaw, and he easily blended into the outlaw underground in the Price area. He reportedly worked undercover as a blacksmith and came to know the outlaws quite well. Watson made periodic reports to Shores, but apparently he had never met Nutter personally.[46] By 1898, he had become so effective in ridding the country of outlaws that Nutter requested a personal meeting with the shadowy character. In a May 28, 1898, letter to his brother in Tennessee, Watson claimed to have killed six men during his detective service for Nutter. Nutter pleaded with Watson to remain in the area to discourage the return of the outlaws, but Watson responded by going on a drunken bender. By July of that year he was dead, killed by two bullets during a gunfight in a Price saloon.[47]

Watson had intended to "give up" the detective business and leave the Price area, but dallied there as he waited for a reward of $20.80—his share of the $500 bounty on the head of the outlaw Joe Walker (see chapter 6). He was paid the reward money in early July, but he promptly spent it in the area saloons, getting into fights and earning the wrath of Carbon County Attorney J. W. Warf, who had earlier given Watson a severe beating over a water rights dispute. The judge had dismissed assault charges against Warf, which prompted snickers from townsfolk that the judge and county attorney were in cahoots.[48]

On July 23, 1898, at 5:45 p.m., Warf and others walked into the Senate Saloon where Watson was already drunk. Insults were exchanged and guns were drawn. Watson was shot once in the groin and once in the buttocks as he tried to crawl away. He died about four hours later. Watson is buried in the Price Cemetery.

It is not surprising that Warf, the county's chief prosecutor, was exonerated of any wrongdoing in the killing,[49] but there were always questions of collusion between Warf and the judge who dismissed the case, Justice J. T. Fitch, the same judge who had earlier dismissed the assault charge against Warf.[50] Warf did not run for reelection. Fitch tied in his reelection bid and won by drawing of lots.[51]

The problem with the Jack Watson story, of course, is the 1898 date. That was four years before Preston Nutter moved into the Nine Mile area. At that time Nutter's massive herds would have been grazing the Uinta Mountain foothills and Strawberry Valley, much closer to Fort Duchesne and Vernal. Yet the histories of Jack Watson specifically state Watson was working undercover for Nutter in Nine Mile Canyon,[52] and newspaper accounts that mention Watson are all from the Price area, not the Vernal newspapers.

Could it be that Nine Mile Canyon was a haven for outlaws—hence it was the source of Preston Nutter's outlaw problem in the Uinta Basin— long before he ever moved to Nine Mile Canyon? Or maybe Preston Nutter had already begun moving his cattle operation into the Nine Mile country four years before he actually acquired a ranch headquarters there in 1902, even though conditions of his Strawberry Valley lease made it illegal for him to do so (see below). Whatever the circumstances of his employ, the death of "detective" Jack Watson was but one bloody reminder of the very fine line that existed between lawful and lawless in those days.

More typical of Nutter's approach to dealing with outlaws, and perhaps even his willingness to bend the truth to suit his own ends, is the story of Peter Nelson (sometimes spelled Nealson or Nielson), a typical Mormon cowboy living in Elsinore, Utah, with a wife, two children, and another on the way. But in March 1897, Pete rode off, deserting his family in search of something more adventurous than farming. He drifted to Robbers Roost where he took the name Pete Logan, and he soon garnered a reputation as a two-bit crook. In his home town, they called him Pete Thief.[53]

At Robbers Roost, Logan met C. L. "Gunplay" Maxwell and was recruited into a gang of a "dozen or so" Roosters planning to rob the Provo bank—a plan that went awry when Nelson, in charge of the relay horses, never got word the holdup had been changed to Springville (see chapter 6). The next time we hear of Pete Logan is 1909 when he was living in Nine Mile Canyon and probably working for Preston Nutter, and a short time later he married Ada Slaugh, Gunplay Maxwell's widow (Gunplay died in 1909 at the hands of Sheriff Ed Johnstone, see chapter 6). According to Nutter's business records, Pete was working for Nutter in 1917 and 1918.[54]

According to an account by Don Wilcox, the grandson of rancher Jim McPherson, himself known to have provided safe haven to outlaws in that day, Pete Logan went to work for Nutter as a ranch foreman, but Nutter found out there was an arrest warrant for Logan. Nutter reportedly went to the county, told officials that he had found Pete Logan dead and his body deteriorated, and then he filled out a death certificate to that effect. A new ranch foreman was then introduced—Pete Nelson.[55]

From Strip to Strawberry

The Triangle operation was obviously successful, but in 1892 or 1893 Nutter hatched an even grander scheme that would vastly increase the size of his holdings. He simultaneously set out to acquire exclusive grazing rights to 665,000 acres of Ute lands in the lush Strawberry Valley *and* acquire a separate operation of similar size on the Arizona Strip—that narrow strip of northern Arizona on the southern border of Utah that is isolated from the rest of Arizona by the Colorado River. The strategic move was mandated because of a condition attached to the Strawberry Valley lease with the federal government: Nutter could own no other holdings in the Utah Territory. The Strawberry Valley was unparalleled summer range but he could not own nearby lands for winter range. Nutter needed winter range, and it needed to be outside the borders of Utah.

Nutter first acquired a five-year lease on the Strawberry Valley in 1893 for $7,100 per year; the lease defined his grazing rights as all lands drained by the Duchesne River, which included not just Strawberry Valley but the Uinta Mountains. He then created the Strawberry Cattle Company, in partnership with Herman and Alfred Schiffer, two acquaintances from his Lake City days who had made their fortunes and returned to New York City. Nutter owned 50 percent of the shares and as president of the company he was responsible for the day-to-day business operations. The Schiffer brothers put up the money. Nutter then sold his existing Utah cattle, reported to be five thousand head, and his interests in the Triangle to the Webster City Cattle Company, his long-time rival in the region. Nutter kept only the "63" brand.

In tandem with this move, Nutter turned his attention to the western Arizona Strip (he did this independent of his financial interests in the Strawberry Cattle Company). His obituary states that he bought out the holdings of Anthony W. Ivins in 1892,[56] whereas his daughter asserts that occurred in 1896.[57] Ivins was himself a large-scale cattle operator, a prominent Mormon apostle and territorial politician. He was also widely viewed as a surrogate for the financially distressed Mormon Church.[58]

Based on the available historical evidence, Nutter did not actually purchase existing rights as much as he recognized a legal loophole of which he took full advantage. The western Strip was open range used in common by a multitude of small ranchers from the St. George area who shared the limited water sources. Other watering holes were claimed by B. F. Saunders, another large cattle operator on the eastern Strip, and yet others were claimed by Ivins as representative of the Mojave Cattle Company. But no one, it seems, had valid title to the lands where the springs were located.

If Nutter could control the water, then he could control vast areas north of the Grand Canyon. Nutter's daughter claims he "developed water holes of his own, and then took the necessary steps to acquire legal titles on some of the land and springs."[59] But that statement glosses over a more unsavory truth: Nutter used a questionable legal maneuver to wrest control of the springs from his rivals large and small. In a letter written in 1935 by Preston Nutter to J. N. Darling, chief of the U.S. Biological Survey, Nutter detailed exactly how he acquired title to the springs:

> The Strip country was public domain and unsurveyed and there was really no way to obtain title to lands until Congress passed a law, known as the Forest Reserve Lieu Selection Act, which allowed citizens to locate 40-acre legal subdivisions on the public domain. This was a great benefit to the cattleman as it gave a person the right to locate springs or water holes. The speculators entered into this game and sold "scrip" covering these lands. I purchased a lot of this scrip and applied it on various 69 selections, and as Arizona began to survey that country, made application for surveys, thus through patents I acquired title to twenty-one 40-acre tracts, all covering springs. Then there were other means of acquiring title. I purchased Sioux Half Breed scrip and in later years bought two 640-acre proven up homesteads, also 80 acres of cultivated land known as Parashant Field, and in more recent years a purchase of land from the Santa Fe Railroad. This gives me more than 7,000 acres patented land practically all of the living water on that range.[60]

While Nutter's approach to land acquisition was technically legal, it was viewed locally with disdain. Historian Juanita Brooks noted, "Just as the Mormons had filched the water from the Indians, so he in turn filched it from the Mormons. They had paid for it, they thought; they held the springs, and in this country possession was all ten points of the law. But they had not taken time and trouble to have their claims surveyed and

Anthony Ivins, a prominent leader and Mormon apostle, operated the Mojave Cattle Company, the largest operation on the western Arizona Strip. Nutter bought out Ivins in about 1892 and eventually controlled the entire area. Used by permission, Utah State Historical Society, all rights reserved.

recorded."[61] An oral history with Reed Mathis, whose father ran cattle in competition with Nutter, indicates Nutter "never did shut the waters off from other cattle.... But he owned it and he let you know it. This country wasn't fenced; the waters weren't even fenced; it was all open range."[62] Virginia Nutter Price hints that Nutter's relationship with local ranchers was not just strained but downright hostile, forcing him to hire Texas "deputies" to protect his interests, which is probably a euphemism for hired guns like Jack Watson. "The Arizona Strip range war against Nutter might have continued on much longer if he had not, after legally acquiring title on all the springs, bought out the opposition."[63]

Indian scrip was, in effect, a government voucher for forty acres of federal land given to Native Americans who had been displaced by white settlers from their homes in the Midwest, usually as part of a treaty. Through a loophole in the law, the scrip could be bought and sold.[64] Speculators would "purchase" the scrip from the Indians and in turn sell it to entrepreneurs like Nutter who would then file a claim. It was a practice rife with fraud, and it eventually landed Nutter in the courtroom as a defendant accused of defrauding the U.S. government. He was never convicted of the charges, and by most accounts he was an unwitting purchaser of the allegedly bogus scrip.

Beckstead makes a point of the feud between Nutter and B. F. Saunders, who tried and failed to run Nutter out of business there. But business is business. By 1894, Saunders was apparently subleasing a portion of the Strawberry Valley to run several hundred head of his own cattle there.[65]

With Arizona Strip winter range locked up and the lease secured on the Strawberry Valley, Nutter set about restocking his herds. He put the word out in southern Arizona that he was buying cattle, and by September of 1893 he had amassed a herd of five thousand head. The problem was how to get the herd across the Colorado River. One of the legendary stories of Nutter's sheer force of will has it that he swam the herd across the river at Scanlon's Ferry without losing a single head or rider. "Nutter was always proud of this feat, but in recounting it in later years would say, with a twinkle in his eyes, 'It is possible we lost a few spectators lined up to watch from the banks. I was too busy to keep an eye on them.'"[66]

The following month, in October 1893, Nutter was indicted by a Salt Lake grand jury.[67] The criminal charges were not specified, and no record was located of any trial in the matter. But it illustrates that not everyone was enamored of the cattle-king-in-the-making.

Over the next several years, Nutter's wranglers would move cattle back and forth between the Strawberry Valley and Arizona Strip. His Strawberry Valley lease expired in 1898, and although he was able to get a one-year extension, the pressure to open the Ute reservation in the Uinta Basin to homesteaders was mounting, as was the clamor to open the Strawberry Valley to sheep men. Most accounts imply that the end was in sight for grazing on tribal lands in the Uinta Basin. The traditional history holds that Nutter responded to that imminent reality by searching out a new base of operations, especially a new summer range for his twenty-five thousand head of cattle.[68]

But that wasn't necessarily the case. Nutter could have continued leasing Ute lands for another five years after his lease expired in 1899, but he appears to have preferred a less expensive alternative. In the spring of 1900, Indian Agent H. P. Myton announced that rights to graze on the same seven hundred thousand acres had been awarded at $18,300 per year for five years—roughly two and a half times what Nutter had paid for the same rights six years before. Nutter had actually submitted a bid on a small portion of the Ute lands, but was far outbid by a consortium of other livestock operators.[69]

With his Strawberry lease expiring in 1899, he was free again to start purchasing Utah properties. And apparently he did so with gusto. He acquired holdings on the Myton Bench near Duchesne and in Emery County south of Price. By some accounts he began buying out small ranches in Nine Mile Canyon, although this has not yet been verified by historical records. And he continued to buy up holdings on the Arizona Strip.

Exactly when he turned his attention to Nine Mile Canyon, Range Creek, and the West Tavaputs Plateau is not clearly articulated in the available histories. By 1899 there was a scattering of ranches up and down Nine Mile Canyon, and most of the prime ranch lands would have already been claimed. There were already major cattle operators in the area, the Range Valley Cattle Company that claimed the entire West Tavaputs Plateau and the Whitmore family, which claimed most of the upper reaches of the Nine Mile Canyon area. Opportunity knocked on October 7, 1901, when Pete Francis—by some accounts an outlaw and by others a

Nine Mile Canyon innkeeper who was simply friendly to outlaws—was killed in his own saloon in a shootout with another Nine Mile rancher, Dave Russell. At that time, Francis's widow had already divorced Pete and she was living in Salt Lake City. She had no interest in running a hotel and saloon for rowdy freighters. She was an eager seller, and by early 1902 Nutter had acquired Francis's holdings, which included the hotel, saloon, several barrels of grain alcohol, and a peacock.[70]

The Francis place, which Pete Francis had acquired from William Brock, was ideally situated at the mouth of Gate Canyon with road access north to the Uinta Basin and west to Price.[71] The pasture lands were well suited for wintering cattle, but they did not solve the problem of summer range. So at the same time he bought out Francis's widow, in 1902, Nutter also bought out the Range Valley Cattle Company holdings, which included Range Creek—a sister drainage to the south, which had an established cattle trail through the lower Price River country to railheads at Woodside—and the lush high country on top of the plateau separating Nine Mile and Range Creek.[72] In addition to his headquarters, he established outlier ranches at Cherry Meadows in Range Creek and at the mouth of Nine Mile Canyon. His new range totaled roughly three hundred thousand acres; he named this operation the Nutter Corporation and instituted a new brand, a circle on the cow's right shoulder and right hip (he kept the "63" brand for his horses and mules). He retained the Arizona Strip holdings as breeding grounds for his livestock, but there was no longer a need to move great numbers of cattle back and forth from Arizona to northeastern Utah.[73]

The Headquarters

Since 1886, Brock's Place had been the commercial hub of Nine Mile Canyon, but Nutter shut it all down in an instant (it shifted to the west to the Edwin Lee Ranch, which became known as Harper). He built a house on his new headquarters site in 1902, which probably surpassed any other in the canyon for opulence, and he closed the saloon and turned the hotel into a bunkhouse for his cowboys. He kept Francis's peacock and even found a mate for it, after which the population of peafowl increased at an alarming rate, much to the bemusement of passersby.[74] For the next six

The house built by Preston Nutter in 1902 as his Nine Mile Canyon headquarters. It later burned to the ground, destroying priceless artifacts and collectibles. Used by permission, Utah State Historical Society, all rights reserved.

Pete Francis brought the first peacock to the ranch. Nutter found a mate for it, and the resulting flock of peafowl was a major curiosity to passersby for decades to come. Used by permission, Utah State Historical Society, all rights reserved.

decades, this locality served as the headquarters for Nutter's expansive cattle operation, first for Nutter himself, later for his widow, and after that for his daughter Virginia and her husband, Howard C. Price Jr. It was no longer a haven for outlaws, gambling, and vice, but instead the Preston Nutter

Ranch now hosted important business leaders, judges, sheriffs, and others from around the state.

Why Nutter chose to put down roots in this isolated wilderness, rather than turn the ranch into just another outpost, is not clearly indicated in the historical record. But it can be surmised that he fell in love with the canyon and its stark beauty. In a 1923 conversation with a newsman, Nutter gushed,

> You hear every day something about the wonders of Bryce Canyon, but we have just over in Nine Mile cliffs and buttes, peaks and spires and deep canyons all profusely colored like the rainbow. In what we call Pinnacle Canyon there is a chimney rock twenty feet at the base pointing three hundred feet up in the air. Only a short distance away where the Green River has cut through seemingly impregnable formation, I have ridden horse-back along the bed of the stream for a distance of seventy-five miles with no possible means of egress except at one end or the other of that great gorge. In places the perpendicular distance from the bed of the stream to the rim of the canyon is three thousand feet.[75]

The remote and rugged qualities of Nine Mile Canyon might have been well suited to a bachelor accustomed to the smells and sounds of livestock, and he probably wasn't much thinking about female companionship at the time he bought the ranch. There is no written record that Nutter had much of a social life, except for the occasional cattle-buying trips to Kansas City and Chicago. That changed suddenly—and probably came as a huge surprise to his loyalists—when a lady happened by the ranch in 1905 who caught his eye. Nutter was fifty-five at the time, and Katherine Fenton was thirty-four.

According to family history, Katherine Fenton was born in Ohio in 1871 and attended Catholic school in Indiana. She came west to Colorado where she became manager of the Colorado Springs Postal Telegraph Station. On a lark, she entered a lottery in 1905 for a homestead in the Uinta Basin, and she drew a claim for a quarter-section near Ioka in Duchesne County. As the family story goes, she was on her way to Ioka through Nine Mile Canyon when the stage driver missed the regular stage stop and the entire stage found itself stranded at Nutter's ranch for the night. Nutter gave up his bed to Miss Fenton and her traveling companion, a school teacher

bound for Vernal. Friendship blossomed, the story goes, but Katherine was determined to "prove up" on her homestead claim, a three-year process of building a cabin, making improvements to the land, and living there without change in marital status. She stayed on the homestead the minimum time required, traveling back and forth from her job in Colorado Springs. They were married in 1908 in Glenwood Springs, Colorado, and had two daughters, Catherine and Virginia. Katherine died in 1965, having survived Preston by almost thirty years, much of that time running the Nutter Ranch herself and earning the title "Cattle Queen."[76]

Katherine Fenton never relinquished her interest in the Ioka homestead and remained involved in the area's politics, serving as secretary of the Dry Gulch Irrigation Company. She was widely respected in the Uinta Basin. One account praised her as "one of the best known homesteaders of the Dry Gulch section. Not every woman has the courage and pluck to come to a new country, endure its hardships and deprivations and finally win the title to a quarter section of good land, and a husband too."[77] She had no qualms about living in Nine Mile among the trail-worn cowboys, and her accommodations there were certainly passable. According to one newspaper account, written much later after the house burned to the ground in 1955, the house was first built in 1902 and was "a 9 room modern dwelling of log construction with knotty pine interior. All contents of the house were destroyed, among which were Navajo rugs from the Byron Cummings collection, a group of firearms including sabers and swords dating from the Crimean War, a library containing valuable archaeological and military volumes..."[78]

But one would be mistaken to assume that Katherine and Preston Nutter lived at the Nine Mile ranch most or even much of the time, and even less so after the daughters were born. The couple soon acquired an "apartment" in Salt Lake City near Fifth East and South Temple—a stone's throw from the palatial mansions of the mining magnates of the day. In Salt Lake, their daughters attended private Catholic schools, and Katherine's name is mentioned frequently in the Salt Lake society pages attending gala events and art exhibits.

Based on entries in Nutter's journals, Nutter spent a fair amount of time in Nine Mile Canyon, often surrounded by extended family. According to the 1910 census, the ranch was occupied by Preston Nutter, along with his wife, Katherine; infant daughter, Catherine; and eight ranch hands, including his long-time foreman, William W. McCoy. It was the only time Preston's wife or either of his children would be listed on the census records for Nine Mile Canyon. Preston Nutter always listed himself as a resident of Nine Mile Canyon.[79]

In 1920, Preston Nutter's household included a nephew, Cleveland Nutter; his wife, Grace Nutter; and two grand-nephews, Jasper Nutter and Harold Nutter. By 1930, the household included Preston and nine hired hands, some with familiar names: three members of the Barney family, who were early settlers of upper Nine Mile; Cecil Rouse, who would go on to acquire the neighboring Eagan ranch; and Lon Alger.[80]

Nutter's wife and daughters seemed much more comfortable with the trappings of wealth that could be better enjoyed in a city environment. Katherine was still living in the Salt Lake City apartment in 1965 at the time of her death at the age of ninety-four.

Life on the Nine Mile ranch was all about raising livestock—either moving cows from one range to another, raising alfalfa to feed the cows, or keeping the cowhands fed. He built and maintained three separate ranch complexes: one at Cherry Meadows in Range Creek, another at the mouth of Nine Mile Canyon, and his ranch headquarters in middle Nine Mile.

Nutter appears to have acquired the lower ranch from the state of Utah, which had acquired it as a "state selection" from the federal government. It was certainly in operation by 1913 when Ed Harmston, the engineer who led a 1913 exploration of the Green River to determine its suitability for a railroad, wrote on August 13 that Preston Nutter was "improving a ranch" at the mouth of Nine Mile Canyon, and "also another at the next bend below here."[81]

Even though the area is overgrown by greasewood today, at one time the lower ranch was a major operation with leveled fields, a network of irrigation ditches, a concrete water diversion tunnel, corrals, and cellars and other outbuildings. A two-track road once extended from the Pace Ranch to Nutter's ranch at the mouth of the canyon. There is also a mine tunnel in the area, perhaps remnants of oil shale prospecting.[82] The lower Nutter Ranch is a popular attraction to river runners today.

Nutter was a willing buyer of stock from local ranchers, and as such a ready source of cash. Newspaper accounts of the day chronicle some of these purchases, but most probably went unnoticed.[83] He stocked his ranch with supplies purchased from local Price and Vernal businesses,[84] and he hired local labor to work the ranch.[85] In 1918, at the height of World War I, Nutter purchased $50,000 in Liberty Bonds, which he credited to Duchesne County.[86] More than just a cattle baron, he was a valuable contributor to local communities and their economies.

The number of employees working for Nutter at any one time cannot be surmised from the available historical record, but it undoubtedly fluctuated by the season. When possible, he hired local labor—something that endeared him to the economically depressed communities of Price and Vernal. He hired cash-strapped ranchers who had also put down roots in Nine Mile—a good-neighbor policy that paid off, for the most part. Descendants of these cowhands today still boast that grandpa so-and-so or uncle so-and-so was a foreman for Nutter—enough so that if all the claims were true Nutter would have had more foremen than actual cowboys.

Nutter's most trusted right-hand man was William Walter McCoy, a New Yorker and fellow bachelor who remained loyal to Nutter for three decades, signing on with Nutter when he moved his first herds into The Triangle. McCoy managed the actual movement and transfers of the large

herds. He died at Nutter's Nine Mile ranch house in 1915.[87] After McCoy's death, Nutter probably struggled to find a trusted replacement for a daily operations manager. One of them might have been L. H. Milton, a veteran of managing other large cattle outfits, including one in The Triangle. Later in life he claimed to have managed Nutter's operations.[88] Another might have been W. G. McGuire, according to an April 14, 1919, notation in Nutter's journal.[89]

There is no doubt that Preston Nutter was a hands-on cattle operator. Photos in the Preston Nutter Corporation Collection depict him engaged in all sorts of the cowboy activities that would be expected: riding, roping, branding. But how much cowboying did Nutter actually do himself? Probably very little. A review of his journals indicates Preston Nutter was a man constantly on the go, rarely staying more than a week in any one

location. Beckstead claims, "Nutter was in the saddle for days on end traveling the vast distances between Arizona and Utah."[90]

But this wasn't true, at least not after he established his ranch in Nine Mile. Rather, Nutter traveled by train. He could catch the train in Price and travel to his home in Salt Lake City, or to the St. George area where his Arizona Strip hands would pick him up and take him to the ranch there. He would inspect the herds for a few days and then it was back on the train. And then there were the cattle-buying train trips to the east: Denver, Omaha, Kansas City, Chicago. At times the family would go along but most times he traveled by himself, almost always by train. He later purchased a car—an Oakland—that he used to quicken the trip to and from the Nine Mile ranch, and on at least one occasion he used it to travel to St. George.[91]

Whereas his wife was immersed in Salt Lake's social scene, there are few references in the journals to Preston's social activities. The family tells a story, related by Katherine, that the only way she could get a honeymoon was to tie it to a cattle-buying trip to the East.[92] On another cattle-buying trip, delays in the transaction led to a short vacation where Preston and Katherine enjoyed the social amenities of Kansas City.[93] Katherine was clearly the social butterfly. Not that Preston was fiercely antisocial, but he never exhibited a penchant for the trappings his wealth could have provided.

His journals instead make references to stopping to dine with other Nine Mile stalwarts, such as John Eagan and Frank Alger. He participated in several local and regional livestock associations, testified at grazing hearings, and even served on a jury where the court docket included two accused burglars and one case of incest.[94] In 1926, he was named to a state delegation sent to Phoenix to recruit an annual convention of the American National Livestock Association.[95]

The Tax Man Cometh

Nutter was generally viewed as a tough but fair operator by local residents, who could find employment at the Nutter Ranch if need be, although there was some grumbling about Nutter's refusal to allow local residents to hunt wildlife on his lands. Nutter's major conflict with the locals, however, had nothing to do with deer hunting. It was a running feud with Carbon County over taxes owed, and the dispute eventually turned nasty, ending up at the Utah Supreme Court. In 1910, a notice was published that Nutter was delinquent on his property taxes related to two separate Nine Mile properties, which were to be sold at public auction to pay the debt.[96] There is no record of such a sale, so Nutter must have ponied up on the delinquent taxes. A few years later, Nutter took umbrage with the Carbon County assessor, who imposed a property tax on 1,500 head of cattle—Nutter claimed to have had only 1,000 head of cattle in Carbon County where the Nutter rangelands amounted to 30,000 acres. The case went all the way to the Utah Supreme Court, where Nutter lost his appeal in 1921.[97]

Nutter's claims of only 1,000 head of cattle raised eyebrows. Nutter never boasted about the size of his herds, but the newspapers of the day commonly commented that Nutter was "the largest individual cattle owner in the west."[98] At 1,000 head, he would have been a small operator indeed, perhaps not even the largest in Carbon County. Nutter also claimed in court testimony that he had only 100 cows in Duchesne County, which included a big chunk of Nine Mile Canyon, and 600 head in Emery County, where his vast Range Creek holdings were. In other words, the cattle baron reported to have herds numbering 10,000 to 20,000 actually had only 1,700 total cows, or so he claimed. Nobody was buying Nutter's story. In 1916, Nutter sold 2,100 steers at $73.50 per animal—a $154,350 gross. Even the newspapermen who had lionized Nutter started to question the veracity of the cattle baron. "If this is true it would be interesting to know just how many cattle Preston Nutter owns or did before this big sale."[99]

The Courtroom Wars

A common myth associated with Preston Nutter is that he loved the courtroom, using attorneys to intimidate trespassers and encroachers, and that he was remarkably successful, losing only once. Nutter's daughter relates a story that her mother once asked her father why he spent so much time in courtrooms, to which he responded, "Because I enjoy winning when I know I'm in the right."[100] And certainly there was a fair amount of that. His penchant for using the courts started as early as 1894, when he sued the Webster City Cattle Company for reneging on certain terms of its purchase of his interests in The Triangle.[101] But just as often he was in the courtroom as a defendant, and he lost frequently, perhaps even more so than he won.[102]

And court documents paint an unflattering portrait of Nutter. In 1900, he was sued by Uinta Basin farmer J. M. Thomas, who claimed that Nutter conspired with Indian Agent H. P. Myton to run him and his family off their small spread south of the reservation. He accused Nutter of running 2,500 head of cattle through his property and then sending Indian police to harass the Thomas family until they left their home.[103]

Some of the suits might have seemed trivial and not worth the protracted legal expense. In 1926, he won a judgment of $64 against E. K. Olsen for trespassing, and he settled another case against Ray Lee for $50.[104] In one instance, Nutter was sued by O. S. Curry for $245.16 for nonpayment of work performed. The judge ordered Nutter to pay $198.16—an insignificant sum to a man like Nutter—but Nutter was incensed and said he did not owe the man a dime. Nutter chose to immediately amend his argument and demanded a jury trial. He lost and was ordered to pay $214.30.[105]

Other court cases had more far-reaching ramifications and garnered considerable media attention. Preston Nutter had learned early on that he who controls the water controls the land around it. He had used various legal maneuvers to secure title to virtually all springs on the western Arizona Strip, choking out his rivals and leaving them little option other than to sell out—to him. If it worked once, could it work again? In about 1915, Nutter used his influence with the state to purchase a one-mile-square section near Elgin south of Price.

The state first acquired the section from the federal government as a "state selection" and then sold it to Nutter. At the center of the parcel was a critical watering hole used by ranchers in a 150-square-mile area. Nutter promptly fenced the watering hole, a cruel slap at the other ranchers in the area who had no other water available. The ranchers appealed to the U.S. Department of Interior, which reversed the state selection, invalidated Nutter's ownership, and ordered him to take down the fence.[106]

Nutter's most stunning courtroom defeat resulted from an inexplicable lack of attention to detail. He had bought out Pete Francis's widow and the Range Valley Cattle Company, essentially locking up the entire West Tavaputs Plateau, but he had never bothered to secure a legal title to the lands and the improvements on them. Nutter had merely purchased squatters rights. As summarized by historians Steve Gerber and James M. Aton, Nutter's troubles began about 1915 when a drifter named John Niles hired on with Nutter. Niles was a typical cowboy of the day, low on cash and always asking Nutter for advances. He would work for Nutter awhile and then drift on to something else, only to return and ask Nutter for his old job back.[107]

Range Creek Canyon, at the time known as Range Valley, was formally surveyed in 1912, making it eligible for claims under the Enlarged Homestead Act of 1909. In 1915, Niles suddenly filed a claim on 160 acres of improved land on Nutter's Range Creek ranch, and he sent Nutter a letter stating "you have 30 days to remove your improvements."[108] Nutter went to a magistrate in Woodside, who promptly ordered Niles off the land. Niles apparently abandoned his plan, joined the navy, was dishonorably discharged, and eventually drifted back to eastern Utah. On February 13, 1917, the first formal plat for Range Creek Canyon was filed, and the same day Niles, a man named Thomas Crick, and a Nutter employee named George Long all filed homestead claims on Nutter lands. The state also filed a claim on the land as a "state selection," with the intent of selling it to Nutter.[109]

The state's claim was dismissed first, then George Long came up empty. "Clearly Long's filing was the result of an agreement he had with Nutter. Both later denied this in court, but sufficient evidence exists to show that Nutter intended to use his ranch hand as his agent to obtain the land."[110] The court found in Niles's favor; subsequent appeals found in favor of Nutter, then Niles, then Nutter, and finally Niles. Nutter's determination to win at any cost was revealed during the lengthy appeals process.

Nutter argued that the land in question was part of an earlier Desert Land Entry Claim made by Charles Van Dusen, which had been invalidated on a technicality. Nutter's attorney traveled to Pennsylvania to find the Van Dusen heirs to convince them to reopen the case and award title to them and they in turn would sell to Nutter. "Nutter swore in court that no deal had been made between the two parties, but there is little doubt that such an agreement existed."[111] Niles won the final appeal in 1923, but within six months he had sold out to Nutter for $6,000 plus another $500 in lost income and damages.

There is some speculation that Niles was originally hired to file the claim as a front-man for Nutter—something that was illegal—but that Niles reneged on the deal.[112] Niles later wrote the court that "Nutter is a land hog, a notorious one and has plenty of money.... There is no limit to what a crook with money can do or is it true that money can do anything in the USA."

A simultaneous case on another piece of Nutter's ranch in Range Creek had a similar result. On February 23, 1917, the same day that Niles filed his homestead claim, another claim for a different parcel of Nutter's property was made by John Darioli, an Italian immigrant with no previous known ties to Nutter and a man of no financial means. That same day, a Nutter employee named Arthur Johnson filed a claim on the same parcel, presumably as an agent for Nutter. The Darioli case, like the Niles case, resulted in a lengthy series of hearings in Utah and Washington, D.C., rulings

Remnants of the John Darioli stone cabin in the heart of Nutter's Range Creek holdings. Darioli, an Italian immigrant, won a protracted court case against Nutter. Photo courtesy of the Colorado Plateau Archaeological Alliance.

and appeals that alternately found for Darioli and Nutter. At the end of the day, Darioli was awarded the title, but not before Nutter attempted a highly questionable legal ploy.

Joe Wing, the first permanent resident of Range Creek in the late 1800s, had proved up on a Desert Land Entry claim on 160 acres near the mouth of Turtle Canyon about two miles below the Darioli homestead claim. Nutter dispatched his attorney to Ohio to convince Wing's heirs to go along with a claim that the location of the Wing lands had been mistakenly placed at Turtle Canyon but that it was actually the same land Darioli claimed that was now in dispute. "It was a foolhardy undertaking, but it was Nutter's last hope. It prolonged the eventual resolution of the case for another five years."[113] Darioli eventually won. In an ironic twist, Nutter's courtroom attempts to prove that Wing's improvements were not at Turtle

Canyon but farther up canyon resulted in the court finding that Joe Wing had made a fraudulent land claim and the title was subsequently invalidated, besmirching Wing's honor in the process.[114] Darioli eventually sold the property but not to Nutter.

Darioli and Niles were not the only ones who were targeting Nutter lands. In 1917, Tom Creek of Sunnyside and J. Buchanan of Salt Lake filed on two separate 160-acre parcels in the heart of Nutter's Nine Mile Canyon ranch—lands already developed and cultivated by Nutter. The two men reportedly "researched" land records and found that Nutter had no legal title and filed their own claims on it. Nutter caught wind, and "it is reported that Nutter appeared in Salt Lake with some of his men to file on this land the day after the other fellows nailed it."[115] It must be assumed that the Tom Creek referred to here is the same Thomas Crick who had filed on the Range Creek parcel.

Gerber and Aton make a convincing case that the efforts to wrest title to Nutter lands were part of a conspiracy by Joseph Barboglio, the founder and president of the Helper State Bank.[116] But the larger question remains: Nutter, who had competent attorneys at his beck and call, had to know of the changes coming down the road with the Homestead Act, and he had to know his vast holdings were at risk. He may have been counting on his connections in state government that Utah would file state selection claims and in turn sell the parcels to him. But the court cases reveal this was a false hope and in most cases the state claims were summarily rejected.

End of an Era

Nutter ultimately survived the attacks on his holdings, although his pride was undoubtedly bruised. By all accounts, his business thrived during World War I as he was a major supplier of beef to the military. When the beef market crashed at the end of the war, he thrived when overextended small ranchers were forced into bankruptcy. By 1928, he was again selling massive herds. One report had it that he sold a "great herd" on the eastern markets for $200,000.[117] His operation, unlike others of the day, survived the Great Depression.

In his later years he became active in various associations trying to deal with the pervasive problem of trespassing of sheepherders on established

cattle ranges. Through these efforts, he became an ardent supporter of the Taylor Grazing Act—the federal government's first attempt to regulate grazing on public lands through allotments. He apparently felt that the act "would put rout [to] the itinerant sheepmen and allow the established, legitimate rancher to manage the feed and forage."[118] By some accounts he was instrumental in the passage of the legislation, but more likely he was an outspoken supporter whose opinions commanded respect even in Washington, D.C.[119]

The frailties of age began creeping up on Nutter. There is no question he liked to ride. In 1926, at the age of seventy-six, a riding accident resulted in a broken leg. The following year, a stream bank caved in on him and his horse, and Nutter's hip was crushed, requiring a convalescence of three months.[120] Another accident in the summer of 1935, at age eighty-five, removed him from the saddle for good (Webb states it was another horseback accident, this one in Range Creek). He died on January 26, 1936, at his Salt Lake apartment and was buried in the Salt Lake Cemetery with full Masonic honors.

His wife took over the cattle operations, but in 1937 she sold the Arizona Strip holdings, at that time called the Nutter Livestock Company (Nutter had hoped it would become a massive game preserve, but that never happened due to the Department of Interior's failure to act). In 1950, she sold the Range Creek holdings.

The Nine Mile holdings, under the name Preston Nutter Corporation, remained in the Nutter family. Katherine was president of the corporation until 1956, when she turned over corporate affairs to her daughter Virginia Nutter Price. Katherine died in 1965, followed a year later by her daughter Catherine Nutter Story. Virginia ran the company until her death in 1977. Her husband, Howard Price Jr.,[121] took over, but in 1980 he sold the Preston Nutter Corporation to the Sabine Corporation of Texas.[122] Old-timers still shake their heads in disbelief as to how the company fell apart under his stewardship.

Preston is buried in Salt Lake City. Katherine is buried more than two thousand miles away in the family cemetery in Ohio.

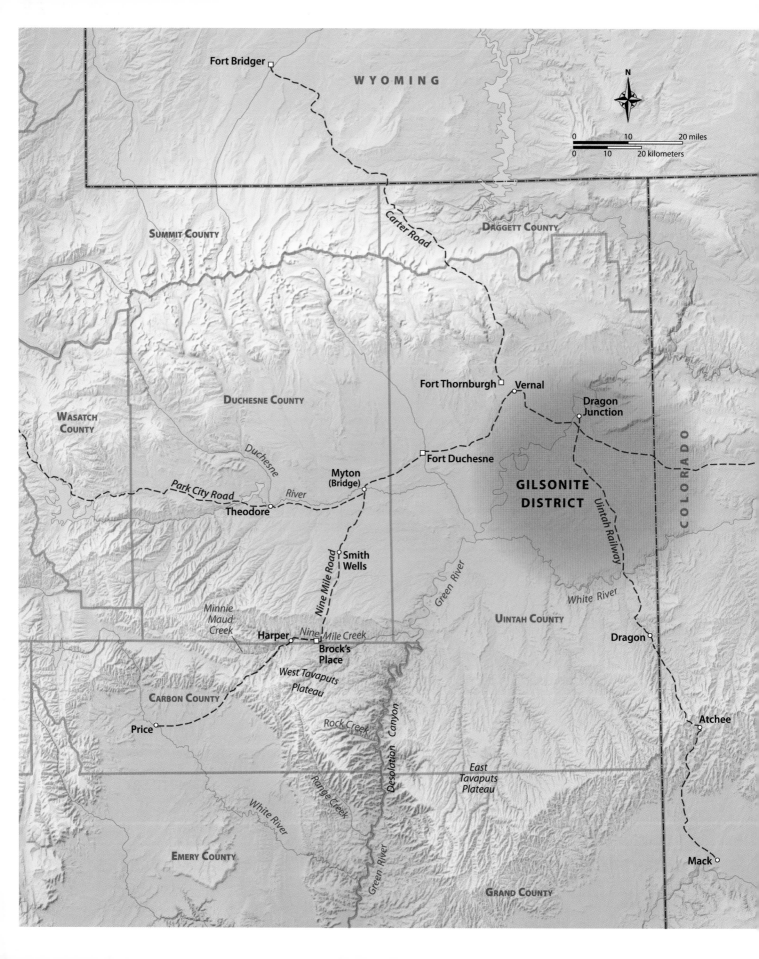

A Perfect Storm
From Boom to Bust on the Nine Mile Road

The years after 1887 were unquestionably halcyon days for Nine Mile Canyon. Farms and ranches were prospering, the road was all a bustle with freighters with money to spend, and hotels, dances, and rodeos provided plenty of social merriment. Families intermarried, children were born, and a tight-knit but ever-changing community was established. The Nine Mile Road had almost instantly become one of the most important economic corridors anywhere in the state. The future seemed bright and only getting brighter.

Even if the locals couldn't hear it, there was a knell in the background tolling the death of their community—a death resulting from unavoidable events occurring in the Uinta Basin to the north. The final chapter of the Nine Mile Road as a major economic corridor was being written almost from the time U.S. Army soldiers first sledged and graded the route to make it passable in 1886.

In some respects, the brief prosperity brought about by the Nine Mile Road fell victim to a harsh reality: the road was not an ideal commercial route to begin with. No one could have foreseen the demand for Gilsonite would explode, and the need to ship tens of thousands of tons of ore would result in traffic jams of monumental proportions—gridlock made worse by the vagaries of weather. Few could have thought Fort Duchesne would devolve into irrelevance as quickly as it did and there would no longer be a need to ship massive quantities of freight to the military post or to the Indian agencies. Few could have foreseen the change in federal Indian policy that would result in the opening of the Ute reservation to Euro-American homesteaders, shifting the balance of political and economic power north to the Uinta Basin.

Stone chimney at the Don Johnston Ranch is a reminder of a once-thriving stopover for freighters and traveling homesteaders on the Nine Mile Road. Photo courtesy of the Colorado Plateau Archaeological Alliance.

Opposite: Map of Uinta Basin 1886–1910.

Nine Mile Canyon in the spring.
Photo by Ray Boren.

In short, the demise of the Nine Mile Road as a major economic thoroughfare was the result of a series of events, some interconnected and others unrelated, beginning in the mid-1890s and continuing through 1905. Sure, the Harper Precinct—the name for the Nine Mile Canyon community at the time—boasted a population of 130 in the 1910 census, the most at any time in Euro-American history. But it all was about to collapse. Harper would soon become a ghost town, the stage route would be shut down, and all except a few of the most determined ranchers would flee to better opportunities elsewhere. Unlike mining boom towns that were abandoned within weeks or months, this was a slow death over many years.

Water Witches and the Withering of Fort Duchesne

Fort Duchesne, manned by scores of infantry and cavalry soldiers, was a veritable beehive of activity in the years after the Nine Mile Road was opened for business in late 1886, and much if not most of the soldiers' efforts at that time were focused on Nine Mile Canyon—Fort Duchesne's primary lifeline to the outside world. There was unending road maintenance, there were winter snowstorms that required troops to spend up to ten days at a time clearing the drifts, and the frigid winters played havoc on the telegraph line, which needed constant repair. What the troops didn't have was any real work to do other than their tasks in Nine Mile Canyon.

The anticipated hostilities that had brought them to the Uinta Basin in the first place never materialized, and as the threat diminished the army began to downsize Fort Duchesne. By November 1892, the army had all but abandoned Fort Duchesne, leaving behind only a two-troop garrison to keep the peace and a cluster of fine buildings that would have made Major Benteen green with envy (see chapter 4). The road maintenance—and presumably the telegraph repairs—eventually fell to Carbon County and the Gilsonite interests.[1]

The Nine Mile Road was clearly a nuisance to the military from the moment it was completed. It might have been better than the Carter Military Road (see chapter 4), but it was still susceptible to long closures due to weather, and soldiers could go weeks without communication with the outside world.[2] And by all accounts Fort Duchesne in the years after 1892 remained a tiny outpost on the edge of a frontier so isolated and unappealing that it earned a reputation as "Fort Damn Shame."[3]

As much as anything, the few soldiers who remained at Fort Duchesne evolved into a federal police force with orders to deter trespassing on Indian lands, to calm the fears of Euro-American settlers, to keep the Indians from leaving the reservation, to protect the growing commerce on the Nine Mile Road, and to keep the peace between three different Ute bands, each with grievances against the others. The road was not the only

route into the Uinta Basin at the time, but it was the best all-season route despite all its problems. And the military did not really have any other practical option for its own freight shipments.

Freighting was especially troublesome along the thirty-seven miles between Brock's Place and the bridge over the Duchesne River (later Myton)—a lonely stretch of desert with no water for human or beast. This mandated that freighters carry barrels of water for their draft animals, enough for the two or three days needed to cross the waterless wasteland. Those heavy barrels took up valuable cargo space and cut into the freighters' profits. Was there a better route? In May 1891, the *Eastern Utah Advocate* reported that the army was set to build a new road "from Nine Mile Canyon commencing 8 miles above Brock's Ranch" and that the "new road is much shorter than the old road and better. Fresh water along entire way."[4]

The location of this new route is not known with any certainty, but there are clues. The newspaper report indicated it was eight miles above Brock's Place and there was fresh water along the entire route. This could be a reference to Argyle Canyon, the only tributary in this area of Nine Mile Canyon that offers year-round flowing water *and* meaningful access to the Uinta Basin. The headwaters of Argyle Canyon are in the high plateau country to the west at elevations above 8,000 feet where deep snows could have been a problem for the freighters, but this route could have been passable to wagons in 1891. There is a decent road today through Argyle Canyon that connects to the Indian Canyon Highway (U.S. 191), now the main connector between Price and Duchesne. The problem with the 1891 account as related in the *Eastern Utah Advocate* is that Argyle Canyon would have been considerably longer than the Gate Canyon route, not shorter, and the ascents would have been much higher. Not surprisingly, nothing came of the idea.

The absence of water along the Gate Canyon segment of the Nine Mile Road was a persistent problem from 1886 to 1892. It would take a miracle to resolve it, which is exactly what happened. In October 1891, Owen Smith, a frequent traveler on the Nine Mile Road, had a "dream" of water in the Gamma Grass Canyon area halfway between Brock's Place and Myton that would become "an oasis in the desert."[5] Smith hired a "water witch" from Price, and the end result was a well 180 feet deep, 6 feet square, and lined with timbers from top to bottom.[6] Smith found the water, but it was

A view of the general store at Smith Wells in about 1904, after the Owen Smith family had sold the establishment. Used by permission, Utah State Historical Society, all rights reserved.

Overview of the Smith Wells station on the Price-to-Myton Road during its heyday in the early 1900s. Used by permission, Utah State Historical Society, all rights reserved.

Owen Smith and family. The photo is identified as the Smith cabin in Myton, but the backdrop of cliffs and the design of the cabin are similar to the "store" at Smith Wells. Used by permission, Uintah County Library Regional History Center, all rights reserved.

highly mineralized—suitable for animals but not potable for humans. Smith devised a complex system of gears and buckets to extract the water.[7]

The location of Smith Wells (or Smith's Well), as it came to be known, was a sound business decision. Not only did he charge the freighters for forage and water for their animals,[8] but he developed overnight

accommodations for the stage passengers. Smith Wells was later expanded to include a general store, a post office, and a log cabin for female employees. Smith sold the operation to I. W. Odekirk near the turn of the century and opened a store at Myton (earlier called Bridge).[9]

Odekirk expanded the frame house to reflect a more hotel-like atmosphere and constructed a bunkhouse used by freighters free of charge. About 1905, Odekirk sold Smith Wells, perhaps to James and Will Hamilton of Nine Mile Canyon (see chapter 9), and then opened a general store in Myton, which had experienced a population boom when some fifteen thousand immigrants arrived to stake their homestead claims in the Uinta Basin. "It was said that one could not travel the old freight road more than a quarter mile without passing someone, either coming or going." Most of these travelers stopped at Smith Wells.[10] Remnants of the site can still be seen along the road.

Remnants of Smith Wells can still be seen along the old Nine Mile Road. Photo by Jerry D. Spangler.

This "Hamilton" inscription at Smith Wells might be attributed to the Hamilton family that purchased the station in about 1906. Photo by Jerry D. Spangler.

Smith's miraculous discovery of water at Gamma Grass might very well have deterred any army intention of building an alternative, more water-friendly route, if it ever really considered it. Or it could have been the army already recognized there was no longer any need for a new military road. Rumors that Fort Duchesne would be closing surfaced the follow year, in 1892. Why would the army invest in transportation infrastructure if it intended to close Fort Duchesne?

Rumors of the closing of Fort Duchesne became a near-annual event. But each time the closure seemed imminent, powerful political interests would intervene on behalf of the settlers in eastern Utah and western Colorado who were fearful that without a military presence the Utes would become unmanageable. But nothing really happened in the 1890s to warrant military intervention, and the number of troops assigned there eventually dwindled to insignificance.[11]

And with the downsizing there was less and less need to ship massive amounts of military supplies. As summarized by Ronald Watt, in 1887, the first full year of military shipments on the Nine Mile Road, two million pounds of freight were sent to Fort Duchesne. By 1891, when the military was considering an alternative route, the freight shipments had dropped to one million pounds, and by 1895, when few soldiers remained at Fort Duchesne, the totals had fallen to 526,870 pounds.[12]

The Uintah Railway

If the Argyle Canyon route (or any other route, for that matter) was indeed shorter and better and had water along the entire route, the Gilsonite interests of the day would most certainly have jumped at the opportunity to build it themselves. Gilsonite was a booming enterprise in the 1890s and there seemed to be insatiable demand for the unique hydrocarbon. New technologies allowed for development of new mines and deeper mining. Boom towns sprouted with names like Dragon and Bonanza and Rainbow. The mining concerns could sell as much Gilsonite as they could produce, and they simply could not get it to market fast enough. An easier transportation route would have meant faster shipments and more profits. But the Gilsonite investors were not interested in another wagon road. They had much bigger plans.

As discussed in chapter 3, the Gilsonite Manufacturing Company, which owned the lion's share of the first Gilsonite claims, was bought out in 1889 for a reported $150,000 to $185,000 by St. Louis investors, who named the new company the Gilson Asphaltum Company. Over the next fifteen years, other Gilsonite mines were started, and as the market continued to expand throughout the 1890s production was increased to meet that demand. The logistics of shipping tens of thousands of tons of ore on a single narrow wagon route became immediately apparent: the Nine Mile Road was a business liability that limited profits by limiting production to only the amount that could be shipped on the narrow bottleneck of a road.

An alternative to the Nine Mile Road had been discussed for years. Not only were timely shipments a problem, it was getting more expensive. In January 1899, the freighters went on strike to raise their compensation from $1.12 per hundredweight to $2 per hundredweight. "Freight companies

Uintah Railway transports
soldiers in the early 1900s
through Baxter Pass, named for
Charles Baxter, the president of
the Gilson Asphaltum Company
and the originator of the Uintah
Railway. Used by permission,

Uintah Railway cars loaded
with two-hundred-pound sacks
of Gilsonite at Thimble Rock.
Used by permission, Uintah

thought that they would easily be able to replace the rigs, but they failed to do so. Within two weeks the wagons were rolling once again and the freighters had won a substantial pay increase."[13]

But there was a long-term cost. At the same time freighters were celebrating their pay raise, the Gilsonite companies were engaged in unsuccessful talks to convince the Denver and Rio Grande Railroad to build a spur line to the Uinta Basin. When that failed, the Gilsonite concerns did more than talk. In 1903, a group of investors incorporated the Uintah Railway Company, and they announced plans to construct a narrow-gauge rail line from the Gilsonite mines at Black Dragon Vein near the Utah-Colorado border to the Denver and Rio Grande railheads at Crevasse, Colorado (near Grand Junction). Among the incorporators was C. O. Baxter, the suspected moneyman behind Sam Gilson and Bert Seaboldt in the earliest Gilsonite claims and the president of Gilson Asphaltum Company, which owned more Gilsonite claims than all other companies combined (see chapter 3).

Not only would the new rail line bypass Nine Mile Canyon altogether, but once the plans were announced the mining companies, for the most part, stopped their shipments on the Nine Mile Road, preferring to stockpile the ores at the mine site in anticipation of the rail line. When ores had to be shipped, they were loaded on wagons and shipped by way of a rough wagon road along the same route where the rail line was being built along the Utah-Colorado border. For all intents and purposes, the Gilsonite companies had had enough of the Nine Mile Road.[14]

The fifty-two-mile-long Uintah Railway was completed in October 1904 amid cheers and high expectations that the Uinta Basin would soon displace Price as the regional economic hub. The hucksters behind the Uintah Railway detailed ambitious plans to extend the railway to Vernal and Fort Duchesne.[15] Rumors were swirling in the Uinta Basin that Anheuser Busch Brewing Company—the owners of Gilson Asphaltum Company—were offering to buy Fort Duchesne from the army and that, once connected to the Uintah Railway, it would become a "bustling metropolis of 15,000 to 25,000 people."[16] Much to the chagrin of Uinta Basin residents, the hoped-for extensions were never built.[17]

The completion of the railroad in 1904 led to the construction of Dragon Junction, which featured a depot, warehouse, hotel, store, and several dwellings. The junction eventually became a bigger town than the mining camp of Dragon, and it might have rivaled many Uinta Basin towns in terms of population. At Dragon Junction, passengers and freight destined for Vernal and Fort Duchesne were transferred from the trains to stagecoaches and freight wagons. The Uintah Railway constructed a toll road and wagon service from Dragon Junction to Vernal and Fort Duchesne. Most of the road construction had been completed by late 1905, after which daily passenger, mail, and freight services were initiated.[18]

Rather than bridge the Green River, the company, "in a characteristic spirit of frugality," built ferries at Ouray on the Bonanza–Fort Duchesne road and at Alhandra (about one mile south of the bridge that crosses the Green River today on U.S. Highway 40). The company acquired their own teams and wagons, and by the end of 1906 it owned more than 160 freight horses. In November 1906, a new subsidiary company, called the Uintah Toll Road Company, was incorporated to manage the business. The toll road continued for at least two more decades before increased automobile access into the Uinta Basin made rail transportation of freight and passengers increasingly uneconomical and inconvenient.[19]

The Uintah Railway immediately became the preferred means of transportation into and out of the Uinta Basin, not just for the valuable ores, but for passengers, for the military seeking to ship supplies to Fort Duchesne and the Indian agency, and for mail deliveries. In effect, the Uintah Railway became everything the Nine Mile Road once was and with greater predictability. The Nine Mile community—and the Price businesses that depended on Uinta Basin commerce through Nine Mile Canyon—would have withered if not for yet another near-simultaneous event: Ute reservation lands were finally opened to a flood of Euro-American homesteaders.

A New Indian Policy

The Mormon Church–owned *Deseret News* had once characterized the Uinta Basin as "one vast continuity of waste, and measurably valueless, except for nomadic purposes, hunting grounds for Indians and to hold the world together,"—hardly a description that would encourage Mormon settlement of the region.[20] A few Mormon and non-Mormon families nonetheless put down roots here, but not many. The communities of Ashley and Vernal were small hamlets, but traditional Mormon colonization by Mormon families dispatched by church leaders to settle the wilderness did not occur here. In 1880, before the Nine Mile Road was built, there were only seventy-nine Euro-Americans in the entire region.[21]

The church's interest in the area took a dramatic turn just as outside interests began to pressure Congress to open the reservation to Euro-American settlers. In 1888, the *Deseret News* glowed,

> Uintah Valley is probably the most beautiful and desirable section of country within a radius of hundreds of miles. It has an even, balmy climate, which is delightful in the extreme. It is well watered by the Uintah and Duchesne rivers and their numerous tributaries, which are generally large brooks, flowing through a rich prairie country, and

which could easily be diverted for purposes of irrigation. The land is very rich and fertile, and mile after mile of it is natural meadow. Timber is abundant and easily accessible, and the region abounds in resources well calculated to tempt the cupidity of would be settlers.[22]

The same 1888 *Deseret News* article also decried the "machinations" of land speculators and stockmen who were behind a move to "despoil" the Utes. "It is a shame that the avarice of the white man should forever be permitted to triumph over the rights of the Indians."[23]

But the clamor to open the reservation to settlement was getting louder with each passing year. A law passed in the late 1890s granted Euro-American farmers the right to divert water from reservation lands to non-Indian farms, and the opening of the reservation to actual homestead claims was viewed as inevitable. The Mormon Church seems to have recognized this inevitability, and when it happened it would bring floods of non-Mormons to their very doorstep. This concern was expressed at the October 1899 General Conference of the church when Mormon apostle Abraham Woodruff exhorted young members to take up farming on

vast tracts of land which I believe the God in Heaven has kept in reserve for this people. They only wait the diversion of the streams from their natural courses to transform them into thrifty farms and settlements. If our people do not take advantage of the vast tracts of

land that are around us...we will ultimately find ourselves surrounded by a people not of us.[24]

According to historian Craig Woods Fuller, the shift in Mormon attitudes toward the Uinta Basin resulted in part from the increased urbanization of Mormon communities elsewhere in Utah—and all the social ills that came with that urbanization—and the fact there were no more agricultural areas left that could be colonized in the typical Mormon pattern. The Uinta Basin was seen as an opportunity "to continue to build Zion in the tops of the mountains" on the agrarian model that had worked so well for fifty years.[25]

The problem, of course, is the Uinta Basin lands were not free for the taking, and the opening of the Uintah Reservation had become part of a much larger federal Indian policy. The only way the church would have a say in how the Uinta Basin would be settled would be through loyal land

Lott Powell and other Powell family members left their inscriptions along the Nine Mile Road. This one is in a narrow stretch of Gate Canyon. Photo by Jerry D. Spangler.

Fort Duchesne soldiers in downtown Vernal. The military presence here was beefed up in 1902 as plans were initiated to open the Ute reservation to white homesteaders. Used by permission, Uintah County Library Regional History Center, all rights reserved.

agents and by encouraging the faithful to apply for homesteads once it was opened. William H. Smart, a Mormon ecclesiastical leader from the Heber Valley, conducted two unauthorized surveys of the Uintah Reservation in 1904, and with the encouragement of Mormon leaders in Salt Lake City, Smart created the Wasatch Development Company to lay the groundwork for Mormon settlement of the Uinta Basin once the reservation was opened to homesteaders.[26] By 1904, the opening of tribal lands to Euro-American settlement was imminent, and faithful members of the church were at the forefront of efforts to claim the lands.[27]

The opening of the Uintah Indian Reservation had its roots in a national reformation movement in the mid-1880s—the same movement castigated by the *Deseret News* in 1888 as a scheme by land speculators and livestock interests. The reformists believed the removal of Indians to isolated reservations was morally wrong; they preferred instead a policy of "assimilation" of Indians into Euro-American culture. Their three-part plan had three objectives: (1) Reservations and the annual government handouts to tribal members would be eliminated, with each tribal member receiving title to a 160-acre homestead with arable lands (and any unalloted lands would then be opened to Euro-American homesteaders). It was thought that individuals would embrace farming if their welfare depended on it, and they would more readily assimilate into the American mainstream by living alongside Euro-American neighbors. (2) Indian culture and traditions were to be replaced through the education of the children, which would involve removal of Indian children to boarding schools where they would be taught English and the Christian religion. (3) Tribal organizations were to be terminated and replaced with individual responsibilities and promises of citizenship.[28]

> Many have assumed that the allotment of Indian lands held the primary goal of opening new lands for white settlement. The reformers claimed otherwise. In their thinking it was true that the Indians would lose a great deal of land but this was for their own good. They argued that reservations discouraged civilizing influences and encouraged white trespass; forcing Indians to take up the responsibility of ownership would encourage assimilation preventing a total loss of their land through encroachment of whites.[29]

In 1887, President Grover Cleveland signed into law the Dawes Severalty Act, which set into motion the objectives of the reformers. But the law required the consent of the tribes. The Uncompahgre Utes accepted their allotments in 1898, but the Uintah and White River Utes in the Uinta Basin had doggedly resisted any allotments of their reservation lands. In 1902, the U.S. Supreme Court ruled that tribal consent was not needed, that the federal government could act unilaterally to sell its surplus lands—and the White River and Uintah Utes had no choice but to submit.[30]

Anticipating a hostile reaction from the Utes, and to police the hordes of homesteaders descending on the reservation, the army ordered reinforcements to Fort Duchesne in 1902, where they remained until 1907. These included two companies of the Twelfth Infantry to complement the two troops of Fifth Calvary already there, and later two companies of the Twenty-Ninth Infantry.[31] It was the first time in almost two decades that Fort Duchesne boasted any sizable military presence.

The Utes were clearly not happy with the forced allotments. In the spring of 1906, the entire White River band, as well as several others—some 321 in all—packed up their belongings, and along with a thousand horses and fifty cows headed east to join up with the Sioux. "After a long sojourn through four states, the Utes finally arrived in the lands of the supposed sympathetic Sioux, but soon realized that they had been duped in their expectation of a grand welcome. They now became a people with no home, friends or Indian rights group supporters."[32] It would take another two years for the government to come up with a plan to return the Utes to their Uinta Basin allotments.

Top: Axle-grease signature in Gate Canyon dating to 1906. This was probably an early homesteader traveling to the Uinta Basin. Photo by Jerry D. Spangler.

Bottom: Axle-grease signature in Nine Mile Canyon dating to 1907 during the height of the land rush in the Uinta Basin. Photo by Jerry D. Spangler.

By July 18, 1905, government officials reported that 774 allotments had been made to Uintah and White River Utes, prompting President Theodore Roosevelt to then issue a proclamation opening the remaining lands to Euro-American homesteaders. The process for getting the lands was a grand lottery. Drawings for 160-acre parcels were held in Provo, Vernal, and Price, Utah, and Grand Junction, Colorado. Thousands of people from all over the United States applied, including a band of gypsies passing through Provo, large numbers of Greek immigrants, a religious sect called Emethaehavahs based in Denver, several performers

One contractor was so confident the new state highway would be built through Nine Mile Canyon that he reportedly stockpiled equipment here. He went bankrupt and the rusted shells along the road are a testament to another shattered dream. Photo by Jerry D. Spangler.

and roustabouts from the Barnum and Bailey Circus, and a prominent clairvoyant.[33]

The lottery was held on August 17, 1905, for an estimated 37,000 applicants. A total of 5,772 names were drawn, with each homesteader agreeing to pay $1.25 an acre. Ironically, 1905 was a year of above-normal precipitation in the Uinta Basin, creating misperceptions among the arriving homesteaders as to what the normal rainfall was. Severe droughts beginning in 1906 prompted hundreds of homesteaders—perhaps as many as one in three families—to abandon the Uinta Basin within a few years, sometimes selling their claims for pennies on the dollar.[34]

Those lucky enough to win a homestead had to travel to the Uinta Basin to stake their claims with the Land Office, make the required improvements, and live on the land for three years in order to earn actual title. And the Nine Mile Road appears to have been a major transportation route for homesteaders going to and from the Uinta Basin. By 1905, the Gilsonite shipments on the Nine Mile Road would have dwindled to next to

Utah Governor Simon Bamberger signed the death warrant for the Nine Mile Road when he chose the Indian Canyon route for a new state highway (it is now a portion of U.S. 191). Used by permission, Utah State Historical Society, all rights reserved.

nothing. But any noticeable decrease in traffic might have gone unnoticed with the increase in traffic resulting from the homesteaders (and in theory increased military freight). Some, like Katherine Fenton, who became Mrs. Preston Nutter after proving up on her homestead claim in Ioka (see chapter 7), first traveled to the Uinta Basin by stagecoach. Others traveled by wagon, based on the dozens upon dozens of axle-grease signatures on the canyon walls with dates of 1906 and the years immediately thereafter. Once the homesteaders began to abandon their claims in the wake of droughts over the next few years, it is assumed some of them would have returned by the same route.[35]

The Nine Mile route was, by some accounts, the most popular one for the homesteaders. George Stewart recalled, "My dad said he stood on a peak at the head of Gate Canyon and from there he could trace the Stage Road all the way to Vernal and the Land Office, by the dust churned up from the turning wheels and pounding hoofs."[36]

By that time, however, the homesteaders would have had various other travel route options besides Nine Mile Canyon. The Uintah Railway was

carrying passengers by 1905, and it was far quicker than wagon travel but certainly more expensive. Many other homesteaders in the Uinta Basin came by way of a new wagon road that bypassed Nine Mile Canyon to the west and linked Castle Gate with the fledgling town of Theodore (now Duchesne).[37] This road is now known as U.S. 191, or the Indian Canyon Highway, although in 1905 it was not much of a road. The Carter Road was still functional in 1905, as was another wagon route to and from Park City (this would become U.S. 40).

The land rush was also a boon to Price businesses that had prospered by selling their wares to Uinta Basin farmers, ranchers, and miners—products that arrived by rail and were then shipped north on the Nine Mile Canyon freight route. The influx of homesteaders—fifteen thousand people by some

accounts—brought an increased demand for these products, even if some could be more easily transported via the Uintah Railway. This prosperity was temporary, however, as enterprising individuals in the newly created towns of Theodore, Roosevelt, and Myton, as well as Vernal, soon opened their own mercantile stores and cooperatives—stores furnished by way of the Uintah Railway, or from Salt Lake City by way of an improved route through Park City and the Heber Valley, or the new wagon route through Indian Canyon, which was connected to the Denver and Rio Grande railhead at Colton.[38]

The great land rush of 1905–1906 might not have been as great as traditionally thought. By some accounts, more than 15,000 people poured into the Uinta Basin at that time, which would have been twice the population of Price and its surrounding towns. If the average homesteader family consisted of two to three people (a lot of homesteaders were single people),

The state chose the Indian Canyon route under political pressure from Duchesne County. The higher elevations proved to be a problem for winter travel during heavy snows. Used by permission, Uintah County Library Regional History Center, all rights reserved.

Paved road through Nine Mile Canyon today (the Nutter Ranch is in the background). Photo by Jerry D. Spangler.

then 15,000 is a reasonable estimate given the 5,772 homestead allotments. Barton believes as many as a third gave up and walked away from their homesteads,[39] which meant roughly 10,000 would have stayed. But he might have greatly underestimated the failure rate: in 1910, the Basin had a population of 7,820 people, which would also have included Uinta Basin old-timers, Gilsonite miners, soldiers, and others with roots that predated the land rush. Carbon County had 8,624 people at the same time.

In 1910, the two regions were similar in size, similar in demographic makeup, and similar in economics. There is no question the Uinta Basin rivaled Carbon County in terms of population and economic importance at this time, and it was a rivalry manifest in the one-upmanship and booster-ism articulated in the local newspapers of the day.

The biggest difference was the Uinta Basin was no longer dependent on Price as its economic lifeline—and that lifeline had been the Nine Mile Road. With the land rush all but over and Uintah Railway delivering supplies and mail, the Nine Mile Road was fast becoming a historical footnote.

Fort Duchesne closed for good in 1912—the same year a stage route was established between Salt Lake City and Duchesne, and the same year stage service through Nine Mile Canyon was discontinued.[40] Some probably held out hope that the Nine Mile Road would somehow survive the downturn, but a final blow came in 1918. The proliferation of privately owned automobiles in Utah had resulted in frantic need for better roads, and as lawmakers have done ever since, they initiated ambitious state highway construction programs across the state. Utah officials determined that an improved road—a highway by standards of that day—was needed to connect Price to the thriving communities in the Uinta Basin: Duchesne, Roosevelt, Vernal, and others. Two routes were under consideration, the Nine Mile Canyon route preferred by Vernal and folks living in the eastern Uinta Basin, and the Indian Canyon route from Castle Gate to Duchesne which was preferred by those in the western part of the Uinta Basin.

Local legend has it that one road contractor was so certain the Nine Mile route would be chosen that he stockpiled equipment and materials at the Harmon Ranch in advance of any decision. The issue was "hotly debated," but the Indian Canyon route was ultimately chosen after considerable political pressure from the community of Duchesne.[41] The local contractor went bankrupt and his equipment now lies rusting along the Nine Mile Road.

In 1918, Governor Simon Bamberger authorized the use of prisoners at the state penitentiary in Salt Lake City to improve the Indian Canyon Highway, and the road was completed the following year. The highway eliminated the need for any commercial travel on Nine Mile Canyon Road,[42] even though the new highway was beset with its own challenges to efficient travel.

More than eight decades would pass before the Nine Mile Road again assumed major economic importance—it is now a paved road to facilitate natural gas development on the high West Tavaputs Plateau. An estimated two million vehicles will travel the road over the next two decades to explore, drill, and service the gas wells. The vast majority will be traveling to and from Duchesne and Roosevelt and Vernal, using the same Gate Canyon route that so bedeviled the freighters with their wagons and teams more than a century ago.

A Genealogy of Place

The Farmers and Ranchers of Nine Mile Canyon

If one believed all that was told, ghosts could be seen walking every night up the road, driving the women crazy...wells were filled with dead men and built over to conceal their secrets.

—Mildred Miles Dillman, 1948

Nine Mile Canyon was bustling with activity from 1886 through the early 1900s—freighters hauling their loads back and forth to the Uinta Basin, cattlemen and cowboys, travelers coming and going on the stage coach, and people both famous and infamous. But lost in the more colorful events that forged the backdrop of Nine Mile Canyon's history are the families who saw in Nine Mile Canyon an opportunity for a place to call their own. For many, this hope was illusory, and they left disappointed after a few years. A few put down roots here, and their descendants today look back proudly on their ancestors' efforts to tame an untamable landscape.

This chapter evolved from years of driving up and down Nine Mile Canyon and pondering the skeletons of log cabins and dilapidated corrals and barns and wondering about the human stories behind them. The story of Nine Mile Canyon may have been shaped by broader events, but its people defined its history. It was a tough land that challenged the resolve of the toughest men and women, and most found it more practical to simply leave. It is a place where children were born, where young adults courted and married—and sometimes divorced amid dramatic acrimony—and where parents grew old and died. It is a genealogy of place where family histories are passed down with varying degrees of accuracy.

Scenic view of the Rabbit Ranch at the mouth of Cottonwood Canyon. Photo by Ray Boren.

Scenic view of the mouth of Cow Canyon where a small community once thrived. Photo by Jerry D. Spangler.

We estimate that maybe five hundred people called Nine Mile Canyon home during the fifty-year heyday of the canyon from 1886 to 1936, though rarely did more than a hundred live here at any one time. Each of those souls had hopes and dreams and aspirations, kinfolk who loved them, others who didn't. And each would have a tale to tell, although few of their stories have survived the passage of time. But tantalizing clues are beginning to surface as to who they were, thanks to the emergence of exhaustive public databases and because of the monumental efforts of the last canyon stalwarts who scramble to collect oral histories before they are gone forever.

For the purposes of this chapter we analyzed the following databases: the Mormon Pioneer Overland Database for 1847 to 1868, maintained by the Church of Jesus Christ of Latter-day Saints (Mormons); the Mormon Migration database maintained by the Harold B. Lee Library at Brigham Young University, which includes immigrants from foreign lands; the Utah Digital Newspaper database, which is an online collection of all early newspapers in Utah; a series of interconnected databases at Ancestry.com that include census records, death records, military service records and even city directories; and the General Land Office database of land patents, maintained by the Bureau of Land Management. And we were given unfettered access to the histories collected over the years by the Nine Mile Canyon Settlers Association.

We took the names of early canyon residents mentioned in accounts by early Nine Mile historian Mildred Dillman and by current keeper of the flame, Norma Dalton, and we cross-referenced those names to all databases, with special attention on census records. This proved very effective but for the absence of 1890 Census records (all national census records for that year were destroyed in a fire).

As our own database of names got exponentially larger, it became necessary to limit it, and we decided, perhaps somewhat arbitrarily, to end the early history of Nine Mile Canyon at 1936, the year that cattle baron Preston Nutter passed away (see chapter 7). This signaled the end of an era and an appropriate end to our history, although the canyon's history in the 1940s and 1950s certainly warrants more detailed examination. The year 1936 also, conveniently, marked fifty years from the time the military first improved the Nine Mile Road to make it passable to freighters.

As we reviewed the various databases, we were able to test a number of statements offered by William Miller, the first scholar to seriously examine social and demographic trends in Nine Mile Canyon (but without the benefit of electronic databases).[1] Miller's conclusions are generally accurate,

and in some cases remarkably so. In other instances they warrant some revisions and augmentations.

Skeletons of old cabins line the Nine Mile Road. Who built them remains a mystery in many cases. Photo by Jerry D. Spangler.

The Black Hawk War

Miller asserts that one motivation behind the settlement of distant places like Nine Mile Canyon was the displacement of Ute Indians from their reservations that opened up new opportunities for settlement. This might have been true to a point, but it must also be clarified. Nine Mile Canyon was never part of an Indian reservation, and as far as we have determined there were never any confrontations here between white settlers and Native Americans living on the reservation in the Uinta Basin in the 1870s and later.

What could have motivated the settlement of Nine Mile Canyon, per-haps as early as 1877, were events that had occurred a decade or so ear-lier when Ute chief Black Hawk rallied disenfranchised peoples from many different Ute and Paiute bands, as well as sympathetic Apaches and Navajos and even a few whites, to resist encroachment on their traditional lands. Between 1865 and 1872, most of central Utah was in an all-out state of war with the Ute warriors, prompting dispersed Utah settlers to retreat into heavily protected forts. The Utah militia was dispatched to chase the Ute marauders, usually with minimal success. And in the process, the mili-tiamen discovered new, unexplored territories ripe for settlement—places like Price River and Castle Valley, and perhaps even Nine Mile Canyon.[2]

Although depredations continued here and there on both sides through 1872, the conflict had all but ended by 1870 when Chief Black Hawk died from tuberculosis. And in 1872 the last remnants of the Ute bands in cen-tral Utah had been removed to the Uinta Basin reservation. This allowed Mormon families unrestricted access to the new territories they had dis-covered during the military campaigns.[3]

References to early Nine Mile settlers serving in the Utah militia during the Black Hawk War are scant. Edwin Lee Sr. was a veteran of the Black Hawk War, and it is possible the conflict brought the elder Lee to the Price region,[4] and that he later told his sons, Arthur and Edwin Jr., about the unsettled place. By 1900 Arthur was living in Price and Edwin Jr. in Nine Mile Canyon, where his ranch just above Argyle Canyon became a favorite stop for freighters and stagecoach passengers.

According to a family history, G. C. "Don" Johnston was a vet-eran of the Black Hawk War "during the uprising in Spanish Fork and Springville," for which he was awarded a monthly pension.[5]

Another possible connection is Nephi Smithson, who with his wife, Barbara, settled in Nine Mile Canyon sometime before 1900. They had one ranch at the mouth of Sulphur Canyon and another near the mouth of Cottonwood Canyon. Nephi's parents, Allen Freeman and Jeanette Smithson, were among the first Mormon pioneers to arrive in the Salt Lake Valley in the Mississippi Company in 1847.[6] Nephi was born in about 1849 or 1850 before the family settled in Washington County. Nephi served in the "Indian Wars" and was awarded a military pension.[7]

It is speculative to assume he discovered Nine Mile Canyon during his military service. He married in 1881, and the couple probably did not arrive to establish their own farm until after that time—or a decade after the end of the Black Hawk War. At the time of the 1900 Census, Nephi, Barbara, and their five children (ages one to sixteen) were all living in Nine Mile Canyon. Nephi died the following year, in 1901, at age fifty-one or fifty-two, and is buried in Price;[8] he took sick and died at the Don Johnston Ranch while traveling to see a doctor in Price. Barbara and the children then moved on to Wasatch County and later to Duchesne County.

The connection between Utah's Indian policy before 1872 and the settlement of Nine Mile Canyon years later remains tenuous, at best. But there is evidence that later Indian policy had a profound effect on the canyon demographics. The opening of the Ute reservation in the Uinta Basin to white homesteaders in 1906 resulted in scores of Nine Mile residents abandoning their Nine Mile farms and ranches for better farmlands in the Uinta Basin (see chapter 8). And these early residents were then replaced by a new generation of families.

Poor Folk Seeking Land

William Miller also claims that the isolated farmstead pattern evident in Nine Mile Canyon resulted from Mormon children coming of age in other areas of Utah. Seeking a place of their own, they scattered into previously unsettled and less optimal farming areas like Nine Mile Canyon. They were generally from poorer families unable to buy farmlands in the communities where they had been raised.[9] Indeed, there is considerable support for this. In 1900, some 82 percent of all canyon residents had been born in Utah, most of them born to parents that had come to Utah in the Mormon migration after 1847. By 1910, the percentage was still 80 percent, even though the catalog of residents had changed dramatically by that time. By 1920 it was 78 percent, and in 1930 it was at 77 percent. In other words, roughly eight out of ten canyon residents during the earliest settlement days were from Utah Mormon families.[10]

Most of these families came from settlements in Sanpete, Sevier, Juab, and Utah Counties. In other words, they migrated east across the Wasatch

The Winn Rock House, later known as the Harmon Rock House and the Wimmer Rock House, first constructed in 1883. Photo by Ray Boren.

Plateau. Only one of the earliest families of Nine Mile Canyon came by a different route, by way of Rich County and Idaho—the Dennis Winn family, who arrived in about 1883.

Dennis Alma Winn was the son of Dennis Wilson Winn, an early Mormon convert and Mormon Battalion veteran who might have been a stonecutter on the Nauvoo Temple before migrating west to Salt Lake City in 1849.[11] Dennis Alma, who is credited with the construction of the "Rock House" at Harmon Canyon, might have learned stonecutting from his father. He was born in Salt Lake City in 1849, and by 1870 he was living in Cache County with his sixteen-year-old wife, Emma Lorena Blair, and an infant son, and by 1880 the family, which then included five children, had settled in nearby Franklin, Idaho.[12] How the family found their way to Nine Mile Canyon by 1883 is not known.

According to family accounts, Dennis stayed in Nine Mile Canyon until the late 1880s or early 1890s when he moved his family to the Uinta Basin, and he leased his squatters' rights to the Nine Mile Canyon ranch rather than sell out. In 1896, Dennis's son John moved back to the Rock House with his wife, Fanny Weeks Winn, where their first child was born on November 25, 1896. In 1898, John and Fanny also returned to Vernal, selling the family ranch and Rock House to Ed Harmon. John and Fanny would return to Nine Mile Canyon in 1932 to build a ranch near the mouth of Argyle Canyon.[13] Dennis and a son are also credited with building the cut-stone saloon on the John Eagan ranch in 1902 (see chapter 6).

More characteristic of Miller's generalization is the John Babcock family, which put down roots near the mouth of Minnie Maud Canyon. According to Miller's genealogical research, the Babcock family lived in five different communities over a thirteen-year period before their arrival in Nine Mile Canyon. All of the communities were in areas that were settled after the Black Hawk War and none were settled under the direction of the central church authorities. The last two settlements were Helper and Vernal, and the main road between these two towns would have passed through Nine Mile Canyon. Miller places their arrival in Nine Mile Canyon at 1891,[14] but this is inconsistent with reports the family moved there to be closer to their daughter, Sarah Hall, who arrived in 1894.

John Babcock lived in Nine Mile Canyon for about thirty-five years, making him one of the longest-term residents in the canyon. John's daughter Mary D. married William E. Casady (sometimes spelled Cassidy), and the couple had two children and a place of their own in Nine Mile Canyon in 1910.[15] John's son Earl stayed in the canyon through 1920, living with and working for Frank Alger at the time.[16] He later married and moved on to Idaho. A daughter Maud married into the Don Johnston family, which had a ranch farther down canyon.[17] The other children all moved away in search of better opportunities. The Babcock farm was eventually sold to Mel Keele.[18]

In about 1920, John Babcock moved down canyon to live with his daughter Josephine, who had married Ed Harmon. The couple had acquired the "Winn Rock House," which then became known as the "Harmon Rock House." They raised four children there over the next three decades. Dillman states this ranch was also a stage stop at one time and that the ranch served as a recreation center for canyon "hoe-downs."[19]

Ed Harmon would become one of the main pioneer figures in the canyon, serving several times as an election judge, working tirelessly to reopen the road after flooding and blizzards, and offering commentary to Price newspapers on happenings in Nine Mile Canyon. He might also have been an unofficial "community leader" charged with keeping civil order. According to one brief 1903 newspaper account, Ed Harmon was assaulted by a man named A. O. Smith during enforcement of a health quarantine imposed in the canyon.[20]

We are not sure how Ed Harmon came to be in Nine Mile Canyon, but he probably arrived sometime in the 1890s. Edwin Lewis Harmon was born between 1851 and 1854 in Maine (different birth years are given on various records), and he was still living in Maine with his parents, Frank and Mary Harmon, as late as 1870. Sometime about 1875, he enlisted in the U.S. Army and served in the "Indian Wars" and was awarded a military pension.[21] There is no record of him in the 1880 or 1900 federal censuses.

He might have arrived in 1898 or about the same time the Winn family left Nine Mile Canyon, and perhaps a year or so before the couple's oldest child was born in 1899. Josephine Babcock was the eighteen-year-old daughter of John Rowley Babcock; Ed would have been about forty-five years old at the time and only a few years younger than his father-in-law. Ed and Josephine were still living at the "Rock House" as late as 1928 when he served as a Harper Precinct election judge.[22] By 1930, Ed and Josephine were living in Myton, where Ed died in 1933.[23]

Sometime in 1928, the Harmon place was leased to Meril Mead, who lived there with a business partner for a time until he married Ellen Workman. Meril worked for Frank Alger, his neighbor to the east. A dispute between Meril and his business partner over the treatment of a team of draft horses led to a coin flip. Meril's unnamed partner won the ranch, and Meril won the team of draft horses. Meril and Ellen moved out of the rock house and lived with Jeremiah (Jerry) Rich through the winter.[24]

This cabin at the mouth of Minnie Maud Canyon is located near the point where the Russell, Hamilton, and Hall families lived in the 1890s. It is not known who built this particular house. Photo by Jerry D. Spangler.

Their son Ben Mead now owns the large ranch operation at the mouth of Cow Canyon, and is the only descendant of the early Nine Mile settlers who still lives in the canyon. The Harmon ranch complex was sold in 1939 to Harold and Neville Wimmer; it is still referred to today as the Wimmer Place or the Wimmer Rock House.[25] A log cabin across the road from the Harmon House, once occupied by a character named Montana Bob, became a school for local children for many years.[26]

The Gooseberry Connection

Particularly intriguing is the connection between Nine Mile Canyon and Gooseberry Valley in Salina Canyon. As we discussed in chapter 3, notorious polygamist hunter Sam Gilson was an early settler of Gooseberry Valley in about 1871, and he was certainly well aware of Nine Mile Canyon by about 1878. Is it just coincidence that his neighbors in Gooseberry Valley were also among the earliest settlers of Nine Mile Canyon? Could Sam Gilson have told them about the canyon?

Two Hamilton brothers, David William and James, established their Nine Mile ranches at or near the mouth of Minnie Maud Canyon,[27] probably in the early 1890s. They were both originally from Nephi, sons of David and Martha Hamilton. Norma Dalton indicates James A. Hamilton lived there seven to ten years before the property was patented on September 7, 1900. This would place his arrival between 1890 and 1893. Dalton indicated, "Those people in the mouth of Minnie Maud were some of the earliest settlers and had productive farms of produce and sold much of it to freighters."[28] Dalton believes James Hamilton later purchased the store at Smith Wells (see chapter 8), citing an October 27, 1909, letter to "J. A. Hamilton, Dealer in General Merchandise," which lists twelve food items and the cost of each.[29]

In 1880 James was still single and living in Gooseberry Valley, and he listed his occupation on census records as "farm help."[30] The 1900 Census records indicate that thirty-eight-year-old James A. Hamilton had by then married Susan Van Wagoner in 1886, and they had four children ranging in ages from two to ten, all living in "Minnie Maud," as Nine Mile Canyon was known at that time.[31]

By 1910, or about the time James would have been involved with Smith Wells, James and Susan also listed their residence as Myton. They apparently put down roots there; the 1920 and 1930 censuses both list their residence as Myton.[32] James died in Duchesne County in 1933 at age seventy. Susan died a year later.

David "Will" Hamilton probably moved to Nine Mile Canyon from Gooseberry Valley with his brother in the early 1890s. By 1900 he was listed on the census with his wife, Eliza "Liza" Bird Hamilton, and eight children ages three to seventeen. His occupation was listed as freighter.[33] Will must have sold out at about the same time as James and perhaps joined him at Smith Wells. The 1910 Census lists their residence as Myton, and the 1920 Census lists their residence as Antelope, Duchesne County.[34] Liza died in 1928 in Bridgeland, Duchesne County. No death record was identified for Will but he must have died about the same time as his name does not appear on the 1930 Census.

The Wiseman family was also living in lower Whitmore Park in about 1900. William Miller states the Wiseman ranch was located six homesteads "up" from James Hamilton, who was located at the mouth of Minnie Maud Canyon. Frank Wiseman, who hailed from Summit County, had married Emma Hamilton, a sister to James and Will, and they had a toddler at the time of the 1900 Census. Also living with them were Martha E. Hamilton, Emma's widowed mother, and Calvin Hamilton, another brother, both of whom came to Nine Mile Canyon from the Gooseberry Valley area of Salina Canyon.[35] They did not follow Emma's brothers James and Will to Myton, but instead moved to Price.

Mildred Dillman states another ranch at the mouth of Minnie Maud belonged to the Russell family, who "are almost as much a part of the canyon as the rocks and cattle, some of them are still native."[36] Norma Dalton indicates that three Russell brothers came to Nine Mile Canyon to establish a ranch at the mouth of Minnie Maud. The ranch was successful and a number of buildings were erected, which stood for decades as sentinels of the Russell family's tenure here. But in recent years the old ranch buildings were dismantled and left decaying in the high sage.[37]

A review of census records reveals there were, in fact, at least four Russell brothers living in Nine Mile Canyon, all of whom arrived with their parents sometime before 1900 from Gooseberry Valley. The family patriarch was Andrew Jackson Russell—known as Daddy Russell—who was one of Utah's original pioneers. Born in Cass County, Illinois, on November 16, 1841, Andrew and thirteen members of the Russell family immigrated to Utah in 1847 in the Abraham O. Smoot Company of Mormon pioneers.[38] The Russell family had settled in Payson at the time of the 1860 Census,[39] and in 1862 Andrew married sixteen-year-old Julia Ann Mott.[40] Julia, born in Wisconsin, had immigrated to Utah as a two-year-old in an unknown pioneer company that arrived in the Salt Lake Valley in 1850.[41] By 1860, the Mott family was living in Spanish Fork.[42]

By 1880, Andrew and Julia had moved on to Gooseberry Valley, where they were raising five children: John W., Charles Henry, Julia, David W., and Myron.[43] Of course, they would have been well acquainted with the James Hamilton family, their neighbors in both Gooseberry and later in Nine Mile Canyon. Exactly when they arrived in Nine Mile Canyon is not known. According to the 1900 Census, sons David, Myron, and Heber were living with Andrew and their mother, Julia, at their Nine Mile ranch at that time.[44]

As discussed in chapter 5, David Wintworth Russell was the stage driver who stopped at Brock's Place in the fall of 1901 and killed Pete Francis with two bullets to the head. Newspaper accounts of the shooting indicated he was a rancher in Nine Mile Canyon, and like many of the local residents he drove the stagecoach for extra cash. Three years before

What remains of the Daddy Russell homestead at the mouth of Minnie Maud Canyon. Photo courtesy of Norma Dalton.

Axle-grease signature left behind by Myron Russell, one of the earliest settlers of Nine Mile Canyon. Photo by Jerry D. Spangler.

the killing, in 1898, Dave Russell had married Emma Brundage, herself from an early Nine Mile ranching family,[45] but by 1900 Dave Russell listed his marital status as single; there is no record they had any children. David was acquitted in the killing of Pete Francis in 1901, and in 1902 his name appeared on a legal document transferring water rights.[46] There is no other record of him in the canyon until 1920, when he was living as a boarder with Alma Z. Thompson.[47]

"Daddy" Russell might have stayed on the family ranch after the death of his wife in 1902. The 1910 Census lists a Jackson Russell, who was living alone at the time. He died in 1917, but not before watching his sons and their families put down roots in Nine Mile Canyon. By 1910, Harrison had returned to Nine Mile Canyon with his wife, Ada Taylor Russell, and their three young children, Olive, Effie, and Kenneth. Harrison's brother Heber was also in the canyon in 1910, along with his wife, Florence, and young sons, Heber Jr. and George.[48] Myron, Harrison, and Harrison's son Kenneth were still living in Nine Mile Canyon as late as 1930.[49] Daddy Russell and his sons Myron and Harrison were fixtures here for more than three decades—certainly among the longest-tenured residents of the canyon. Daddy Canyon is named for Daddy Russell.

The Russell and Hamilton families were not the only ones to stake a claim at the mouth of Minnie Maud Canyon. Charles and Sarah Babcock

Hall arrived in the spring of 1894, hailing from Escalante in Garfield County. This family is noteworthy because of two twin daughters, Minnie and Maud. Local legends persist that Minnie Maud Canyon was named after the twins, even though the name Minnie Maud Creek had been used since 1876 (see chapter 1). The Hall family had three children when they arrived in Nine Mile Canyon, and three more were born while there. Minnie Hall's son, Leonard Brown, has kept alive the legend that the canyon was named for his mother and his aunt. The family of eight reportedly lived in a one-room log house at the mouth of Minnie Maud Canyon.[50]

According to a later newspaper interview with Minnie, the Hall family also lived at Cow Canyon and Coal Creek before taking over the Soldier Creek Station on the Price-to-Vernal stage line (at the mouth of Soldier Creek Canyon just below the current coal mine location). Minnie recalled, "Mother had to have dinner ready at 10 a.m. in the morning and again at 2 p.m. in the afternoon for the stage-coach passengers. Dad kept fresh horses ready. I used to tend the other children in the back room while mother served the meals. Sometimes there would be a flood and the stage would have to turn back and we would have to make beds all over the floor."[51]

The Hall family did not remain in Nine Mile all that long. Sarah died in 1905 at age thirty, leaving behind six children ages six to thirteen.[52] Charles died in 1932 in Duchesne County, but his name does not appear on any census records after 1900. None of the family members are listed on census records for Nine Mile Canyon after 1900, although their relatives, the Babcock family, remained through at least 1910.

The Cow Canyon Community

William Miller, using General Land Office maps, also made the argument that Nine Mile ranches were spaced, on average, about a mile apart in the more densely occupied portion of the canyon along the freight road. In contrast to the rectangular grid of the "Mormon Village," Nine Mile featured a linear pattern with the farms located directly on the farmlands and spaced along the canyon bottom.[53] This is contingent on the accuracy of the map and whether the surveyor indicated the presence of all farms on the map (we did not identify the maps he used in his analysis).[54]

Our reconstruction of the farm and ranch locations confirms Miller's statement to be generally accurate for the canyon as a whole, but there were three areas—the mouth of Minnie Maud Canyon (discussed above), the mouth of Cow Canyon, and the mouth of Argyle Canyon—where ranches were clustered much closer together. In these areas there might have been four to seven families living in close proximity to one another at any given time in the early years of settlement.

The clustering of ranches certainly had economic and social advantages. Neighbors could, if called upon, assist one another, and tasks like digging ditches, constructing diversion dams on the creek, raising barns, and building fences were, in a real sense, community endeavors that were beneficial to all. Many of these families were bonded by blood and marriage, and family trees became more like family vines: intertwined and tangled.

Perhaps the best example of social and economic clustering is found at the mouth of Cow Canyon where there were six or seven families living close to one another. Cow Canyon is the first major tributary on the south side of Nine Mile Canyon just below the mouth of Minnie Maud Canyon. It is fairly broad, the slopes are quite forested, and there are expansive pastures at the mouth of the canyon. This area is currently the site of the Nine Mile Ranch, owned by Ben and Myrna Mead, and the former Houskeeper Ranch, currently owned by the Hammerschmid family.

In the 1890s, this area was a veritable beehive of activity. Among the families living here at the time were those of John A. Powell, one of the original pioneers of Price; Lon and Gett Alger, two brothers who had arrived here by way of Orangeville in Emery County; the Charles Smith family and the Theodore Houskeeper families, both related to the Algers; the John Babcock family, related to the Hall family living just up canyon; and the Carl Johnston family, which married into the Babcock and Houskeeper families. Divining exactly where each of these ranches was located is nigh impossible as there are no land records from the 1890s and there was probably no legal claim to the lands at that time.

As discussed above, the Charles Hall family moved to Nine Mile Canyon in 1894, and soon thereafter the Hall family was joined by Sarah Hall's parents, Augusta Mae and John Rowley Babcock, who built a ranch near the mouth of Cow Canyon. John Babcock was born in Missouri in about 1846, and he might be the John Babcock who arrived in 1847 as a four-year-old traveling in the Edward Hunter–Joseph Horne Company of Mormon pioneers, although there is a slight discrepancy in the age.[55]

Augusta Mae Hanchette was born in 1856 in San Bernadino, California, but immigrated to Utah from Wisconsin with her parents sometime after 1870. She married John Rowley Babcock and they had settled in Piute County by 1880; Sarah Babcock Hall was their oldest child.[56] Augusta died in 1897 at age forty shortly after the family arrived in Nine Mile Canyon.[57] John, who became a widower with four small children at home, continued to live on his own farm in Nine Mile Canyon through 1910,[58] but by 1920 the sixty-five-year-old was living with his brother-in-law, Edwin Harmon, who had acquired the Rock House at the mouth of Harmon Canyon.[59] John died in 1928 and is buried in Price.[60]

Mildred Dillman indicates the Carl Johnston family had the ranch to the east of the Russell family, and it can be inferred that the Johnston ranch was also located near the Babcock place (Dillman suggested their ranch was later purchased by Lon and Gett Alger). The Johnston family is probably the Cyrenus C. Johnston (or Johnstun) family listed in the 1900, 1910, and 1920 censuses for Nine Mile Canyon. Cyrenus and Maud Babcock Johnston were both born in Utah, and they raised six children in Nine Mile Canyon. In 1900 Carl's profession was listed as "freighter." There are almost no cross-references in the Ancestry.com database for these family members, and little is known about them other than they would have been among the first residents of the canyon and they would have left the canyon sometime before 1930.[61] Carl's father and two brothers also lived in the canyon.

Also arriving here in the 1890s was the family of Charles and Luna Alger Smith. Ralph Smith, a son, indicated he was born in Emery County in November 1896, and three weeks later his parents took him "back" to their homestead in Nine Mile Canyon. This implies the Smith family was there prior to that time, but how much sooner? The couple was married in St. George in 1885 and they could have been looking for their own place at that time. The Smith farm on the south side of Nine Mile Creek at the mouth of Cow Canyon had a large veranda, year-round running water, and easily cultivated farmland. Within a short time, Luna's brothers, Lon and Gett Alger, had built their own two-room cabin at the mouth of Cow Canyon and began clearing fields. Ralph Smith recalled, "The Alger boys,

Lon and Gett, were cantankerous and hard to reason with." The Smith family had had enough of the bullying, and in 1898 they sold their farm for the price of a team of horses and wagon and moved to Wyoming.[62]

The successor to the Smiths was the Houskeeper family, which has one of the longest and richest traditions in Nine Mile Canyon. According to Craig Houskeeper, Theodore F. Houskeeper, Craig's great-grandfather, was one of the original homesteaders in upper Nine Mile Canyon, perhaps shortly after the Nine Mile Road was opened to freight traffic in 1886, although a date of 1898 or 1899 seems more likely.

At that time, the Houskeeper family was probably squatting on public land but they later filed legal homestead claims. The Houskeeper family eventually married into the Alger family, which also had major holdings in the canyon. The Houskeepers were farmers and ranchers, but when occasion called they dabbled in other ventures, such as a family sawmill that provided timber to coal mines.

The family patriarch, Theodore, was born in about 1843 in Pennsylvania, and he is probably the Theodore Frelinghuysen Houskeeper who arrived in the Salt Lake Valley in 1852 as part of the Harmon Cutler Company of Mormon pioneers that had embarked on the overland journey from Council Bluffs, Iowa.[63] In 1860, the Houskeeper family was living in Provo in a house shared by at least two other families. Sometime in the late 1860s, Theodore married Sarah Butler, who had immigrated to Utah from England in 1853 by way of New Orleans.[64] In 1880, Sarah and Theodore were living in Emery County with their seven children,[65] but by 1900 they had moved to Nine Mile Canyon with five of their children, all of them young adults. Their oldest daughter, Rosetta, had married Theodore Kelsey, and in 1900 the couple had four children and their own ranch in Nine Mile Canyon.[66]

According to the Houskeeper family history, the site of the Houskeeper ranch was originally owned by Charles and Luna Smith, who sold out to a man named Kimball, who then sold it to Theodore F. Houskeeper.[67] The Charles Smith family had the place through 1898, which would mean the Houskeepers did not arrive before that time.

By 1910, Theodore Sr. and Sarah had moved back to Orangeville, Utah, with their son William. Most of their other children moved on to better opportunities elsewhere. But Theodore Jr. inherited the ranch, perhaps not all that willingly (he had wanted to study music and law). In 1910, Theodore lived on the family ranch with his wife, Clarissa Alger, and their young daughters Fern and Sarah. Clarissa, who went by Clara, might have helped smooth relations with her ornery brothers, but apparently not a lot.

Theodore, Lon, and Gett had built a dam on Nine Mile Creek to divert water onto their adjacent fields. "However the brothers were always stealing Theodore's irrigation water. More to torment him than anything else, I believe. Trip after trip he made to the dam. Then there was a brawl, and because Theodore was a mild mannered man, not given to fisticuffs, the thought prevailed that the Alger brothers cleaned his plow. The water problems ceased at any rate."[68]

By 1920, Clarissa was living in Wellington with six children and her mother, Jane Alger.[69] Theodore B. is listed on the census records for both Wellington and Nine Mile Canyon at that time. According to family histories, the Houskeepers lived in Wellington so the children could attend school there. By 1930, the family included a nephew, Ralph R. Smith, a son of Charles and Luna Smith, who had first come to Nine Mile Canyon as an infant.[70]

The Houskeeper family remained in Nine Mile Canyon through 1963. Young Theodore B. would have arrived in Nine Mile Canyon as a teenager (or younger) and he remained in the canyon for most of the next fifty years. He died in 1944 at age seventy-one and is buried in Price.[71] His son, also named Theodore B., built a road in the years after World War II that ascends the north wall of Nine Mile Canyon and leads to the family sawmill. Craig Houskeeper indicates his father used a large Case International cattle truck to haul the logs (it was the only vehicle the family owned). The steepness of the grade was a constant worry, and the descent involved wedging the driver's door open for an easy exit if the truck should go out of control.[72]

Also warranting mention here is the arrival sometime before 1920 of William and Catherine Hammerschmid. It is not known where in the canyon they lived in 1920 or how long they stayed, but in 1963 the Hammerschmid family bought out the Houskeeper ranch. The Hammerschmid family still owns the ranch today.

The history of Nine Mile Canyon would be woefully incomplete without the story of the Alger brothers: Frank, Alonzo, Gerrett, and Joseph, three

Sarah and Theodore F. Houskeeper in 1867. They were among the earliest settlers in the Cow Canyon area in the 1890s. Photo courtesy of the Craig Houskeeper family.

Theodore B. Houskeeper inherited the ranch from his father, married into the Alger family, and lived most of his life in Nine Mile Canyon. Photo courtesy of the Craig Houskeeper family.

Jane Burnett Alger was the fourth wife of John Alger. She had had enough of the polygamist lifestyle and moved with her children to Emery County. Photo courtesy of the Craig Houskeeper family.

Clarissa (Clara) Alger was the younger sister of brothers Frank, Lon, and Gett, and wife of Theodore B. Houskeeper. Photo courtesy of the Craig Houskeeper family.

of whom had their own farms up and down the canyon. Frank, a lifelong bachelor, had his own spread just east of Harmon Canyon (more on him later). Alonzo and Gett owned the old Johnston place at the mouth of Cow Canyon, where they were neighbors of the Charles Smith and Theodore Houskeeper families (see above).

The brothers all came from Mormon polygamist stock. Their father, John Alger, was one of the first immigrants to Utah in 1850, and he lived for a time in Farr West with his three wives. By the late 1850s or early 1860s the family had been sent to settle in Washington County, where John married his fourth wife, Jane Ann Burnett, on October 26, 1861. In 1864, John Alger moved Jane's family to a new homestead on the Santa Clara River, where the children—Franklin, Edmund, Alonzo (Lon), Gerrett (Gett), Clarissa, and Joseph Eli—were raised.

According to the family history, "Jane and her family often did not have enough to eat and were seldom visited by her husband, John Alger. The boys became bitter about the way he neglected their mother." On one occasion, the boys had managed to kill and butcher a wild cow, but their father, upon hearing of the family's good fortune, arrived on the scene, loaded the meat into his buggy, and drove away. The Alger brothers harbored resentment toward their father the rest of their lives.[73]

At age sixteen, Frank Alger worked at a timber mill north of St. George where he earned enough to buy a wagon and team of horses. Two years later, in about 1885, he loaded his mother (and presumably his siblings) and their belongings and moved them to Orangeville in Emery County where Jane's parents lived. John Alger tried to convince Jane to return to Washington County, but she never did. The brothers worked to buy a place for their mother in Cleveland, also in Emery County, and about this time the brothers found work in the coal mines at Sunnyside.[74] It is not known exactly when the brothers arrived in Nine Mile Canyon, but it would have been in the mid-1890s at the same time their sister Luna was living there with her family (see Charles Smith discussion above).

Family tradition has it that Frank Alger and his brothers initially worked for Shadrach Lunt, building a log house and sheds at Lunt's ranch near Gate Canyon (now the Nutter Ranch), and that they later built the hotel and saloon when William Brock bought the place from Lunt.[75] The saloon and hotel were in place by about 1887—or at least five years before the Alger family lived in the canyon. The brothers also are credited with building the stagecoach barn on the Edwin Lee ranch.[76]

Little is known about Lon and Gett Alger. Gett was reportedly riding shotgun on a stagecoach carrying a military payroll when he thwarted a holdup attempt in Gate Canyon.[77]

Lon Alger was a professional card player well known in the saloons of Price, and even did a bit of dealing in Las Vegas.[78]

At one time, the three brothers also got sucked into a story of an easterner looking for gold treasure reportedly pilfered during a train robbery years before by the man's grandfather. The man had a penciled map, and the brothers recognized the location at the head of Devil's Canyon and agreed to take the man there. Of course, no gold was ever found, although a lot of Nine Mile cowboys have spent a fair amount of time looking for it. The tale of cached outlaw gold remains deeply engrained in the lore of the canyon.[79]

None of the Alger brothers are listed on the 1900 census for Nine Mile Canyon. Lon Alger was at that time living with his sister Luna and her family in Wyoming.[80] Frank was also living in Wyoming, although not with Lon and Luna.[81] There is no record of Gett Alger anywhere in the 1900 census. By 1910, Frank was listed as a single head of household in Nine Mile Canyon, whereas his brothers Lon, Gett, and Joseph were living together in Nine Mile Canyon with their elderly mother, Jane.[82]

Lon Alger apparently returned to Wyoming, where he is listed in the 1920 census, and later that year, at age forty-seven, he married Margaret Burns, a Kansas girl he met in Wyoming.[83] They lived for a spell in Mason City, Iowa,[84] but he was back in Nine Mile Canyon in 1930, working for Preston Nutter; he and Margaret had split. He died in Price in 1949.[85] There is no record as to what became of Margaret.

By 1920, Gett had also married and moved on, first to the Hill Creek country of the East Tavaputs Plateau (an area very much like Nine Mile Canyon) and later to Helper.[86] Almost nothing is known of Joseph, the only other brother to live in Nine Mile Canyon. He died in 1915.[87]

Lon Alger with his wife in happier times. The couple split up after she lost a baby. Photo courtesy of Norma Dalton.

Family Vines

Miller also hints at the interconnectedness of the families in Nine Mile Canyon, wherein families living in the canyon would encourage other family and friends living elsewhere in Utah to join them. More often than not, these families were—or would soon become—related through marriage. Our review of the census data revealed that most Nine Mile families were related in some way to at least one other local family, and in some instances to two or three other families. There are a handful of instances where families did not marry into the local families, such as the Edwin Lee and John Olsen families, but these were anomalies.

A good example of the intertwined family trees is the Powell family, which had arrived with the first settlers of Price in 1878. The John A. Powell family's tenure in Nine Mile Canyon is based mostly on the recollections of Leonard Brown, who was close friends with Sheridan Powell, John's son by his third wife, Rosealtha. Brown indicated the Powell place was a quarter mile east of the homestead of Charles Hall, Brown's grandfather. "With the Powell's house being within 50 feet of the road, they got to see and hear it [freight traffic] all night and day.... Sherd then told me how a big part of everything they raised was sold to the old freighters, especially garden produce and feed for their animals. It was a year round business."[88]

John A. Powell is credited in family lore with guiding the army soldiers through Nine Mile Canyon in 1886 in search of a route for freight wagons to supply Fort Duchesne (see chapter 4). It is probable the family was living in Nine Mile Canyon in the late 1890s and early 1900s, although John A., a polygamist with three large families, also had places in Sunnyside and Price at the time. By 1910, Rosealtha Powell and her brood were living in Price.[89]

Also living in the canyon at the time, in the Whitmore Park area, was Frederic Grames and his wife, Martha Ellen Powell, a sister to John A. Powell. Frederic Grames once owned a big chunk of downtown Price, and he was probably well acquainted with the Whitmore brothers and perhaps partnered with them in the Price business community. It is quite possible they actually bought their Nine Mile ranch from the Whitmore brothers. Dillman indicates the Grames family arrived before 1890, and that "everybody remembers Freddy and that his Dad '[f]ell off the farm when he died and Freddy would rather have lost the best cow on the ranch than poor old Dad.'"[90]

Dillman's reference is confusing, but it offers enough clues to reconstruct who the Grames family was. Frederic Emper Grames was born

This cabin at the mouth of Sulphur Canyon is at or near where John A. Powell established a ranch with his third wife, Rosealtha, in about 1900. Photo by Jerry D. Spangler.

August 19, 1851, in Findon, Sussex, England, and presumably immigrated to Utah with other Mormon converts, although his name does not appear on LDS immigration records. In the 1870 census, he was nineteen years old and living with his parents, Charles and Maria Grames, in Payson.[91]

In January 1878, Caleb Rhoades, Caleb's former brother-in-law Frederic Grames, and Fred's brother Charles Grames, arrived from Payson to settle along the Price River. The Grames brothers chose a spread in a grove of cottonwood trees next to the river, living in a dugout that was eventually replaced by a log cabin—the first structures built in what would become Price.[92] Fred's wife, Martha Powell Grames, arrived in June 1879. According to the 1880 Census, the couple had two daughters at that time, Martha, age two, and a younger sister, Jemima, who would die a few years later.[93]

Fred was one of the icons of early Price settlement. In March 1879, Fred, along with Robert A. Powell, William Davis, Levi Simmons, William Z. Warrant, Caleb B. Rhoades, and Lyman Curtis, developed the first irrigation canal in the Price area, called the Pioneer Ditch Number One (they later built Pioneer Ditch Number Two on the other side of the Price River).[94]

Grames is credited with the emergence of a genuine business district when he sold for one dollar a small piece of his property to the Denver and Rio Grande Railroad for a depot. He had his own thriving store near the depot. Fred was described as "an Englishman, local entrepreneur and community leader, [he] opened a store near the depot, hauled freight to the communities south of Price, served as the town's first postmaster and was a precinct constable and Emery County deputy sheriff. Grames also built a bowery where early community events were held."[95]

In 1885, Grames sold his store and, according to Watts, "returned to farming until he sold his farm [presumably the family farm in Price] to James M. Whitmore and moved to Nine Mile Canyon."[96] This reference is intriguing because the Grames ranch in Nine Mile Canyon was probably in Whitmore Park, which were lands claimed by the Whitmore brothers. The sale of the family farm to James Whitmore might well have been a trade of Grames's farm in Price for a ranch in Whitmore Park. Fred died August 12, 1897, in Nine Mile Canyon.[97] At the time, he had a son with the exact same name, born in 1883, who could have been the "Freddy" referred to by Dillman. Martha Powell Grames died in 1925 and is buried next to Fred in the Price Cemetery.

After Fred's death in 1897, the widow Martha and her children might have left Nine Mile Canyon (there is no record of them in the 1900 census), but by 1910 she had returned to live there with her daughter, also named Martha, and her son-in-law, Alma Z. "Al" Thompson, who also had a ranch in Nine Mile Canyon. She lived with the Thompson family, which included three daughters and an eleven-year-old son named Earl Hall, through at least 1920.[98] By 1910, the younger "Freddy," then twenty-nine and a bachelor, had also returned to Nine Mile Canyon.[99]

In 1920, the younger Martha was listed on the census records as a divorced mother of three girls.[100] Divorces have been a part of family relationships since the beginning of the human experience, but this one must have been bitter by the standards of the day. Even though Al Thompson always had a reputation as a cantankerous man, the entire canyon residency sided with him. Almost a hundred years later, the old-timers speak of his ex-wife Martha with contempt, though they are circumspect as to just why.

Freddy might have continued to live in Nine Mile as late as 1935; the 1940 census lists his residence in 1935 as "rural Carbon County," although by 1940 he was divorced and living with relatives, the Lott Powell family, who had a homestead in Altonah, Duchesne County.[101] He died in 1950 in Price.

Also in the canyon at the same time was the Warren family, which had a ranch in the Argyle Canyon area sometime before 1900. Census records indicate the presence of Parley P. Warren, a thirty-year-old "trapper," who Dillman said "returned" to the canyon in 1899 from the Klondyke Gold Rush. She also indicated that Bill Warren and his wife and six children moved there, that Bill died shortly after arriving, and that "Mrs. Warren made a heroic struggle to raise her large family alone."[102]

Bill Warren must have arrived after 1900 (or he did not participate in the census) and died sometime prior to 1910. A further review of the 1910 Census records reveals some errors of fact in Dillman's statement. Mrs. Warren did not raise her children alone, but rather she soon remarried James H. Blaine, who was listed as the stepfather to her six children ages seven to twenty-one.[103] By 1920 she was again a widow, living in Bluebell in the Uinta Basin with her two youngest children from Bill Warren and a nine-year-old son, Rulon, from James Blaine.[104]

Mrs. Warren was actually Mariah Powell, a daughter of John A. Powell who had the ranch at Sulphur Canyon.[105] She had been born and raised in Utah County, a daughter of John's second wife, Sarah Jane Shields.[106] James H. Blaine was raised in Sanpete County, the son of English parents who immigrated to Utah in the 1850s.[107] Although there is only circumstantial evidence, Parley Warren might have been the younger brother to Bill Warren, and might have been the first to arrive before 1900, with his older brother following shortly thereafter. By 1910, Parley had married Sarah Blaine, the sister of James H. Blaine, and they had two small children.[108] By 1920, Parley and his family had moved on to Price, where he proved up on a homestead entry near Wellington in 1929. He died in 1938.[109]

Alma Z. Warren, the oldest of Bill Warren's children, served in World War I[110] and then returned to Nine Mile Canyon through at least 1920, when he was listed as a single man and farmer. By 1930 he had married and moved on to the Uinta Basin.[111] His son, Noral, later returned to Nine Mile Canyon, proving up on a forty-one-acre Homestead Act claim in 1939 at the mouth of Argyle Canyon.[112]

According to Francis Bowen, another son, Roy Warren, was a noted cowboy in Nine Mile Canyon who also answered the call for troops during World War I but never survived the war.[113] This account is unlikely since he was only sixteen years old at the time of the war, and by 1930 he was a sheepherder living in Nevada.[114]

Everything 4 Sale

Whenever city slickers express romanticism about the idea of ranching, real cowboys are likely to grimace, grin, and offer the following advice: the way to be paid a million dollars for cattle is to start with two million. Ranching is and always has been a tough way to make a living. And it was no different in the 1880s and 1890s when farmers rushed to claim the Nine Mile Canyon bottomlands. They were largely undercapitalized and always outflanked by cattle barons like George and James Whitmore, Preston Nutter, and the Range Valley Cattle Company who tolerated the small operators, but only to a point.

Scenic view of old fence line. Photo by Ray Boren.

It is not surprising that the first to settle in Nine Mile Canyon engaged in a lot more than just ranching. Many, if not most, of the residents here sold goods and services to the steady stream of freighters passing by: fresh produce, water and feed for the draft animals, dry goods, and more. Many of them were freighters, as well. Entrepreneurs along the road included the John A. Powell family, who sold fresh produce; the Johnston family, who opened their ranch to freighters for camping and hot meals; the Ed Lee family, who opened a hotel for weary travelers; Frank Alger, who had a dry-goods store; and John Eagan and Pete Francis (see chapter 5), who catered to the more rough-and-tumble elements of the freight traffic.

The Don Johnston ranch became a popular stopover for freighters because of the fine cooking offered by an Indian woman named Martha.[115] Dillman indicates Don's initials were "GC,"[116] which is probably a reference to George Carlos Johnston, who is listed on the 1910 Census as a sixty-two-year-old farmer from Iowa; he was married, but his wife, Melissa Taylor, was not living there at the time.[117] By 1920, he was living at the Nine Mile

The Don Johnston clan, including Martha Brown and members of the Houskeeper family. Photo courtesy of Norma Dalton.

Not much remains of the original G. C. "Don" Johnston ranch. This old barn might be part of the original ranch or it might have been built later. Photo by Jerry D. Spangler.

ranch with his son Charles and daughter-in-law, Cecilia Downard, and two grandchildren.

The census also lists Martha Brown, a seventy-year-old Native American "cook" who boarded with the family.[118] According to the family history, when the Johnston family was living in Manti, Don's wife was in poor health and they brought in an Indian girl, Martha Beal, to help with household chores. The girl had arrived in Manti as a captive to some Indians that were seeking to sell her. She was purchased by a Mr. Beal for the price of one pig.[119] When she went to work for the Johnston family, she took the name Martha Johnston. She later married a drifter named John Brown, but soon returned to the Johnston family and remained with them the rest of her life.[120] By 1930, the Johnston clan was all living in Price; George C. "Don" Johnston was eighty-two years old at that time.[121]

G. C. Johnston is not listed on the 1900 census, but the family history claims Don Johnston arrived in Nine Mile Canyon in 1896. Also living in Nine Mile Canyon in 1900, but listed as separate heads of household, were two of Johnston's sons, Carl (Cyrenus C.) and John M., although the latter is not listed in the catalog of children in the family history of Don Johnston. As discussed above, Carl and his wife, Maud, initially had a place at the mouth of Cow Canyon. His younger brother John and his wife, Florence, also had a place, but its location is not known. And a sister Lenora later married into the Houskeeper family.

Deciphering who George C. Johnston was is a difficult task due to the commonness of the name and the fact he went by Don Johnston. He is probably the George C. Johnston who was living in Manti in 1870 who was born in Iowa.[122] According to Norma Dalton, the first to file legal claims on the ranch were Don Johnston and his son Sam, who homesteaded there in the early 1900s. There may have been even earlier owners, although the historical record is not clear on this point. By 1939, the ranch had been leased to Bill Lines, a long-time canyon resident whose wife had earlier died under mysterious circumstances.[123] The ranch was later sold to Doyle Barney, who eventually sold it to Tom Christensen. It is commonly referred to as the Christensen Ranch today. The ranch is now the site of the Cottonwood Glen Picnic Area.

Of interest is the absence of any "Sam" Johnston in the census records for Nine Mile Canyon and in the catalog of family names in the family

The hotel on the Edwin Lee ranch, which became known as Harper, was the center of community activities in Nine Mile Canyon. The hotel later burned to the ground. Photo courtesy of Norma Dalton.

history of Don Johnston. If George C. went by "Don," it does not stretch the imagination to think one of his sons might also have used a different name such as "Sam." The family history indicates Don had five sons, all of whom were engaged in the freighting business.[124]

Another entrepreneur was Edwin Lee, who had a big ranch about a half mile above the mouth of Argyle Canyon, one of the largest and broadest drainages that feed into Nine Mile Canyon. It features a permanent flowing creek that was diverted for irrigation. It is ideal grazing country and it appears to have drawn families from the earliest days of settlement.

Dillman states the ranch was co-owned by J. K. W. Bracken and Harry Sherman of Salt Lake, whereas William Miller states Edwin Lee moved to the canyon in the early 1890s from Utah County and that his partner was Joseph Bracken, a wealthy doctor from Price.[125] This is probably the "Bracken Lee" ranch referred to in newspaper accounts of Butch Cassidy's famous holdup of the Castle Gate mine (see chapter 6). This location offered a hotel, and was a stagecoach stop and the Harper Post Office in the early days, and where Effie Lee became renowned as "a most charming hostess."[126]

Edwin Lee grew up in Utah County with seven brothers and sisters, and parents who had immigrated to Utah from England.[127] One of his brothers was Arthur J. Lee,[128] whose son (Edwin's nephew) would later become Utah governor J. Bracken Lee.[129] Edwin married Effie Box, also from Utah County, in about 1890, and it is assumed Edwin would not have been in Nine Mile Canyon before then. How and why Edwin arrived in Nine Mile Canyon is not known, but the family was in the canyon well before 1900.

The Edwin Lee family must have been quite well-to-do, at least enough so that they had two full-time ranch hands living with them, Frank Taylor and Neal Hanks, and a maid, a Danish girl named Annie Larson. Some of their children went on to college, which was quite rare for children in Nine Mile Canyon in that day. None of their eight children married into the Nine Mile families with whom they were socially intertwined. Edwin also bought out two ranches in lower Nine Mile, one belonging to the Desborough family and the other a Babcock homestead.[130] Dillman states Edwin sold out in 1919 to the Murray Sheep Company.[131] Edwin died in Utah County in 1949 at age eighty-six,[132] while Effie died in 1956 in Carbon County at age eighty-three.[133]

Down canyon to the east another few miles was a store operated by Frank Alger, one of the most beloved characters in the canyon's brief history. According to one account, Frank Alger arrived in 1893 or 1894 and remained there forty-five years.[134] By another account, he "began to work his property" in 1895.[135] Frank Alger's place was expanded over the years, and Frank eventually had a blacksmith shop, a large cellar, a saddle shop, and a dry goods store that catered to the canyon residents and passing freighters. He sold grain to the passing teamsters, he planted a sixty-five-tree orchard, and he constructed bins for storing apples, pears, and plums, although he never charged travelers for the apples. According to Norma Dalton's recollections of her uncle's place,

> That store room carried food and household articles, especially nice, good, inexpensive yard goods, cloth for women to sew. He then made a shed the full length of the first rooms and filled it with straw. Ice was cut from the creek all winter and stored in the straw. Ice was used for refrigeration to keep meat and milk cool and for making ice cream in July.[136]

Among the goods he sold were kerosene, canned foods, spare parts used to repair farm equipment, freshly butchered pigs, fresh produce, eggs, and jelly beans. Beef was seldom eaten, as "the cattle were raised to sell to pay the mortgage payments and purchasing items for the store."[137]

Mildred Dillman states that after Preston Nutter closed down Brock's Place in 1902, the social center of the canyon shifted to the Frank Alger place where there was a post office and hotel.[138] Norma Dalton, Frank's niece and a childhood resident there, says this simply wasn't true.

The hotel was on the Ed Lee place. By the time Uncle Frank had buildings enough to house sleeping guests, he did accommodate as many as possible when needed. He also drove the stage at times and helped wherever he was needed. His ice room was soon converted into a single very long room which offered dining and sleeping space. However, it was never referred to as a hotel.[139]

As the only dry goods store in the canyon at the time, the Frank Alger place was most certainly a gathering place for canyon residents. But Dalton is probably correct that the social center of the canyon was actually the Edwin Lee ranch farther to the west. The post office had been moved there prior to 1900 (see chapter 5), and it had become a regular stage stop by the time Frank Alger was getting his place started.

Frank Alger never married or had children of his own, but he was a family man. When his sister Clarissa Alger Houskeeper was killed in 1925 in a buggy accident, Frank and his sister Luna Alger Smith helped raise Clara's children and provided for their education. Thorald Rich and his wife, Lucille, and Al Hancock and his wife, Janie, who was Lucille's sister, also raised their families at the Frank Alger place. Frank helped them with their own ranches nearby.

Frank Alger died in his sleep in 1938, and Thorald Rich and Al Hancock inherited the Frank Alger place upon his death. A few fruit trees are all that remain of Frank's establishment.

As discussed in chapter 5, the freighters sometimes sought strong drink to numb the loneliness of the road. And when Brock's Place was closed, John Eagan built a saloon to cater to those needs. Eagan, a bachelor during most of his tenure in the canyon, owned the ranch in between Brock's Place and the Frank Alger ranch. We know he was present in the canyon as early as 1889 when he was a witness in the murder trial of William

Frank Alger was a life-long bachelor and one of the most iconic pioneers in the history of Nine Mile Canyon. Photo courtesy of Norma Dalton.

Lucille Houskeeper in front of Frank Alger's general merchandise store. Photo courtesy of Norma Dalton.

Brock (see chapter 5). But he is not listed on the 1900 Census as a canyon resident, although he most certainly was there at the time. In about 1902, he began construction on his own roadhouse to cater to the needs of the freighters (remnants of the stone structure are still visible next to the road). According to Dillman, it was a hotel that was never finished,[140] although canyon residents all knew it was a functioning saloon.

According to Norma Dalton, the Eagan family hired Dennis Winn and his son Jack, who were early homesteaders in the Harmon Canyon area, to construct the building. Eagan's place was originally a three-room structure with a saloon, a blacksmith shop, and bunkhouse. The Eagan family also constructed a fine house at the site,[141] and the watering hole became a stage stop for a time.[142]

We do not know much about John Eagan or how he came to be in Nine Mile Canyon at such an early date. He was probably John H. Eagan, born in 1859 in Indiana to Dennis and Maza Eagan. In 1880, the twenty-two-year-old John was still living in Indiana with his parents and ten siblings.[143] His older brother, Gilbert, moved on to Iowa, but there is no record that John went with him. John probably arrived in Nine Mile Canyon shortly after the road was opened in 1886. He seems to have been a bachelor for much of the time, but around 1900 he married a Kansas-born woman named Catherine, and their first child, John, was born in 1903. Another son was born in 1906 and a daughter was born the following year.

John must have died shortly thereafter, at about age fifty, inasmuch as Catherine is listed as a widow and head of household in the 1910 Census. Living with her at the Nine Mile ranch in 1910 were her three young children, her brother-in-law, Gilbert Eagan, and a boarder named Charles Brown.[144] Indiana death records indicate John H. Eagan died on October 6, 1909, in New Garden, Indiana,[145] but if this is the same John Eagan then his family was living more than a thousand miles away in Nine Mile Canyon at that time.

Dalton indicates the Eagan house later burned to the ground in the 1920s and the Eagan family sold the ranch to Frank "Mental" Taylor, one of four partners with mining and ranching interests in the canyon. Taylor constructed a large house on the property. Sometime between 1936 and 1939, the ranch was sold to the Stratman family, who stayed at the ranch until about 1942 when their house also burned to the ground. The ranch

Catherine Eagan and Fern Shaw in front of the Eagan ranch house. Photo courtesy of Norma Dalton.

was then sold to Cecil Rouse. Norma Dalton's father, Thorald "Cotton" Rich, helped Rouse construct the new house, and in about 1946 Rich bought out Rouse and began adding rooms onto the cabin. The Rich family lived at the ranch until 1956. The house alongside the road today is the same one originally constructed in about 1942 by Cecil Rouse and then modified in 1946 by Cotton Rich.

There is no census data to support the idea that Catherine Eagan and her children remained in Nine Mile Canyon through the 1920s. By 1930, her sons, John L. and Eugene, were both living with the Patrick Creaham family in San Francisco.[146] There are no records as to what became of Catherine and her daughter, Mazie, after 1910.

Divorce, Death, and Drama

Not everything in Nine Mile Canyon was sunshine and roses. Whenever humans coalesce into groups there are bound to be incidents of sadness and tragedy—all part of the tapestry of the human experience. And Nine Mile Canyon was no different. Yes, the families living here were bonded, often by blood but certainly by sweat. Women died in childbirth, residents young and old alike were struck down by killer "black" flus. People died in horseback-riding accidents and horse-and-buggy accidents and incidents that might not have been accidents at all.

Like when Bill Lines wife was shot to death. On June 18, 1929, the *Salt Lake Telegram* reported Amy Catherine Lines had died when a rifle held by her husband accidentally discharged, the bullet passing under her right arm and through her torso. She died before a physician could be summoned.[147] Bill was never charged in the death, but whispers that Bill had committed a black deed spread throughout the canyon, and old-timers to this day are skeptical of the official finding that the death was accidental.

The Lines family, which included four small children, was living in a cabin in Whitmore Park at the time. At some point in the 1920s or 1930s, Bill Lines had snatched the property from the Whitmore family (see chapter 5) in a tax sale. The Whitmore family later reacquired the property.

Additional canyon drama was provided courtesy of two best friends, Henry "Hank" Stewart and Neal Hanks, both among the earliest settlers of Argyle Canyon. Stewart may well have been one of the first "river rats" in the area. In 1906, Hank was an oarsman in a disastrous attempt to float Desolation Canyon as part of an expedition to see if Gilsonite could be floated to Green River. By 1913 he was again at the oars, this time as part of an expedition to determine if a railroad could be built through the canyon.[148] From 1911 to 1920, he operated a ferry on the Green River at Tia Juana Bottom, where he had an altercation with a Ute rebel named Red Moon. According to James Aton's history of the Green River, Red Moon shot at the ground around Hank's feet, and "the ferryman grabbed the Indian, threw him to the ground, held a pistol to his head, and threatened to kill him. Red Moon begged for his life, and the Anglo let him go."[149]

John Henry "Hank" Stewart was born in Mona, Utah, in 1868. His father, Simeon (or Simion), was a dentist for the nearby Eureka mines. Hank and his brother George lived for a time in the Puget Sound area of Washington, and both later attended All Hallows College in Salt Lake City. According to his son Arden, all Hank ever wanted to be was a cowboy. As a youth he had devoured dime-store westerns and yearned to be part of the legendary life. In 1897, the brothers came to Castle Valley, where Hank became acquainted with Butch Cassidy and Elza Lay (Hank's horse was allegedly "borrowed" by the Wild Bunch during one getaway).[150]

On October 16, 1898, Hank married Minerva Van Wagoner, and the couple started a ranch in Argyle Canyon. Minerva was a sister to Susan Van Wagoner, the wife of James Hamilton, who had the ranch at the mouth of Minnie Maud Canyon (see above).[151]

Hank worked for various cattlemen in the area, including Preston Nutter, and also rounded up wild mustangs and mavericks. In 1904, he partnered with Frank Fiske in a large cattle operation with several hundred head that wintered near Wellington and summered in Nine Mile Canyon. In 1905, he feuded with Nutter over water rights on Nine Mile Creek. And sometime after 1910 he divorced Minerva. According to Aton, "She got the ranch in Nine Mile and custody of the children; Stewart got the freedom to pursue mining and ferry ventures with his brother George."[152]

She also got Hank's best friend. Just down the road was a young cowboy named Neal Hanks, who was living with and working for Edwin Lee. Neal was probably a frequent guest at the Stewart ranch over the years. By 1910, Hank and Minerva had three children: Eva, Rex, and Van. After

Hank and Minerva divorced, Minerva married Neal Hanks, and together they had a daughter, Donna.[153]

Dillman called Neal Hanks the most "beloved" of the Nine Mile cowmen. "He worked for almost every cattle man in the canyon, becoming the foreman of Nutter's for many years, but finally, a short time before his death, owned and operated his own cattle outfit."[154] Neal and Minerva had a place just east of Balanced Rock (Pig Rock), and later they proved up on a homestead claim at the mouth of Cottonwood Canyon. The couple lived in the canyon until 1945, when they sold out and moved to Price.[155] It is not known for sure who Neal Hanks was, but he could be the Kneel Hanks who was born in Kane County in 1879.[156]

Hank and Neal apparently remained close friends even after Neal married Minerva. Hank and Neal were oarsmen together on the 1913 exploration of the Green River to determine its suitability for a railroad. Dillman also mentions that Hank Stewart and Neal Hanks had "homesteaded" a ranch in the Cottonwood Canyon area, which became known as the Rabbit Ranch.[157] Neal died in 1946 and Minerva died in 1951; both are buried in Price.[158]

Hank Stewart would go on to leave his name throughout the history of upper Desolation Canyon as a river runner, ferryman, miner, and dreamer. In 1919, Hank, then fifty-one, met and married Elsie Wardle, who was only fifteen years old at the time. In 1920 (or 1921), the newlyweds started a new ferry operation at Sand Wash (the Stewart cabins are still there today). The ferry was a thriving business operation, but Hank grew weary of it and sold out in 1925, moving on to Willow Creek where he bought out Elsie's father.[159] Hank drowned in 1937 when a ferry loaded with farm equipment flipped while he was trying to cross the Green River.

Homesteaders and Squatters

William Miller believes that difficult farming conditions resulted in a highly mobile population where families did not put down lasting roots. He notes that less than one-third of the families listed in the 1900 federal census appeared again in the 1910 census. He argues that because most of the settlers were there temporarily, the majority of the homestead claims

Old structures at the site of the Neal and Minerva Hanks homestead at the mouth of Cottonwood Canyon. Photo by Jerry D. Spangler.

Hank Stewart's cabin at Sand Wash where he brought his fifteen-year-old bride to live. Photo by Jerry D. Spangler.

were never completed and patented. "In fact, most of the settlers never even applied for a homestead claim."[160]

Our review of the census data revealed that 81 percent of the individuals listed on the 1910 Census were not living in the canyon during the 1900 Census. And by 1920, roughly 90 percent of the individuals living there had not been present in either the 1900 or 1910 censuses. In other words, the vast majority of canyon residents stayed less than a decade before moving on to better opportunities. Only a few early residents ever returned once they left.

Miller's review of Homestead and Desert Land Entry filings is insightful. He notes there are several possibilities for this lack of formal paperwork to obtain title to the lands. First, it might have resulted from settlers being unaware of the rules or unable to travel to the land office to file a claim. However, the 1900 census reported more than 95 percent of the adults could read. The nearest newspaper, the Eastern Utah Telegraph, carried advertisements of people who offered to go to the land office and fill out a claim so that the settlers would not need to make this trip. "These advertisements would have been common knowledge for the settlers. It is unlikely that lack of awareness or travel difficulties were the cause."[161]

A second reason, Miller believes, is that the settlers felt that they did not need to file. In the 1900 census, nineteen of the twenty-eight heads of household reported that they owned their homes.[162] However, the General Land Office records show that only five Homestead or Desert Land entries had been filed before 1900.

> The third and most likely reason for the lack of homestead claims is the majority of the settlers realized that they were only going to be there temporarily and it was not worth the risk of giving up their one chance of getting land. They could farm the land tax-free and when they were ready to move on to a new community they could sell their squatter's rights. For over twenty years this land was being settled, bought, sold, and rented without obtaining legal ownership. For whatever reason, the settlers in Nine-Mile did little to gain ownership of the land they were farming, which added to the low rate of permanence.[163]

Miller asserts that only one land claim was ever patented by 1900, but this is not accurate. James Hamilton certainly proved up on his claim to 151 acres at the mouth of Minnie Maud Canyon on September 7, 1900.[164] But the extended Whitmore family (see chapter 5) was also actively securing title to roughly 600 acres in the Whitmore Park area—the heart of their massive summer range. In 1897, Mary Whitmore proved up on 80 acres,[165] Samuel Whitmore proved up on 120 acres,[166] and Elizabeth C. Whitmore provided up on 80 acres.[167] Elizabeth L. G. Whitmore purchased another

120 acres from the government in 1898 in a cash sale.[168] With the exception of the cash purchase, these claims were all filed under the Desert Land Act, and all were family members acting on behalf of George and James M. Whitmore, who had the largest cattle operation in the region.

George Whitmore later purchased from the federal government another 80 acres in lower Whitmore Park in 1900,[169] and his brother James M. Whitmore purchased another 160 acres in the same area, also in 1900 (he also received a patent for 160 acres on the site of the family's Sunnyside ranch at this time).[170]

Beginning in 1908, there was a flurry of claims filed under the enlarged Homestead Act. Some were made by long-time canyon residents, like Lon Alger and Theodore Houskeeper and Neal Hanks, seeking legal title to lands they had been farming for a decade or more. Other claims were filed by the children of the original settlers, like Harrison Russell and Myron Russell. Yet others were filed by "newcomers" like Lucretia Miles and Alva Lee and Charles C. Rich. For all intents and purposes, the days of squatting on "free" land were over by 1910.

Family Farms

By and large, the early residents of Nine Mile Canyon were family farmers—and some of the families were quite large with the age range of children running from toddlers to young adults. In 1900, there were nineteen families living in Nine Mile Canyon that accounted for 116 of the 122 canyon residents living there. Ten years later, there were twenty-four families that accounted for 111 of the 130 people living there at the time. Most of the others who were present in 1910 were employees of Preston Nutter's cattle operation, although there was a smattering of miners, trappers, hired cowboys, and domestic help. Nine Mile Canyon was, for the most part, all about small family farms and ranches.[171]

Of course, any conclusions are contingent on the accuracy of the census itself, and there is good reason to believe some canyon residents never bothered with the census. John Eagan was one of the earliest canyon residents, and he lived there for at least two decades, but his name appears nowhere on the census records. Some residents also maintained part-time households elsewhere and may have been absent during the Nine Mile

census but otherwise lived in the canyon most of the time. In some cases, canyon residents were counted twice, once for Nine Mile Canyon and once for their house in Price or Sunnyside or elsewhere. The census figures we use here—122 people in 1900, 130 in 1910, 80 in 1920, and 65 in 1930—should be considered minimum numbers.

Based on census data, we concluded roughly half of the Nine Mile population was under the age of eighteen, which would place the adult population at any one time at thirty to sixty individuals. A handful of adults were bachelor men trying to establish a ranch, but the vast majority of households were comprised of couples with children and, in some instances, extended family. Based on this demographic trend, there might have been twenty to thirty ranches during the canyon's population zenith in the 1900s and 1910s, and ten to twelve ranches in the 1930s during the canyon's population decline.

The destruction of the 1890 Census is unfortunate, but some estimates can be offered. According to a July 1895 Carbon County school census, there were thirty-five children attending school in Nine Mile Canyon.[172] Most children of that day attended school through the eighth grade, or about age fourteen, although some continued their education rather than work on the family farm. If the thirty-five students represents two-thirds of the minors under age eighteen, and the ratio of half-adults-to-half-children was valid in the 1890s as it was in later decades, we can estimate the population of Nine Mile Canyon in the 1890s at about one hundred people. And if the patterns hold true, roughly eighty to ninety of them would have moved on to greener pastures by the time of the 1900 census.

The fluidity of the population here was such that many families could have come and gone and never been counted in any census, leaving little, if any, evidence of their passing. For example, Dillman mentions that a man named Desbrough and his wife had a small homestead,[173] presumably at or near the mouth of the canyon that carries that family name today. The Desbrough name does not appear in the database of Mormon pioneers of that era, and census records do not list a Desbrough family living anywhere in Utah in the late 1800s or early 1900s. Dillman indicates they did not stay long and sold out to Edwin Lee, who sold to William Miles, who sold to Al Pace, and that it eventually ended up in the hands of Preston Nutter.[174]

Another family that came and went with scarcely a trace was that of John H. Olsen, his wife, Olive, and their five children. They warrant mention here because a major southern tributary to Nine Mile Canyon is named Olsen Canyon, and it is assumed they lived near that location about a half-mile east of the Nutter Ranch. They were present during the 1900 census and it is assumed they arrived sometime before that.[175]

John H. was born in either Norway or Sweden (it is listed differently on different census records) and he could be the John Hendrick "Henry" Olsen who immigrated to Utah in the Canute Peterson Company of Mormon pioneers in 1856.[176] The Olsen family settled in Sanpete County and remained there through at least 1880. By 1900, they were in Nine Mile Canyon, and a decade later they had settled in Idaho. Given the proximity of Olsen Canyon to the Nutter Ranch, they might have been bought out by Nutter (or been pushed out). There is no record the children intermarried with the other families of the early Nine Mile settlers.

Greener Pastures

As we discussed in chapter 8, the opening of the Ute Indian reservation in the Uinta Basin to white homesteaders in 1906 created new opportunities for families to acquire their own farmlands. And there was an exodus of Nine Mile Canyon families to the more fertile Uinta Basin lands at that time. But as these families packed up and left Nine Mile Canyon, there were other families waiting in the wings to take over their Nine Mile ranches. These new arrivals were not bonded by blood to those already in the canyon, but many would intermarry with children of the first families, continuing the genealogy of place that had begun two or three decades before.

One of these new arrivals was Charles Coulson Rich III, who bought a portion of the Don Johnston ranch (it is known today as the Upper Rich Ranch). According to Norma Dalton, Charles (her grandfather) bought the property from Don and Sam Johnston in 1923. Norma's father, Thorald "Cotton" Rich, was nine years old when the family moved to Nine Mile Canyon from the Uinta Basin, and he was raised at the ranch and also worked as a gardener for the Nutter Ranch as a child. The Rich family later sold that particular ranch to Tom Christensen in the mid-twentieth century.[177]

The Rich family is especially prominent in Mormon history. Charles Colson Rich I served as a bodyguard to church leaders and as an apostle, and he was eventually sent to establish Mormon settlements in Sacramento. He also settled the Centerville and Bear Lake areas. Rich County in northeastern Utah is named after him.

According to the Rich family history, Charles Coulson Rich III "traded" an eighty-acre homestead in Roosevelt for an eighty-acre one in Nine Mile Canyon. A later survey indicated their Nine Mile parcel was actually located up on the canyon slopes and ledges, and Charles was forced to apply for a second eighty-acre allotment to homestead the canyon bottom where his fields were located. His mother, Jane, homesteaded another eighty acres to the east to enlarge the family holdings.[178]

Charles Rich III, who hailed from the Uinta Basin, may have purchased the ranch, but he is not listed on any of the census records for the canyon. According to 1930 Census records, his son Jeremiah (Jerry) Rich was living there with his wife, Wanda, and their three young sons, along with Thorald, his sixteen-year-old brother. Also in the canyon were another brother, Arbun Rich, and his wife, Thelma.[179] Their father, Charles, was living in Sunnyside at the time,[180] but by 1939 Charles had moved back to Vernal. Jeremiah eventually moved on to Price and Sunnyside; Arbun

Old cabin at the mouth of Desbrough Canyon. Photo by Jerry D. Spangler.

moved back to the Uinta Basin. In 1933, Thorald "Cotton" Rich married Lucille Houskeeper, daughter of Theodore B. and Clara Houskeeper; Norma Dalton is their daughter.

At the time of Thorald's marriage to Lucille, he was a nineteen-year-old range cowboy for Preston Nutter. He and Lucille honeymooned at Sand Wash on the Green River where Thorald went to work for Ray Thompson as a ferry operator, while Lucille cooked for the ferry operation. They eventually returned to Nine Mile where Thorald went to work for his bachelor uncle, Frank Alger, as did Al Hancock, a Nutter cowboy who had married Lucille's sister, Janie Houskeeper. When Frank Alger died in 1938, Thorald and Al inherited the Alger ranch, although it was heavily mortgaged.

Alvis "Al" Hancock, who was noted for wearing a sidearm, had an interesting story to tell in his own right. Turns out he had killed a man in Texas during a barroom brawl and fled to Utah where he found safe haven working for Preston Nutter's outfit, leaving behind a wife and four children. While in Nine Mile Canyon, he met and fell in love with Janie Houskeeper, and it was only then he decided to return to Texas to face the consequences.

He served a spell in prison for the killing, divorced his wife, made amends with his four children, and finally returned to Nine Mile Canyon after seven long years in Texas. Janie had waited for him patiently, and

they were married immediately. They had two children, a girl, Clara, and a boy, Alvis, who died of stomach cancer at only six months old. Al died just three years after he was reunited with Janie.[181]

For years, Thorald supported his own family and that of his sister-in-law. Thorald lived on the ranch from 1923 until 1956 when the family finally sold out.[182] Thorald later moved to lower Nine Mile Canyon, where he managed ranch holdings for the Flying Diamond Corporation through 1976. A nephew continued to manage the properties through 1979, which marked the end of the Rich family's fifty-six-year tenure in Nine Mile Canyon.

The Barney family also represents a second generation to seek its fortune in Nine Mile Canyon. Delbert Barney arrived sometime before 1920 with his wife, Mary Elizabeth Anderson, and their seven children, including seventeen-year-old twin sons Doyle and Dayle, and twin daughters Reva and Reta.[183] By 1930 only Doyle was listed on the census, along with his wife, Dolly Russell, and a young daughter.

According to Barney family history, the Barneys were among the earliest to arrive in Nine Mile Canyon, and in some respects they never left.

Descendants of Virgil and Doyle Barney still own property in the canyon. Delbert, who had a family farm in Ferron, was on occasion a ranch hand for Preston Nutter, and at other times he hauled coal. The Barney family sold their farm in Emery County, and in about 1918 they moved to Nine Mile Canyon where they took up quarters at the old Eagan ranch. The family moved frequently, first to the mouth of Argyle Canyon and then near the mouth of Minnie Maud Canyon; each move was made so the children could be close to a school. At one point they even lived in tents next to a school.[184]

Doyle, his older brother, Virgil, and a younger brother Oral lived in the canyon on and off for three decades. Doyle married Dolly Russell, the daughter of Harrison Russell and granddaughter of Andrew Jackson and Julia Mott Russell—one of the earliest blood lines to settle in the canyon. Virgil married Crystal Thompson, the daughter of Alma Z. and Martha Grames Thompson, who were also among the earliest arrivals.[185]

Apparitions and Isolation

Very little is known of the settlement of Nine Mile Canyon below the point where the road turns north to go up Gate Canyon. Unlike the canyon corridor above, where farmers and freighters interacted daily and farmers could sell their produce, there was simply no freight traffic below the mouth of Gate Canyon. Those who settled here would have been on the outer fringes of Nine Mile social life, and there would have been few opportunities to capitalize on commerce with the freighters. The ranches in this area were, for the most part, widely spaced and situated near the mouths of prominent side canyons such as Dry Canyon, Cottonwood Canyon, Desbrough Canyon, Franks Canyon, and Maxies Canyon. Preston Nutter owned the entire upper area between the mouth of Currant Canyon and the mouth of Prickly Pear Canyon—a distance of about eight miles—and any family living below his holdings would have routinely crossed the Nutter Ranch on their way to Price or the Uinta Basin. Because of its social and economic isolation, only a few ranches were ever established here.

One ranch was located at the mouth of Daddy Canyon about eight miles from the Nutter Ranch headquarters. Mildred Dillman indicates this ranch was a homestead belonging to Myron Russell,[186] whereas Norma Dalton indicates it belonged to his brother, Harrison Russell.[187] A major canyon entering from the south is called Dry Canyon, and another on the north is called Daddy Canyon, which is named after Andrew Jackson "Daddy" Russell, the father of Myron and Harrison (see above). Dillman states Myron Russell later sold it to a mining company, which in turn sold it to Oliver Rasmussen who lived there until his death.[188]

Norma Dalton relates a story told by her father that Harrison Russell was approached by two men who claimed to be miners. They told him they wanted to buy that particular homestead, but Harrison said it wasn't for sale. The miners told him it was for sale and just how much they would give for it. Harrison could accept their terms or he could die. He sold. Norma's father believed the miners were a front for cattle baron Preston Nutter who wanted the entire lower canyon.[189] The Russell homestead was the neighboring private parcel to the east.

The large rock shelter at this location is noted for its rich ancient Indian deposits and painting of a large red elk. It is still called Rasmussen Cave today, and it has been the focus of archaeological investigations since at least 1931.[190]

The Rabbit Ranch was located another couple of miles to the east of Daddy Canyon in the Cottonwood Canyon area. Dillman indicated it was farmed by a succession of settlers, including Joe Thompson, Hank Stewart, and Neal Hanks. She also mentions that the Nephi Smithson family once lived there, and that Mrs. Smithson planted rare roses, grapes, and fruit trees.[191] Neal Hanks was the first to actually prove up on the homestead claim here. Their farm was apparently bought and sold several times, eventually ending up in the hands of the Miles family (see below) and later the Thorald Rich family. Thorald is credited with rerouting the stream channel from the north to the south side of the canyon at this point.[192]

Somewhere in the Desbrough Canyon or Franks Canyon area was the Clark Elmer ranch, located between Devils Canyon and Desbrough Canyon. According to Dillman, "it was the home of the outlaws, and almost every cowhand had a weird tale about the 'stills' that operated underground. If one believed all that was told, ghosts could be seen walking every night up the road, driving the women crazy, whose tunnels full of rustled cattle, butchered and taken to market at Sunnyside,

Rasmussen Cave at the site of the Russell homestead at Daddy Canyon has been the focus of archaeological investigations since 1931. Photo by Ray Boren.

covered the ranch, wells were filled with dead men and built over to conceal their secrets."[193]

Clark A. Elmer was a young man when he came to Nine Mile Canyon, probably in the late 1890s. He married Harriett Foster in 1898 in Price, and by the time of the 1900 Census the couple was living in Nine Mile Canyon with two toddlers.[194] Clark and Harriett soon moved on to settle in the Uinta Basin. Little is known of where Clark and the English-born Harriett came from before they landed in lower Nine Mile Canyon. Interestingly, the 1900 Census records list the Clark Elmer family of four living in Nine Mile Canyon, but it also lists Harriett and the same two children, Ethel and Alva, living in Pleasant Grove with the David Baxter family.[195]

Entering the scene about that time was William A. Miles, who bought from unspecified sellers the ranch near the mouth of Maxies Canyon in 1907. He must have had financial means as he bought out every ranch between Cottonwood Canyon on the west and Bull Canyon on the east, which included about ten miles of canyon bottom. Dillman indicates he bought out Clark Elmer, the Desbroughs, Edwin Lee, the Babcocks, and the "Taylor Place,"[196] which made him one of the largest landowners in Nine Mile Canyon, rivaling even Preston Nutter. As local legend has it, William Miles had seven daughters, and along with his wife, Lucretia, they constituted the "Nine Miles," from which the canyon got its name (see chapter 1).

Although the canyon was most certainly not named after the Miles family, one part of the legend is true: William and Lucretia had seven daughters, although the older two daughters might never have lived in Nine Mile Canyon. William A. Miles was born and raised in Missouri, but it is unknown how he came to be living in Salt Lake City in 1900 with Lucretia and their seven daughters.[197] Lucretia Wightman was a native Utahn, having been born and raised in the Payson area. She was single in 1880, with her occupation listed as music teacher.[198]

William and Lucretia would have been about forty-seven years old when they arrived in Nine Mile Canyon; their oldest daughters, Donna and Martha, would have been twenty-four and twenty-two years old, respectively, and both were married and living elsewhere by 1910. The Miles family apparently did not stay all that long. By 1920, the family had moved on to the Uinta Basin, where William died in 1923.[199]

According to Dillman, the Miles ranch became "home" to all of the cowboys in the canyon. "Mrs. Miles proved Nine Mile could produce bounteous fruits and vegetables. Mr. Miles brought with him several pure blooded animals."[200] Their daughter, Mildred Miles Dillman, wrote the first history of Nine Mile Canyon.

Dillman states the Miles family sold out to John A. Pace, but exactly when this occurred is not known. The Miles family was gone from the canyon by 1920, but John Pace is not listed on the census records until 1930. John Albert Pace was from a large family living in the Price area. He married Ada Cottam sometime after 1900, probably around 1904, and in 1910 they were living in Price with their three small children. They were still in Price in 1920 and the clan had grown to seven children.[201] The 1930 Census records indicate John was living alone in lower Nine Mile Canyon and at the same time in Price with Ada and their children.[202] There is no indication Ada and the children ever lived in Nine Mile Canyon.

Local legend has it that Pace was a serious taskmaster, even constructing a high perch with a rocking chair from which he could order around his hired hands.[203] Norma Dalton contends the perch was constructed by Pace's ranch hand, Dave Nordell, as a prop for "many amusing photographs," for which Nordell was famous. In 1931, the Pace Ranch became the base camp for the Claflin Emerson Expedition from Harvard University. This archaeological expedition was one of the most famous in

View of the William Miles–
Albert Pace Ranch. Photo by
Jerry D. Spangler.

Utah archaeological history.[204] Local legend also has it that Pace, despondent due to the combined effects of the Great Depression and his social isolation, committed suicide at the ranch during one particularly brutal winter, by some accounts slitting his own throat. Death records indicate he died in 1937 and is buried in Price.[205]

Al's son, Carlyle Pace, then took over the ranch and hired a foreman named Dave Nordell, a hard-drinking cowboy and one of the most colorful individuals in the history of the canyon. He was a notorious looter of ancient Indian sites, and he had an endless appetite for self-promotion. Among many legendary fetes attributed to him, which may or may not be true, was an incident where he was reputed to have lassoed and ridden a mountain lion,[206] although those familiar with the story say the photo was faked. Nordell left the canyon in 1958.

The Pace Ranch was later sold to the Flying Diamond Corporation, which hired Thorald Rich and his son, Bus Rich, to manage their holdings. Thorald and Lucille constructed a new home at the mouth of South Maxies Canyon that had running water and flush toilets—a rare treat for the hardened Nine Mile pioneers. Members of the Rich family managed the ranch through at least 1979.[207] It is now owned by the Russell Evans family.

The Northern Fringe

The Nine Mile Road today begins in Wellington where it trends north toward the base of the Book Cliffs. But in 1887 (or thereabouts) it originated at the northeast edge of Price and angled northeast toward Soldier Canyon across the bench areas north of Wellington. The ascent through the Book Cliffs through Soldier Canyon provided access into Whitmore Park and the upper reaches of Nine Mile Canyon. The climb to the summit was short, steep, and susceptible to winter snow drifts, and it was perhaps the most difficult stretch of the Nine Mile Road to maintain. The road then trended gradually to the east from the headwaters of Nine Mile Creek toward its confluence with its main tributary, Minnie Maud Creek.

Famous perch on the Pace Ranch. Some accounts have it that Pace supervised his workers from this perch, others that it was a prop for staged photographs by ranch hand Dave Nordell. Photo courtesy of Norma Dalton.

Foundation of an old stone cabin near the mouth of Bull Canyon. No one knows who built it or when. Photo by Jerry D. Spangler.

The Soldier Canyon area was the location of a military camp in 1887 where soldiers from Fort Duchesne lived while working to improve the road to make it passable to the heavy freight wagons. The canyon derives its name from the soldiers who camped there.

This area is on the extreme northern fringe of Nine Mile Canyon, and purists might say it was not really part of the canyon itself. But those who put down roots here were indelibly part of the economic fabric of Nine Mile Canyon, and all families living along the Nine Mile Canyon Road northeast of Price considered themselves part of the canyon. Their ranches were stagecoach stops, they marketed their farm products to passing freighters, and they were counted in the census records as part of Nine Mile Canyon.

The Edwards family had become established in the Wellington area by about 1900, when Caleb Elisha Edwards worked at the recently established Soldier Canyon coal mine caring for blind horses used in the underground mining operation. He was also a renowned violinist who was in demand to perform at community events throughout the region. According to the family history, Caleb was just starting out for a performance in Myton in 1903 when he stopped at a fledgling ranch at the mouth of Soldier Canyon.[208] The homesteader confided that his wife was miserable with the pioneering life, and within moments the two had struck a bargain: Caleb would give the homesteader his wagon and team, and Caleb got a rock house and irrigated fields.

Caleb moved to the ranch with his wife, Margaret Maria Sorenson, and their children, among them Caleb Jr. and his wife, Elvina (or Eliva), and their three small children. This ranch is not mentioned by Dillman and she might not have considered it part of Nine Mile Canyon, although the Edwards family was part of the Harper Precinct for census purposes. By 1910, only the younger Caleb and his family were listed on the census for the area, although other family members were probably living there at the time.[209]

The Edwards family developed the ranch into a way station for traveling freighters and homesteaders on their way to the Uinta Basin. They sold hay and grain to the teamsters, as well as five-gallon cans of honey harvested from their own hives on the ranch.[210]

The elder Caleb was devoutly religious, but he also hated riding in cars. This required him to walk several miles to attend church in Wellington. In 1926, he was walking home from church in the dark when he was hit by a car and dragged a considerable distance. He died a short time later.[211] Caleb Jr. and Elvina remained in the Soldier Canyon and Wellington area for the next thirty years and raised six children there.[212] Their son Archie later took over the family ranch.

Norma Dalton recalls the "Lee family" also had a cabin in Soldier Creek Canyon, but it was just that, a cabin with no associated farm. "I remember my dad picking up Mrs. Lee when she climbed off the mountain to the road, and taking her to Price. She would be dressed to go to 'town,' and knew when the mail truck would be coming by. Sometimes she caught a ride home with us and was dropped off near the little canyon called Cottonwood, just past Pine Canyon."[213]

This could be the Alva Lee family listed on the 1920 Census for the Harper Precinct. Alva and Lillie Lee had four sons, as well as a young girl named Iola Russell, living with them at the time. The genealogy of the Lee family is somewhat confusing. In 1910, Alva was single and living in the Uinta Basin at the Gilsonite fields at Dragon Junction. By 1920, he was married to Lillie Russell and had four or five children, the oldest being eighteen years old. Alva died in 1925, and the following year Lillie remarried George Westwood and moved to Columbia, a small coal-mining town near Sunnyside.[214] Family records indicate Lillie (or Lillia) was the daughter of Andrew Jackson Russell and Julia Mott, a long-time Nine Mile Canyon family discussed above,[215] but her name is not listed on the census records for the Russell family in Nine Mile Canyon.

End of an Era

The skeletons of history outlined above represent only a small portion of the people who lived in Nine Mile Canyon. Most of the stories of the first settlers are now forgotten, or at best they are lost among family treasures awaiting a descendant with interest enough to trace the family history back to Nine Mile Canyon. There are families like Ira and Elizabeth Lyman, who with their five children arrived before 1900, when Ira was

Old corral on the Don Johnston Ranch. Photo by Ray Boren.

"government station keeper," perhaps the civilian hired to operate and maintain the Nine Mile telegraph stations. By 1910, the family had moved on to the Uinta Basin.

And there is the Joseph B. and LaBertha Brundage family, who arrived in Nine Mile Canyon in the 1890s with six children ranging in age from eight to twenty-one. They stayed through at least 1910 and their children intermarried with other early pioneers here. But their history is now largely unknown even to the most ardent students of the canyon's history.

The database used here offers only the briefest of glimpses into the families who settled this land: who they were, where they came from, and in some instances where they went after leaving. It tells us nothing of the toils of farming in a desert, where flash floods filled the irrigation ditches and covered the fields in rocks.

It only hints at the flu epidemics and small pox outbreaks that took the lives of the young and old, or of the dangers of simple accidents that could turn deadly without quick medical care. Nine Mile Canyon was a community, much of it related through marriage, that cared for its own. But it was an isolated community, nonetheless, one that was vulnerable to the influences of national economies and unpredictable climates and social pressures that lured their young away to a softer life in the cities.

People who lived here were proud cowboys and cowboys' wives, whose children became adults very young, boys by age fourteen when they were old enough to work on the farm, girls by age sixteen when they began to marry off into the life of a rancher's wife. Gardens provided food for the entire year, clothes were made by hand, fuel wood was cut with axes, and cows had to be roped and branded and shipped to market with the hope that cattle prices would be high enough to pay the suffocating mortgages.

With few exceptions, no one got rich living here. Preston Nutter, Edwin Lee, and William Miles might have had big herds, and greater potential for profits, but most of the ranchers were small operators with a few hundred head, at best. Thorald Rich, the largest of the cattle operators in the twilight years from the 1930s to 1950s, ran seven hundred to nine hundred head of cattle—a far cry from the ten thousand or so head attributed to Preston Nutter.

Throughout the early twentieth century, economic depression and drought were the twin devils of anyone trying to make a living here. Quite simply, the farmers and ranchers were cash-strapped and heavily mortgaged, working odd jobs whenever possible to keep the family farm afloat. Very few managed to make it work. Most drifted off to work in the coal mines of Carbon County or to the Uinta Basin where better farms could be had.

The last of the original pioneer families eventually sold out—the Rich family in 1956 and the Houskeeper family in 1963. There are few remaining links to the Old West that once was Nine Mile Canyon. Ben Mead, whose father once leased the Rock House at Harmon Canyon, now has his own place at Cow Canyon. The Barney family retains title to parcels in upper Nine Mile Canyon. And George Fasselin, who was raised on the West Tavaputs Plateau among descendants of the Jim McPherson clan and has spent more than six decades in the region, now lives in Nine Mile Canyon as a caretaker for corporate interests that now own most of the private land there.

There are others still alive who once lived in Nine Mile Canyon in the 1930s and 1940s and even into the 1950s, but there are fewer of them every year. Descendants of those early pioneers—primarily the Houskeepers, the Riches, and the Wimmers—are scrambling to collect their stories of early Nine Mile Canyon before they are lost forever. And through their efforts, perhaps another chapter will be written.

Postscript

By and large, Nine Mile Canyon is a sleepy backwater these days. You might see George and Gloria Fasselin out in the fields cutting and baling hay to feed their cows in the coming winter. There are occasional service trucks with their squawking Jake brakes—a reminder that another boom in natural gas drilling could be just around the corner. And you sometimes can hear the giggles of children—tourists discovering the wondrous array of prehistoric rock art that has made the canyon famous throughout the world.

And if you listen close enough, you can hear the ghosts of generations long gone—witnesses to one of the most colorful, albeit brief, periods in Utah history. As hard as it is to imagine now, Nine Mile Canyon was a noisy, crowded, and sometimes rowdy place with outlaws and miners and freighters and merchants and sodbusters aching for a place to call their own. They were all, in some respects, the last vestiges of the Old West, of a time when land and grass were free for the taking, when the uniform of the day included Colt six-shooters and one or two reliable Winchesters, and folks both good and bad and in between could be left alone to live their lives on their own terms.

The Old West had been dying for years before Shadrach and Alfred Lunt first pushed their herds into Nine Mile Canyon in the summer of 1877. In fact, the Old West had been dying in fits and spurts since the arrival of the transcontinental railroads and telegraphs that had revolutionized the very concept of transportation and communication. The mass production of the internal combustion engine signaled yet a new era of travel—one that could make farm life easier but also one that could whisk the children off to the bright lights and creature comforts of Provo and Salt Lake City and beyond. And it might well have been the final nail in the coffin of what had once been a vibrant community filled with optimism.

In the 1820s, fur trappers flooded into the region in search of beaver pelts they hoped would make them rich. They instead found unbridled freedom to live out their lives unfettered by law or social convention. Within two decades, all the rivers and streams had been trapped out. And the burning of Fort Robidoux in 1845 signaled the end of one era of the Old West. Nine Mile Canyon would have witnessed this death, perhaps from afar. It was probably one of the last places to be explored, where beaver were never that plentiful.

By the late 1870s, Nine Mile Canyon had been rediscovered, both by government surveyors like Almon Harris Thompson and Augustus Ferron and by cattlemen seeking range for their large and growing herds that numbered in the thousands. The high meadows of the West Tavaputs Plateau provided ideal summer forage, the floodplains of Nine Mile Creek and Range Creek were suitable winter ranges. And these newcomers seem to have arrived en masse between 1877 and 1879: a large herd brought by the Argyle brothers, perhaps as many as twenty-five hundred head by the Lunt brothers, several thousand more by the Whitmore brothers, and untold numbers by Lord Elliott and the Range Valley Cattle Company. By some accounts, the Whitmore brothers ran more than ten thousand head of cattle here, as did Preston Nutter, the successor to the Whitmore cattle empire.

Not surprising, that much beef on the hoof brought another element to the area—the cattle rustler. Rustling was rampant in the day, and if historian Charles Kelly is to be believed, even the honest cattle ranchers were not that averse to a little thievery on the side. Rustling was a fact of life in Nine Mile Canyon and elsewhere in Utah. Preston Nutter hired an assassin, Jack Watson, to eliminate the problem, and he was successful to a point. But most folks chalked it up to a cost of doing business.

And if rustling was not bad enough, the large cattle operators were faced with a new problem. Family farmers had begun to arrive with their own small herds in Nine Mile Canyon by 1883, fencing off their claims and limiting the previously unrestricted winter range. These small herds also added to the summer range—accentuating the rampant overgrazing. If each small rancher had one or two hundred head, they would have combined for another three to six thousand head on the range. And by the 1890s, the sheep men had begun pushing their own flocks into the area, making the problem even worse. It was open range, and coexistence was not always possible. The old-timers still recall the stories passed down of range wars more than a century ago, and the occasional bleached human skull with a bullet hole that might have been a cowboy or sheepherder who never made it home.

The big cow outfits throughout the West would typically strangle the small operators financially, running off their cattle and closing off the water sources, and if need be they hired nasty men willing to do even nastier deeds. Preston Nutter was a master at this, filing claims and fencing off critical water sources. But in Nine Mile Canyon there were simply too many family farmers to run them all away—as many as a hundred souls by the 1890s. Violence was not so much an option here as there was also a regular military presence, courtesy of a new freight road improved in 1886 to handle tens of thousands of tons of supplies bound for the Uinta Basin and many times that weight in Gilsonite ore coming back the other way.

Sure, the families living in Nine Mile were all cash-strapped and farming marginal lands more suitable for rabbits and gophers, and it should not have taken much to send them running. But the cattle barons could not starve them out. These farmers were also in the freighting business and they were merchants and saloon owners, catering to all the wants and needs of teamsters. And they earned hard cash in return—cash that could keep the family farm afloat regardless of the economics of cattle ranching.

Into this environment arrived an outlaw element that got larger and more brazen with each passing year. It was rumored that more than a hundred heavily armed outlaws lived at Robbers Roost. Rustling got so bad in the Nine Mile Canyon area by 1895 that the Lunt brothers threw up their hands and sold what little was left of their herds. And with so many cattle on the range, the cows were easy pickings for outlaws like Joe Walker and C. L. "Gunplay" Maxwell and perhaps even Pete Francis, the saloon owner at Brock's Place who was long rumored to be part of a criminal enterprise. Sheriffs were hired to stem the wave of outlawry, and one was fired because he could not.

Many of the crimes of that day and age were laid at the feet of Butch Cassidy and his Wild Bunch, although truth told Cassidy and his crew were more interested in robbing trains and banks and payrolls where the risk was high and the reward even higher. It was seen as taking from the rich and giving to the poor, and in that regard they were lionized, in some cases given safe haven, by poor farmers in the grips of economic depression. Outside of the well-heeled establishment there was not much sympathy for bankers like James and George Whitmore, who were also the largest cattle outfit in Nine Mile Canyon and Sunnyside.

The tide began to turn in the late 1890s when the governors of Wyoming, Colorado, and Utah signed an agreement to rid the hinterlands of the outlaws once and for all. One by one, lawmen began to eliminate the most famous of the outlaws. Joe Walker and George "Flat Nose" Curry were both killed in Desolation Canyon, Elza Lay was imprisoned in New Mexico, Butch and Sundance Kid headed to South America. Matt Warner turned lawman, and others, like Pete Logan, changed their names and criminal ways and walked the straight and narrow. Gunplay Maxwell, perhaps the most inept of the bunch but one with the closest ties to Nine Mile Canyon, survived longer than most, but he also met a violent death at the hands of Sheriff Ed Johnstone in 1907. Unlike Butch and Elza and Matt, who were respected by the poor farmers, Maxwell's death brought cheers and offers of rewards. The era of dime-store outlaw heroes was over and so was another chapter of Nine Mile Canyon.

There were certainly other characters whose history is closely tied to the history of Nine Mile Canyon who operated within the law, such as it was at the time. The canyon might not have become what it was if not for Sam Gilson, a deputy U.S. marshal who made a name for himself hunting polygamists in the 1880s. But he seems to have spent far more time prospecting for minerals than he ever did wearing a badge, and through Gilson's efforts and those of his partners he managed not only to lock up rich deposits of hydrocarbons, but to get legislation passed taking them away from the Utes. And he got rich doing it.

And there was famed Indian fighter Major Frederick Benteen, a bigot and drunk who boasted of his hatred of Mormons, who was assigned in 1886 to build Fort Duchesne but was hamstrung by the fact supplies had not yet been delivered by way of the Nine Mile Road. There is a certain irony that he was arrested in 1887 and taken to his court martial on the very road that would have saved his career. Fort Duchesne would later prosper because of the Nine Mile Road, due in large part to the dedication of the

Ninth Cavalry—the famous buffalo soldiers who earned the admiration and respect of everyone living along the road.

In short, the entire length of the Nine Mile Road was bustling, a veritable beehive of activity where fortunes could be made with teams of horses and wagons and enough capital to cater to the needs of those who did. Everything was sold here, from garden produce to jelly beans. There were blacksmiths and carpenters. There were barkeeps and ladies of questionable repute. There were more and more and more people. And just as quickly as prosperity arrived it took wings.

Undoubtedly the combined herds of the cattle barons and the family farmers led to wanton overgrazing of the rangelands, although sheep men got most of the blame. And as the open range edged toward worthlessness, the government stepped in with the Taylor Grazing Act—the first effort of its kind to limit the number of livestock on the range and to assign allotments to each rancher. Thus came to an end the days of free grass.

There is no question that the arrival of regional rail lines, such as the Uintah Railway, was a death knell to traditional freighting with horses and wagons. Or that politics would later favor an alternative route through Indian Canyon that would bypass Nine Mile Canyon altogether and relegate the canyon to irrelevance. Or that there was no more free land for the taking and that rule and law would govern the landscape, not grit and determination.

Why do we say Nine Mile Canyon is the place the Old West came to die? Quite simply, everything about its brief history is a metaphor for the past colliding with an industrialized, urbanized present.

- The era of the cattle baron ended here with Preston Nutter, who died in 1936 as the Taylor Grazing Act put an end to overgrazing. No longer would herds of tens of thousands of cows roam here.
- The era of free land ended here with modifications to the Homestead Act that required squatters to secure legal right to their farms and ranches. No longer could young families carve out their own places by sheer will.
- The opening of reservation lands in the Uinta Basin to homesteaders marked the last great American land rush—but unfortunately not the last disenfranchisement of the American Indians.

- The development of the Gilsonite deposits in the Uinta Basin—and the road needed to transport the ores—occurred through unabashed bribery of government officials, a common practice in the day that would warrant prison time today.
- The outlaws who operated here in the 1890s were the last of a breed. Most would be dead, in prison, or reformed by the turn of the century.
- The canyon was characterized by the proliferation of free-wheeling saloons and card games, only to be followed by circumspection and Prohibition.
- It was an era of superstition and whispers of ghosts, when water witches actually delivered on their promises.
- It marked the last military presence intended to quell a feared Indian revolt—something that never happened (although threatened closures of Fort Duchesne prompted the same kind of dire warnings that military base closures do today).
- It was the end of the Mormon pioneer era—a time in Nine Mile Canyon when the first religious refugees rubbed shoulders with the second and third generations who had never known the travails of crossing the plains but who shared in this common heritage.

Most of all, the period of time considered here marked an era when men and women established their own community on their own terms and in their own way. It was far removed from "civilization," and here a Mormon was free to chew tobacco and a non-Mormon was unfettered by theocratic rules and regulations. Sure, there were codes most everyone lived by: honor, courage, hard work. But there were no zoning laws, no environmental laws, no paperwork—and success or failure was determined by sheer will—the embodiment of the Old West. Those days are long gone.

Rest in peace.

Biographical Register

Adams, Della A. (Brundage). 1891 (Utah)–1926 (Carbon County) Married: Orson W. Adams; Nine Mile: 1890s to at least 1900; Census 1900: Nine Mile Canyon; Census 1920: Duchesne, Duchesne County. Della married Orson Adams, the younger brother of Daniel Adams, who was the husband of her sister Emma. The Adams family was from Orangeville. Della was a daughter of Joseph B. and Libby Brundage, who were early settlers above the mouth of Minnie Maud Canyon.

Adams, Emma L. (Brundage). 1889 (Utah)–1966 (Carbon County) Married: ca. 1907, Daniel Adams (before 1930, James Hartzell); Nine Mile: 1890s to at least 1900; Census 1900: Nine Mile Canyon; 1910: Myton, Duchesne County; 1920: Duchesne, Duchesne County; 1930: Wattis, Carbon County. Vital records indicate that an Emma Brundage was married to Dave Russell, but might have divorced him in ca. 1901 when he was arrested for the killing of Pete Francis. The Emma who married Dave Russell is not this this particular Emma Brundage, but is probably a relative (and perhaps namesake). This Emma married Daniel Adams before 1910 and moved to Duchesne County. Emma was a daughter of Joseph B. and Libby Brundage, early settlers

above the mouth of Minnie Maud Canyon in the 1890s. Daniel Adams was a brother of Orson Adams, who was married to Emma's sister, Della.

Addley, Lorena (Warren). 1892–1929 (Price, Carbon County) Married: ca. 1911, Elmer Addley, and 1927, John Patrick Marlsey; Nine Mile: ca. 1900 to 1910; Census 1910: Nine Mile Canyon; Census 1920: Price, Carbon County. Death records list her name as Lorena Warren Addley, but there is a marriage record to indicate she remarried John Patrick Marlsey in 1927, two years before she died. In 1920, she had four small children with Elmer Addley. There is no record that Elmer Addley lived in Nine Mile Canyon, and Lorena might have left the canyon in about 1911 when she married. She was the daughter of William and Mariah Warren, early settlers of Argyle Canyon. She was raised by her stepfather, James H. Blaine.

Alger, Alonzo. 1874 (Washington County)–1949 (Carbon County) Married: Margaret Burns; Nine Mile: ca. 1893 to after 1930; Census 1880: Santa Clara River, Washington County; Census 1900: Coyote Creek, Wyoming; Census 1910: Nine Mile Canyon; Census 1930: Nine Mile Canyon. Lon Alger was one of the

earliest settlers in Nine Mile Canyon, and one of four Alger brothers to live there. In about 1893, Lon and his brother Gett started a ranch near the mouth of Cow Canyon, where Charles Smith, married to their sister, Luna, also had a ranch. Lon and Gett had notorious reputations for being cantankerous, especially over irrigation water. Lon was reportedly an expert gambler and was well known in the saloons in Price. His earnings allowed him to purchase a car long before most other canyon residents.

Alger, Frank. 1868 (Washington County)–1938 (Nine Mile Canyon) Nine Mile: 1893–1938; Census 1870: St. George, Washington County; Census 1880: Santa Clara River, Washington County; Census 1900: Carbon, Wyoming; Census 1910: Nine Mile Canyon; Census 1920: Nine Mile Canyon; Census 1930: Nine Mile Canyon. Frank Alger was one of the earliest settlers in Nine Mile Canyon, and one of four brothers to live there. He arrived in about 1893 at the same time his brothers Lon and Gett had a place at the mouth of Cow Canyon. In about 1895, Frank started developing his own ranch farther down canyon. It eventually evolved into a general store, barns, and corrals for the freight teams, orchards, and cellars. It was a major commercial center for canyon residents after 1901, but contrary to some accounts there was never a hotel here. He was appointed postmaster in 1913. Frank was a life-long bachelor who, according to his obituary, lived in Nine Mile Canyon for about forty-five years, which would have placed his arrival in the canyon in 1893 or 1894.

Alger, Gerrett. 1877 (Washington County)–1957 (Price, Carbon County) Married: Caldonna "Donna" Skelton; Nine Mile: ca. 1893 to after 1920; Census 1880: Santa Clara River, Washington County; Census 1910: Nine Mile Canyon; Census 1920: Hill Creek, Uintah County; Census 1930: Helper, Carbon County. Gett (pronounced "Jet") Alger was one of the earliest settlers in Nine Mile Canyon, and one of four Alger brothers to live there. In about 1893, Gett and his brother Lon started a ranch near the mouth of Cow Canyon, where Charles Smith, married to their sister, Luna, had a ranch. Lon and Gett had notorious reputations for being cantankerous, especially over irrigation water. Census records indicate that Donna and Gett had two children, born in 1902 and 1905 in Arkansas. Donna and the children were not living with Gerrett at the time of the 1910 census, but they were all living together in Hill Creek in 1920. The children might have been Gett's stepchildren, as the oldest son Eugene's death records give his surname as Chancellor. Eugene died in Carbon County and is buried in Price. The daughter might have died in Salt Lake City in 1959. There is no indication that Donna and the two children ever lived in Nine Mile Canyon. The 1920 census indicates Gett was the father. If so, he would have married

Donna in about 1902, but in 1910 he was still listed as a single man.

Alger, Jane A. (Burnett). 1941 (New York)–1934 (Price, Carbon County) Married: John Alger; Nine Mile: ca. 1910; Census 1850: St. Louis, Missouri; Census 1860: Salt Lake City; Census 1870: St. George, Washington County; Census 1880: Santa Clara River, Washington County; Census 1910: Nine Mile Canyon; Census 1920: Wellington, Carbon County; Census 1930: Wellington, Carbon County. Jane was a polygamous wife of John Alger, and she raised her family along the Santa Clara River in Washington County. In about 1885, her son Frank loaded her and his siblings into a wagon and moved them to Orangeville, where her parents were living. Her sons were estranged from their father, and John's attempts to convince his wife to move back to Washington County were unsuccessful. She was living with her sons Lon, Gett, and Joseph in Nine Mile Canyon in 1910, but later moved to Wellington to live with her daughter, Clara Houskeeper.

Alger, John. ?–?
Nine Mile: ca. 1889. The name John Alger is given as a witness in the William Brock murder investigation and trial in 1889 and 1890. He was living at Brock's Place at the time, perhaps working for William Brock. This individual is apparently unrelated to the Alger brothers who arrived in Nine Mile Canyon in about 1893. The brothers' father was named John, but they were estranged from him, and it is unlikely that a Mormon patriarch would have been living at a roadhouse in Nine Mile Canyon. Nothing is

known of this John Alger and how he came to be in the canyon.

Alger, Joseph. Ca. 1883 (Washington County)–1913 (Salt Lake) Nine Mile: ca. 1910; Census 1910: Nine Mile Canyon. Joseph was the youngest of the Alger brothers to have lived in Nine Mile Canyon. He was a twenty-seven-year-old single man in 1910, and there are no vital records after that time to indicate where he went or if he married. He would have been a toddler when his brother Frank took the family from Washington County to Orangeville to live with their mother's family.

*Alger, Luna Luella. See **Smith, Luna Luella (Alger)***

Anderson, David R. 1909 (Nine Mile Canyon?)–? Nine Mile: 1909 to ca. 1910; Census 1910: Nine Mile Canyon. David R. was the son of David S. and Sarah Anderson, and the grandson of Erastus Anderson. He might have been born in Nine Mile Canyon. There is no record of David R. after the 1910 census.

Anderson, David S. Ca. 1882 (Utah)–? Married: Sarah Matilda Foster; Nine Mile: before 1910 to after 1930; Census 1900: Price, Carbon County; Census 1910: Nine Mile Canyon; Census 1920: Price, Carbon County; Census 1930: Nine Mile Canyon. David S. was the son of Erastus and Mary Anderson, who were also in Nine Mile Canyon at the time of the 1910 census. David S. was married and starting his own family at the time. He might have left Nine Mile Canyon for a time, but he was back by 1930. By the 1940s, the family was living in the Miller Creek area.

Anderson, Erastus Soren. 1858 (Utah)–1935 (Carbon County)
Married: Mary Edmiston; Nine Mile: ca. 1910 to after 1930; Census 1860: Ephraim, Sanpete County; Census 1880: Ephraim, Sanpete County; Census 1900: Price, Carbon County; Census 1910: Nine Mile Canyon; Census 1930: Nine Mile Canyon. Erastus was the father of David S., and Lisle Anderson, all of whom were in Nine Mile Canyon in 1910. He would have been about fifty-two years old at the time. He died in Carbon County and is buried in Price.

Anderson, Laura Jane. *See Thompson, Laura Jane (Anderson)*

Anderson, John Lisle. 1898 (Utah)–?
Nine Mile: ca. 1930; Census 1900: Price, Carbon County; Census 1910: Price, Carbon County; Census 1930: Nine Mile Canyon. John Lisle was a younger brother of David S. and Leo C. Anderson, and a son of Erastus and Mary Anderson. He would have been about twelve years old when his parents and brothers lived in Nine Mile Canyon in 1910, but he did not accompany them. Instead, he stayed with relatives Albert and Hannah Anderson in Price. He was present in the canyon in 1930 when he was living there with his father, Erastus, and brother, David S. He was a thirty-two-year-old single man at the time, and there are records to indicate he married.

Anderson, Leo Charles. Ca. 1892 (Price, Carbon County)–?
Nine Mile: ca. 1910; Census 1900: Price, Carbon County; Census 1910: Nine Mile Canyon; Census 1920: Arcadia, Florida; Census 1930: Santa Monica, California. Leo was the younger brother of

David S. Anderson and the son of Erastus Anderson, who were all living together as extended family in Nine Mile Canyon in 1910. By 1920 Leo was in the military, and by 1930 he had married but was living alone in California. There are no records of him after the 1930 census.

Anderson, Mary E. *See Barney, Mary E. (Anderson)*

Anderson, Sarah Matilda (Foster). 1882 (St. George)–1969 (Salt Lake City)
Married: David S. Anderson; Nine Mile: ca. 1910; Census 1900: St. George, Washington County; Census 1910: Nine Mile Canyon; Census 1920: Price Carbon, County; Census 1930: Price (?). Sarah was the wife of David S. Anderson, and some of her children might have been born in Nine Mile Canyon. David returned to Nine Mile in 1930 with his brother Lisle and father, Erastus, but Sarah is not listed on the census records for the canyon. She probably remained behind at the family home in Price. By 1940 Sarah and David were living in the Miller Creek area.

Ashton, Eva (Stewart). Ca. 1899 (Nine Mile Canyon?)–?
Married: Ray Ashton; Nine Mile: 1899 to after 1910; Census 1900: Nine Mile Canyon; Census 1910: Nine Mile Canyon; Census 1920: Roosevelt, Duchesne County; Census 1930: Vernal, Uintah County. Eva was the daughter of Hank and Minerva Stewart, and she lived on the Stewart ranch in Argyle Canyon. She was later raised by her stepfather, Neal Hanks, a long-time cowboy and Nutter Ranch foreman in Nine Mile Canyon.

Babcock, Augusta Mae (Hanchett). 1857 (California)–1897 (Carbon County)
Married: John Rowley Babcock; Nine Mile: ca. 1891 to 1897; Census 1860: Payson, Utah County; Census 1870: Albany, Wisconsin; Census 1880: Greenwich, Piute County. Family history indicates they followed their daughter, Sarah J. (Babcock) Hall and her family to Nine Mile Canyon so the mother could be closer to her daughter. The Hall family arrived in 1894, and it is assumed the Babcock family arrived at about the same time. A different account has it the Babcock family arrived in 1891, or three years before the Hall family arrived there. If this is correct, their daughter Sarah might have moved her family to Nine Mile to be closer to her parents (not the other way around). Augusta died in 1897 within a year of the birth of her youngest son, Lorenzo. She probably died in Nine Mile Canyon.

Babcock, Belle. *See Curtis, Belle (Babcock)*

Babcock, Dora J. *See Taylor, Dora (Babcock)*

Babcock, Earl Lorenzo. 1896 (Utah)–1971 (Myton, Duchesne County)
Married: Faith "Fay" Curtis; Nine Mile: ca. 1896 to ca. 1922; Census 1900: Nine Mile Canyon; Census 1910: Nine Mile Canyon; Census 1920: Nine Mile Canyon; Census 1930: Myton, Duchesne County. Earl Lorenzo was the youngest son of John Rowley and Augusta Mae Babcock, among the earliest settlers in Nine Mile Canyon. He was probably born in Nine Mile Canyon, and he spent his entire childhood and young adult years there. His mother died within a year of his birth. Lorenzo and his

father have the longest history in Nine Mile among the Babcock family. He probably married in about 1922 and moved to Myton, where his wife's family lived and where they raised their own family. There is no record that Faith and Lorenzo lived in Nine Mile Canyon.

Babcock, John Rowley. 1850 (Missouri)–1928 (Carbon County) Married: Augusta Mae Hanchett; Nine Mile: ca. 1891 to 1928; Census 1860: Manti, Sanpete County; Census 1870: Mount Vernon, Tooele County; Census 1880: Greenwich, Piute County; Census 1900: Nine Mile Canyon; Census 1910: Nine Mile Canyon; Census 1920: Nine Mile Canyon. The Babcock family patriarch arrived with his family perhaps as early as 1891. Family history indicates they followed their daughter Sarah J. (Babcock) Hall and her family to Nine Mile Canyon so the mother could be closer to her daughter. The Hall family arrived in 1894. Another account has it they arrived in 1891, which if true would mean Sarah and her family followed the parents to Nine Mile Canyon. John's wife, Augusta, died in 1897, leaving John to raise the children alone. John appears to have never left Nine Mile Canyon. By 1920, he was living with Edwin Harmon, who had married John's daughter Josephine.

Babcock, John Roy. 1891 (Utah)–1916 (Duchesne County) Nine Mile: ca. 1891 to after 1900; Census 1900: Nine Mile Canyon; Census 1910: Hagerman, Idaho. John Roy was the son of John Rowley and Augusta Mae Babcock, who were among the earliest settlers of Nine Mile Canyon. He died at age twenty-four, and there is no record he was married. If his parents arrived in Nine Mile Canyon in 1891, as one account has it, John Roy might have been born in Nine Mile Canyon or he arrived as an infant.

Babcock, Josephine. *See* **Harmon, Josephine (Babcock)**

Babcock, Mary Adelia. *See* **Casady, Mary Adelia (Babcock)**

Babcock, Maud M. *See* **Johnston, Maud R. (Babcock)**

Babcock, Sarah A. *See* **Hall, Sarah A. (Babcock)**

Banning, Charles A. "Rowdy Dowdy." 1871 (Colorado)–? Nine Mile: 1901; Census 1900: Helper, Carbon County. Charles Banning was a cook, bartender, and handyman hired by Pete Francis to help with the saloon at Brock's Place. He was a witness in the murder trial of Dave Russell, who killed Francis during a barroom brawl in late 1901. A year before he was working as a cook at a boarding house in Helper. There are no other records linked to him.

Barney, Clarence Adelbert. 1875 (Utah)–1943 (Carbon County) Married: Mary Elizabeth Anderson; Nine Mile: 1910s to 1930s; Census 1880: Kanosh, Millard County; Census 1900: Kanosh, Millard County; Census 1910: Ferron, Emery County; Census 1920: Nine Mile Canyon; Census 1930: Nine Mile Canyon. Delbert and Mary arrived in Nine Mile Canyon with their six children sometime before 1920, and it is uncertain how long they remained. Local history suggests they were long-time residents. In 1930, Delbert was a ranch hand for Preston Nutter, although it is unknown where Mary was at the time. The family ranch was above the mouth of Minnie Maud Canyon. Their son Doyle started his own family in Nine Mile Canyon.

Barney, Crystal Ellen (Thompson). 1904 (Nine Mile Canyon?)–1998 (Duchesne County) Married: Virgil Barney; Nine Mile: 1904 to after 1920; Census 1910: Nine Mile Canyon; Census 1920: Nine Mile Canyon; Census 1930: Price, Carbon County. Crystal was the daughter of Al and Martha Thompson, and granddaughter of Martha and Frederic Grames, both long-time ranch families in Nine Mile Canyon. She married Virgil Barney, the oldest son of Delbert and Mary Barney, who arrived in Nine Mile Canyon before 1920. It is assumed Crystal and Virgil met in Nine Mile Canyon and were married sometime after 1920. Virgil and Crystal had returned to live in Nine Mile Canyon in 1940. Crystal might have been born in Nine Mile Canyon.

Barney, Dolly (Russell). 1906 (Utah)–1981 (?) Married: Oscar Doyle Barney; Nine Mile: ca. 1906 to 1930s; Census 1930: Nine Mile Canyon. Dolly was the wife of Doyle Barney and daughter of Harrison Russell. They probably married about 1928. There are no other vital records beyond the 1930 census. The database links her to a Dolly Barney who died in New York in 1981, but this might not be the same person.

Barney, Oscar Doyle. 1903 (Utah)–? Married: Dolly Barney; Nine Mile: ca. 1918 to 1930s; Census 1910: Ferron, Emery County; Census

1920: Nine Mile Canyon; Census 1930: Nine Mile Canyon. Doyle was a son of Delbert and Mary Barney, who arrived in Nine Mile Canyon before 1920 with his parents. He is listed in the 1920 census for Nine Mile Canyon as a boarder with Al Thompson. He had a twin brother named Dayle. Doyle married Dolly in about 1928, and they were living in the canyon in 1930 with their daughter, Ada. There is no record of Doyle and Dolly after the 1930 census. Doyle was a long-time ranch hand for Preston Nutter.

Barney, Janie. 1918 (Nine Mile Canyon?)–1998 (Price, Carbon County)
Married: Ephraim Henri; Nine Mile: 1918 to 1920s; Census 1920: Nine Mile Canyon; Census 1930: Price, Carbon County (in 1935). Janie, or Jennie, was a daughter of Delbert and Mary Barney, and was a toddler in 1920. Her parents arrived sometime before 1920, and she might have been born in Nine Mile Canyon. She married sometime before 1940 to Ephraim Henri, and they were living in the Miller Creek area at the time of the 1940 census.

Barney, Mary E. (Anderson). 1878 (Utah)–1927 (Carbon County)
Married: Clarence Adelbert (Delbert) Barney; Nine Mile: before 1920 to ca. 1927; Census 1880: Kanosh, Millard County; Census 1900: Kanosh, Millard County; Census 1910: Ferron, Emery County; Census 1920: Nine Mile Canyon. Delbert and Mary arrived in Nine Mile Canyon with their six children sometime before 1920, and it is uncertain how long they remained. Local history suggests they were long-time residents. The family is not listed on any census for

1930, but it is possible they were still in the canyon at that time, although Mary died in 1927. The family ranch was above the mouth of Minnie Maud Canyon. Their son Doyle started his own family in Nine Mile Canyon. The Barney family retains land holdings in the canyon.

Barney, Oral. 1910 (Utah)–1986 (Provo?)
Nine Mile: 1910s to 1920s; Census 1920: Nine Mile Canyon. Oral was a son of Delbert and Mary Barney, who arrived in Nine Mile Canyon sometime before 1920. Oral would have been a young child at the time, and might have grown up in Nine Mile Canyon. There is very little information about him beyond the 1920 census.

Barney, Reta Elizabeth. *See* **Quinn, Reta Elizabeth (Barney)**

Barney, Reva Armanda. *See* **Cox, Reva (Barney)**

Barney, Virgil. Ca. 1899–?
Married: Crystal Thompson; Nine Mile: 1910s to 1920s; Census 1900: Kanosh, Millard County; Census 1910: Ferron, Emery County; Census 1920: Nine Mile Canyon (?); Census 1930: Nine Mile Canyon. Virgil was a son of Delbert and Mary Barney, who arrived in Nine Mile Canyon sometime before 1920. He is not listed on the 1920 census for Nine Mile Canyon, but he was probably there. He met and married Crystal Thompson in about 1920, and the couple might have had children there before moving to Price by 1930. Virgil is also listed in the 1930 census for Nine Mile Canyon. By 1940, Virgil and Crystal were back living in Nine Mile Canyon. Crystal

was probably born and raised in Nine Mile Canyon. Virgil was a long-time ranch hand for Preston Nutter. His first name is sometimes spelled "Virgal."

Barney, William Lee. 1906 (Utah)–1965 (Carbon County)
Nine Mile: 1910s to 1930s; Census 1910: Ferron, Emery County; Census 1920: Nine Mile Canyon; Census 1930: Nine Mile Canyon. Lee was a son of Delbert and Mary Barney, and would have arrived in Nine Mile Canyon with his parents sometime before 1920. He remained in the canyon through at least 1930, when he was a ranch hand for Preston Nutter. There are no records of him after 1930 until his death in 1965. He is buried in Price.

Beach, Floyd. Ca. 1905 (Utah)–?
Nine Mile: ca. 1930; Census 1930: Nine Mile Canyon. Floyd was a twenty-five-year-old ranch hand working for Preston Nutter at the time of the 1930 census. He indicated he was married. There are no cross-references in the database as to who he was, who he married, or what became of him.

Bentley, Vivian L. (Hamilton). 1893 (Gordon Creek, Carbon County)–1972 (Price, Carbon County)
Married: Elba Bentley (1913); Nine Mile: 1890s to 1900s; Census 1900: Nine Mile Canyon; Census 1910: Myton, Duchesne County; Census 1920: Antelope, Duchesne County; Census 1930: Hayden, Uintah County. Vivian was the daughter of William and Liza Bird Hamilton, who were early settlers in the Minnie Maud Canyon area. The Hamilton family arrived sometime after 1893

by way of Gooseberry Valley and Gordon Creek, and they sold out in the early 1900s and moved to Duchesne County. Vivian probably spent her childhood in Nine Mile Canyon.

Benton, Lucius. ?–?
Nine Mile: ca. 1887. Lucius Benton owned a "whiskey ranch" in the Soldier Creek Canyon area that catered to freighters traveling the road. In 1887, Benton witnessed two soldiers killing and butchering a cow belonging to George Whitmore, and he was the star witness in the trial of the men. Both men were acquitted despite rather convincing evidence. Nothing is known about who Lucius Benton was, how he came to be in Nine Mile Canyon, or what became of him after the 1887 incident.

Bird, Eliza Jane. *See Hamilton, Eliza Jane (Bird)*

Blaine, James Hillary. 1870 (Utah)–1915 (Bluebell, Duchesne County)
Married: Mariah Powell Warren; Nine Mile: ca. 1910; Census 1880: Spring City, Sanpete County; Census 1910: Nine Mile Canyon. James married the widow Mariah Powell Warren and helped to raise her seven children. They had one child of their own, but it is unknown if this child was born in Nine Mile Canyon. The Warren ranch was in Argyle Canyon. It is unknown if James took over the Warren place or if he had a place of his own. The family moved on to Duchesne County where James died in 1915.

Blaine, Mariah (Powell-Warren). 1868 (Utah)–?
Married: William Warren; James H. Blaine; Nine Mile: 1900s to 1910s; Census 1870: Pondtown, Utah County; Census 1880: Salem, Utah County; Census 1910: Nine Mile Canyon; Census 1920: Bluebell, Duchesne County; Census 1930: Bluebell, Duchesne County. Mariah was the daughter of John A. and Sarah J. Powell, early settlers of Price. Her father also had a place in Nine Mile Canyon in the late 1890s or early 1900s near Minnie Maud Canyon. Mariah would have married William Warren sometime before 1890, and it is possible they moved to Nine Mile Canyon about that time. William Warren died sometime before 1910, at which time Mariah married James Blaine. She had a child with him in about 1913. Many of Mariah's six children with William Warren might have been born in Nine Mile Canyon.

Blaine, Rulon H. 1911 (Nine Mile Canyon?)–1985 (Price, Carbon County)
Nine Mile: 1910s; Census 1920: Bluebell, Duchesne County. There is no official record that Rulon lived in Nine Mile Canyon, but he was born one year after the 1910 census when his family was all living in Nine Mile, so it is possible he was born in Nine Mile. There are no census records related to him after 1920.

Blohm, Charles. Ca. 1886 (Arizona)–?
Nine Mile: ca. 1910; Census 1910: Nine Mile Canyon. Charles was a ranch hand working for Preston Nutter at the time of the 1910 census. There are no cross-references in the database as to who he was or what became of him.

Brock, William. 1859 (New York)–1932 (Grand County)
Married: Edith Brinkerhoff (1890); Nine Mile: 1887 to 1889; Census 1900: Tucker, Utah County; Census 1910: Elgin, Grand County; Census 1930: Elgin, Grand County. William Brock was one of the more colorful figures in Nine Mile Canyon history. He acquired squatter's rights to Shadrach Lunt's ranch (now the Preston Nutter Ranch) in late 1886 or 1887, and constructed a saloon and hotel there to capitalize of the growing freight traffic between Price and the Uinta Basin. It became known as Brock's Place. In 1889, Brock killed a local resident named Frank Foote in a barroom dispute, and Brock was tried for murder in Provo. He was acquitted after only fifteen minutes of deliberation. He sold the operation to Pete Francis in 1890 to pay for his defense. He never returned to live in Nine Mile Canyon.

Broderick, Joseph. 1901 (Emery County)–1950 (Huntington Park, California)
Married: Lola Mae Henningsen; Nine Mile: ca. 1930; Census 1910: Emery, Emery County; Census 1920: Emery, Emery County; Census 1930: Nine Mile Canyon. Joseph was a twenty-nine-year-old ranch hand working for Preston Nutter at the time of the 1930 census. He might be the same Joseph Alston Broderick who was born and raised in Emery County. He had returned to Emery County by 1935.

Brown, Charles. Ca. 1865 (Illinois)–?
Nine Mile: ca. 1910; Census 1910: Nine Mile Canyon. Charles was a forty-five-year-old boarder living with Catherine Eagan, the widow of John Eagan, her three small children, and her brother-in-law, Gilbert Eagan. There are no cross-references in the database as to who he was or what became of him.

Brown, Martha. Ca. 1850 Utah–? Nine Mile: before and after 1920; Census 1860: Manti (?); Census 1870: Manti (?); Census 1920: Nine Mile Canyon. Martha is listed as a Native American "cook" who was boarding with George C. "Don" Johnston, his son Charles W., and daughter-in-law Celia. Martha was renowned among Nine Mile Canyon teamsters for her fine cooking. The Johnston ranch (now the Cottonwood Glen Picnic Area) was a popular stop for freighters. Given that her state of birth was listed as Utah, it is likely she was of Northern Ute or Paiute ancestry. According to family history, she was a captive to slave traders and was adopted by a Mormon family in Nephi. She went by Martha Johnston until she married a drifter named Brown.

Brown, Mary Mae (Hall). 1892 (Utah)–? Married: Joseph Brown; Nine Mile: 1894 to 1900s; Census 1900: Nine Mile Canyon; Census 1910: Huntington, Emery County; Census 1920: Huntington, Emery County. Mary Mae was the oldest of the six children born to Charles and Sarah Babcock Hall, and she would have been about two years old when the family migrated from Escalante to Nine Mile Canyon. She married and moved on to Emery County.

Brown, Minnie (Hall). 1893 (Escalante, Garfield County)–? Married: John W. Brown; Nine Mile: 1894 to 1900s; 1900: Nine Mile Canyon; Census 1910: Huntington, Emery County; Census 1920: Huntington, Emery County; Census 1930: Huntington, Emery County. Sisters Minnie and Maude sparked the legend that the canyon was

named after the twin girls. Minnie is the daughter of Charles and Sarah Babcock Hall. She was born in November 1893 and the family came to Nine Mile Canyon the following spring. She married and moved on to Emery County.

Brundage, Ada (Hamilton). 1884 (Utah)–? Married: Joseph Brundage; Nine Mile: 1890s to 1910s; Census 1900: Nine Mile Canyon; Census 1910: Nine Mile Canyon; Census 1930: Antelope, Duchesne County. Ada was also known as Zada. She married Joe Brundage, from the Joseph B. and Libby Brundage family, who were early settlers in Nine Mile Canyon. She was the daughter of William and Eliza Bird Hamilton, who also had an early ranch above the mouth of Minnie Maud Canyon. Her sister, Hettie, married Joe's brother, George.

Brundage, Della A. *See Adams, Della A. (Brundage)*

Brundage, Emma L. *See Adams, Emma L. (Brundage)*

Brundage, George S. 1882 (Utah)–1964 (Salt Lake) Married: Hettie Maud Hamilton; Nine Mile: 1890s to 1900s; Census 1900: Nine Mile Canyon; Census 1910: Myton, Duchesne County; Census 1920: Antelope, Duchesne County; Census 1930: Price, Carbon County. George was the son of Joseph B. and Libby Brundage, early settlers of Nine Mile Canyon in the 1890s. His wife, Maud, was the daughter of William Hamilton, also among the earliest settlers of Nine Mile Canyon in the Minnie Maud Canyon area.

Brundage, Hettie Maud (Hamilton). 1886 (Utah)–1920 (Duchesne County) Married: George S. Brundage; Nine Mile: 1890s to 1900s; Census 1900: Nine Mile Canyon; Census 1910: Myton, Duchesne County; Census 1920: Antelope, Duchesne County. Maud was a daughter of William and Liza Hamilton, among the earliest settlers of Nine Mile Canyon in the Minnie Maud Canyon area. It is unlikely that any of her children were born in Nine Mile Canyon. Their oldest was a newborn at the time of the 1910 census when they were living in Myton. Hettie's sister, Ada, married George's brother, Joe.

Brundage, John A. 1886 (Utah)–1966 (Utah County?) Married: Ethel Foy; Nine Mile: 1890s to 1900s; Census 1900: Nine Mile Canyon; Census 1910: Myton, Duchesne County; Census 1920: Antelope, Duchesne County. John A. was the son of Joseph B. and Libby Brundage. His wife, Ethel Foy, was from Green River, and there is no evidence the Foy family was in Nine Mile Canyon.

Brundage, Joseph A. 1880 (Spanish Fork, Utah County)–1966 (Utah County) Married: Zada Mary Hamilton; Nine Mile: 1890s to 1910s; Census 1900: Nine Mile Canyon; Census 1910: Nine Mile Canyon; Census 1930: Antelope, Duchesne County. Joe was the son of Joseph B. and Libby Brundage, who settled in Nine Mile Canyon before 1900. He was married to Ada (also called Zada) Hamilton, daughter of William and Liza Hamilton, who were also among the earliest settlers in the Minnie Maud Canyon area at the same time.

Brundage, Joseph B. 1840 (New Jersey)–before 1910
Married: LaBertha Brundage (1876); Nine Mile: 1890s to 1900s; Census 1850: Utah (?); Census 1860: Fillmore, Millard County (?); Census 1870: Parowan, Iron County; Census 1900: Nine Mile Canyon. The family name is sometimes spelled Brondage, Brundege, or Brundige. The database also links Joseph B. to the name Joseph B. Mulford with the same birth year and birthplace. In 1850, Mulford was in Utah (unspecified) and in 1860 he was in Fillmore. By 1870, the Brundage name was being used. It is unknown if Joseph B. Mulford changed his name to Joseph B. Brundage, or whether this is a quirk in the database and the individuals are unrelated. He would have been sixty years old at the time of the 1900 Nine Mile Canyon census. His name does not appear after that point. By 1910, his wife, Libby, was a widow living in Myton. Two daughters married into the Hamilton family, which also had deep roots in Nine Mile Canyon.

Brundage, Labertha (Taylor). 1854–1937 (Myton, Duchesne County)
Married: Joseph B. Brundage (1876); Richard B. Thompson (1913); Nine Mile: 1890s to 1900s; Census 1860: Davis County; Census 1880: Spanish Fork (?); Census 1900: Nine Mile Canyon; Census 1910: Myton, Duchesne County. Labertha, who also went by Liberty or "Libby" Brundage, was married to Joseph B. Brundage for about thirty years. In 1910, she was a widow living in Myton. In 1913, she remarried to Richard B. Thompson in Uintah County. Thompson was a widower who in 1910 was listed as

a sixty-seven-year-old farm laborer working for Preston Nutter.

Brundage, Mary L. *See* **Liddell, Mary L. (Brundage)**

Brundage, Rhoda Evelyn. *See* **McCourt, Rhoda B. (Brundage)**

Brundage, Viola M. *See* **Shepard, Viola M. (Brundage)**

Brundage, William. 1908 (Green River)–1948 (Salt Lake City)
Married: Christina Giles; Nine Mile: 1908 to 1910s; Census 1910: Nine Mile Canyon; Census 1930: Antelope, Duchesne County. Family records indicate he was born in Green River, but he was probably raised in Nine Mile Canyon. He was the son of Joe and Zada Hamilton Brundage.

Bunts, Homer. ?–?
Nine Mile: late 1890s or early 1900s. School census records indicate Homer Bunts was a teacher in Nine Mile Canyon. There are no other records associated with this individual.

Burgess, Donna J. (Miles). 1883 (Utah)–?
Married: Ernest Burgess; Nine Mile: 1907(?); Census 1900: Salt Lake City; Census 1910: Lund, Nevada; Census 1920: Roosevelt, Duchesne County; Census 1930: Cedar City, Iron County. There is no convincing evidence that Donna ever lived in Nine Mile Canyon. She was married by 1910 when her parents and siblings were living in Nine Mile Canyon. She was one of seven Miles daughters that contribute to the legend that Nine Mile Canyon was named after the Miles family. She was a daughter of William A. and Lucretia Wightman Miles.

Burnett, Jane A. *See* **Alger, Jane A. (Burnett)**

Burns, Albert. 1825 (New York)–1922 (Carbon County)
Nine Mile: ca. 1900; Census 1900: Nine Mile Canyon. Albert was seventy-four years old when he was living in Nine Mile Canyon with his son Edward. He listed his occupation as a trapper. He must have remained in the area because he died in 1922 in Carbon County. Nothing else is known about him or how he came to be in Nine Mile Canyon at such an elderly age.

Burns, Edward Everett. 1865 (Nevada)–1900 (Vernal, Uintah County)
Nine Mile: ca. 1900; Census 1900: Nine Mile Canyon. Edward was a single man living with his elderly father, Albert, in Nine Mile Canyon in 1900. Later that year, he must have moved to the Uinta Basin, where he died in October. He listed his occupation as a trapper. Nothing else is known of him or how he came to be in Nine Mile Canyon.

Butler, Sarah. *See* **Houskeeper, Sarah (Butler)**

Caffreg, Mattio. ?–?
Nine Mile Canyon: 1897. School census records indicate Mattio was a teacher in Nine Mile Canyon in 1897. There are no vital records linked to this person.

Casady, Mary Adelia (Babcock). 1889 (Utah)–1965 (Springville, Utah County)
Married: William E. Casady, Claire Whareham; Nine Mile: 1890s to 1910s; Census 1900: Nine Mile Canyon; Census 1910: Nine Mile

Canyon; Census 1920: Castle Gate, Carbon County; Census 1930: Price, Carbon County. Sometimes the family name is spelled Casidy or Cassady. Mary was a daughter of John Rowley and Augusta Mae Babcock, among the earliest settlers in Nine Mile Canyon. William and Mary had their own ranch in Nine Mile Canyon.

Casady, William Everton. 1870 (Emery, Emery County)–1923 (Castle Gate, Carbon County)
Married: Mary Adelia Babcock (1906); Nine Mile: 1900s to 1910s; Census 1910: Nine Mile Canyon; Census 1920: Castle Gate, Carbon County. William married Mary Adelia Babcock, daughter of John Rowley and Augusta Mae Babcock, and by 1910 they had their own ranch in Nine Mile Canyon. Castle Gate was a coal-mining town and it is possible they moved there so he could work in the mines.

Casady, Edna. *See* ***Robinson, Edna (Casady)***

Casady, Fern. *See* ***Morgan, Fern (Casady)***

Christensen, Charles. ?–?
Nine Mile: 1904. County land records indicate he bought out the James Hamilton homestead in the early 1900s, but his name does not appear on any census records for the canyon. Due to the commonness of the name, there are no convincing records of this individual in the database.

Collins, Vondella (Kelsey). Ca. 1907 (Nine Mile Canyon?)–1976 (Taylor, Idaho)
Married: Triece Collins; Nine Mile: 1900s; Census 1910: Basalt, Idaho; Census 1920: Basalt, Idaho; Census

1930: Hawthorne, California. There is no positive record that Della was in Nine Mile Canyon, but she was born in Utah, her family was in Nine Mile Canyon in 1900, and she could have been born there before the family moved to Idaho. She was a daughter of Theodore and Rosetta Houskeeper Kelsey. The Houskeeper family was among the earliest to arrive in Nine Mile Canyon in the 1890s.

Cook, Ada (Barney). 1928 (Nine Mile Canyon?)–2005 (Uintah County)
Married: (?) Cook; Nine Mile: 1928 to 1930s; Census 1930: Nine Mile Canyon. Ada was the daughter of Doyle and Dolly Barney, and she might have been born in Nine Mile Canyon. There are very few records of her after the 1930 census. Ada would have been the granddaughter of Delbert and Mary Barney, who arrived in the canyon sometime before 1920.

Cook, Allen L. Ca. 1918 (Utah)–1967 (not indicated)
Married: Alta Boswell (1938); Nine Mile: ca. 1930; Census 1920: Bluebell, Duchesne County; Census 1930: Nine Mile Canyon; Census 1940: Colorado. Allen would have been a child when he accompanied his parents, James Hyrum and Calista Cook, to Nine Mile Canyon sometime before 1930. The Cook family had lived in the Uinta Basin for more than twenty years before briefly relocating to Nine Mile Canyon, and they had returned to Bluebell by 1940. Allen married in 1938 in Duchesne, and the couple had moved on to Colorado by 1940.

Cook, Barbara. *See* ***Smithson, Barbara (Cook)***

Covert, Calista. *See* ***Cook, Calista (Covert)***

Cook, Calista (Covert). Ca. 1879 (Utah)–?
Married: James Hyrum Cook; Nine Mile: ca. 1930; Census 1880: Granite, Salt Lake County; Census 1900: South Ashley, Uintah County; Census 1910: Naples, Uintah County; Census 1920: Bluebell, Duchesne County; Census 1930: Nine Mile Canyon. James and Calista Cook moved to the Uinta Basin shortly after their marriage and they raised a large family in the Vernal and Bluebell area over more than two decades. Sometime before 1930, they moved to Nine Mile Canyon with three of their younger children and one older son. It is unknown how long they remained, but by 1940 James, Calista, and their youngest son, William, were living in Bluebell, Duchesne County.

Cook, Theora. Ca. 1915 (Utah)–?
Nine Mile: ca. 1930; Census 1920: Bluebell, Duchesne County; Census 1930: Nine Mile Canyon. Theora accompanied her parents, James Hyrum and Calista Cook, to Nine Mile Canyon as a teenager. The Cook family had lived in the Uinta Basin for more than twenty years before relocating to Nine Mile Canyon sometime before 1930. The family had returned to Bluebell by 1940. There are no records related to Theora after the 1930 census.

Cook, James Hyrum. Ca. 1876 (Utah)–?
Married: Calista Covert; Nine Mile: ca. 1930; Census 1880: Salina, Sevier County; Census 1900: South Ashley, Uintah County; Census 1910: Naples, Uintah County; Census 1930: Nine

Mile Canyon. James and Calista Cook moved to the Uinta Basin shortly after their marriage and they raised a large family in the Vernal and Bluebell area over more than two decades. Sometime before 1930, they moved to Nine Mile Canyon with three of their younger children and one older son. It is unknown how long they remained, but by 1940 James, Calista, and their youngest son, William, were living in Bluebell, Duchesne County.

Cook, James O. Ca. 1899 (Utah)–?
Nine Mile: ca. 1930; Census 1900: South Ashley, Uintah County; Census 1910: Naples, Uintah County; Census 1930: Nine Mile Canyon. James O. was thirty-one years old and single when he accompanied his parents to Nine Mile Canyon. There are no vital records related to him after the 1930 census. He was the son of James Hyrum and Calista Cook, who had lived in the Uinta Basin for more than twenty years before relocating to Nine Mile Canyon. The family had returned to Bluebell by 1940.

Cook, William Wiley. 1920 (Bluebell, Duchesne County)–?
Nine Mile: ca. 1930; Census 1920: Bluebell, Duchesne County; Census 1930: Nine Mile Canyon. William was a child when he accompanied his parents, James Hyrum and Calista Cook, to Nine Mile Canyon sometime before 1930. The Cook family had lived in the Uinta Basin for more than twenty years before relocating to Nine Mile Canyon, and they had returned to Bluebell by 1940. William enlisted in the military in 1943. There are no records of him after that time.

Cox, Martha Jane (Hamilton). 1883 (Utah)–1910 (Wasatch County)

Married: W. E. Cox; Nine Mile: 1890s to 1900s; Census 1900: Nine Mile Canyon; Census 1910: Myton, Duchesne County. Martha Jane was only twenty-seven when she died, leaving behind five children. It is possible some of the children were born in Nine Mile Canyon. She was the daughter of William and Liza Hamilton, early settlers in the Minnie Maud Canyon area.

Cox, Reva Armanda (Barney). 1908 (Utah)–1985 (Carbon County)
Married: Van Cox; Nine Mile: 1910s to 1920s; Census 1910: Ferron, Emery County; Census 1920: Nine Mile Canyon; Census 1930: Antelope, Duchesne County. Reva was the daughter of Delbert and Mary Barney, who arrived in Nine Mile Canyon before 1920, when Reva was a teenager. She married Van Cox, the son of W. E. Cox and Martha Jane Hamilton, a daughter of William and Liza Hamilton, early settlers in the Minnie Maud Canyon area. It is unknown if Van and Reva ever lived together in Nine Mile Canyon. Reva's death records indicate she later remarried a man named Dockstader.

Crawford, Jedediah. Ca. 1902 (Utah)–?
Married: Margaret (?); Nine Mile: 1920s?; Census 1920: Ogden, Weber County; Census 1930: Boneta, Duchesne County. Local histories indicate Jedediah Crawford owned the "first ranch past the summit" in Nine Mile Canyon, which could place it in the Whitmore Park area. There are no vital records to indicate he lived in the canyon. By 1930, he lived in Duchesne County where he remained through at least 1940.

Crawford, Margaret. Ca. 1903 (Utah)–?
Married: Jedediah Crawford; Nine Mile: 1920s?; Census 1930: Boneta, Duchesne County. Local histories indicate Jedediah and Margaret Crawford owned the "first ranch past the summit" in Nine Mile Canyon, which could place it in the Whitmore Park area. There are no vital records to indicate she lived in the canyon. By 1930, she lived in Duchesne County where she remained through at least 1940.

Curtis, Belle (Babcock). 1895 (Nine Mile Canyon?)–1987 (Myton, Duchesne County)
Married: Erastus Curtis; Nine Mile: 1890s to 1910s; Census 1900: Nine Mile Canyon; Census 1910: Nine Mile Canyon; Census 1930: Myton, Duchesne County. Belle also went by Belva. She was a daughter of John Rowley and Augusta Mae Babcock, among the earliest settlers in Nine Mile Canyon in the Cow Canyon area. The Babcocks might have arrived by 1891, and Belle might have been born in Nine Mile Canyon. It is unknown if Belle and her husband lived together in Nine Mile Canyon.

Curtis, Hattie Elizabeth. 1884 (Moroni, Sanpete County)–?
Nine Mile: 1899. School census records indicate a Hattie Curtis was a teacher in Nine Mile Canyon in 1899. This could be the Hattie Elizabeth Curtis who was born in Moroni. There are no other records associated with this person.

Desbrough, (?). ?–?
Nine Mile: early 1900s (?). Mildred Dillman indicates that a family named Desbrough owned a ranch in lower Nine Mile Canyon, probably

in the Desbrough Canyon area. Not enough information is provided to know who they might have been, and there are no Desbrough names listed in the Utah censuses for the late 1800s and early 1900s.

Dillman, Mildred (Miles). 1893 (Utah)–1980 (Salt Lake City) Married: Ray Dillman; Nine Mile: 1907 to 1910s; Census 1900: Salt Lake City; Census 1910: Nine Mile Canyon; Census 1920: Roosevelt, Duchesne County; Census 1930: Roosevelt, Duchesne County. Mildred was a daughter of William A. and Lucretia Wightman Miles, and one of seven daughters, from which the legend of the "nine miles" was derived. Only five of the daughters might actually have lived in Nine Mile Canyon. Mildred wrote the first historical account, published in 1948, of Nine Mile Canyon, and much of it is derived from personal recollections.

Downward, Cecilia (or Celia). *See **Johnston, Georgiana Cecelia (Downard)***

Downard, Ida (Warren). 1902 (Nine Mile Canyon?)–1960 (Price, Carbon County) Married: Lee Downard; Nine Mile: 1900s to 1910s; Census 1910: Nine Mile Canyon; Census 1920: Price, Carbon County; Census 1930: Price, Carbon County. Ida was the oldest child of Parley P. and Sarah Warren, who settled in Argyle Canyon. Her father might have been in the canyon before 1900, at which time he was listed on the census. Ida was born two years later, perhaps in Nine Mile Canyon.

Draper, Rose. ?–?

Nine Mile: 1900. School census records indicate she was a teacher in Nine Mile Canyon in 1900. There are no other vital records that are clearly linked to this person.

Dummer, George H. Ca. 1866 (New York)–? Nine Mile: ca. 1887; Census 1880: Brighton, Salt Lake County. George was a hired ranch hand working for James and George Whitmore in 1887. At that time he was living in a cabin in Whitmore Park in upper Nine Mile Canyon. He provided testimony in a cattle rustling case against two soldiers accused of killing and butchering a Whitmore cow. The soldiers were acquitted despite rather convincing testimony. Nothing much is known about him after that time.

Eagan, Catherine. 1873 (Kansas)–? Married: John H. Eagan (ca. 1900?), Patrick Creaham (?); Nine Mile: ca. 1900 to 1910; Census 1910: Nine Mile Canyon; Census 1920: Ogden, Weber County; Census 1930: San Francisco. Catherine, or "Kate," married John Eagan in about 1900. John was one of the original settlers in Nine Mile Canyon in the 1880s. The couple had three children before his death sometime before 1910. Kate and the children later moved to Ogden. She later married Patrick Creaham and they were living in San Francisco with her adult children at the time of the 1930 census. By 1940 she was still living in San Francisco, a widow by then, with her sons John and Eugene. There are very few vital records related to Kate.

Eagan, Eugene V. 1905 (Nine Mile Canyon?)–1981 (San Francisco) Nine Mile: 1906 to 1910s; Census 1910: Nine Mile Canyon; Census 1920: Ogden, Weber County; Census

1930: San Francisco. There is no indication Eugene ever married, and he appears to have lived with his mother for more than thirty years. He was the son of John H. Eagan, one of the earliest settlers in Nine Mile Canyon. He might have been born in Nine Mile Canyon.

Eagan, Gilbert S. Ca. 1857 (Indiana)–? Married: Catherine (?); Nine Mile: ca. 1910; Census 1860: Centre, Indiana; Census 1870: Centre, Indiana; Census 1900: Sand Creek, Iowa; Census 1910: Nine Mile Canyon; Census 1920: Ogden, Weber County. Gilbert was the brother of John Eagan, who had a ranch and saloon a few miles above Brock's Place. Both Gilbert and his brother John married women named Catherine. In 1910 Gilbert, a widower, was living with John's wife Catherine, who is also listed as a widow, and her three young children. There are minimal vital records related to Gilbert after he arrived in Utah.

Eagan, John H. Ca. 1859 (Indiana)– after ca. 1906 Married: Catherine Eagan; Nine Mile: ca. 1889 to ca. 1906; Census 1860: Centre, Indiana; Census 1870: Centre, Indiana; Census 1900: Nine Mile Canyon. John Eagan was one of the earliest settlers of Nine Mile Canyon. The family name is also spelled Agan. There are no vital records for John Eagan in Utah, but there are numerous historical accounts. He was present at the time William Brock killed Frank Foote at Brock's saloon in 1889, and there are references to him having dinner with Preston Nutter (after 1901). John constructed his own saloon after Nutter closed down the roadhouse at Brock's Place. A planned hotel was never completed. He might have died in Indiana.

Eagan, John L. 1903 (Nine Mile Canyon?)–?
Nine Mile: 1903 to 1910s; Census 1910: Nine Mile Canyon; Census 1920: Ogden, Weber County; Census 1930: San Francisco. There is no indication John L. ever married, and he appears to have lived with his mother, Catherine, for more than thirty years. He is the son of John H. Eagan, one of the earliest settlers in Nine Mile Canyon. He might have been born in Nine Mile Canyon.

Eagan, Mazie Ellen. 1907 (Utah)–?
Nine Mile: 1907 to 1910s; Census 1910: Nine Mile Canyon; Census 1920: Ogden, Weber County; Census 1930: San Francisco. There is no indication Ellen ever married, and she appears to have lived with her mother, Catherine, for about thirty years. She was the daughter of John H. Eagan, one of the earliest settlers in Nine Mile Canyon. She might have been born in Nine Mile Canyon.

Edwards, Archie L. 1908 (Nine Mile Canyon)–2001 (Manti, Sanpete County)
Nine Mile: 1908 to 1930s; Census 1910: Nine Mile Canyon; Census 1920: Wellington, Carbon County; Census 1930: Nine Mile Canyon. Archie was the son of Caleb and Elvina Edwards, early settlers in the Soldier Creek Canyon area. He might have been born at the family ranch along the road near where it enters Soldier Creek Canyon. There is no record that he married.

Edwards, Caleb Elisha. 1879 (Utah)–1946 (Carbon County)
Married: Elvina Jensen; Nine Mile: 1900s to 1930s; Census 1880: Levan, Juab County; Census 1900: Emery, Emery County; Census 1910: Nine Mile Canyon; Census 1920: Wellington, Carbon County; Census 1930: Nine Mile Canyon. Caleb, the family patriarch, was one of the longest-term residents of the area, arriving before 1910 and living there through the 1930 census, although the 1920 census lists him living in Wellington. He had a ranch along the road near where it enters Soldier Creek Canyon, and he sold supplies and produce to passing freighters. Their children might have been born there.

Edwards, Clinton J. 1907 (Nine Mile Canyon?)–1974 (Price, Carbon County)
Married: Ethel May (after 1930); Nine Mile: 1907 to 1930s; Census 1910: Nine Mile Canyon; Census 1920: Wellington, Carbon County; Census 1930: Nine Mile Canyon. Clinton was the son of Caleb and Elvina Edwards, long-time early residents of the canyon. He might have been born at the family ranch near Soldier Creek Canyon. There is no indication he raised his family in or near Nine Mile Canyon.

Edwards, Elda M. 1905 (Nine Mile Canyon)–1977 (Salt Lake City)
Married: (?) Anderson; Nine Mile: 1900s to 1910s; Census 1910: Nine Mile Canyon; 1920: Wellington, Carbon County. Elda is also listed as Ella Mae. She was listed as Elda Anderson at the time of her death, but no marriage records were identified. She is the daughter of Caleb and Elvina Edwards, long-time early residents of the canyon. She might have been born at the family ranch near where the road enters Soldier Creek Canyon. There are few records related to her after the 1920 census.

Edwards, Elvina (Jensen). 1888 (Utah)–?
Married: Caleb Edwards; Nine Mile: 1900s to 1930s; Census 1900: Emery, Emery County; Census 1910: Nine Mile Canyon; Census 1920: Wellington, Carbon County; Census 1930: Nine Mile Canyon. Elvina, the family matriarch, was one of the longest-term residents of the canyon, arriving before 1910 and living there through the 1930 census, although the 1920 census lists her living in Wellington. Her children might have been born at the family ranch near where the road enters Soldier Creek Canyon.

Edwards, Grant Odell. 1913 (Nine Mile Canyon?)–1997 (Price, Carbon County)
Married: Martha (after 1930); Nine Mile: 1913 to 1930s; Census 1920: Wellington, Carbon County; Census 1930: Nine Mile Canyon. Grant was the son of Caleb and Elvina Edwards, long-time early residents of the canyon. He might have been born at the family ranch along the road near where it enters Soldier Creek Canyon.

Edwards, June Leroy. 1917 (Nine Mile Canyon?)–2000 (Price, Carbon County)
Nine Mile: 1917 to 1940s; Census 1920: Wellington, Carbon County; Census 1930: Nine Mile Canyon. June was the son of Caleb and Elvina Edwards, long-time early residents of the canyon. He might have been born at the family ranch along the road near where it enters Soldier Creek

Canyon. He was still farming there at the time of the 1940 census.

Edwards, Martha Jane (Miles). 1885 (Utah)–?
Married: Homer Percival Edwards; Nine Mile: (1907?) to 1910s; Census 1900: Salt Lake City; Census 1910: Salt Lake City; Census 1920: Roosevelt, Duchesne County; Census 1930: Roosevelt, Duchesne County. There is no convincing evidence that Martha ever lived in Nine Mile Canyon. She was already married by 1910 when her parents and siblings were living in Nine Mile Canyon. She is one of seven Miles daughters that contribute to the legend that Nine Mile Canyon was named after the Miles family. She is a daughter of William A. and Lucretia Wightman Miles.

Edwards, Melvin. 1910 (Nine Mile Canyon?)–1977 (North Salt Lake, Davis County)
Nine Mile: 1910 to 1930s; Census 1910: Nine Mile Canyon (?); Census 1920: Wellington, Carbon County; Census 1930: Nine Mile Canyon. Melvin was the son of Caleb and Elvina Edwards, who had a ranch along the road near where it enters Soldier Creek Canyon. There is no record that he married. He might have been born here.

Ellis, Minervia. ?–?
Nine Mile: 1899. School census records indicate Minervia was a schoolteacher in Nine Mile Canyon in 1899. There are no other records that are conclusively linked to this person.

Elmer, Alvin D. 1900 (Nine Mile Canyon?)–?
Nine Mile: ca. 1900. Nothing is known about the Clark and Hariette

Elmer family, how they came to be in Nine Mile Canyon, or where they went after 1900. Alvin was of an age where he could have been born in Nine Mile Canyon. There are no cross-references to this person in the database.

Elmer, Clark. 1870 (Utah)–?
Married: Hariette; Nine Mile: ca. 1900; Census 1900: Nine Mile Canyon. Little is known about the Clark and Hariette Elmer family, how they came to be in Nine Mile Canyon, or where they went after 1900. Both the children are of an age where they could have been born in Nine Mile Canyon. There are no cross-references to Elmer in the database. Dillman indicates they owned a ranch in lower Nine Mile Canyon in the Desbrough or Franks Canyon area.

Elmer, Ethel. 1898 (Nine Mile Canyon?)–?
Nine Mile: ca. 1900; Census 1900: Nine Mile Canyon. Little is known about the Clark and Hariette Elmer family, how they came to be in Nine Mile Canyon, or where they went after 1900. Ethel was of an age where she could have been born in Nine Mile Canyon. There are no cross-references to this person in the database.

Elmer, Hariette. 1872 (England)–?
Married: Clark Elmer; Nine Mile: ca. 1900; Census 1900: Nine Mile Canyon. Nothing is known about the Clark and Hariette Elmer family, how they came to be in Nine Mile Canyon, or where they went after 1900. Both the children are of an age where they could have been born in Nine Mile Canyon. There are no cross-references to Harriett in the database.

Evans, Lucretia (Miles). Ca. 1892–1977 (Salt Lake City)
Married: Edmund P. Evans; Nine Mile: 1907 to 1910s; Census 1900: Salt Lake City; Census 1910: Nine Mile Canyon; Census 1920: Roosevelt, Duchesne County; Census 1930: Salt Lake City. Lucretia was a daughter of William A. and Lucretia Wightman Miles. She is one of seven Miles daughters who contribute to the legend that Nine Mile Canyon was named after the Miles family. The Miles ranch was in lower Nine Mile Canyon at Maxies Canyon. She would have been a teenager at the time her father bought the ranch in 1907.

Evans, R. O. ?–?
Nine Mile: 1899. School census records indicate this person was a teacher in Nine Mile Canyon in 1899. There are no other records related to this person.

Ewell, Elvira Lillian. 1877 (Utah)–1952 (Salt Lake City)
Married: William W. Ewell (1894); Nine Mile: ca. 1930; Census 1880: Gunlock, Washington County; Census 1900: Helper, Carbon County; Census 1910: Price, Carbon County; Census 1920: Salt Lake City; Census 1930: Nine Mile Canyon. The Ewell family lived variously in Carbon County and the Salt Lake Valley. They arrived in Nine Mile Canyon sometime before 1930, and they did not stay long. Nothing is known as to how the family came to be in Nine Mile Canyon or why they left.

Ewell, Lois. 1917 (Utah)–2001 (Sandy, Salt Lake County)
Married: James L. Washburn; Nine Mile: ca. 1930; Census 1920: Salt

Lake City; Census 1930: Nine Mile Canyon. Lois was the youngest of the Ewell children to accompany her parents, William and Lillian Ewell, to Nine Mile Canyon. She returned to the Salt Lake Valley where she married and raised a family.

Ewell, Thelma A. 1910 (Utah)–1990 (Denton, Texas)
Married: Lavell Kemp; Nine Mile: ca. 1930; Census 1920: Salt Lake City; Census 1930: Nine Mile Canyon. Thelma was about nineteen years old at the time of the 1930 census when she was living as a single woman with her parents, William and Lillian Ewell, in Nine Mile Canyon. She returned to the Salt Lake Valley where she married and raised a family.

Ewell, Walter L. Ca. 1909 (Utah)–1993 (Salt Lake City)
Married: Ida Marie; Nine Mile: ca. 1930; Census 1910: Price, Carbon County; Census 1920: Salt Lake City; Census 1930: Nine Mile Canyon. Walter was twenty-one years old at the time of the 1930 census when he was a single man living with his parents, William and Lillian Ewell, in Nine Mile Canyon. He returned to the Salt Lake Valley where he married and raised a family.

Ewell, William W. 1870 (Goshen, Utah)–1950 (Salt Lake City)
Married: Elvira Lillian Bigelow (1894); Nine Mile: ca. 1930; Census 1870: Santaquin, Utah County; Census 1880: Santaquin, Utah County; Census 1900: Helper, Carbon County; Census 1910: Price, Carbon County; Census 1920: Salt Lake City; Census 1930: Nine Mile Canyon. The Ewell family lived variously in Carbon County and the

Salt Lake Valley. They arrived in Nine Mile Canyon sometime before 1930 but did not stay long. William would have been sixty years old in 1930, and his children were grown. William's profession was listed as farmer. Nothing is known about how the family came to be in Nine Mile Canyon or why they left.

Farrow, Ervin W. Ca. 1880 (Texas)–?
Nine Mile: ca. 1930; Census 1930: Nine Mile Canyon. Almost nothing is known of Ervin. In 1930, he was a ranch hand working for Preston Nutter and living at the Nutter Ranch. There are no other records cross-referenced to him.

Fausett, Clara B. (Smithson). 1896 (Utah)–1980 (Price, Carbon County)
Married: Ervin Fausett; Nine Mile: 1890s to 1900s; Census 1900: Nine Mile Canyon; Census 1910: Packard, Wasatch County; Census 1920: Neola, Duchesne County; Census 1930: Price, Carbon County. Clara might have been born in Nine Mile Canyon after the family migrated here from Arizona. She was the daughter of Nephi and Barbara Cook Smithson. The Smithson family had a ranch in the Sulphur Canyon area and another at the mouth of Cottonwood Canyon.

Fitt, Annie E. (Houskeeper). 1881 (Utah)–?
Married: William W. Fitt; Nine Mile: 1890s to 1900s; Census 1900: Nine Mile Canyon; Census 1910: Orangeville, Emery County; Census 1920: Orangeville, Emery County. Annie was probably a teenager or young adult when her father brought her to Nine Mile Canyon. She soon married and moved back to Emery County. She was the daughter of

Theodore Sr. and Sarah Butler Houskeeper, who were among the earliest residents of the canyon in the 1890s.

Foote, John Franklin. Ca. 1863 (Nephi, Juab County)–1889 (Nine Mile Canyon)
Nine Mile: ca. 1889; Census 1880: Nephi, Juab County. Very little is known about Frank Foote other than he was from Nephi where his dad was a judge, he had a ranch in upper Nine Mile Canyon, and he was married with a small child. He was twenty-six years old when he was killed in November 1889 by William Brock during a saloon brawl at Brock's Place, now the Preston Nutter Ranch. Brock was acquitted of murder charges. It is not known what happened to his wife and child after his death. He is buried in Nephi.

Foster, Sarah R. See Anderson, Sarah Matilda (Foster)

Fowler, Ida (Harmon). 1899 (Nine Mile Canyon?)–1945 (Myton, Duchesne County)
Married: Earle R. Fowler; Nine Mile: 1899 to 1910s; Census 1900: Nine Mile Canyon (?); Census 1910: Nine Mile Canyon; Census 1920: Myton, Duchesne County; Census 1930: Myton, Duchesne County. Ida would have been born about the same time her parents acquired the Rock House at the mouth of Harmon Canyon. Family records indicate she was born in Wellington, but the family could have been living in Nine Mile Canyon. She was a daughter of Edwin and Josephine Babcock Harmon, and she grew up in Nine Mile Canyon.

Francis, Alice (Elston). April 1872 (Minnesota)–?
Married: Pete Francis, (?) Bradley; Nine Mile: 1890s to ca. 1900; Census 1880: Columbus, Nebraska; Census 1900: Nine Mile Canyon; Census 1910: Monterrey, California. Alice married Pete about the same time he acquired the saloon and hotel from William Brock in about 1890. Both of their children were probably born in Nine Mile Canyon. Pete was killed in 1901, and newspaper accounts indicated he was divorced from Alice at that time, and that she was living in Salt Lake City with their two sons. She later married a man named Bradley, but by 1910 she was again divorced. There are no vital records related to her after 1910.

Francis, Pete. 1862 (Texas)–1901 (Nine Mile Canyon)
Married: Alice Elston; Nine Mile: ca. 1890 to 1901; Census 1900: Nine Mile Canyon. Pete was closely associated with the outlaw element in Nine Mile Canyon, including Gunplay Maxwell. He operated a saloon and hotel at what is today the Nutter Ranch. He was killed by Dave Russell in 1901 during a dispute in the saloon, traditionally called Brock's Place. There are no vital records related to him prior to the 1900 census. He lived at the roadhouse with his wife, Alice, and two sons, Forrest and Fredie.

Francis, Forrest. 1891 (Nine Mile Canyon?)–?
Nine Mile: 1891 to ca. 1900; Census 1900: Nine Mile Canyon; Census 1910: Monterrey, California. Forrest was the oldest son of Pete and Alice Francis. He was probably born in Nine Mile Canyon and lived at the roadhouse referred to as Brock's

Place. There are no vital records related to him after the 1910 census. In 1901, he was living with his divorced mother in Salt Lake City.

Francis, Fredie. 1892 (Nine Mile Canyon?)–?
Nine Mile: 1892 to ca. 1900; Census 1900: Nine Mile Canyon; Census 1910: Monterrey, California; Census 1930: Monterrey, California. Fredie was the son of Pete and Alice Francis. He was probably born in Nine Mile Canyon and lived at the roadhouse, referred to Brock's Place. There are no vital records related to him after the 1930 census.

Franklin, Edna W. Ca. 1902 (Grand Junction, Colorado)–1935 (St. George, Washington County)
Nine Mile: ca. 1910; Census 1910: Nine Mile Canyon; Census 1920: Mount Trumbull, Arizona; Census 1930: St. George, Washington County. Edna was the daughter of Edward Benjamin and Winnifred Franklin. Very little is known about the Benjamin Franklin family. They lived in Nine Mile Canyon briefly, and were present for the 1910 census when Edna was eight years old. They eventually moved on to the Arizona Strip. Winnifred and Edna moved to St. George after the death of Benjamin, and were living there at the time of the 1930 census.

Franklin, Edward Benjamin. Ca. 1860 (Texas)–before 1930
Married: Winnifred (?); Nine Mile: ca. 1910; Census 1910: Nine Mile Canyon; Census 1920: Mount Trumbull, Arizona. Very little is known about the Benjamin Franklin family. They lived in Nine Mile Canyon briefly, and were present

for the 1910 census. They eventually moved on to the Arizona Strip. Winnifred and Edna moved to St. George after the death of Benjamin, and were living there at the time of the 1930 census.

Franklin, Winnifred A. Ca. 1887 (Colorado)–?
Married: Edward Benjamin Franklin; Nine Mile: ca. 1910; Census 1910: Nine Mile Canyon; Census 1920: Mount Trumbull, Arizona; Census 1930: St. George, Washington County. Very little is known about the Benjamin Franklin family. They lived in Nine Mile Canyon briefly, and were present for the 1910 census. They eventually moved on to the Arizona Strip. Winnifred and Edna moved to St. George after the death of Benjamin, and were living there at the time of the 1930 census. Winnifred's name is spelled Winferd in the 1910 Census.

Grames, Frederic Emper. Ca. 1850 (Findon, England)–1897 (Nine Mile Canyon)
Married: Martha Powell; Nine Mile: ca. 1886 to 1897; Census 1850: England; Census 1870: Payson, Utah County; Census 1880: Huntington, Emery County. Frederic was one of the earliest settlers of Price, in 1878, and he is credited with starting the first commercial district there. In 1885 he sold his general store and returned to the family farm, presumably in Price where he had large landholdings. Shortly after, he sold the farm to James Whitmore and moved to a ranch in Nine Mile Canyon, probably located in the Whitmore Park area. He was one of the first white settlers in the canyon. He died on his Nine Mile Canyon ranch.

Grames, Frederic Emper "Freddie."
Ca. 1884 (Price, Carbon County)–1950
(Price, Carbon County)
Nine Mile: ca. 1886 to 1910s; Census
1910: Nine Mile Canyon. Freddie
probably arrived in Nine Mile
Canyon in about 1886 as a young toddler. He might have returned to Price
after the death of his father in 1897,
but he had returned by 1910 when he
was listed as a single head of household. His mother and sister were also
living in the canyon at the time with
Al Thompson. There are very few
vital records related to Freddie.

Grames, Martha E. *See* **Thompson,**
Martha E. (Grames)

Grames, Martha Ellen (Powell). 1850
(Iowa)–1925 (Price, Carbon County)
Married: Frederic Grames; Nine
Mile: ca. 1886 to after 1910; Census
1850: Keokuk, Iowa; Census 1870:
Payson, Utah County; Census 1880:
Huntington, Emery County; Census
1910: Nine Mile Canyon. Martha
Ellen Powell would have been one of
the first white residents of Nine Mile
Canyon. She might have returned
to Price after the death of her hus-
band in 1897, but she was back in 1910,
living with her daughter, Martha
Thompson. Martha was a sister to
John A. Powell, also an early settler
of Price in 1878; John and his third
wife also had a ranch in Nine Mile
Canyon. A niece also had a ranch in
the canyon.

Gwyther, William. 1883 (Utah)–1941
(Carbon County)
Nine Mile: ca. 1930; Census 1900:
North Ashley, Uintah County;
Census 1930: Nine Mile Canyon.
William was living with Neal and
Minerva Hanks as a boarder at the
time of the 1930 census. There is no

indication he has any other ties to
Nine Mile Canyon, and there are few
vital records related to him. He was
still living with Neal and Minerva in
1940.

Hadley, Elmer. Ca. 1882 (England)–?
Nine Mile: ca. 1910; Census 1910:
Nine Mile Canyon. Little is known
of Elmer Hadley, a twenty-eight-
year-old single man at the time of
the 1910 census. He listed his occupation as sheepherder. There are no
other cross-references to him in the
database.

Hall, Alvin J. 1899 (Nine Mile
Canyon?)–1962 (Los Angeles,
California)
Married: Martha Hall; Nine Mile:
1894 to 1900s; Census 1900: Nine
Mile Canyon; Census 1930: Chicago,
Illinois. Alvin was the youngest son
of Charles and Sarah Babcock Hall.
He was probably born in Nine Mile
Canyon. Alvin was only about five
years old when his mother died. It is
not known where he grew up in the
years after, but it appears his other
siblings were sent to live with relatives at that time.

Hall, Charles. 1863 (Utah)–1932
(Duchesne County)
Married: Sarah A. Babcock (1891);
Nine Mile: 1894 to 1900s; Census
1870: Panaca, Washington County;
Census 1880: Escalante, Garfield
County; Census 1900: Nine Mile
Canyon. Charles and his wife, Sarah,
reportedly moved from Escalante
to Nine Mile Canyon in the spring
of 1894. Their daughters Minnie
and Maude sparked the legend that
Minnie Maud Canyon was so named
after the twin girls. Sarah died in
1905 and Charles might have moved
on to the Uinta Basin where he died

in 1932. It appears the children were
sent to live with relatives. There are
no vital records of Charles after the
1900 census. The Hall ranch was
located at the mouth of Minnie Maud
Canyon. Family histories indicate the
family also operated the stage stop at
the mouth of Soldier Creek Canyon
after selling their ranch.

Hall, Charles Earnest. 1897 (Nine
Mile Canyon?)–1982 (Salt Lake City)
Married: Leda Peterson; Nine Mile:
1897 to 1900s; Census 1900: Nine
Mile Canyon; Census 1910: Escalante,
Garfield County; Census 1920:
Richfield, Sevier County; Census
1930: Salt Lake City. Charles Earnest
was the son of Charles and Sarah
Babcock Hall. He might have been
born in Nine Mile Canyon. After his
mother died in 1905, Earnest went to
live with relatives John and Eliza Roe
in Escalante. He apparently never
returned to Nine Mile Canyon.

Hall, Earl E. Ca. 1899–1957 (Price,
Carbon County)
Nine Mile: 1900s to 1910s; Census
1910: Nine Mile Canyon. Earl was
the son of Martha E. Grames, who
later married Al Thompson. There are
very few vital records related to Earl,
and it is unknown if he married. It
is unknown who his father was, or if
he was related to the Hall family that
settled at the mouth of Minnie Maud
Canyon.

Hall, Jessie Myrtle. *See* **Lloyd, Jessie**
Myrtle (Hall)

Hall, Mary Mae. *See* **Brown, Mary**
Mae (Hall)

Hall, Maude. *See* **Potter, Maude**
(Hall)

Hall, Minnie. *See **Brown, Minnie (Hall)***

Hall, Sarah A. (Babcock). 1875 (Utah)–1905 (Nine Mile Canyon?)
Married: Charles Hall (1891); Nine Mile: 1894 to 1900s; Census 1880: Greenwich, Piute County; Census 1900: Nine Mile Canyon. Charles Hall and his wife, Sarah Babcock, reportedly moved from Escalante to Nine Mile Canyon in the spring of 1894. Their daughters Minnie and Maude sparked the legend that Minnie Maud Canyon was named after the twin girls. Sarah died in 1905, leaving behind six young children. Sarah was the daughter of John and Augusta Mae Babcock, who were among the earliest settlers in Nine Mile Canyon. After Sarah's death, Charles sent some of the children to live with relatives.

Hamilton, Ada. *See **Brundage, Ada (Hamilton)***

Hamilton, Calvin. 1869 (Utah)–1925 (Duchesne County)
Married: Carmelia Hunt (1907); Nine Mile: 1890s to 1900s; Census 1870: Nephi, Juab County; Census 1880: Gooseberry Valley, Sevier County; Census 1900: Nine Mile Canyon; Census 1910: Giles, Wayne County. Calvin was the younger brother of James and David Hamilton and Emma Hamilton Wiseman. He might have joined the extended Hamilton family who migrated to Nine Mile Canyon in the 1890s from the Gooseberry Valley area. In 1900, he was single and living with his sister, Emma, in Nine Mile Canyon. He married a Wayne County girl in 1907 and appears to have stayed in Wayne County through at least 1910.

Hamilton, David William. 1860 (Utah)–?
Married: Eliza Jane Bird; Nine Mile: 1890s to 1900s; Census 1870: Nephi, Juab County; Census 1880: Gooseberry Valley, Sevier County; Census 1900: Nine Mile Canyon; Census 1910: Myton, Duchesne County; Census 1920: Antelope, Duchesne County. David William "Will" Hamilton was one of the earliest settlers of upper Nine Mile Canyon, where he had a ranch just above the mouth of Minnie Maud Canyon. His profession in 1900 was listed as freighter. He arrived in Nine Mile Canyon before 1900 with his brother, James, and sister, Emma (Wiseman), who also had ranches in the same area. He later moved on to Myton, and he might have been in business with his brother, who had purchased Smith Wells.

Hamilton, James Alma. Ca. 1864 (Utah)–1933 (Duchesne County)
Married: Susan Van Wagoner; Nine Mile: 1890s to 1900s; Census 1870: Nephi, Juab County; Census 1880: Gooseberry Valley, Sevier County; Census 1900: Nine Mile Canyon; Census 1910: Myton, Duchesne County; Census 1920: Myton, Duchesne County; Census 1930: Myton, Duchesne County. James and Susan moved to Nine Mile Canyon in the 1890s along with the extended Hamilton family, including brothers William and Calvin, sister Emma, and widowed mother, Martha. They came by way of Gooseberry Valley, but might have settled in the Gordon Creek area before migrating to Nine Mile Canyon. James had a ranch near his brother, William, at the mouth of Minnie Maud Canyon. He proved up on a homestead claim on the family ranch and then sold it in 1906. He

appears to have purchased the store at Smith Wells, a stage stop south of Myton.

Hamilton, James Andrew. Ca. 1899 (Nine Mile Canyon?)–1954 (Duchesne County)
Nine Mile: 1899 to 1900s; Census 1900: Nine Mile Canyon; Census 1910: Myton, Duchesne County; Census 1920: Myton, Duchesne County. James was the son of James and Susan Van Wagoner Hamilton. He was probably born in Nine Mile Canyon. There is no record that he married. His family would have left Nine Mile Canyon when he was just a toddler.

Hamilton, Martha E. (Bennett). Ca. 1842 (Illinois)–1917 (Myton, Duchesne County)
Married: David F. Hamilton; Nine Mile: ca. 1900; Census 1850: Salt Lake City (?); Census 1870: Nephi, Juab County; Census 1880: Gooseberry Valley, Sevier County; Census 1900: Nine Mile Canyon; Census 1910: Myton, Duchesne County. The database cross-references Martha to a Martha E. Bennett, born in Missouri and living in Salt Lake City in 1850. In 1900, she was living with her daughter, Martha Wiseman, and son Calvin Hamilton in Nine Mile Canyon. It also indicates she was living with her son William in Myton in 1910. William is probably the David W. Hamilton listed as the oldest son.

Hamilton, Martha Jane. *See **Cox, Martha Jane (Hamilton)***

Hamilton, Eliza Jane (Bird). 1863 (Mendon, Cache County)–1928 (Duchesne County)

Married: William Hamilton; Nine Mile: 1890s to 1900s; Census 1880: Gooseberry Valley, Sevier County; Census 1900: Nine Mile Canyon; Census 1910: Myton, Duchesne County; Census 1920: Antelope, Duchesne County. Liza's father, Kelsey Bird, moved the family to Gooseberry Valley where the Birds came in contact with the Hamilton family. There is no record of other members of the Bird family in Nine Mile Canyon. Liza married William Hamilton, probably David W. Hamilton, and they had a ranch near the mouth of Minnie Maud Canyon. They left Nine Mile Canyon in about 1900.

Hamilton, Ellen Pearl. *See Mair, Ellen Pearl (Hamilton)*

Hamilton, Hettie Maud. *See Brundage, Hettie Maud (Hamilton)*

Hamilton, Latessy "Tessie." Ca. 1896 (Nine Mile Canyon?)–?
Nine Mile: 1890s to 1900s; Census 1900: Nine Mile Canyon; Census 1910: Myton, Duchesne County. Tessie was the daughter of James A. and Susan Van Wagoner Hamilton, and she might have been born in Nine Mile Canyon. Her family sold the Nine Mile ranch in the early 1900s and moved to Smith Wells and later Myton. There are no records of her after the 1910 census.

Hamilton, Louis. Ca. 1898 (Nine Mile Canyon?)–1949 (Duchesne County)
Nine Mile: ca. 1898 to 1900s; Census 1900: Nine Mile Canyon; Census 1910: Myton, Duchesne County; Census 1920: Antelope, Duchesne County. Louis might have been born in Nine Mile Canyon. He was the son

of William and Liza Bird Hamilton. There is no record that he married. He would have been a small child when his family moved to Myton after 1900.

Hamilton, Maude. *See Warren, Maude (Hamilton)*

Hamilton, Nellie M. *See Taylor, Nellie M. (Hamilton)*

Hamilton, Sarah A. 1888 (Utah)–1925 (Carbon County)
Married: (?) Stansfield; Nine Mile: 1890s to 1900s; Census 1900: Nine Mile Canyon. There are very few vital records related to Sarah. She was the daughter of William and Liza Bird Hamilton, and was probably raised in Nine Mile Canyon. Her family left the canyon in about 1900. She is buried in Myton.

Hamilton, Susan (Van Wagoner). Ca. 1869–1934 (Duchesne County)
Married: James A. Hamilton; Nine Mile: 1890s to 1900s; Census 1880: Gooseberry Valley, Sevier County; Census 1900: Nine Mile Canyon; Census 1910: Myton, Duchesne County; Census 1920: Myton, Duchesne County; Census 1930: Myton, Duchesne County. James and Susan moved to Nine Mile Canyon in the 1890s along with the extended Hamilton family, including brothers William and Calvin, sister Emma, and widowed mother, Martha. They came by way of Gooseberry Valley, but might have settled in the Gordon Creek area before migrating to Nine Mile Canyon. They had a ranch at the mouth of Minnie Maud Canyon.

Hamilton, Vivian L. *See Bentley, Vivian L. (Hamilton)*

Hamilton, William. 1892 (Utah)–1931 (Duchesne County)
Married: Cora Barbieri; Nine Mile: 1890s to 1900s; Census 1900: Nine Mile Canyon; Census 1920: Neola, Duchesne County; Census 1930: Wellington, Carbon County. William was the son of William and Liza Bird Hamilton, and he probably grew up on the family ranch near the mouth of Minnie Maud Canyon. He was probably not born in the canyon. His family moved to Myton in about 1900.

Hammerschmid, Kathryn. Ca. 1899–?
Married: William Hammerschmid; Nine Mile: ca. 1920; Census 1920: Nine Mile Canyon; Census 1930: Roosevelt, Duchesne County. Her name is listed as Kathryn on marriage records, but Catherine in census records. Willie married Kathryn in 1915 in Kansas, and by 1920 they were living in Nine Mile Canyon. How they came to know about Nine Mile Canyon is not known. They arrived in late 1919, and they did not stay long; by 1930 the family was living in Roosevelt. They later returned and bought out the Houskeeper ranch at the mouth of Cow Canyon in 1963. It is still in the Hammerschmid family today.

Hammerschmid, Minnie. Ca. 1921 (Nine Mile Canyon?)–?
Nine Mile: ca. 1921; Census 1930: Roosevelt, Duchesne County. Minnie was born one year after her family arrived in Nine Mile Canyon, and it is possible she was born there before her family moved to Roosevelt. There are no other vital records related to her in the database.

Hammerschmid, Rosanna (or Rosina). Ca. 1856 (Germany)–1933 (Duchesne County)
Married: Karl Hammerschmid; Nine Mile: ca. 1920; Census 1910: Tonganoxie, Kansas; Census 1920: Nine Mile Canyon; Census 1930: Roosevelt, Duchesne County. Rosie accompanied her son, Willie, and daughter-in-law, Kathryn, to Utah from Kansas. She was a German by birth, and in 1918 Rosie registered as an "alien enemy" at the outbreak of World War I. There are few records in the database related to her.

Hammerschmidt, Rosina (or Katherine). Ca. 1919 (Colorado)–?
Nine Mile: ca. 1920; Census 1920: Nine Mile Canyon; Census 1930: Roosevelt, Duchesne County. This person is listed as Rosina in the 1920 census for Nine Mile Canyon and as Katherine in the 1930 census for Roosevelt. It is possible they are two separate persons with slightly different birth years, but both were born in Colorado one year apart. There are no records cross-referenced in the database to either Rosina or Katherine.

Hammerschmid, William. Ca. 1895–?
Married: Kathryn Pellman (1915); Nine Mile: ca. 1920; Census 1910: Tonganoxie, Kansas; Census 1920: Nine Mile Canyon; Census 1930: Roosevelt, Duchesne County. Willie married Kathryn in 1915 in Kansas, and by 1920 they were living in Nine Mile Canyon. It is possible they moved there after their marriage and that their children were born there. How they came to know about Nine Mile Canyon is not known. They did not stay long, and by 1930 the family was living in Roosevelt. They later returned and bought out the Houskeeper ranch at the mouth of Cow Canyon. It is still in the Hammerschmid family today.

Hammerschmidt, William. Ca. 1916 (Kansas)–?
Nine Mile: ca. 1920; Census 1920: Nine Mile Canyon; Census 1930: Roosevelt, Duchesne County. Willie Jr.'s birthplace in Kansas in about 1916 and his sister's birthplace in Colorado in about 1919 suggest the Hammerschmid family did not arrive here until just before the 1920 census. It is unknown how long Willie Jr. stayed in Nine Mile Canyon before moving to Roosevelt. There are no other records cross-referenced to him.

Hampton, Armon (or Alvah). Ca. 1903 (Utah)–1977 (Utah County)
Married: Ovena Jensen; Nine Mile: ca. 1920; Census 1910: Glendale, Kane County; Census 1920: Nine Mile Canyon; Census 1930: Lehi, Utah County. Armon was the son of George and Minerva Hampton of Kane County. He came to Nine Mile Canyon with his two brothers, Theodore and George, and they were boarding with the Pierre and Janet Perry family in 1920. His occupation was listed as farm laborer. A year later he married Elma Perry, the daughter of his landlords, and moved to Utah County. All three brothers are also listed on the 1920 census for Abraham, Millard County, where their parents had moved.

Hampton, Elma (Perry). Ca. 1899 (Utah)–1958 (El Paso, Texas)
Married: Alvah Hampton (1921); Nine Mile: ca. 1920; Census 1900: Farmer, Salt Lake County; Census 1910: Mill Creek, Salt Lake County; Census 1920: Nine Mile Canyon; Census 1930: Cottonwood, Salt Lake County. Her husband, Alvah Hampton, was listed as a boarder in the Perry household in the 1920 census. A year later, Alvah and Elma were married in Salt Lake City. Elma was one of several grown children who accompanied their parents to Nine Mile Canyon from the Salt Lake Valley. Elma and Alvah do not appear to have stayed in the canyon very long.

Hampton, George M. Ca. 1897 (Utah)–1952 (Utah County)
Married: Jeanetta Lowe; Nine Mile: ca. 1920; Census 1910: Glendale, Kane County; Census 1920: Nine Mile Canyon; Census 1930: Caliente, Nevada. George was the son of George and Minerva Hampton of Kane County. He came to Nine Mile Canyon with his two brothers, Theodore and Armon, and they were boarding with the Pierre Perry family. His occupation was listed as farm laborer. He later married and moved to Nevada with his in-laws. All three brothers are also listed on the 1920 census for Abraham, Millard County, where their parents had moved.

Hampton, Theodore. Ca. 1899 (Utah)–1976 (Utah County)
Married: Mertle (?); Nine Mile: ca. 1920; Census 1910: Glendale, Kane County; Census 1920: Nine Mile Canyon; Census 1930: Maybell, Colorado. Theodore was the son of George and Minerva Hampton of Kane County. He came to Nine Mile Canyon with his two brothers, George and Armon, and they were boarding with the Pierre Perry family. His occupation was listed as farm laborer. He later married and moved to Colorado. All three brothers are also listed on the 1920 census for Abraham, Millard County, where their parents had moved.

Hancock, Alvis Morris. Ca. 1893 (Texas)–1939 (Carbon County) Married: Sarah Jane Houskeeper (1936); Nine Mile: 1930s; Census 1900: Riverdale, Texas; Census 1910: Justice, Texas; Census 1930: El Centro, California. Al Hancock was a Texas-born cowboy working for the Preston Nutter Ranch in the 1920s when he met and fell in love with Sarah Jane ("Janie") Houskeeper, daughter of Clara Alger and Theodore B. Houskeeper. Al was, at the time, on the run for a killing in Texas, and after meeting Janie he returned there to answer to the charges. After serving time in prison, he returned to Nine Mile Canyon seven years later, and he and Janie were married in 1936. Al then went to work for Jane's uncle, Frank Alger. When Frank died in 1938, Al and Jane, together with Jane's sister, Lucille, and her husband, Thorald Rich, inherited the Frank Alger ranch. Al died the following year and the ranch remained in the Rich family through the 1950s.

Hancock, Sarah Jane (Houskeeper). 1910 (Nine Mile Canyon?)–1970 (Weber County) Married: Al Hancock (1936); Raymond Newbill (1948); Nine Mile: 1910 to 1930s; Census 1910: Nine Mile Canyon; Census 1920: Wellington, Carbon County; Census 1930: Nine Mile Canyon. Sarah was probably born and raised in Nine Mile Canyon. She was the daughter of Theodore B. and Clara Alger Houskeeper. In 1936, she married Al Hancock, a Texas-born cowboy working for Preston Nutter. They lived at and worked for Jane's uncle, Frank Alger, and with her sister, Lucille Rich, they inherited the ranch

when Frank died in 1938. Al died in 1939.

Haney, Grace (Olsen). Ca. 1884 (Utah)–1982 (Yakima, Washington) Married: Charles Haney; Nine Mile: 1890s to 1900s; Census 1900: Nine Mile Canyon; Census 1910: Blackfoot, Idaho; Census 1920: Orchard Homes, Montana; Census 1930: King County, Washington. Grace was a teenage daughter of John Henry and Olive Olsen when she moved to Nine Mile Canyon. She was married by 1910 and had moved to Idaho with most members of her family.

Hanchett, Augusta Mae. *See Rowley, Augusta Mae (Hanchett)*

Hanks, Donna. Ca. 1915 (Nine Mile Canyon?)–? Nine Mile: ca. 1915 to 1930s; Census 1920: Roosevelt, Duchesne County; Census 1930: Nine Mile Canyon. Donna was the daughter of Neal and Minerva Hanks. Neal was a long-time cowboy in Nine Mile Canyon and good friend to Minerva's first husband, Hank Stewart. There are no vital records related to Donna after the 1930 census.

Hanks, Minerva A. (Van Wagoner). Ca. 1876 (Utah)–? Married: Hank Stewart, Neal Hanks; Nine Mile: 1890s to 1930s; Census 1880: Gooseberry Valley, Sevier County; Census 1900: Nine Mile Canyon; Census 1910: Nine Mile Canyon; Census 1920: Roosevelt, Duchesne County; Census 1930: Nine Mile Canyon. Minerva married Hank Stewart and had two children, then divorced Hank and married Hank's friend, Neal Hanks. She lived most of her adult life in Nine Mile Canyon. Minerva was a sister of

Susan Van Wagoner, who had married James Hamilton, a long-time resident of Nine Mile Canyon in the Minnie Maud Canyon area.

Hanks, Neal. Ca. 1880 (Utah)–? Married: Minerva Van Wagoner; Nine Mile: 1890s to 1930s; Census 1880: Bellevue, Kane County; Census 1900: Nine Mile Canyon; Census 1920: Roosevelt, Duchesne County; Census 1930: Nine Mile Canyon. Little is known of Neal before his arrival in Nine Mile Canyon sometime before 1900. By one account, he came in the 1890s with Hank Stewart to wrangle wild cattle. In 1900, he was a cowboy working for Edwin Lee, and his friend Hank Stewart had a place nearby. After Minerva divorced Hank Stewart, she married Neal and they had a daughter together. Hank and Neal remained good friends. Neal had a ranch near Balanced Rock and another at the mouth of Cottonwood Canyon.

Harmon, Eda. Ca. 1906 (Nine Mile Canyon?)–? Nine Mile: 1906 to 1920s; Census 1910: Nine Mile Canyon; Census 1920: Nine Mile Canyon. There are no vital records related to Eda after the 1920 census. She was the daughter of Edwin and Josephine Babcock Harmon, and she was probably born in Nine Mile Canyon. She was raised at the Rock House.

Harmon, Edwin L. Ca. 1855 (Maine)–1933 (Duchesne County) Married: Josephine Babcock; Nine Mile: ca. 1898 to 1926; Census 1860: Detroit, Maine; Census 1900: Nine Mile Canyon (?); Census 1910: Nine Mile Canyon; Census 1920: Nine Mile Canyon; Census 1930: Myton, Duchesne County. Edwin acquired the "Rock House" from the Winn family in the late 1890s or early 1900s and lived there with his family for more than twenty years. Edwin was married to Josephine Babcock, daughter of John Rowley Babcock, another long-time Nine Mile settler. Very little is known of Edwin until he arrived in Nine Mile Canyon. Harmon Canyon is named after him. The previous occupant of the Rock House, John Winn, left in 1898 and Edwin and Josephine could have moved in at that time. But they are not listed on the 1900 census for Nine Mile Canyon.

Harmon, Ida. *See* **Fowler, Ida (Harmon)**

Harmon, Josephine (Babcock). Ca. 1880 (Utah)–?
Married: Edwin Harmon (1898); Nine Mile: 1890s to 1926; Census 1900: Nine Mile Canyon (?); Census 1910: Nine Mile Canyon; Census 1920: Nine Mile Canyon; Census 1930: Myton, Duchesne County. Josephine Babcock was a daughter of John Rowley Babcock, who was among the earliest settlers in Nine Mile Canyon. John Babcock was living with Josephine and Edwin at the time of the 1920 census. She was eighteen years old when they married, Edwin was forty-three years old.

Harmon, John. Ca. 1916 (Nine Mile Canyon?)–?
Nine Mile: 1916 to 1920s; Census 1920: Nine Mile Canyon; Census 1930: Myton, Duchesne County. There are no vital records of John after the 1930 census. He was a son of Edwin and Josephine Babcock Harmon, and he might have been born and raised at the Rock House in Nine Mile Canyon.

Harmon, Lewis. Ca. 1918 (Nine Mile Canyon?)–?
Nine Mile: 1918 to 1920s; Census 1920: Nine Mile Canyon. There are no vital records of Lewis after the 1920 census. He was a son of Edwin and Josephine Babcock Harmon, and he might have been born and raised at the Rock House in Nine Mile Canyon.

Harmon, Ross. Ca. 1912 (Nine Mile Canyon?)–?
Married: Fern (?); Nine Mile: 1912 to 1920s; Census 1920: Nine Mile Canyon; Census 1930: Myton, Duchesne County. There are very few vital records related to Ross. He was probably born and raised at the Rock House in Nine Mile Canyon. He was a son of Edwin and Josephine Babcock Harmon.

Harmon, Vera. Ca. 1904 (Nine Mile Canyon?)–1973 (Ogden, Weber County)
Married: (?) Wilson; Nine Mile: 1904 to 1920s; Census 1910: Nine Mile Canyon; Census 1920: Nine Mile Canyon; Census 1930: Hurricane, Washington County. Vera was a daughter of Edwin and Josephine Babcock Harmon. She was probably born and raised at the Rock House in Nine Mile Canyon. She might have married a man named Wilson, but there are no marriage records.

Hartvizden, Joseph R. Ca. 1879 (Utah)–?
Nine Mile: ca. 1910; Census 1910: Nine Mile Canyon. Joseph was a ranch hand for Preston Nutter at the time of the 1910 census. There are no cross-references to him in the database, and nothing is known of where he came from or what became of him. There is some confusion on the

spelling of his last name, and it might not be as indicated here.

Hatch, Mary Leona (Miles). Ca. 1889–1975 (Idaho Falls, Idaho)
Married: Henry Hatch; Nine Mile: 1907 (?) to 1910s; Census 1900: Salt Lake City; Census 1910: Salt Lake City; Census 1920: Salt Lake City. There is no convincing evidence that Mary Leona ever lived in Nine Mile Canyon. She was married by 1910 when her parents and siblings were living in Nine Mile Canyon. She is one of seven Miles daughters that contribute to the legend that Nine Mile Canyon was named after the Miles family.

Hill, Minnie. ?–?
Nine Mile: 1900. School census records indicate a Minnie Hill was a teacher in Nine Mile Canyon in 1900. There are no other records conclusively linked to this person.

Holdaway, David William. 1851 (Utah)–1939 (Utah)
Married: Bertha (?); Nine Mile: 1890s or 1900s; Census 1860: Mount Pleasant, Sanpete County; Census 1870: Provo, Utah County; Census 1880: Beaver, Beaver County; Census 1900: Price, Carbon County. D. W. was listed on a school census as a board member of the school district in Nine Mile Canyon, which infers he lived there. There are no other records to indicate he actually lived there.

Hollands, John R. Ca. 1878 (England)–?
Nine Mile: ca. 1910; Census 1910: Nine Mile Canyon. John R. was a ranch hand for Preston Nutter at the time of the 1910 census. He immigrated to the United States in 1887, later married and divorced, and found

his way to the Nutter Ranch. There are no cross-references to him in the database.

Houskeeper, Annie E. *See* **Fitt, Annie E. (Houskeeper)**

Houskeeper, Clarissa (Alger). Ca. 1879 (Washington County)–1925 (Carbon County)
Married: Theodore B. Houskeeper; Nine Mile: 1890s to 1925; Census 1880: Santa Clara River, Washington County; Census 1900: Nine Mile Canyon (?); Census 1910: Nine Mile Canyon; Census 1920: Wellington, Carbon County. Clara was the sister of the Alger brothers (Lon, Gett, Frank, and Joseph). She married Theodore B. Houskeeper, who inherited the family ranch at the mouth of Cow Canyon. Her brothers Lon and Gett had a neighboring ranch at the mouth of Cow Canyon, and there were ongoing disputes over irrigation water. Clara split her time between the farm in Nine Mile and a home in Wellington. She would have been five or six years old when her brother Frank moved her to Orangeville, where they were neighbors of the Houskeeper family. She died in 1925 in a horse-and-buggy accident.

Houskeeper, David. 1879 (Utah)–?
Married: Lenora Johnston; Nine Mile: 1890s to 1900s; Census 1880: Castledale, Emery County; Census 1900: Nine Mile Canyon; Census 1910: Boneta, Wasatch County; Census 1920: Mountain Home, Duchesne County; Census 1930: Mountain Home, Duchesne County. David was a young man when his father brought him to Nine Mile Canyon. He soon married a daughter of G. C. "Don" Johnston and moved on to Duchesne County. He is the

son of Theodore Sr. and Sarah Butler Houskeeper, who were early settlers in the Cow Canyon area in the 1890s.

Houskeeper, Eliza Lucille. *See* **Rich, Eliza Lucille (Houskeeper)**

Houskeeper, Emma J. *See* **Smith, Emma J. (Houskeeper)**

Houskeeper, Fern L. *See* **Shaw, Fern Luella (Houskeeper)**

Houskeeper, John C. 1918 (Utah)–1982 (Wellington, Carbon County)
Nine Mile: 1918 to 1930s; Census 1920: Wellington, Carbon County; Census 1930: Nine Mile Canyon. John was probably born and raised in Nine Mile Canyon, but there are few vital records related to him. He was the son of Theodore B. and Clarissa Alger Houskeeper, early settlers of the Cow Canyon area in the 1890s.

Houskeeper, Rosetta. *See* **Kelsey, Rosetta (Houskeeper)**

Houskeeper, Sarah (Butler). Ca. 1843 (England)–1920 (Emery County)
Married: Theodore Fielding Houskeeper; Nine Mile: 1890s to 1900s; Census 1850: England; Census 1880: Castledale, Emery County; Census 1900: Nine Mile Canyon; Census 1910: Orangeville, Emery County; Census 1920: Orangeville, Emery County. Sarah immigrated to the United States from England and married Theodore F. Houskeeper. With their children, they were among the earliest settlers in Nine Mile Canyon, and her son Theodore remained longer than most. They arrived in Nine Mile Canyon sometime in the mid-1890s and settled near the mouth of Cow Canyon.

Houskeeper, Sarah Jane. *See* **Hancock, Sarah Jane (Houskeeper)**

Houskeeper, Theodore B. 1873 (Utah)–1944 (Carbon County)
Married: Clarissa Alger; Nine Mile: 1890s to 1930s; Census 1880: Castledale, Emery County; Census 1900: Nine Mile Canyon; Census 1910: Nine Mile Canyon; Census 1920: Nine Mile Canyon; Census 1930: Nine Mile Canyon. Theodore B. was among the longest-term residents of Nine Mile Canyon. He arrived as a young man in the mid-1890s and remained there the rest of his life. His wife was a sister of Lon, Gett, and Frank Alger. The Algers were neighbors of the Houskeeper family in the Orangeville and Nine Mile areas. Theodore B. was the son of Theodore F. and Sarah Butler Houskeeper. In 1920, he was listed on the census for both Wellington and Nine Mile Canyon.

Houskeeper, Theodore B. Jr. Ca. 1912 (Nine Mile Canyon?)–1992 (Price, Carbon County)
Nine Mile: 1912 to 1960s; Census 1920: Wellington, Carbon County; Census 1930: Nine Mile Canyon. Theodore Jr. was the son of Theodore and Clara Houskeeper, who were among the longest-term residents of Nine Mile Canyon and had settled at the mouth of Cow Canyon. He could have been born and raised in Nine Mile Canyon. He remained in the canyon much of his life, and even operated a family sawmill that provided timber to the coal mine in Soldier Creek Canyon.

Houskeeper, Theodore F. 1843 (Pennsylvania)–1915 (Emery County)
Married: Sarah Butler; Nine Mile: 1890s to 1900s; Census 1850:

Pottawattamie, Iowa; Census 1860: Provo, Utah County; Census 1880: Castledale, Emery County; Census 1900: Nine Mile Canyon; Census 1910: Orangeville, Emery County. Theodore F., the patriarch of the Houskeeper family, was one of the first settlers in Nine Mile Canyon in the mid-1890s, and his son Theodore retained the family ranch long after the father had moved back to Emery County. He originally settled in the Orangeville area where he was neighbors of the Burnett-Alger family, where the Alger children were living with their grandparents.

Houskeeper, William. 1874 (Utah)–? Married: Martha (?); Nine Mile: 1890s to 1900s; Census 1880: Castledale, Emery County; Census 1900: Nine Mile Canyon; Census 1910: Orangeville, Emery County; Census 1930: Orangeville, Emery County. William was the son of Theodore F. and Sarah Houskeeper, who were among the first residents of Nine Mile Canyon in the 1890s. He was a brother of Theodore B. Houskeeper, who inherited the ranch. William had returned to Emery County by 1910.

Huntington, Edward. Ca. 1888 (Utah)–? Nine Mile: ca. 1910; Census 1910: Nine Mile Canyon. In 1910, Edward was living with and working for William Miles in lower Nine Mile Canyon, probably as a cowboy on the large ranch. There are no cross-references in the database, and nothing is known of where he came from or what became of him.

Javier, Fredrick. Ca. 1886 (Indiana)–? Nine Mile: ca. 1920; Census 1920: Nine Mile Canyon. Fred was listed

as a boarder with Frank Whitmore in the 1920 census, and he listed his occupation as a farmer. There are no cross-references in the database to know how he came to be in Nine Mile Canyon or what became of him.

Jensen, Olive (Russell). Ca. 1901 (Nine Mile Canyon?)–? Married: Alfred S. Jensen; Nine Mile: ca. 1901 to 1910s; Census 1910: Nine Mile Canyon; Census 1920: Desert Lake, Emery County. Olive might have been born in Nine Mile Canyon. She was the daughter of Harrison and Ada Russell, and she was living in the canyon with her parents in 1910. She later moved to Emery County with her husband. In 1920, there was a boarder living with them named George Westwood. He later married Olive's aunt, Lillie Russell.

Johnson, Mary Ruth (Kelsey). 1893 (Nine Mile Canyon?)–? Married: Orvil Johnson; Nine Mile: ca. 1893 to 1900s; Census 1900: Nine Mile Canyon; Census 1910: Basalt, Idaho; Census 1920: Basalt, Idaho; Census 1930: Emmett, Idaho. She was the daughter of Theodore and Rosetta Houskeeper Kelsey, who were early residents of the canyon. Given the early arrival of the Houskeeper family, Ruth might have been born in Nine Mile Canyon.

Johnston, Beulah. Ca. 1897 (Nine Mile Canyon)–? Nine Mile: ca. 1897 to 1900s; Census 1900: Nine Mile Canyon. Beulah was the daughter of John M. and Florence Johnston. She is buried in Price, but no death date is given. There are no other vital records related to her. She might have been born in Nine Mile Canyon. Her father was probably the

son of G. C. "Don" Johnston, one of the earliest settlers in the 1890s.

Johnston, Blanch M. Ca. 1898 (Nine Mile Canyon?)–? Nine Mile: ca. 1898 to 1910s; Census 1900: Nine Mile Canyon; Census 1910: Nine Mile Canyon. Blanch was the daughter of Carl and Maud Babcock Johnson, and granddaughter of G. C. "Don" Johnston, one of the earliest settlers in the 1890s. There are no other vital records linked to this individual. She was probably born in Nine Mile Canyon.

Johnston, Burke D. Ca. 1915 (Nine Mile Canyon?)–1988 (Wellington, Carbon County) Married: June (?); Nine Mile: ca. 1915 to 1920s; Census 1920: Nine Mile Canyon; Census 1930: Roosevelt, Duchesne County. Burke was the son of Carl and Maud Babcock Johnson, and he might have been born in Nine Mile Canyon. He was a grandson of G. C. "Don" Johnston, one of the earliest settlers in the 1890s. By the time he was a teenager, the family was living in the Uinta Basin.

Johnston, Charles W. 1883 (Utah)–1955 (Carbon County) Married: Cecilia or Celia Downward; Nine Mile: 1900s to 1920s; Census 1910: Price, Carbon County; Census 1920: Nine Mile Canyon; Census 1930: Price, Carbon County. Charles was the son of G. C. "Don" Johnston. Along with his wife and children, he lived with his father at the Johnston ranch in 1920, now the Cottonwood Glen Picnic Area. Charles was presumably from Sanpete County, but there are no records of him prior to 1910. He was a rancher and a freighter.

Johnston, Cyrenus C. "Carl." Ca. 1871 (Utah)–1939 (Duchesne County) Married: Maud M. Babcock; Nine Mile: 1890s to 1920s; Census 1880: Petty, Sanpete County; Census 1900: Nine Mile Canyon; Census 1910: Nine Mile Canyon; Census 1920: Nine Mile Canyon; Census 1930: Roosevelt, Duchesne County. Carl or Carlos was a son of G. C. "Don" Johnston, and a brother of John and Charles Johnston, all of whom were in the canyon at the same time. The family name is sometimes spelled Johnson or Johnstun in the historical record, but it is consistently spelled Johnston in the census records. Carl was married to Maud Babcock, daughter of John Rowley and Augusta Mae Babcock, who were among the earliest settlers in the Cow Canyon area.

Johnston, Elzina (Smithson). 1887 (Arizona)–1974 (Bountiful, Davis County) Married: John M. Johnston; Nine Mile: 1890s to 1900s; Census 1900: Nine Mile Canyon; Census 1910: Vernal, Uintah County; Census 1920: Bluebell, Duchesne County. Elzina (or Alzina) was the daughter of Nephi and Barbara Smithson, who were among the early settlers of Nine Mile Canyon. She was the second wife of John Johnston and they raised their family in the Uinta Basin.

Johnston, Ernest Wayne. Ca. 1913 (Nine Mile Canyon?)–? Married: Florence McDonald (1932); Nine Mile: 1913 to 1920s; Census 1920: Nine Mile Canyon; Census 1930: Roosevelt, Duchesne County. Wayne was the son of Carl and Maud Babcock Johnston, and he might have been born in Nine Mile Canyon. He

had moved to the Uinta Basin by the time he was a teenager.

Johnston, Florence E. 1878 (Utah)–? Married: John M. Johnston; Nine Mile: 1890s to 1900s; Census 1900: Nine Mile Canyon. Florence was the wife of John M. Johnston. There are no other vital records related to her. She might have died, or the couple divorced, after 1900. By 1910, John had married Elzina Smithson and had moved to the Uinta Basin. Their daughter, Beulah, was not listed in John Johnston's households after 1900.

Johnston, George C. "Don." Ca. 1848 (Iowa)–? Married: Melissa or Emily (?); Nine Mile: 1890s to 1920s; Census 1850: Sanpete County (1856 state census); Census 1870: Manti, Sanpete County; Census 1880: Petty, Sanpete County; Census 1910: Nine Mile Canyon; Census 1920: Nine Mile Canyon; Census 1930: Price, Carbon County. Don Johnston might have been one of the earliest settlers of Nine Mile Canyon in the 1890s, along with his sons John and Carl, who were both living in the canyon with their families by the 1890s. Don was married, but there is no indication his wife ever lived with him in Nine Mile Canyon. His ranch, now the Cottonwood Glen Picnic Area, was a favorite stopping point for freighters on the Nine Mile Road. A Native American woman named Martha Brown lived at the ranch and was renowned for her cooking. The Johnston family was originally from Manti.

Johnston, Georgiana Cecilia (Downard). Ca. 1886 (Utah)–1966 (Price, Carbon County)

Married: Charles W. Johnston; Nine Mile: ca. 1920; Census 1900: Price, Carbon County; Census 1910: Price, Carbon County; Census 1920: Nine Mile Canyon; Census 1930: Price, Carbon County. Celia was married to Charles W. Johnston, son of G. C. "Don" Johnston. Charles's brothers, John and Carl, were also in Nine Mile Canyon at the time and were among the earliest residents. She was the daughter of George and Mena Downard.

Johnston, Harold. 1907 (Price, Carbon County)–1988 (Price, Carbon County) Married: Leona Wall; Nine Mile: 1907 to 1920s; Census 1910: Nine Mile Canyon; Census 1920: Nine Mile Canyon; Census 1930: Roosevelt, Duchesne County. Harold was the son of Carl and Maud Babcock Johnston. He could have been born in Nine Mile Canyon, although death records indicate he was born in Price. By the time he was a young man he had moved to the Uinta Basin.

Johnston, John Floyd. Ca. 1909 (Price, Carbon County)–1959 (Salt Lake City) Nine Mile: 1909 to 1920s; Census 1910: Nine Mile Canyon; Census 1920: Nine Mile Canyon; Census 1930: Roosevelt, Duchesne County. John was the son of Carl and Maud Babcock Johnston. There are no other vital records linked to this individual. He could have been born in Nine Mile Canyon, although death records indicate he was born in Price. His family had moved to the Uinta Basin by the time he was a teenager or young man.

Johnston, John M. 1873 (Utah)–1920 (Duchesne County)

Married: Florence (?); Elzina J. Smithson; Nine Mile: 1890s to 1900s; Census 1880: Petty, Sanpete County; Census 1900: Nine Mile Canyon; Census 1910: Vernal, Uintah County; Census 1920: Bluebell, Duchesne County. John M. was the son of G. C. "Don" Johnston, who also had a ranch in Nine Mile (now the Cottonwood Glen Picnic Area). John had his own place by at least 1900 when he was married to a woman named Florence. By 1910, he had married Elzina J. Smithson, a daughter of Nephi and Barbara Smithson, also early arrivals in Nine Mile Canyon, and had moved on to the Uinta Basin.

Johnston, Loren R. 1917 (Nine Mile Canyon?)–2005 (Salt Lake City
Nine Mile: 1917 to 1920s; Census 1920: Nine Mile Canyon; Census 1930: Roosevelt, Duchesne County. Loren was the son of Carl and Maud Babcock Johnston, and he might have been born in Nine Mile Canyon. There are no records that he married. By the time he was a teenager the family was living in the Uinta Basin.

Johnston, Maud M. (Babcock). 1877 (Utah)–before 1930
Married: Cyrenus Carl Johnston; Nine Mile: 1890s to 1920s; Census 1880: Greenwich, Piute County; Census 1900: Nine Mile Canyon; Census 1910: Nine Mile Canyon; Census 1920: Nine Mile Canyon. Maud was the daughter of John and Augusta Mae Babcock, one of the earliest Nine Mile pioneer families in the 1890s in the Cow Canyon area. She married Carl Johnston, another early arrival here, and spent most of her adult life in Nine Mile Canyon, where she raised her family.

Johnston, Milda. Ca. 1914 (Utah)–?
Nine Mile: ca. 1920; Census 1920: Nine Mile Canyon. Milda was the daughter of Charles W. and Celia Downward Johnston, and granddaughter of G. C. "Don" Johnston. There are no records of her after the 1920 census, and nothing more is known about her.

Johnston, Rosa. Ca. 1907 (Nine Mile Canyon?)–?
Married: Gilbert Murray (1923); Nine Mile: ca. 1907; Census 1910: Vernal, Uinta County; Census 1920: Bluebell, Duchesne County. Rosa was the oldest child of John M. and Elzina Smithson Johnston. She might have been born in Nine Mile Canyon before the family moved to the Uinta Basin. There are no records of her after the 1920 census.

Johnston, Wallace Leroy. Ca. 1911 (Utah)–1925 (Carbon County)
Nine Mile: 1910s to 1925; Census 1920: Nine Mile Canyon. Wallace died at the age of fourteen in an unspecified location in Carbon County, perhaps Nine Mile Canyon. He was the son of Charles W. and Celia Downward Johnston.

Justison, Elmer P. Ca. 1878 (Utah)–?
Married: Sarah Allred; Nine Mile: ca. 1910; Census 1900: Ephraim, Sanpete County; Census 1910: Nine Mile Canyon. Elmer was working as a ranch hand for Preston Nutter in 1910. He hailed from Sanpete County, and he later returned there and raised his own family in Spring City. The surname is sometimes spelled Justinson or Justesen.

Keele, Mervel "Mel." 1919 (Neola, Duchesne County)–1981 (Provo, Utah County)

Married: Jennie Sorensen; Nine Mile: 1930s; Census 1920: Hiawatha, Carbon County; Census 1930: Heber, Wasatch County. Mel bought out the John Rowley and Augusta Mae Babcock homestead near Cow Canyon in the 1930s. It is unknown what years he might have lived there with his wife, Jennie. He is not listed on any census records for Nine Mile Canyon.

Kelsey, Argent Golden. 1903 (Nine Mile Canyon?)–1915 (Basalt, Idaho)
Nine Mile: ca. 1903; Census 1910: Basalt, Idaho. There is no positive record that Argent was in Nine Mile Canyon, but he was born in Utah and his family was in Nine Mile Canyon in 1900, and he might have been born there. He was a son of Theodore and Rosetta Houskeeper Kelsey. The Houskeeper family was among the earliest to arrive in Nine Mile Canyon in the 1890s. He was only twelve years old when he died.

Kelsey, Claude M. 1901 (Nine Mile Canyon?)–1985 (Idaho Falls)
Married: Nettie Singleton (1921); Nine Mile: 1901 (?); Census 1910: Basalt, Idaho; Census 1920: Basalt, Idaho; Census 1930: Shelley, Idaho. There is no positive record that Claude was in Nine Mile Canyon, but he was born in Utah and his family was in Nine Mile Canyon in 1900, so he might have been born there. However, the database links to an unnamed Kelsey child born to parents of similar names in 1901 in Sanpete County. He was a son of Theodore and Rosetta Houskeeper Kelsey. The Houskeeper family was among the earliest to arrive in Nine Mile Canyon.

Kelsey, Ernest T. 1900 (Nine Mile Canyon?)–?
Married: Beatrice (?); Nine Mile: 1900s; Census 1900: Nine Mile Canyon; Census 1910: Basalt, Idaho; Census 1920: Basalt, Idaho; Census 1930: Simms, Montana. Ernest was an infant at the time of the 1900 census when his family lived in Nine Mile Canyon. He was a son of Theodore and Rosetta Houskeeper Kelsey. The Houskeeper family was among the earliest to arrive in Nine Mile Canyon in the 1890s.

Kelsey, Florence. 1883 (Utah)–?
Nine Mile: 1899; Census 1900: Price, Carbon County. A school census indicates Florence Kelsey was a teacher in Nine Mile Canyon in 1899. This could be the Florence Kelsey who lived with her parents in Price in 1900, although she would have been quite young to be a teacher in 1899.

Kelsey, Francis Earl. 1895 (Nine Mile Canyon?)–?
Married: Emily Gregerson; Nine Mile: ca. 1895 to 1900s; Census 1900: Nine Mile Canyon; Census 1910: Basalt, Idaho; Census 1920: Basalt, Idaho; Census 1930: Basalt, Idaho. Earl was the son of Theodore and Rosetta Houskeeper Kelsey and. Given the early arrival of the Houskeeper family, he might have been born in Nine Mile Canyon.

Kelsey, Mary Ruth. *See **Johnson, Mary Ruth (Kelsey)***

Kelsey, Rosetta (Houskeeper). Ca. 1871–1950 (Shelley, Idaho)
Married: Theodore Kelsey; Nine Mile: 1890s to 1900s; Census 1880: Castledale, Emery County; Census 1900: Nine Mile Canyon; Census 1910: Basalt, Idaho; Census 1920:

Basalt, Idaho; Census 1930: Shelley, Idaho. Rosetta was the daughter of Theodore and Sarah Houskeeper, who were among the earliest settlers in Nine Mile Canyon in the 1890s. Rosetta and her family migrated to Idaho sometime after 1900. Her brother, Theodore B. Houskeeper, inherited the Nine Mile family ranch.

Kelsey, Sarah E. 1898 (Nine Mile Canyon?)–?
Nine Mile: ca. 1898 to 1900s; Census 1900: Nine Mile Canyon; Census 1910: Basalt, Idaho. She was the daughter of Theodore and Rosetta Houskeeper Kelsey. There are no records of her after the 1910 census. Given the early arrival of the Houskeeper family in the 1890s, she might have been born in Nine Mile Canyon.

Kelsey, Theodore. 1871 (Utah)–?
Married: Rosetta Houskeeper; Nine Mile: 1890s to 1900s; Census 1880: Fairview, Sanpete County; Census 1900: Nine Mile Canyon; Census 1910: Basalt, Idaho; Census 1920: Basalt, Idaho; Census 1930: Shelley, Idaho. Theodore married Rosetta Houskeeper, a daughter of Theodore and Sarah Houskeeper, who were among the earliest settlers in Nine Mile Canyon in the 1890s. The Kelsey family had their own place in the canyon, but the family migrated to Idaho sometime after 1900.

Kelsey, Vondella. *See **Collins, Vondella (Kelsey)***

Krissman, Amber M. (Thompson). Ca. 1910 (Nine Mile Canyon?)–?
Married: Frank Krissman; Nine Mile: 1910 to 1920s; Census 1910: Nine Mile Canyon; Census 1920: Nine Mile Canyon; Census 1930:

Spring Glen, Carbon County. Amber was the daughter of Al and Martha Thompson, and granddaughter of Martha and Frederic Grames, who were among the earliest settlers of Price in 1878. She might have been born in Nine Mile Canyon. Her parents divorced, and she was raised by her mother.

Larsen, Annie. 1877 (Denmark)–?
Nine Mile: ca. 1900; Census 1900: Nine Mile Canyon. The Danish-born Annie was listed on the 1900 census for Nine Mile Canyon as a house servant for the Edwin and Effie Box Lee family, which had a ranch at the mouth of Argyle Canyon. There are no other vital records linked to this person, and nothing more is known about her.

Lee, Alva C. Ca. 1876 (Utah)–1925 (Carbon County)
Married: Lillie M. Russell; Nine Mile: ca. 1920 to ca. 1925; Census 1900: Naples, Uintah County; Census 1910: Dragon, Uintah County; Census 1920: Nine Mile Canyon. Alva married Lillie Russell, daughter of Andrew Jackson and Julia Mott Russell, among the earliest settlers in Nine Mile Canyon. He might have died in Nine Mile Canyon. It is unknown if he was related to Edwin Lee, who had a ranch in the canyon from the late 1890s through about 1920.

Lee, Charles B. Ca. 1899 (Nine Mile Canyon?)–?
Nine Mile: 1899 to ca. 1920; Census 1900: Nine Mile Canyon; Census 1910: Nine Mile Canyon. Charles was a son of Edwin and Effie Box Lee, who arrived in Nine Mile Canyon in the 1890s and established a thriving ranch just above the mouth of

Argyle Canyon. He would have spent most of his childhood in Nine Mile Canyon. There are no convincing records of Charles after the 1910 census.

Lee, Claude D. 1907 (Nine Mile Canyon?)–1983 (Los Angeles)
Married: Barbara (?); Nine Mile: 1907 to ca. 1920; Census 1910: Nine Mile Canyon; Census 1920: Price, Carbon County; Census 1930: Price, Carbon County. Claude was a son of Edwin and Effie Box Lee, who arrived in Nine Mile Canyon in the 1890s and established a thriving ranch just above the mouth of Argyle Canyon. He would have spent most of his childhood in Nine Mile Canyon, and might have been born there. By 1940 he was in California. He used the middle initials "D" and "E" on various vital records.

Lee, Clifton C. 1892 (Utah)–1960 (Price, Carbon County)
Married: Thelma (?); Nine Mile: 1890s to ca. 1920; Census 1900: Nine Mile Canyon; Census 1910: Nine Mile Canyon; Census 1920: Price, Carbon County; Census 1930: Wilson, Uintah County. Clifton was a son of Edwin and Effie Box Lee, who arrived in Nine Mile Canyon in the 1890s and established a thriving ranch just above the mouth of Argyle Canyon. He would have spent most of his childhood in Nine Mile Canyon.

Lee, Clyde E. Ca. 1908 (Nine Mile Canyon?)–?
Nine Mile: 1908 to ca. 1920; Census 1910: Nine Mile Canyon; Census 1920: Price, Carbon County. Clyde was a son of Edwin and Effie Box Lee, who arrived in Nine Mile Canyon in the 1890s and established

a thriving ranch just above the mouth of Argyle Canyon. He would have spent most of his childhood in Nine Mile Canyon, and might have been born there. There is no positive record of him after the 1920 census, but he might have moved on to California.

Lee, Cora A. 1895 (Utah)–?
Nine Mile: ca. 1895 to ca. 1920; Census 1900: Nine Mile Canyon; Census 1910: Nine Mile Canyon. Cora was a daughter of Edwin and Effie Box Lee, who arrived in Nine Mile Canyon in the 1890s and established a thriving ranch just above the mouth of Argyle Canyon. She would have spent most of her childhood in Nine Mile Canyon. There is no record of her after the 1910 census. She might have been born in Nine Mile Canyon or arrived as a small child.

Lee, Edward. 1902 (Utah)–?
Nine Mile: 1902 to ca. 1920; Census 1920: Nine Mile Canyon. Edward was the oldest son of Alva and Lillie Russell Lee. There are no other vital records related to him besides the 1920 census when he was eighteen years old. It is possible that Edward Lee is actually James Edward Taylor, who was born in the canyon in 1901. Edward Lee's mother was married to Charles Franklin Taylor, and she had a son named James Edward in 1901.

Lee, Edwin C. 1863 (Utah)–1949 (Utah County)
Married: Effie D. Box; Nine Mile: 1890s to ca. 1920; Census 1880: Springville, Utah County; Census 1900: Nine Mile Canyon; Census 1910: Nine Mile Canyon; Census 1920: Price, Carbon County; Census 1930: Price, Carbon County. Ed Lee was among the most prominent ranchers in Nine Mile Canyon

for two decades. The Lee ranch just above the mouth of Argyle Canyon became a social headquarters, stage stop, and post office, which later became known as Harper. He married Effie Box, and most of their children were born and raised in Nine Mile Canyon. He was from Utah County and reportedly kept a house there. In addition to his holdings in Argyle Canyon, he bought out the Rabbit Ranch and other small ranches in lower Nine Mile Canyon.

Lee, Edwin Ray. 1890 (Springville, Utah County)–1964 (Orem, Utah County)
Married: Mina Manchester; Nine Mile: 1890s to ca. 1920; Census 1900: Nine Mile Canyon; Census 1910: Nine Mile Canyon; 1920: Price, Carbon County; Census 1930: Price, Carbon County. Ray was the oldest child of Edwin and Effie Box Lee, who arrived in Nine Mile Canyon in the 1890s. He would have spent most of his childhood in Nine Mile Canyon at the family ranch just above the mouth of Argyle Canyon.

Lee, Effie Blanche. *See* **Taylor, Effie Blanche (Lee)**

Lee, Effie Doret (Box). Ca. 1874 (Utah)–1956 (Price, Carbon County)
Married: Edwin C. Lee; Nine Mile: 1890s to ca. 1920; Census 1880: Payson, Utah County; Census 1900: Nine Mile Canyon; Census 1910: Nine Mile Canyon; Census 1920: Price, Carbon County; Census 1930: Price, Carbon County. Effie was married to Ed Lee, who was among the most prominent ranchers in Nine Mile Canyon for two decades. The Lee ranch at the mouth of Argyle Canyon became a social headquarters, stage stop, and post office, later

known as Harper. Most of their children were born and/or raised in Nine Mile Canyon. Effie was noted as an exceptional hostess to travelers on the Nine Mile Road.

Lee, Eldredge. Ca. 1908 (Utah)–?
Nine Mile: ca. 1908 to 1920s; Census 1920: Nine Mile Canyon. Eldredge was the son of Alva and Lillie Russell Lee. There are no other records of him besides the 1920 census, and nothing more is known about him.

Lee, Lillie (Russell). 1882 (Gooseberry Valley, Sevier County)–1966 (Salt Lake City)
Married: Charles Franklin Taylor (1898), Alva Lee (after 1901), George Westwood (1926); Nine Mile: 1890s to ca. 1925; Census 1900: Nine Mile Canyon; Census 1920: Nine Mile Canyon; Census 1930: Columbia, Carbon County. Lillie was the daughter of Andrew Jackson and Julia Mott Russell, who were among the earliest settlers in Nine Mile Canyon. She married in 1898 to Charles Franklin Taylor. She must have married her second husband, Alva, after about 1901. He died in 1925 and she then married George Westwood the following year. She is not listed on any census records for the Russell family, and it is unknown when she might have arrived in Nine Mile Canyon. In 1901 she gave birth to a son, James Edward Taylor, in Nine Mile Canyon.

Lee, Martin Sharp. 1911 (Nine Mile Canyon?)–? (Craig, Colorado)
Married: Marie Louise Villard; Nine Mile: 1911 to ca. 1920; Census 1920: Price, Carbon County; Census 1930: Price, Carbon County. Martin was a child of Edwin and Effie Box Lee, who arrived in Nine Mile Canyon

in the 1890s. He would have spent much of his childhood in Nine Mile Canyon on the family ranch just above the mouth of Argyle Canyon. He might have been born there.

Lee, Thelbert. Ca. 1904 (Utah)–?
Nine Mile: 1900s to 1920s; Census 1920: Nine Mile Canyon. Thelbert was the son of Alva and Lillie Russell Lee. There are no other records of him besides the 1920 census, and nothing more is known about him.

Lee, Thesrilda. Ca. 1922 (Nine Mile Canyon?)–?
Nine Mile: 1922 to ca. 1925; Census 1930: Columbia, Carbon County. There are no records that link Thesrilda to Nine Mile Canyon, but she could have been born there. She was born three years before her father, Alva Lee, died (perhaps in Nine Mile Canyon). After 1925, she went to live with her mother, Lillie Russell, and stepfather, George Westwood, in Columbia. By 1940, she was a divorced woman living in Price. There are no other vital records related to her.

Lee, Veloy. 1914 (Utah)–1993 (Coos Bay, Oregon)
Married: Valencia Timothy; Nine Mile: ca. 1914 to ca. 1925; Census 1920: Nine Mile Canyon; Census 1930: Columbia, Carbon County. Veloy was a son of Alva and Lillie Russell Lee. His father died when Veloy was eleven years old, and Veloy moved to Columbia with his mother and stepfather, George Westwood.

Lee, Walter Scott. 1900 (Nine Mile Canyon?)–1934 (Price, Carbon County)
Married: Leah Pace; Nine Mile: 1900 to ca. 1920; Census 1900: Nine Mile

Canyon; Census 1910: Nine Mile Canyon; Census 1920: Price, Carbon County; Census 1930: Huntington Beach, California. Walter was a child of Edwin and Effie Box Lee, who arrived in Nine Mile Canyon in the 1890s. He would have spent most of his childhood in Nine Mile Canyon. He was an infant at the time of the 1900 census and might have been born in Nine Mile Canyon on the family ranch just above the mouth of Argyle Canyon. His wife might have been distantly related to John A. Pace, who ranched in lower Nine Mile Canyon.

Liddell, Charlotte. ?–?
Nine Mile: 1930s. Local histories indicate Charlotte was a teacher in Nine Mile Canyon in the 1930s. There are no records that are clearly linked to this person, and it is unknown if she was related to John Liddell, who married into the Brundage family, which had a ranch above Minnie Maud Canyon.

Liddell, Mary L. (Brundage). 1909 (Nine Mile Canyon?)–1999 (Orem, Utah County)
Married: John Liddell; Nine Mile: 1909 to 1910s; Census 1910: Nine Mile Canyon; Census 1930: Antelope, Duchesne County. Mary was the daughter of Joe and Zada Hamilton Brundage. Mary might have been born in Nine Mile Canyon.

Lisonbee, Alva Leonidas "Lee." Ca. 1872 (Utah)–1947 (Duchesne County)
Married: Mary Merrill (1894); Nine Mile: 1890s?: Census 1880: Glenwood, Sevier County; Census 1900: Riverdale, Uintah County; Census 1920: Myton, Duchesne County; Census 1930: LaPoint, Uintah County. Little is known about

the Lisonbee family other than a few family recollections. Lee Lisonbee was reportedly a stage driver on the Nine Mile Road, and with his wife they thwarted a robbery attempt by the Wild Bunch by hiding the military payroll beneath soiled baby diapers. If the story is accurate, this probably occurred in the 1890s when outlaws were active in the area. Lee's son, Shelby, proved up on a 640-acre claim at the head of Cow Canyon.

Lisonbee, Elva (Christiansen). 1905 (Utah)–2001 (Salt Lake County) Married: Shelby Lisonbee; Nine Mile: 1920s?; Census 1910: Monroe, Sevier County; Census 1930: Lawrence, Emery County. Elva was the wife of Shelby Lisonbee. As newlyweds, they lived on their homestead claim at the head of Cow Canyon. Shelby had been working for Preston Nutter, but was fired when he got married (Nutter reportedly did not like to employ married men).

Lisonbee, Shelby. Ca. 1901 (Utah)–2000 (Salt Lake County) Married: Elva Christiansen; Nine Mile: 1920s?; Census 1920: Myton, Duchesne County; Census 1930: Lawrence, Emery County. Little is known about the Lisonbee family other than a few family recollections. Shelby proved up on a 640-acre claim at the head of Cow Canyon. It is unknown if he lived there with his family while proving up on the claim, but according to a family history he was working for Preston Nutter, who fired him when he married, stating he "wouldn't keep a married man on." Shelby reportedly lived on the homestead with his new wife and no job. Shelby was the son of Lee Lisonbee, a stage driver on the Nine Mile Road.

Lloyd, Jessie Myrtle (Hall). 1896 (Nine Mile Canyon?)–1972 (Salt Lake City) Married: William Lloyd; Nine Mile: 1896 to 1900s; Census 1900: Nine Mile Canyon; Census 1910: Huntington, Emery County; Census 1920: Red Cap, Duchesne County; Census 1930: Lake Fork, Duchesne County. Myrtle was only about nine years old when her mother died in 1905. In 1910, at age fourteen, she was working as a housemaid for the Monson family in Huntington. She was the daughter of Charles and Sarah Babcock Hall, and she might have been born in Nine Mile Canyon.

Lunt, Alfred. Ca. 1847 (England)–1922 (Nephi, Juab County) Married: Priscilla Pitt; Nine Mile: ca. 1877; Census 1850: England; Census 1860: Nephi, Juab County; Census 1870: Nephi, Juab County; Census 1880: Nephi, Juab County; Census 1900: Nephi, Juab County; Census 1910: Nephi, Juab County; Census 1920: Nephi, Juab County. An 1878 survey map of Nine Mile Canyon indicates the presence of the Alfred Lunt Ranch at the mouth of Minnie Maud Canyon. This is the only ranch indicated in the canyon at the time. There is some doubt that Alfred actually had a ranch complex there or whether it was summer range for his herds that were seasonally moved from Nephi to Nine Mile. Alfred lived his whole life in Nephi. Alfred was from a well-to-do family in Nephi and they might have been associated with James and George Whitmore, who moved their herds into the same area in about 1877–1878.

Lunt, Shadrach. 1850 (England)–1933 (Juab County)

Married: Anne Pitt (1872); Nine Mile: 1877 to ca. 1930; Census 1880: Nephi, Juab County; Census 1900: Nephi, Juab County; Census 1910: Nephi, Juab County; Census 1920: Nephi, Juab County; Census 1930: Nephi, Juab County. The title of first resident of Nine Mile Canyon is commonly bestowed on Shadrach Lunt, who arrived in 1877, constructed a ranch near the mouth of Gate Canyon (now known as the Nutter Ranch), became the first rancher in Desolation Canyon, and in his later years worked as a range cowboy for Preston Nutter. Shadrach was known and loved throughout Nine Mile Canyon for more than fifty years. Vital records indicate he had a wife and six children in Nephi, which was probably his home during the winter months. But most of his life was spent in Nine Mile Canyon. There is no reference that any of his children joined him in Nine Mile Canyon.

Lyman, Chester. Ca. 1894 (Utah)–1963 (Price, Carbon County) Married: Laura Partridge; Nine Mile: ca. 1900; Census 1900: Nine Mile Canyon; Census 1910: Randlette, Uintah County; Census 1920: Price, Carbon County; Census 1930: Duchesne, Duchesne County. Chester was a son of Ira D. and Elizabeth Lyman. He served in the military in 1917 and later returned to Price. He is incorrectly listed on the 1910 census as Esther, a female.

Lyman, Claude E. Ca. 1893 (Utah)–? Nine Mile: ca. 1900; Census 1900: Nine Mile Canyon; Census 1910: Randlette, Uintah County; Census 1920: Dragon, Uintah County; Census 1930: Fruita, Colorado. Claude was a son of Ira D. and Elizabeth Lyman. He would have spent his childhood in Nine Mile Canyon. There is no record that he married.

Lyman, Edna C. Ca. 1898 (Nine Mile Canyon?)–?
Nine Mile: ca. 1898 to 1900s; Census 1900: Nine Mile Canyon; Census 1910: Randlette, Uintah County; Census 1920: Dragon, Uintah County. Edna was a daughter of Ira D. and Elizabeth Lyman. She might have been born in Nine Mile Canyon. There are no records of her marriage or death.

Lyman, Elizabeth A. Ca. 1857 (Utah)–?
Married: Ira D. Lyman; Nine Mile: 1890s to 1900s; Census 1880: Kanosh, Millard County; Census 1900: Nine Mile Canyon; Census 1910: Randlette, Uintah County; Census 1920: Dragon, Uintah County; Census 1930: Fruita, Colorado. Elizabeth married Ira D. Lyman in Millard County. After his death in 1917, she moved in with her children Edna and Claude, who were living in Dragon, and she later moved to Colorado with Claude.

Lyman, Ira D. 1855 (California)–1917 (Uintah County)
Married: Elizabeth (?) (1878); Nine Mile: 1890s to 1900s; Census 1870: Fillmore, Millard County; Census 1880: Kanosh, Millard County; Census 1900: Nine Mile Canyon; Census 1910: Randlette, Uintah County. Ira D. was raised in Millard County and has no apparent family ties to others in Nine Mile Canyon. The 1900 census lists him as a government station keeper, perhaps the telegraph operator. He later moved on to the Uinta Basin.

Lyman, George. Ca. 1885 (Utah)–?
Nine Mile: 1890s to 1900s; Census 1900: Nine Mile Canyon; Census 1910: Randlette, Uintah County. George was a son of Ira D. and Elizabeth Lyman, and he would have been a teenager when living in Nine Mile Canyon where his father worked as a government station keeper. There is no record of him after the 1910 census.

Lyman, Mabel. *See* **O'Fallon, Mabel (Lyman)**

McClain, Isaac. 1849 (England)–?
Nine Mile: ca. 1900; Census 1900: Nine Mile Canyon. Isaac was listed as a fifty-year-old head of household in the 1900 census for Nine Mile Canyon. He listed his occupation as a miner. There are no other vital records linked to this person, and nothing more is known about him.

McCourt, Rhoda B. (Brundage). 1879–1962 (Carbon County)
Married: Joshua McCourt; Nine Mile: 1890s (?); Census 1880: Spanish Fork, Utah County; Census 1900: Nine Mile Canyon; Census 1910: Sunnyside, Carbon County; Census 1920: Antelope, Duchesne County; Census 1930: Columbia, Carbon County. Rhoda was the oldest daughter of Joseph B. and Libby Brundage. She was twenty-one years old at the time of the 1900 census and was probably already married and not living in the canyon. She is also listed on the 1900 census for Sunnyside as Mrs. Joshua McCourt. There is no record that her husband lived in Nine Mile Canyon. Joshua died in 1937 and Rhoda remarried to a man named Delamater.

McCoy, Fred M. Ca. 1887 (New Mexico)–1957 (Bayfield, Colorado)
Married: Julia Amy (?); Nine Mile: ca. 1910; Census 1900: Flora Vista, New Mexico; Census 1910: Nine Mile Canyon; Census 1920: Columbus, Colorado; Census 1930: LaPlata, Colorado. Fred was married to Julia Amy (unknown last name). They apparently had no family connections to those living in Nine Mile Canyon at the time, and they apparently did not stay long. Fred came to Nine Mile with his cousin Linn or "Den." Fred moved on to Colorado, and Linn moved back to New Mexico. It is unknown how they came to be in Nine Mile Canyon. It is possible that Fred was somehow related to William McCoy, Preston Nutter's long-time ranch manager.

McCoy, Julia Amy. 1890 (Oregon)–1976 (Bayfield, Colorado)
Married: Fred McCoy; Nine Mile: ca. 1910; Census 1910: Nine Mile Canyon; Census 1920: Columbus, Colorado; Census 1930: LaPlata, Colorado. Amy was married to Fred M. McCoy, and she came to Nine Mile Canyon with her husband and his cousin. They apparently had no family connections to those living in Nine Mile Canyon at the time, and they apparently did not stay long. All of Julia's children were born after they left Utah.

McCoy, Linn H. Ca. 1885–?
Married: Dora Larick; Nine Mile: ca. 1910; Census 1900: Aztec, New Mexico; Census 1910: Nine Mile Canyon; Census 1920: Crown Point, New Mexico; Census 1930: Aztec, New Mexico. Linn apparently had no family connections to those living in Nine Mile Canyon at the time, and he apparently did not stay long.

Linn came to Nine Mile with his cousin Fred McCoy. Fred moved on to Colorado, and Linn moved back to New Mexico. It is unknown if Linn was somehow related to William McCoy, who was Preston Nutter's long-time ranch manager.

McCoy, William W. Ca. 1836 (Vermont)–?
Married: Jane (?); Nine Mile: ca. 1901 to 1915; Census 1900: Salt Lake City; Census 1910: Nine Mile Canyon. On the 1910 census, William listed himself as a seventy-four-year-old cook living with Preston Nutter. This greatly understates his role as Nutter's right-hand man and manager from the beginnings of Nutter's ranching empire. Historical accounts indicate he was a life-long bachelor, but in 1900 he was apparently married and living in Salt Lake City. He died on the Nutter Ranch.

McIntire, John O. 1847 (Illinois)–1906 (Carbon County)
Nine Mile: ca. 1900; Census 1900: Nine Mile Canyon. There are database links to John O. McIntire in Iron County in 1870 and Washington County in 1880, but the birth year and birthplaces are not consistent, and it is unknown if this is the same person. John O. McIntire died in Carbon County in 1906, perhaps in Nine Mile Canyon, and he was buried in Price. This is probably the same person. Nothing else is known about him other than he was divorced at the time he was living in Nine Mile Canyon.

McKee, Almira. Ca. 1880 (Millard County)–?
Nine Mile: 1899. School census records indicate an Almira McKee was a teacher in Nine Mile Canyon

in 1899. This could be Elmira Mckee, born in Holden, but there are no other records associated with this person.

Madson, Christian. Ca. 1889 (Denmark)–?
Married: Maud (?); Nine Mile: ca. 1910; Census 1910: Nine Mile Canyon; Census 1920: Minneapolis, Minnesota; Census 1930: Minneapolis, Minnesota. In 1910, Christian was a twenty-one-year-old ranch hand living with and working for Preston Nutter. The database links suggest Christian moved on to Minnesota where he married and raised a family.

Mair, Ellen Pearl (Hamilton). 1891 (Utah)–?
Married: Daniel Mair; Nine Mile: 1890s to 1900s; Census 1900: Nine Mile Canyon; Census 1920: Heber, Wasatch County; Census 1930: Heber, Wasatch County. Pearl was the daughter of William and Liza Bird Hamilton, and she was probably raised in Nine Mile Canyon at the family ranch near the mouth of Argyle Canyon.

Mead, Ellen (Workman). 1911 (Utah)–1999 (Carbon County)
Married: Meril Mead (1928); Nine Mile: ca. 1928; Census 1920: Roosevelt, Duchesne County; Census 1930: Sunnyside, Carbon County. Ellen was the wife of Meril Mead, who worked as a ranch hand for Preston Nutter in the 1920s. By 1928, he had leased the Rock House at the mouth of Harmon Canyon (commonly called the Harmon House or the Wimmer House) with a business partner. About the same time, he married Ellen Workman and moved her into the Rock House. He

was working for Frank Alger at the time. After a dispute with his business partner, Meril and Ellen moved out of the Rock House and lived with Jerry Rich for a time, but by 1930 they were living in Sunnyside. Their son, Ben, currently owns the Nine Mile Ranch at the mouth of Cow Canyon.

Mead, Meril E. 1906 (Utah)–1997 (Carbon County)
Married: Ellen Workman (1928); Nine Mile: 1920s; Census 1910: Green River, Emery County; Census 1930: Sunnyside, Carbon County. Meril worked as a ranch hand for Preston Nutter in the 1920s. By 1928, he had leased the Rock House at the mouth of Harmon Canyon (commonly called the Harmon House or the Wimmer House) with a business partner. About the same time, he married Ellen Workman and moved her into the Rock House. He was working for Frank Alger at the time. After a dispute with his business partner, Meril and Ellen moved out of the Rock House and lived with Jerry Rich for a time, but by 1930 they were living in Sunnyside. Their son, Ben, currently owns the Nine Mile Ranch at the mouth of Cow Canyon.

Miles, Donna J. *See* ***Burgess, Donna J. (Miles)***

Miles, Lorenea (or Lorenza). Ca. 1887 (Utah)–?
Nine Mile: 1907 to 1910s; Census 1900: Salt Lake City; Census 1910: Nine Mile Canyon. The database incorrectly links this individual to Mary Leona Miles, who was already married and living in Salt Lake City at the time of the 1910 census. What became of Lorenea after 1910 is not known. She was a daughter of William A. and Lucretia Wightman

Miles, and is part of the legend that Nine Mile Canyon was named after the Miles family.

Miles, Lucretia. 1860 (Utah)–1923 (Idaho Falls, Idaho)
Married: William Allen Miles; Nine Mile: 1907 to 1910s; Census 1860: Payson, Utah County; Census 1880: Payson, Utah County; Census 1900: Salt Lake City; Census 1910: Nine Mile Canyon; Census 1920: Roosevelt, Duchesne County. Lucretia and William Allen Miles had seven daughters, from whence the legend arose that Nine Mile Canyon was named for the nine Miles. This is not accurate. Only four or five daughters lived in Nine Mile Canyon, which had that name long before the Miles family arrived. Lucretia and William acquired a ranch in lower Nine Mile Canyon in 1907, but they retained their home in Salt Lake City. Lucretia also proved up on a homestead claim in lower Nine Mile Canyon.

Miles, Lucretia. See **Evans, Lucretia (Miles)**

Miles, Martha Jane. See **Edwards, Martha Jane (Miles)**

Miles, Mary Leona. See **Hatch, Mary Leona (Miles)**

Miles, Mildred. See **Dillman, Mildred (Miles)**

Miles, Ruby V. Ca. 1895–?
Nine Mile: ca. 1907 to 1910s; Census 1900: Salt Lake City; Census 1910: Nine Mile Canyon. Ruby was a daughter of William A. and Lucretia Wightman Miles, and she would have arrived with her parents in 1907. There are no records of Ruby after the

1910 census. She is part of the legend that Nine Mile Canyon was named after the Miles clan.

Miles, William Allen. 1850 (Missouri)–1923 (Duchesne County)
Married: Lucretia Wightman; Nine Mile: 1907 to 1910s; Census 1900: Salt Lake City; Census 1910: Nine Mile Canyon; Census 1920: Roosevelt, Duchesne County. Lucretia and William Allen Miles had seven daughters, from whence the legend arose that Nine Mile Canyon was named for the nine Miles. This is not accurate. Only four or five daughters lived in Nine Mile Canyon, which had that name long before the Miles family arrived. William and Lucretia acquired their ranch in lower Nine Mile Canyon in 1907, but they retained their home in Salt Lake City. William bought out all of the neighboring ranches in lower Nine Mile Canyon and had private landholdings that rivaled those of Preston Nutter.

Millett, Matthew F. Ca. 1881 (Minnesota)–?
Nine Mile: ca. 1910; Census 1910: Nine Mile Canyon. In 1910, Matthew was a twenty-nine-year-old ranch hand living with and working for Preston Nutter. There are no other vital records linked to this person, and nothing more is known about him.

Mills, Jerald. Ca. 1908 (Utah)–?
Nine Mile: ca. 1930; Census 1930: Nine Mile Canyon. In 1930, Jerald was a boarder living with Harrison and Ada Russell. There are no other vital records linked to this person.

Mitchell, Thomas. ?–?

Nine Mile: ca. 1889. Thomas Mitchell might have been working for William Brock at the Brock's Place road house in the late 1880s. He was a witness at the 1889 murder investigation and 1890 trial of Brock on murder charges. Nothing else is known about him or how he came to be in Nine Mile Canyon.

Morgan, Ellen Gertrude (Smithson). Ca. 1885 (Pahreah, Wayne County)–1948 (Springville, Utah County)
Married: William R. Morgan (1901); Nine Mile: 1890s to 1900s; Census 1900: Nine Mile Canyon; Census 1910: Wellington, Carbon County; Census 1920: Mount Emmons, Duchesne County; Census 1930: Armona, California. Ellen was the daughter of Nephi and Barbara Cook Smithson. She married in 1901, the same year her father died, and might have left the canyon at that time.

Morgan, Fern (Casady). 1909 (Nine Mile Canyon?)–1927 (Carbon County)
Married: (?) Morgan; Nine Mile: 1909 to 1910s; Census 1910: Nine Mile Canyon; Census 1920: Castle Gate, Carbon County. Fern might have been born in Nine Mile Canyon. She was the granddaughter of John Rowley and Augusta Mae Babcock, who were among the earliest settlers in Nine Mile Canyon. Additional siblings are listed on the 1920 census that could have been born in Nine Mile Canyon after 1910.

Morris, Charles E. Ca. 1858 (Maine)–?
Nine Mile: ca. 1920; Census 1920: Nine Mile Canyon; Census 1930: Nine Mile Canyon. The database indicates a Charles Marse lived here

in 1920 and a Charles Morris in 1930, but these are clearly the same person with the same birth year and birthplace. Charles was a sixty-two-year-old widower living in Nine Mile Canyon at the time. He listed his occupation as carpenter. No other vital records are convincingly linked to this person, and nothing more is known about him.

Mott, Julia Ann. *See* **Russell, Julia Ann (Mott)**

Murray, Bernard. 1833 (New York)–? Nine Mile: ca. 1900; Census 1900: Nine Mile Canyon. Bernard was listed as a sixty-seven-year-old head of household in the 1900 census for Nine Mile Canyon. He listed his occupation as miner. There are no other vital records linked to this person, and nothing more is known about him.

Nutter, Grace (Gordon). 1890 (Colorado)–1986 (Los Angeles) Married: Talmadge Cleveland Nutter; Nine Mile: ca. 1920; Census 1900: Gunnison, Colorado; Census 1920: Nine Mile Canyon; Census 1930: Long Beach, California. Grace was the wife of Cleveland Nutter, a nephew of Preston Nutter. They and their two young sons lived briefly with Preston Nutter at the Nine Mile ranch.

Nutter, Harold Stanley. 1918 (New Mexico)–1987 (Los Angeles, California) Nine Mile: ca. 1920; Census 1920: Nine Mile Canyon; Census 1930: Long Beach, California. Stanley was the son of Cleveland Nutter, a nephew of Preston Nutter. He lived briefly at the Nutter Ranch with his parents and great-uncle Preston. There is no record that he married.

Nutter, Jasper. 1914 (New Mexico)–2000 (Davis, California) Nine Mile: ca. 1920; Census 1920: Nine Mile Canyon; Census 1930: Long Beach, California. Jasper was the son of Cleveland Nutter. He lived briefly at the Nutter Ranch with his parents and great-uncle Preston. There is no record that he married.

Nutter, Katherine (Fenton). 1871 (Ohio)–? Married: Preston Nutter (1908); Nine Mile: 1905 to 1965; Census 1900: Colorado (?); Census 1910: Nine Mile Canyon; Census 1920: Salt Lake City; Census 1930: Salt Lake City. Historical accounts list her name as Katherine, but it is spelled Catherine on all census records. Katherine was a telegraph operator in Colorado when she won a lottery for a homestead in the Uinta Basin. On her way there, the stage she was riding in was forced to stop for the night at the Nutter Ranch, where she spent the night. After she proved up on her Duchesne County homestead, she then married Preston Nutter. She lived at the Nine Mile Ranch in the early years of their marriage, but she preferred their apartment in Salt Lake City where she raised their two daughters. She is listed on the 1910 census for both Nine Mile Canyon and Salt Lake City.

Nutter, Katherine. 1910 (Utah)–? Nine Mile: 1910 to 1970s; Census 1910: Nine Mile Canyon; Census 1920: Salt Lake City; Census 1930: Salt Lake City. Katherine was an infant at the time of the 1910 census, and she is listed on that census for both Nine Mile Canyon and Salt Lake City. She spent summers at the ranch, but she was raised and educated in Salt Lake City. She was the older daughter of Preston and Katherine Fenton Nutter.

Nutter, Preston. Ca. 1855 (West Virginia)–1936 (Salt Lake City) Married: Catherine Fenton (1908); Nine Mile: 1901 to 1936; Census 1880: Lake City, Colorado; Census 1910: Nine Mile Canyon; Census 1920: Nine Mile Canyon; Census 1930: Nine Mile Canyon. Preston Nutter acquired the Pete Francis place in late 1901 or early 1902, closed the saloon, and turned the hotel into a bunkhouse for his ranch hands. He split his time between the Nine Mile ranch and an apartment in Salt Lake City. He was one of the largest cattle barons of his day, running tens of thousands of cows between his sprawling operation on the Arizona Strip and northeastern Utah. He came to Nine Mile after he lost his leases on Indian lands in the Uinta Basin. He met Katherine Fenton when she was a stage passenger on her way to claim a homestead in Ioka in 1905. She was present for the 1910 census, but she lived most of the time in their Salt Lake apartment where she raised their two daughters. Preston is listed on the 1910 and 1930 census for both Nine Mile Canyon and Salt Lake City.

Nutter, Talmage Cleveland. 1886 (West Virginia)–1967 (Los Angeles, California) Married: Grace Boyd; Nine Mile: ca. 1920; Census 1900: Troy, West Virginia; Census 1910: Dawson, New Mexico; Census 1920: Nine Mile Canyon; Census 1930: Long Beach, California. Cleveland was the son of Jasper Nutter, Preston's brother. He had moved west with his parents to

New Mexico, and in 1920 he was living with his uncle Preston. He was recently married and brought his wife, Grace, and their two young sons to the Nutter Ranch. It is not known how long they stayed at the Nutter Ranch. Preston Nutter had a cordial relationship with Jasper, and there are several letters in the Special Collections files between the two of them.

Nutter, Virginia F. *See* **Price, Virginia F. (Nutter)**

O'Fallon, Mabel (Lyman). Ca. 1889 (Utah)–?
Married: Owen O'Fallon; Nine Mile: ca. 1900; Census 1900: Nine Mile Canyon; Census 1910: Randlette, Uintah County; Census 1920: Gunnison, Colorado. Mabel was a daughter of Ira D. and Elizabeth Lyman. She later moved with her family to the Uinta Basin, then married and moved to Colorado. Her father was a government station keeper in the canyon in 1900.

Olsen, Blaine. 1889 (Utah)–?
Nine Mile: 1890s to 1900s; Census 1900: Nine Mile Canyon; Census 1910: Clayton, Idaho. Blaine was ten years old when he moved to Nine Mile Canyon. There are no vital records of him after the 1910 census. He was a son of John Henry and Olive Olsen, who had a ranch near Olsen Canyon.

Olsen, Byron L. Ca. 1873 (Utah)–1944 (King County, Washington)
Married: Frances (?); Nine Mile: 1890s to 1900s; Census 1880: Mount Pleasant, Sanpete County; Census 1900: Nine Mile Canyon; Census 1920: Seattle, Washington; Census 1930: King County, Washington.

Frank was an adult son of John Henry and Olive Olsen when he moved to Nine Mile Canyon with his parents. He later moved on to Washington State. The Olsen family ranch was probably located at Olsen Canyon.

Olsen, Frank H. 1871 (Utah)–?
Nine Mile: 1890s to 1900s; Census 1880: Mount Pleasant, Sanpete County; Census 1900: Nine Mile Canyon. Frank was an adult son of John Henry and Olive Olsen when he moved to Nine Mile Canyon with his parents. There are no other vital records related to him after the 1900 census. The family ranch was probably located at Olsen Canyon.

Olsen, Grace. *See* **Haney, Grace (Olsen)**

Olsen, John Henry. 1848 (Norway)–before 1930
Married: Olive (?); Nine Mile: 1890s to 1900s; Census 1880: Mount Pleasant, Sanpete County; Census 1900: Nine Mile Canyon; Census 1910: Clayton, Idaho; Census 1920: Missoula, Montana; Census 1930: Missoula, Montana. By 1920, John had changed the family surname to Allison. Olsen Canyon in middle Nine Mile Canyon is named for the Olsen family, who were among the early settlers here, arriving sometime before 1900. The family farm in Nine Mile might have been bought out by Preston Nutter in about 1902.

Olsen, Marian. 1881 (Utah)–?
Married: (?) McCall; Nine Mile: 1890s to 1900s; Census 1900: Nine Mile Canyon; Census 1910: Blackfoot, Idaho; Census 1920: Glendale, California; Census 1930: Missoula, Montana. Marian was

widowed before 1910 at a young age and remained a widow the rest of her life. In 1930, her elderly mother was living with her in Montana. She was an adult daughter of John Henry and Olive Olsen when she moved to Nine Mile Canyon in the late 1890s. The Olsen family ranch was probably near Olsen Canyon.

Olsen, Olive. 1849 (Iowa)–after 1930
Married: John H. Olsen; Nine Mile: 1890s to 1900s; Census 1880: Mount Pleasant, Sanpete County; Census 1900: Nine Mile Canyon; Census 1910: Clayton, Idaho; Census 1920: Missoula, Montana; Census 1930: Missoula, Montana. Olive was the Olsen family matriarch. By 1920, John and Olive had changed the family surname to Allison. Olsen Canyon in middle Nine Mile Canyon is named for the Olsen family, who were among the early settlers here sometime before 1900. They might have been bought out by Preston Nutter.

Pace, John Albert. 1881 (Bluff, San Juan County)–1937 (Duchesne County)
Married: Ada Cottam; Nine Mile: 1920s to 1937; Census 1900: Price, Carbon County; Census 1910: Price, Carbon County; Census 1920: Price, Carbon County; Census 1930: Nine Mile Canyon. Albert is also listed on the 1930 census for Price, where his wife and children lived. Local legend has it Albert committed suicide in Nine Mile Canyon during a particularly cold winter. This might not be accurate.

Perry, Eldwin B. Ca. 1906–?
Married: Ethel (?); Nine Mile: 1910s to 1920s; Census 1910: Mill Creek, Salt Lake County; Census 1920: Nine

Mile Canyon; Census 1930: Salt Lake City. Eldwin was a teenager when he came to Nine Mile Canyon with his parents and siblings sometime before 1920. The Perry family does not appear to have stayed long in the canyon. Eldwin became a chemist and raised a family in the Salt Lake Valley.

Perry, Elma. *See* **Hampton, Elma (Perry)**

Perry, Janet. Ca. 1870 (Utah)–1948 (Salt Lake County)
Married: Pierre O. Perry; Nine Mile: 1910s to 1920s; Census 1880: South Cottonwood, Salt Lake County; Census 1900: Farmer, Salt Lake County; Census 1910: Mill Creek, Salt Lake County; Census 1920: Nine Mile Canyon; Census 1930: Salt Lake City. The Perry family arrived in Nine Mile Canyon from the Salt Lake Valley sometime before 1920, but they did not stay long before returning to Salt Lake City. Nothing is known about the Perry family, why they came here, or why they left.

Perry, Kenneth B. Ca. 1909 (Utah)–?
Nine Mile: 1910s to 1920s; Census 1910: Mill Creek, Salt Lake County; Census 1920: Nine Mile Canyon; Census 1930: Salt Lake City. Kenneth was the youngest of the Perry children to accompany their parents to Nine Mile Canyon. The Perry family does not appear to have stayed long in the canyon before returning to the Salt Lake Valley. There are no death or marriage records for Kenneth.

Perry, Pierre O. Ca. 1871 (Utah)–1949 (Salt Lake County)
Married: Janet Bradford; Nine Mile: 1910s to 1920s; Census 1900: Farmer,

Salt Lake County; Census 1910: Mill Creek, Salt Lake County; Census 1920: Nine Mile Canyon; Census 1930: Salt Lake City. The Perry family arrived in Nine Mile Canyon from the Salt Lake Valley sometime before 1920, but they did not stay long before they returned to Salt Lake City. Nothing is known about the Perry family, why they came here, or why they left.

Perry, Pierre W. Ca. 1901 (Utah)–1969 (Roswell, New Mexico)
Nine Mile: 1910s to 1920s; Census 1910: Mill Creek, Salt Lake County; Census 1920: Nine Mile Canyon; Census 1930: Salt Lake City. Pierre W. was a young man when he came to Nine Mile Canyon with his parents and older siblings. The Perry family does not appear to have stayed long in the canyon. There are no marriage records for Pierre. He later moved to Chicago.

Perry, William R. Ca. 1903 (Utah)–?
Nine Mile: 1910s to 1920s; Census 1910: Mill Creek, Salt Lake County; Census 1920: Nine Mile Canyon; Census 1930: Salt Lake City. William was a teenager when he came to Nine Mile Canyon with his parents and older siblings. The Perry family does not appear to have stayed long in the canyon. There are no death or marriage records for William.

Potter, Maude (Hall). 1893 (Escalante, Garfield County)–1946 (Salt Lake City)
Married: George Elza Potter; Nine Mile: 1894 to 1900s; Census 1900: Nine Mile Canyon; Census 1920: Talmage, Duchesne County; Census 1930: Talmage, Duchesne County. Sisters Minnie and Maude, daughters of Charles and Sarah Babcock

Hall, sparked the legend that the canyon was named after the twin girls. Maude was born in November 1893 in Escalante, and the family came to Nine Mile Canyon the following spring. Family histories indicate she died of cancer at about age fifty-three.

Powell, Ada J. Ca. 1901–?
Nine Mile: ca. 1901 to ca. 1905; Census 1910: Price, Carbon County. Ada was the daughter of John A. and Rosealtha Allred Powell. There are no vital records to prove she lived in Nine Mile Canyon, but historical accounts suggest the family was living there in the late 1890s and/or early 1900s. Ada would have been a young child at the time. There are no records of Ada after the 1910 census. She might have been born in Nine Mile Canyon. Her mother was the third wife of John A. Powell.

Powell, Clarence. 1892 (Utah)–1948 (Carbon County)
Married: Lillie E. (?); Nine Mile: ca. 1895 to 1905; Census 1900: Nine Mile Canyon (?); Census 1910: Price, Carbon County; Census 1920: Price, Carbon County; Census 1930: Riverside, California. Clarence was the son of John A. and Rosealtha Allred Powell. There are no vital records to prove he lived in Nine Mile Canyon, but historical accounts suggest the family was living there in the late 1890s and/or early 1900s. Clarence would have been about eight years old if the family lived there in 1900. His mother was the third wife of John A. Powell.

Powell, Earl Herbert. 1898 (Utah)–1928 (Carbon County)
Nine Mile: ca. 1898 to ca. 1905; Census 1900: Nine Mile Canyon (?);

Census 1910: Price, Carbon County; Census 1920: Price, Carbon County. Earl was the son of John A. and Rosealtha Allred Powell. There are no vital records to prove he lived in Nine Mile Canyon, but historical accounts suggest the family was living there in the late 1890s and/or early 1900s. Elmer would have been a small child if the family lived there in 1900. His mother was the third wife of John A. Powell.

Powell, Elmer W. 1890 (Utah)–1959 (Carbon County)
Married: Gertrude Roberts; Nine Mile: ca. 1895 to ca. 1905; Census 1900: Nine Mile Canyon (?); Census 1910: Price, Carbon County; Census 1920: Price, Carbon County; Census 1930: Price, Carbon County. Elmer was the son of John A. and Rosealtha Allred Powell. There are no vital records to prove he lived in Nine Mile Canyon, but historical accounts suggest the family was living there in the late 1890s and/or early 1900s. Elmer would have been about ten years old if the family lived there in 1900. His mother was the third wife of John A. Powell.

Powell, Ethel N. 1894 (Utah)–1926 (Price, Carbon County)
Married: Gordon A. Leonard; Nine Mile: ca. 1895 to ca. 1905; Census 1900: Nine Mile Canyon (?); Census 1910: Price, Carbon County; Census 1920: Price, Carbon County. Ethel was the daughter of John A. and Rosealtha Allred Powell. There are no vital records to prove she lived in Nine Mile Canyon, but historical accounts suggest the family was living there in the late 1890s and/or early 1900s. Ethel would have been about six years old if the family lived there

in 1900. Her mother was the third wife of John A. Powell.

Powell, Grant. 1903 (Price, Carbon County)–1975 (Kenilworth, Carbon County)
Married: Ruby (Thompson?); Nine Mile: ca. 1903 to ca. 1905; Census 1910: Price, Carbon County; Census 1920: Price, Carbon County. Grant was the son of John A. and Rosealtha Allred Powell. There are no vital records to prove he lived in Nine Mile Canyon, but historical accounts suggest the family was living there in the late 1890s and/or early 1900s. Grant might have been born in Nine Mile Canyon or after the family returned to Price. Records indicate he married a woman named Ruby. This could be Ruby Thompson, daughter of Al and Martha Grames Thompson. Records indicate she married an unspecified person named Powell.

Powell, John Ammon, Sr. Ca. 1846 (Missouri)–1928 (Salt Lake County)
Married: Rosealtha Jane Allred; Nine Mile: ca. 1895 to ca. 1905; Census 1870: Pondtown, Utah County; Census 1880: Salem, Utah County; Census 1900: Nine Mile Canyon (?); Census 1910: Price, Carbon County; Census 1920: Price, Carbon County (?). There are no vital records to verify that John A. Powell Sr. ever lived in Nine Mile Canyon, but family history indicates he had a ranch at Sulphur Canyon in the late 1890s or early 1900s with his third wife, Rosealtha. Family legend has it John A. Powell guided U.S. Army troops through Nine Mile Canyon when they were looking for a freight route between the Uinta Basin and Price. John A. had three very large families and thirty-one children. Rosealtha died in 1932. The catalog of Powell

family members who might have been in the canyon is derived from the 1910 census when the family was living in Price. The 1910 census indicates they were living both in Price and in Hiawatha. They might have retained ownership of their Nine Mile properties well into the 1940s. The Powells were neighbors of John Rowley and Augusta Mae Babcock.

Powell, Rosealtha Jane (Allred). Ca. 1863 (Utah)–1932 (Carbon County)
Married: John A. Powell Sr.; Nine Mile: ca. 1895 to ca. 1905; Census 1870: Spring City, Sanpete County; Census 1880: Spring City, Sanpete County; Census 1900: Nine Mile Canyon (?); Census 1910: Price, Carbon County; Census 1920: Price, Carbon County; Census 1930: Price, Carbon County. Rosealtha was the third wife of John A. Powell Sr. and they raised their family in Price. There are historical accounts that they had a place next to the Nine Mile Road between the mouth of Minnie Maud and the mouth of Cow Canyon. By inference, the Powells would have been in Nine Mile Canyon in the late 1890s or early 1900s. There is minimal evidence that any of her children married into the established families in Nine Mile Canyon. One son might have married the daughter of Al and Martha Grames Thompson, who would have been a distant cousin. According to one account attributed to her son Sheridan, most of her children were born in Nine Mile Canyon.

Powell, Ruby M. (Thompson). 1905 (Nine Mile Canyon?)–1983 (Price, Carbon County)
Married: (Grant) Powell; Nine Mile: 1905 to 1920s; Census 1910: Nine Mile Canyon; Census 1920: Nine Mile

Canyon. Ruby was the daughter of Al and Martha Thompson. She was probably born in Nine Mile Canyon. Her death records indicate her last name was Powell, and she might have married Grant Powell, son of John A. and Rosealtha Allred Powell. The Powell family has a long history in Nine Mile Canyon. Her grandmother was Martha Powell Grames.

Powell, Sheridan R. 1896 (Utah)–1965 (Carbon County)
Married: Jessie Fay Barker; Nine Mile: ca. 1896 to ca. 1905; Census 1900: Nine Mile Canyon (?); Census 1910: Price, Carbon County; Census 1920: Storrs, Carbon County; Census 1930: Kenilworth, Carbon County. Sheridan, or "Sherd," was the son of John A. and Rosealtha Allred. There are no vital records to prove he lived in Nine Mile Canyon, but historical accounts suggest the family was living there in the late 1890s and/or early 1900s. Sherd would have been about four years old if the family lived there in 1900. He is named specifically in one historical account as living there.

Price, Virginia F. (Nutter). 1913 (Utah)–?
Married: Howard C. Price Jr.; Nine Mile: 1913 to 1970s; Census 1920: Salt Lake City; Census 1930: Salt Lake City. Virginia was born in Salt Lake City. She spent summers at the ranch, but she was raised and educated in Salt Lake City. She was the younger daughter of Preston and Katherine Fenton Nutter, and heiress to the Nutter empire. Her husband, Howard Price, ran the Nutter Ranch after the death of her mother.

Quinn, Reta Elizabeth (Barney). 1908 (Utah)–1971 (Carbon County)

Married: William Quinn; Nine Mile: 1910s to 1920s; Census 1910: Ferron, Emery County; Census 1920: Nine Mile Canyon; Census 1930: Price. Reta was the daughter of Delbert and Mary Barney, who moved to Nine Mile Canyon sometime before 1920. Reta would have been a child at the time. She married William Quinn and moved to Price. Her death records give her last name as Leger, suggesting she remarried at some point.

Rasmussen, Oliver. 1877 or 1879 (Utah)–1947 (Carbon County)
Nine Mile: ca. 1930 to 1940s; Census 1880: Manassah, Sanpete County; Census 1900: Cleveland, Emery County; Census 1930: Nine Mile Canyon. Oliver's birth date is listed as 1877 on his World War I draft registration and as 1879 on his death record. He was the son of Cornelius and Hannah Rasmussen, who were living in Emery County in 1900. In 1930, he was listed as a single head-of-household farmer in Nine Mile Canyon. The Rasmussen Ranch was located at Daddy Canyon, where a large rock shelter is still called Rasmussen Cave. Oliver sold out to Humbert Presett in 1960. Presett was responsible for painting the (misspelled) "no trespassing" on the back of Rasmussen Cave.

Revoir, Henry. Ca. 1885 (France or Italy)–?
Married: Mary (?); Nine Mile: ca. 1910; Census 1910: Nine Mile Canyon; Census 1920: Price, Carbon County. Henry immigrated to the United States in 1900, and census records indicate he was born in France and was working in Nine Mile Canyon as a sheepherder, perhaps in partnership

with Oscar Warcham. By 1920, he was living in Price with his wife, Mary, and a young child, and he listed his place of birth as Italy. By 1940, he had moved on to Colorado. There is no information as to why he came to Nine Mile Canyon, where he lived there, or why he left.

Rich, Arbun. 1911 (Utah)–1969 (Utah)
Married: Thelma (?); Nine Mile: ca. 1923 to 1935; Census 1920: Altonah, Duchesne County; Census 1930: Nine Mile Canyon. Arbun was the son of Charles C. Rich III, and he was twelve years old when he accompanied his parents to Nine Mile Canyon. He married a woman named Thelma at or just before 1930, and they had their own household in Nine Mile Canyon. By 1935, Arbun and Thelma were still in "rural Carbon County," probably Nine Mile Canyon, but by 1940 they had moved back to the Uinta Basin with their three small children. It is unknown if any of their children were born in Nine Mile Canyon.

Rich, Arthur. 1920 (Utah)–2002 (Carbon County)
Nine Mile: 1920 to ca. 1940; Census 1930: Sunnyside, Carbon County. Arthur would have been about three years old when his parents, Charles and Jane Rich, brought him to live in Nine Mile Canyon. Family histories indicate he grew to adulthood there, but there are no census records to indicate that. In 1930, he was living with his parents in Sunnyside (the family had a second home there). He was a veteran of World War II, and he was living in Wellington at the time of his death. No other vital records are listed in the database.

Rich, Charles Coulson. 1924 (Nine Mile Canyon?)–1938 (Carbon County)
Nine Mile: 1924 to ca. 1935; Census 1930: Nine Mile Canyon. Charles C. was the son of Jerry and Wanda Rich, and he was probably born and raised in Nine Mile Canyon. He was only fourteen years old when he died.

Rich, Charles Coulson, III. 1866 (Idaho)–1935 (Salt Lake City)
Married: Theodocia Jane Clark; Nine Mile: ca. 1923 to 1935; Census 1880: Garden City, Rich County; Census 1900: Vernal, Uintah County; Census 1910: Roosevelt, Duchesne County; Census 1920: Altonah, Duchesne County; Census 1930: Sunnyside, Duchesne County. Charles C. Rich III was among the prominent settlers of the Uinta Basin in the early 1900s. In 1923, he traded a homestead there for an eighty-acre parcel in Nine Mile Canyon and moved his wife, Jane, and their younger children to the canyon. When a survey indicated their eighty acres was not on the valley floor, Charles filed a second eighty-acre claim on the valley floor where the ranch was located, and his wife filed a second eighty-acre claim next to it. There are no vital records to indicate Charles lived in the canyon, but family histories indicate both he and Jane were there after 1923. By 1930, they were living in Sunnyside (they might have had a second home there). Family histories indicate they left Nine Mile Canyon in the late 1930s and returned to the Vernal area.

Rich, David Harvey. 1917 (Utah)–1969 (Utah)
Nine Mile: 1923 to 1930s; Census 1920: Altonah, Duchesne County; Census 1930: Sunnyside, Carbon County. David would have been about five years old when his parents, Charles and Jane Rich, brought him to live in Nine Mile Canyon. Family histories indicate he grew to adulthood there, but there are no census records to indicate that. In 1930, he was living with his parents in Sunnyside (the family had a second home there). He is buried in Wellington.

Rich, Eliza Lucille (Houskeeper). 1916 (Utah)–1990 (Vernal?)
Married: Thorald Rich; Nine Mile: 1916 to 1950s; Census 1920: Nine Mile Canyon; Census 1930: Nine Mile Canyon. Lucille was the daughter of Theodore B. and Clara Alger Houskeeper, who were among the earliest settlers in Nine Mile Canyon. She was raised on the Houskeeper ranch near the mouth of Cow Canyon. She married Thorald Rich in 1933 and the couple lived with Lucille's bachelor uncle, Frank Alger. Lucille and Thorald inherited the Alger Ranch (and all its debt), and expanded the Rich ranch holdings to include the John Eagan ranch, where some of the Rich children were raised as children. Lucille and Theodore met at a rodeo held at the Edwin Lee ranch at the mouth of Argyle Canyon.

Rich, Guadine. Ca. 1931 (Nine Mile Canyon?)–?
Nine Mile: 1931 to ca. 1935. There are no vital records to indicate Guadine lived in Nine Mile Canyon, but the 1940 census indicates her parents, Jerry and Wanda Rich, were living in "rural Carbon County" in 1935, presumably in Nine Mile Canyon. Guadine was probably born there and was four or five years old when her parents had a place in Wellington. There are no other vital records for her besides the 1940 census. Family histories indicate Jerry and Wanda had daughters living in the canyon. This is probably a reference to Guadine.

Rich, Jane Susanna (Stock). 1846 (South Africa)–1925 (Vernal, Uintah County)
Married: Charles C. Rich II; Nine Mile: 1923 to ca. 1925; Census 1860: Omaha, Nebraska; Census 1870: Paris, Rich County; Census 1880: Garden City, Rich County; Census 1900: Vernal, Uinta Basin; Census 1920: Roosevelt, Duchesne County. Jane was the mother of Charles C. Rich III, who acquired a Nine Mile Canyon homestead in 1923. When a survey indicated the homestead was in the cliff ledges and not on the valley floor, Charles III filed an eighty-acre claim on the valley floor. Jane filed a second eighty-acre claim on an adjoining piece. A cabin was built on this second parcel and it was known as the Jane Rich cabin. But it is unknown if Jane actually lived in it; she would have been seventy-seven years old at the time. There are no vital records indicating she actually lived in Nine Mile Canyon.

Rich, Jeremiah. 1903 (Utah)–1983 (Salt Lake City)
Married: Wanda Lamar Alexander; Nine Mile: ca. 1923 to 1935; Census 1910: Roosevelt, Duchesne County; Census 1920: Altonah, Duchesne County; Census 1930: Nine Mile Canyon. Jerry Rich was twenty years old when he came with his parents to Nine Mile Canyon, and as the oldest of the Charles Rich children in the canyon the ranching duties fell to him. He married Wanda Alexander shortly after arriving, and by 1930 he was listed as the head of household with three small children. Also living

with him was his younger brother, Thorald. By 1935, Jerry and Wanda were living in Wellington.

Rich, Kenneth Grant. 1922 (Utah)–1993 (Uintah County)
Nine Mile: 1923 to ca. 1940; Census 1930: Sunnyside, Carbon County. Kenneth was just a baby when his parents, Charles and Jane Rich, brought him to live in Nine Mile Canyon. Family histories indicate he grew to adulthood there, but there are no census records to indicate that. In 1930, he was living with his parents in Sunnyside (the family had a second home there). By 1940, he had moved back to the Uinta Basin with his parents. He was a veteran of World War II, and he was living in Vernal at the time of his death. No other vital records are listed in the database.

Rich, Lazon. 1933 (Nine Mile Canyon?)–2011 (Salt Lake County?)
Married: (?) Allen; Nine Mile: 1933 to ca. 1935. There are no vital records to indicate Lazon lived in Nine Mile Canyon, but the 1940 census indicates her parents, Jerry and Wanda Rich, were living in "rural Carbon County" in 1935, presumably in Nine Mile Canyon. Lazon was probably born there a year or two before her parents moved to Wellington. Family histories indicate Jerry and Wanda had daughters living in the canyon. This is probably a reference to Lazon (also spelled La Zon or LaZon).

Rich, Lorence D. Ca. 1929 (Nine Mile Canyon?)–?
Nine Mile: 1929 to ca. 1935; Census 1930: Nine Mile Canyon. Lorance was the son of Jerry and Wanda Rich, and he might have been born in Nine Mile Canyon, where he was listed on the 1930 census. By 1940, he was

living in Wellington with his parents. There are no other records of him after that time.

Rich, Robert A. 1926 (Altonah, Duchesne County)–?
Nine Mile: 1926 to ca. 1935; Census 1930: Nine Mile Canyon. In 1926, Jerry and Wanda Rich were living in Nine Mile Canyon. But military service records indicate Robert was born in Altonah (Wanda's parents might have still been there). He was living in Nine Mile Canyon in 1930, and by 1940 he had moved to Wellington with his parents. Robert served in World War II. There is no record of him after that time.

Rich, Thelma "Babe" (Russell). Ca. 1912 (Utah)–?
Married: Arbun Marlow Rich; Nine Mile: ca. 1930 to 1935; Census 1930: Nine Mile Canyon. There are very few vital records related to Thelma Rich. In 1930, she was married to Arbun Rich and living in Nine Mile Canyon, but they had not yet had any children. They were still living there in 1935, but by 1940 they had moved on to LaPoint in the Uinta Basin. There are no death records for her in the database. She is the daughter of Harrison Russell, who was among the original settlers near the mouth of Minnie Maud Canyon in the 1890s.

Rich, Thorald "Cotton." 1914 (Utah)–1987 (Utah)
Married: Lucille Houskeeper (1933); Nine Mile: 1923 to 1950s; Census 1920: Altonah, Duchesne County; Census 1930: Nine Mile Canyon. Thorald was nine years old when he moved with his family from the Uinta Basin to Nine Mile Canyon. Thorald stayed the longest of any of the Rich brothers, expanding the family holdings

to include the John Eagan ranch. Thorald inherited the Frank Alger place from his wife's uncle. As a child, he worked for Preston Nutter as a gardener, and later as a young man as a range cowboy. His wife was the daughter of Clara Alger and Theodore B. Houskeeper, who owned the ranch near the mouth of Cow Canyon. His children were all raised in Nine Mile Canyon, among them Norma Rich Dalton, who remains the leading canyon historian. Thorald was called "Cotton" for his distinctive white hair which was his trademark throughout his life. He met Lucille at a rodeo at the Edwin Lee ranch at the mouth of Argyle Canyon.

Rich, Theodocia "Jane." 1882 (Utah)–1969 (Uintah County)
Married: Charles C. Rich; Nine Mile: ca. 1923 to 1950s; Census 1900: Vernal, Uintah County; Census 1910: Roosevelt, Duchesne County; Census 1920: Altonah, Duchesne County; Census 1930: Sunnyside, Duchesne County. Theodocia, or "Jane," was the wife of Charles C. Rich III. They were among the prominent early settlers of the Uinta Basin. In 1923, they traded their homestead there for eighty acres in Nine Mile Canyon. When it turned out that the eighty-acre homestead was not in the valley bottom but on the side of the canyon, Charles filed on a second eighty acres in the canyon bottom and Jane filed on another eighty acres next to it. Jane is not listed on any of the vital records as living in Nine Mile Canyon, but family histories indicate she was there after 1923. By 1930, she was living in Sunnyside. Family histories indicate they left Nine Mile Canyon in the late 1930s and moved back to the Vernal area.

Rich, Theodocia Pearl. 1908 (Utah)–1929 (Carbon County)
Married: Gerald Mills; Nine Mile: 1923 to ca. 1929; Census 1910: Roosevelt, Duchesne County; Census 1920: Altonah, Duchesne County. Pearl would have been about fourteen years old when her parents, Charles and Jane Rich, brought her to live in Nine Mile Canyon. Family histories indicate she grew to adulthood there. She died in 1929 before the 1930 census. Family histories indicate she worked for Preston Nutter, probably as domestic help at the Nutter Ranch. She was only twenty-one years old when she died. She is buried in Price. Family histories indicate she and her newborn baby died of small pox.

Rich, Wanda. 1902 (Maeser, Uintah County)–1966 (Vernal, Uintah County)
Married: Jeremiah Rich (1923); Nine Mile: 1923 to ca. 1935; Census 1920: Altonah, Duchesne County; Census 1930: Nine Mile Canyon. Wanda married Jerry Rich in 1923, the same year the Rich family traded their homestead in the Uinta Basin for an eighty-acre ranch in Nine Mile Canyon. By 1930, the couple was living in the canyon with their three small children, all of whom might have been born in Nine Mile Canyon. They were still there in 1935, but by 1940 they had moved back to the Uinta Basin.

Robinson, Edna (Casady). 1908 (Utah)–2001 (Price, Carbon County)
Married: Otto Robinson; Nine Mile: 1908 to 1910s; Census 1910: Nine Mile Canyon; Census 1920: Castle Gate, Carbon County; Census 1930: Price, Carbon County. Edna might have been born in Nine Mile Canyon. She is also listed as Edna Casady Averett.

She was the granddaughter of John Rowley and Augusta Mae Babcock, among the earliest settlers in Nine Mile Canyon. Additional siblings are listed on the 1920 census that could have been born in Nine Mile Canyon after 1910.

Robinson, Rhoda W. (Smithson). 1892 (Layton, Arizona)–?
Married: (?) Mitchell, Francis Robinson (1933); Nine Mile: 1890s to 1900s; Census 1900: Nine Mile Canyon; Census 1910: Packard, Wasatch County; Census 1930: Lake Fork, Duchesne County. Rhoda married a man named Mitchell after 1910, but he died before 1930. She remarried in 1933 to Francis Robinson. She was the daughter of Nephi and Barbara Cook Smithson, who had a ranch at the mouth of Sulphur Canyon and another at the mouth of Cottonwood Canyon.

Rouse, Cecil. Ca. 1900 (Utah)–?
Nine Mile: ca. 1930 to ca. 1940; Census 1930: Nine Mile Canyon. In 1930, Cecil was working as a ranch hand for Preston Nutter. He eventually bought the neighboring ranch to the west, once owned by John Eagan, and he later sold out to Cotton Rich. There are no other records positively linked to him, although there is a Cecil E. Rouse in Colorado in 1940, but with a different birthplace.

Russell, Ada. Ca. 1881 (Utah)–?
Married: Harrison Russell; Nine Mile: ca. 1906 to 1930s; Census 1910: Nine Mile Canyon; Census 1920: Desert Lake, Emery County; Census 1930: Nine Mile Canyon. Ada was married to Harrison Russell and raised her children in Nine Mile Canyon over two decades. Most were probably born in the canyon.

Russell, Andrew Jackson. 1840 (Illinois)–1917 (Carbon County)
Married: Julia Ann Mott (1864); Nine Mile: 1890s to 1917; Census 1860: Payson, Utah County; Census 1870: Chicken Creek, Juab County; Census 1880: Gooseberry Valley, Sevier County; Census 1900: Nine Mile Canyon; Census 1910: Nine Mile Canyon. Andrew Jackson "Daddy" Russell was one of the original pioneers of Nine Mile Canyon, along with his wife, Julia Mott, and at least four grown sons and a daughter. He arrived in the 1890s and probably died in Nine Mile Canyon in 1917. He is buried in Price. Daddy Canyon is named after him.

Russell, Charles Henry. Ca. 1868 (Payson, Utah County)–1944 (Carbon County)
Married: Sabrina King (1893); Nine Mile: 1890s?; Census 1870: Chicken Creek, Juab County; Census 1880: Gooseberry Valley, Sevier County; Census 1910: Arbon, Idaho. There are no vital records to indicate Charles lived in Nine Mile Canyon, but it is probable he moved there with his brothers in the 1890s. Mildred Dillman lists him as one of the brothers residing there, but she does not indicate dates. He was a son of Andrew Jackson and Julia Mott Russell, original settlers in the Minnie Maud Canyon area.

Russell, David Wintworth. 1874 (Utah)–1929 (Carbon County)
Married: Emma Brundage (1874); Nine Mile: 1890s to 1929; Census 1880: Gooseberry Valley, Sevier County; Census 1900: Nine Mile Canyon; Census 1920: Nine Mile Canyon. David was the son of Andrew Jackson and Julia Mott Russell. He achieved notoriety in

1901 when he killed Pete Francis in a saloon brawl at Brock's Place. He was acquitted on murder charges. There are legal documents dated 1902 with his name on them, but there is no record of him in the canyon until 1920, when he was living as a boarder with Al Thompson. He was briefly married in 1898, but by 1900 he was single. He might have died in Nine Mile Canyon.

Russell, Dolly. *See* **Barney, Dolly (Russell)**

Russell, Effie L. Ca. 1905 (Utah)–? Nine Mile: 1905 to 1910s; Census 1910: Nine Mile Canyon. Effie was a daughter of Harrison and Ada Russell, and she might have been born in Nine Mile Canyon. There are no other vital records related to her besides the 1910 census.

Russell, Emma (Brundage). 1878–? Married: 1899 (Dave Russell); Nine Mile: 1890s. Marriage records indicate Emma was married to David Wintworth Russell in 1899, but a year later Dave is listed on the 1900 census as a single man living with his parents in Nine Mile Canyon. Dave was a life-long resident of Nine Mile Canyon, and Emma probably lived there with him during their brief marriage. Nothing is known about her. She might have been a sister of Joe Brundage, one of the earliest settlers in Nine Mile Canyon. She should not be confused with Emma Russell, the daughter of Andrew Jackson and Julia Mott Russell.

Russell, Florence (Thompson). 1888 (Utah)–? Married: Heber Russell (1905); Claude McGuire; Nine Mile: 1900s; Census 1900: Elgin, Grand County; Census 1910: Nine Mile Canyon; Census 1920: Salt Lake City. Florence was married to Heber Russell, and after his death in a train accident she married Claude McGuire and raised her children in Salt Lake City.

Russell, George. 1910 (Utah)–? Nine Mile: 1910s; Census 1910: Nine Mile Canyon; Census 1920: Salt Lake City; Census 1930: Klamath Falls, Oregon (?). George was the son of Heber and Florence Thompson Russell. He might have been born in Nine Mile Canyon. He later grew up with his stepfather, Claude McGuire, in Salt Lake City. There is no convincing record of George after the 1920 census, but two Russell brothers named George and Richard were living in Klamath Falls in 1930.

Russell, James Harrison. Ca. 1885–1938 (Carbon County) Married: Ada Taylor; Nine Mile: 1890s to 1930s; Census 1910: Nine Mile Canyon; Census 1920: Desert Lake, Emery County; Census 1930: Nine Mile Canyon. Harrison was a son of Andrew Jackson and Julia Mott Russell, who were among the earliest pioneers in Nine Mile Canyon in the 1890s. He would have been a child when he first arrived in the canyon. Along with his brother Myron, Harrison remained in Nine Mile Canyon longer than the other Russell brothers.

Russell, Heber. 1884 (Utah)–? Married: Florence Thompson; Nine Mile: 1890s to ca. 1915; Census 1900: Nine Mile Canyon; Census 1910: Nine Mile Canyon. Heber was the youngest son of Andrew Jackson and Julia Mott Russell, who were among the original pioneers of Nine Mile Canyon in the 1890s. He would have been a child when he arrived here. There is no unequivocal record of him after the 1910 census. Mildred Dillman indicates Heber was killed by a train in Price, and that he was one of the Russell brothers who lived in the canyon.

Russell, Heber Richard. 1906 (Utah)–? Nine Mile: 1906 to 1910s; Census 1910: Nine Mile Canyon; Census 1920: Salt Lake City; Census 1930: Klamath Falls, Oregon (?). Richard was the son of Heber and Florence Thompson Russell. He was probably born in Nine Mile Canyon. He later grew up with his stepfather, Claude McGuire, in Salt Lake City. There is no convincing record of Richard after the 1920 census, but two Russell brothers named George and Richard were living in Klamath Falls in 1930.

Russell, Iola. Ca. 1914 (Utah)–? Nine Mile: 1910s to 1920s; Census 1920: Nine Mile Canyon. Iola is listed as a foster daughter of Alva and Lillie Russell Lee in the 1920 census. It is unknown if she was related to Lillie. There are no other records related to her.

Russell, John W. 1866 (Utah)–1946 (Shelley, Idaho) Married: Mary F. Cook; Nine Mile: 1890s?; Census 1870: Chicken Creek, Juab County; Census 1880: Gooseberry Valley, Sevier County; Census 1900: North Ashley, Uintah County; Census 1910: Iona, Idaho; Census 1920: Iona, Idaho; Census 1930: Woodville, Idaho. John W. was the son of Andrew Jackson and Julia Mott Russell, who were among the original pioneers of Nine Mile Canyon in the 1890s. There are no vital records to indicate John lived in Nine Mile Canyon, but Mildred

Dillman relates that "Uncle Jack" was one of the Russells living there. That could be a reference to his father, Andrew Jackson Russell, but the father was known to all as "Daddy" Russell. It could have been John W. to whom she was referring.

Russell, Julia Ann (Mott). Ca. 1848 (Wisconsin)–1902 (Carbon County) Married: Andrew Jackson Russell; Nine Mile: 1890s to 1902; Census 1850: Salt Lake City; Census 1860: Spanish Fork, Utah County; Census 1870: Chicken Creek, Juab County; Census 1880: Gooseberry Valley, Sevier County; Census 1900: Nine Mile Canyon. Julia Mott Russell was one of the original pioneers of Nine Mile Canyon in the 1890s, along with her husband, Andrew Jackson "Daddy" Russell, and at least four grown sons and a daughter. She died in 1902, probably in Nine Mile Canyon, and is buried in Price.

Russell, Kenneth. Ca. 1909–? Nine Mile: 1909 to 1930s; Census 1910: Nine Mile Canyon; Census 1920: Desert Lake, Emery County; Census 1930: Nine Mile Canyon. There are no vital records for Kenneth after the 1930 census when he was a boarder living with his parents, Harrison and Ada Russell, who had returned to Nine Mile Canyon from Emery County.

Russell, Lillie. See **Lee, Lillie (Russell)**

Russell, Myron A. 1878 (Utah)–1956 (Carbon County) Nine Mile: 1890s to 1930s; Census 1880: Gooseberry Valley, Sevier County; Census 1900: Nine Mile Canyon; Census 1930: Nine Mile Canyon. Myron was a son of Andrew Jackson and Julia Mott Russell, and

he was one of two Russell brothers who remained the longest in Nine Mile Canyon. There are no records indicating he was married. He would have been a young man when he first arrived in Nine Mile Canyon.

Russell, Olive L. See **Jensen, Olive (Russell)**

Shaw, Fern Luella (Houskeeper). Ca. 1908 (Utah)–1985 (Price, Carbon County) Married: C. Lee Shaw (1925); Nine Mile: 1908 to 1910s; Census 1910: Nine Mile Canyon; Census 1920: Wellington, Carbon County; Census 1930: Wattis, Carbon County. She might have been born in Nine Mile Canyon. She was the daughter of Theodore B. and Clara Alger Houskeeper.

Shepard, Viola M. (Brundage). 1907 (Emery, Emery County)–1966 (Roosevelt, Duchesne County) Married: Willis Shepard; Nine Mile: 1907 to 1910s; Census 1910: Nine Mile Canyon; Census 1930: Antelope, Duchesne County. Family records indicate she was born in Emery, but she was probably raised in Nine Mile Canyon. She was the daughter of Joe and Zada Hamilton Brundage, early settlers above the mouth of Minnie Maud Canyon.

Smith, Charles F. 1886 (Utah)–? Married: Martha J. Bird; Nine Mile: ca. 1893 to ca. 1898; Census 1900: Coyote Creek, Wyoming; Census 1920: Bluebell, Duchesne County; Census 1930: Bluebell, Duchesne County. Charles F. was the son of Charles M. and Luna Alger Smith, who had a ranch at the mouth of Cow Canyon in the early 1890s. The family sold out after a few years and

moved to Wyoming. There are no vital records that link Charles to Nine Mile Canyon, but there are historical accounts. Charles would have been a small child when his family moved to Nine Mile Canyon. It is unknown if Martha Bird was related to Eliza Jane Bird, who married William Hamilton. William and Eliza were ranching in the canyon about the same time as Charles's parents and within a few miles of the Smith ranch.

Smith, Charles M. Ca. 1861 (Utah)–? Married: Luna L. Alger; Nine Mile: ca. 1893 to ca. 1898; Census 1880: St. George, Washington County; Census 1900: Coyote Creek, Wyoming; Census 1920: Bluebell, Duchesne County; Census 1930: Wellington, Carbon County. Charles M. was married to Luna Alger, a sister of the Alger brothers (Lon, Gett, and Frank). Together they had a ranch at Cow Canyon that neighbored a ranch owned by Lon and Gett Alger, his brothers-in-law. The Smith family arrived in the early 1890s, but after a few years of fighting with the brothers over water they sold out, and it was later acquired by Luna's sister and her husband, Theodore F. Houskeeper. Charles then moved to Wyoming. There are no vital records linking him to Nine Mile Canyon, but there are numerous historical accounts. They had four children who could have been born and/or raised in Nine Mile Canyon.

Smith, Emma J. (Houskeeper). Ca. 1885 (Utah)–? Married: Abraham O. Smith; Nine Mile: 1890s to 1900s; Census 1900: Nine Mile Canyon; Census 1910: Myton, Duchesne County; Census 1920: Myton, Duchesne County;

Census 1930: Myton, Duchesne County. Annie was a teenager when her father brought her to Nine Mile Canyon. She soon married and moved to Duchesne County. She is the daughter of Theodore F. and Sarah Butler Houskeeper.

Smith, Lella E. *See* **Wardle, Lella E. (Smith)**

Smith, Luna Luella (Alger). 1864 (Washington County)–? Married: Charles M. Smith; Nine Mile: ca. 1893 to ca. 1898; Census 1870: St. George, Washington County; Census 1900: Coyote Creek, Wyoming; Census 1920: Bluebell, Duchesne County; Census 1930: Wellington, Carbon County. Luna was a sister of the Alger brothers (Lon, Gett, and Frank), and with her husband, Charles Smith, they had a ranch at Cow Canyon that neighbored a ranch owned by Lon and Gett. The Smith family arrived in the early 1890s, but after a few years of fighting with the brothers over water they sold out. It was later acquired by Luna's sister and her husband, Theodore F. Houskeeper. The Smith family then moved to Wyoming. There are no vital records linking Luna to Nine Mile Canyon, but there are numerous historical accounts.

Smith, Mae. ?–? Nine Mile: 1901 to 1902. School census records indicate Mae was a teacher in Nine Mile Canyon from 1901 to 1902. There are no other records that are clearly associated with this person.

Smith, Mervin. Ca. 1895 (Price, Carbon County)–? Married: Fay (?); Nine Mile: 1895 to ca. 1898; Census 1900: Coyote Creek, Wyoming; Census 1920: Castle Gate, Carbon County; Census 1930: Castle Gate, Carbon County. Mervin was a son of Charles M. and Luna Alger Smith, who had a ranch at the mouth of Cow Canyon in the early 1890s. The family sold out after a few years and moved to Wyoming. There are no vital records that link Mervin to Nine Mile Canyon, but there are historical accounts. Mervin could have been born in Nine Mile Canyon, but his 1917 military records indicate he was born in Price. By 1920, he was boarding with more than forty others in Castle Gate (they were probably miners). By 1930, he was married and still living there.

Smith, Ralph R. Ca. 1897 (Utah)–? Nine Mile: ca. 1930; Census 1930: Nine Mile Canyon. Ralph is listed as a nephew of Theodore B. and Clara Alger Houskeeper. He was the son of Charles and Luna Smith, early residents of Nine Mile Canyon who owned a ranch at the mouth of Cow Canyon and who were also related to the Alger brothers. In 1930, Ralph was living with his aunt Lucille Houskeeper in Wellington. Ralph might have been born in Nine Mile Canyon before the family sold out and moved to Wyoming. He might have been born in 1893.

Smith, Vernon. March 1892 (Utah)–? Nine Mile: ca. 1893 to ca. 1898; Census 1900: Coyote Creek, Wyoming. Vernon was a son of Charles M. and Luna Alger Smith, who had a ranch at the mouth of Cow Canyon in the early 1890s. The family sold out after a few years and moved to Wyoming. There are no vital records that link Vernon to Nine Mile Canyon, but there are historical accounts. Vernon would have been a baby or small child when his family moved to Nine Mile Canyon.

Smithson, Allen F. Ca. 1901–1945 (Carbon County) Nine Mile: ca. 1901; Census 1910: Packard, Wasatch County; Census 1920: Neola, Duchesne County. There are no vital records linking Allen to Nine Mile Canyon, but he was born the same year his father died, perhaps in Nine Mile Canyon. His family later moved on to Wasatch and Duchesne Counties. He was the son of Nephi and Barbara Cook Smithson, who had a ranch at the mouth of Sulphur Canyon and another at the mouth of Cottonwood Canyon.

Smithson, Barbara E. (Cook). 1861 (Utah)–1934 (Carbon County) Married: Nephi Smithson; Nine Mile: 1890s to 1900s; Census 1870: Washington, Washington County; Census 1900: Nine Mile Canyon; Census 1910: Packard, Wasatch County; Census 1920: Neola, Duchesne County. Barbara was the wife of Nephi Smithson, who had two ranches in Nine Mile Canyon in the 1890s. Nephi died in 1901, and Barbara eventually moved with her children to Wasatch and Duchesne Counties. They had a ranch at the mouth of Sulphur Canyon and another at the mouth of Cottonwood Canyon.

Smithson, Clara B. *See* **Fausett, Clara B. (Smithson)**

Smithson, David C. 1899 (Nine Mile Canyon?)–1985 (Price, Carbon County) Nine Mile: 1899 to 1900s; Census 1900: Nine Mile Canyon; Census 1910: Packard, Wasatch County;

Census 1920: Neola, Duchesne County. David was probably born in Nine Mile Canyon. His father died when he was two years old, and the family moved on to Wasatch and Duchesne Counties. In 1940, he was living in Miller Creek with his brother Allen. He was the son of Nephi and Barbara Cook Smithson, who had a ranch at the mouth of Sulphur Canyon and another at the mouth of Cottonwood Canyon.

Smithson, Ellen G. *See Morgan, Ellen Gertrude (Smithson)*

Smithson, Elzina. *See Johnston, Elzina (Smithson)*

Smithson, Nephi. 1850 (Utah)–1901 (Carbon County)
Married: Barbara E. Cook; Nine Mile: 1890s to 1901; Census 1850: Utah (unspecified); Census 1860: Washington, Washington County; Census 1900: Nine Mile Canyon. Nephi and Barbara Smithson were among the earliest settlers in Nine Mile Canyon, arriving in the 1890s. Nephi died in 1901, probably in Nine Mile Canyon, and his family drifted north to Wasatch and Duchesne Counties. The family had a ranch at the mouth of Sulphur Canyon and another at the mouth of Cottonwood Canyon. Family histories indicate the Smithsons arrived in Nine Mile Canyon by way of Arizona. Nephi died at the G. C. "Don" Johnston place while traveling to Price to see a doctor.

Smithson, Nephi, Jr. Ca. 1896 (Utah)–1970 (Salt Lake City)
Married: Violet Wall; Nine Mile: before and 1900s; Census 1900: Nine Mile Canyon; Census 1910: Packard, Wasatch County; Census 1920:

Neola, Duchesne County; Census 1930: Neola, Smithson. Nephi might have been born in Nine Mile Canyon after the family migrated here from Arizona. He was the son of Nephi and Barbara Cook Smithson, who had a ranch at the mouth of Sulphur Canyon and another at the mouth of Cottonwood Canyon.

Smithson, Rhoda W. *See Robinson, Rhoda W. (Smithson)*

Sprouse, Essie L. Ca. 1936–?
Nine Mile: ca. 1936. Essie was the daughter of Kenneth and Ruth Sprouse, who might have been living in lower Nine Mile Canyon in about 1935. It is possible she was born there, although this is speculative. There are no other records related to her.

Sprouse, Kenneth L. 1905 (Utah)–1964
Married: Ruth (?); Nine Mile: 1930s; Census 1920: Roosevelt, Duchesne County; Census 1930: Helper, Carbon County. Local histories indicate Ken Sprouse owned the lower Nine Mile ranch, sometimes referred to as the Miles Ranch or Pace Ranch. The 1940 census indicates that he was living in rural Carbon County in 1935, which could be a reference to Nine Mile Canyon. If it is, he probably acquired the ranch from Al Pace, who owned it in the late 1920s and early 1930s.

Sprouse, Ruth. Ca. 1908 (Wyoming)–?
Married: Kenneth L. Sprouse; Nine Mile: 1930s; Census 1930: Helper, Carbon County. Local histories indicate Ken Sprouse owned the lower Nine Mile ranch, sometimes referred to as the Miles Ranch or Pace Ranch. The 1940 census indicates that he and his wife, Ruth, were living in rural Carbon County in 1935, which could

be a reference to Nine Mile Canyon. There is no record of her after the 1940 census when she and Kenneth were living in Neola. If the family was living in Nine Mile Canyon in 1935, it is possible their daughter Essie L. was born there.

Stewart, Eva. *See Ashton, Eva (Stewart)*

Stewart, John Henry. Ca. 1868 (Utah)–1937 (Uintah County)
Married: Minerva Van Wagoner; Nine Mile: 1890s to 1910s; Census 1880: Tintic, Juab County; Census 1900: Nine Mile Canyon; Census 1910: Nine Mile Canyon; Census 1920: Randlett, Uintah County; Census 1930: Willows, Uintah County. Hank arrived in the Nine Mile area with his friend Neal Hanks and established a ranch in Argyle Canyon. After divorcing Minerva, Hank became a renowned figure along the Green River, operating two different ferries and rowing for and guiding early river expeditions. He built the cabins still evident at Sand Wash. He apparently remained friends with Neal Hanks even after Neal married his ex-wife.

Stewart, Minerva (Van Wagoner). *See Hanks, Minerva A. (Van Wagoner)*

Stewart, Rex. Ca. 1904 (Nine Mile Canyon)–1926 (Carbon County)
Nine Mile: 1904 to 1910s; Census 1910: Nine Mile Canyon; Census 1920: Roosevelt, Duchesne County. Rex was a son of Hank and Minerva Stewart. After his mother divorced Hank Stewart, she got custody of the three children. Rex was raised by Minerva's second husband, Neal Hanks. He died a very young man.

Stewart, Van. Ca. 1906 (Nine Mile Canyon?)–1973 (Pocatello, Idaho) Married: Evelyn Parker; Nine Mile: 1906 to 1910s; Census 1910: Nine Mile Canyon; Census 1920: Roosevelt, Duchesne County; Census 1930: Salt Lake City. Van was a son of Hank and Minerva Stewart. After his mother divorced Hank Stewart and got custody of the three children, Van was raised by Minerva's second husband, Neal Hanks.

Stratman, Art. ?–?
Nine Mile: 1930s. Local histories indicate that Art Stratman built a school in Nine Mile Canyon in the 1930s. There are no other records convincingly linked to this person, although there was an Art Stratman living in Wyoming in 1924.

Taylor, Addie. Ca. 1901 (Utah)–?
Nine Mile: 1900s; Census 1910: Nine Mile Canyon. There are no additional vital records related to Addie beyond the 1910 census. She was the daughter of Frank and Nellie Taylor.

Taylor, Annie (Peterson). Ca. 1856 (Utah)–?
Married: Frank Horace; Nine Mile: ca. 1930; Census 1870: Levan, Juab County; Census 1880: Levan, Juab County; Census 1900: Salina, Sevier County; Census 1910: Salina, Sevier County; Census 1920: Salina, Sevier County; Census 1930: Nine Mile Canyon. Annie was the mother of Frank M. Taylor, who lived in the canyon in 1930. Frank H. and his wife, Annie, were in their seventies when they left Sevier County to live with their son in Nine Mile Canyon.

Taylor, Charles Franklin. 1877 (Manti, Sanpete County)–1911 (Price, Carbon County)

Married: Lillie Russell (1898); Nine Mile: ca. 1900; Census 1900: Nine Mile Canyon. There are no vital records linking Charles to Nine Mile Canyon, but he was certainly there in 1900 if not before. Family records indicate he was married to Lillie Russell, and their son James Edward was born in the canyon in 1901. Lillie eventually remarried to Alva Lee and raised a family with him, also in Nine Mile Canyon. Charles and Lillie either divorced in the early 1900s and Lillie had four children with her new husband, Alva Lee, or it is possible she married Alva after Charles Franklin Taylor died in 1911. Any children she had with Charles Franklin are listed with the Lee surname in the 1920 census. That 1920 census includes an Ed Lee with the same birth year as James Edward Taylor, whose mother was Lille Russell Taylor Lee. If it is the same person, he is listed two times in the 1920 census. It also raises the possibility that Ed Taylor's two brothers, Thelbert and Eldredge, are actually Taylors.

Taylor, Dora J. (Babcock). 1885 (Utah)–?
Married: Albert E. Taylor; Nine Mile: 1890s to 1900s; Census 1900: Nine Mile Canyon; Census 1910: Chapin, Idaho; Census 1920: Eureka, Juab County. Dora was a daughter of John Rowley and Augusta Mae Babcock, who were among the earliest settlers in Nine Mile Canyon in the 1890s.

Taylor, Effie Blanche (Lee). Ca. 1906 (Nine Mile Canyon)–?
Married: George E. Taylor; Nine Mile: 1906 to ca. 1920; Census 1900: Nine Mile Canyon; Census 1910: Nine Mile Canyon; Census 1920: Randlette, Duchesne County. Effie B. was fourteen years old when she married George E. Taylor and moved into his parents' house in the Uinta Basin. By 1940, she was divorced. She was a child of Edwin and Effie Box Lee, who arrived in Nine Mile Canyon in the 1890s. She would have spent most of her childhood in Nine Mile Canyon, and she might have been born there.

Taylor, Eldredge. Ca. 1908 (Nine Mile Canyon?)–?
Nine Mile: 1908 to 1910s; Census 1910: Nine Mile Canyon. There are no other vital records related to Eldredge besides the 1910 census. He was the son of Frank and Nellie Taylor.

Taylor, Frank. Ca. 1877 (Utah)–?
Married: Nellie (?); Nine Mile: ca. 1910; Census 1880: Manti, Sanpete County; Census 1910: Nine Mile Canyon. There are no additional vital records related to Nellie or Frank Taylor after the 1910 census. There were other Frank Taylors living in Nine Mile Canyon in 1910 and 1930, but the database indicates these are different individuals, based on different birthplaces and birth years. Nellie Taylor should not be confused with Nellie Hamilton Taylor, who was living with her husband, Frank S. Taylor, in Myton in 1910.

Taylor, Frank A. Ca. 1877 (Kansas)–?
Married: Jessie (?); Nine Mile: ca. 1900; Census 1900: Nine Mile Canyon; Census 1910: Haddam, Kansas; Census 1920: Haddam, Kansas; Census 1930: Manhattan, Kansas. In 1900, Frank A. Taylor was a twenty-year-old farm laborer, born in Kansas, who was living with and working for the Edwin Lee family. Although the commonness of the

name is problematic, it appears that he returned to Kansas, married and lived out his life there. He should not be confused with the Frank M. Taylor who was boarding with the Miles family in 1910 and also living in the canyon in 1930 with his father, also named Frank. Nor is this the same Frank Taylor who was born in Utah, married a woman named Nellie, and was living in the canyon in 1910 with his own family.

Taylor, Frank Horace. Ca. 1855 (California)–?
Nine Mile: ca. 1930; Census 1860: Springville, Utah County; Census 1870: Levan, Juab County; Census 1880: Levan, Juab County; Census 1900: Salina, Sevier County; Census 1910: Salina, Sevier County; Census 1920: Salina, Sevier County; Census 1930: Nine Mile Canyon. Frank H. was the father of Frank M. Taylor, who lived in the canyon in 1930. Frank H. and his wife, Annie, were in their seventies when they left Sevier County to live with their son in Nine Mile Canyon.

Taylor, Frank Mennel. Ca. 1877 (Utah)–?
Nine Mile: 1900s to 1930s; Census 1880: Levan, Juab County; Census 1900: Salina, Sevier County; Census 1910: Nine Mile Canyon; Census 1920: Roosevelt, Duchesne County; Census 1930: Nine Mile Canyon. Frank M. was the son of Frank H. and Annie Taylor, who were long-time residents of Sevier County. In 1910, Frank M. was a boarder and farm laborer working for William Miles. By 1930, he had his own place and brought his elderly parents to live with him in Nine Mile Canyon. There is no indication that he ever married. Frank M. was commonly

referred to as Mennel or "Mental" Taylor. He should not be confused with the Frank Taylor from Kansas who worked for the Ed Lee family in 1900, or the Frank Taylor who married Nellie and was living in the canyon with his family in 1910.

Taylor, James Edward. 1901 (Nine Mile Canyon)–1980 (East Carbon, Carbon County)
Married: Clara Verlillian Waymon (1922); Nine Mile: 1901 to 1920s; Census 1920: Nine Mile Canyon. According to family records, Ed was born in Nine Mile Canyon in 1901. In 1920, he was an eighteen-year-old single man living with Al Thompson, Doyle Barney, and Dave Russell. Russell might have been a relative. He was the son of Charles Taylor and Lillie May Russell, herself the daughter of Andrew Jackson and Julia Mott Russell.

Taylor, Jesse. Ca. 1900 (Utah)–1942 (Carbon County)
Married: Molly Holman; Nine Mile: ca. 1910; Census 1910: Nine Mile Canyon; Census 1920: Thompson, Grand County (?); Census 1930: Columbia, Carbon County (?). It is uncertain if the Jesse Taylor who lived in Nine Mile Canyon is the same Jesse F. Taylor in the 1920 and 1930 censuses. He was the son of Frank and Nellie Taylor.

Taylor, LaBertha "Libbie." See Brundage, LaBertha (Taylor)

Taylor, Lillie M. (Russell). See Lee, Lillie (Russell)

Taylor, Nellie M. (Hamilton). Ca. 1890 (Utah)–?
Married: Frank S. Taylor; Nine Mile: 1890s to 1900s; Census 1900: Nine

Mile Canyon; Census 1910: Myton, Duchesne County; Census 1920: Myton, Duchesne County. Nellie was the daughter of James A. and Susan Van Wagoner Hamilton, some of the original settlers at the mouth of Minnie Maud Canyon in the 1890s. She would have spent her childhood in Nine Mile Canyon. She was married to Frank S. Taylor, who apparently has no other ties to Nine Mile Canyon. Her husband should not be confused with at least four other Frank Taylors who lived in Nine Mile Canyon between 1900 and 1930.

Taylor, Nellie. 1883 (Utah)–?
Married: Frank Taylor; Nine Mile: ca. 1910; Census 1910: Nine Mile Canyon. There are no additional vital records related to Nellie or Frank Taylor after the 1910 census. This could be the same Nellie Hamilton who was married to Frank Taylor in 1900, but the birth years are not close. They were also living in different places in 1910. We assume it is coincidence that two individuals named Frank Taylor married women named Nellie. The database does not link this Nellie to Nellie Hamilton.

Taylor, Thelbert. Ca. 1904 (Utah)–?
Married: Zelpha (?); Nine Mile: ca. 1910; Census 1910: Nine Mile Canyon; Census 1930: Columbia, Carbon County. Thelbert was the son of Frank and Nellie Taylor. There are very few vital records related to him. He would have been a child when he lived in Nine Mile Canyon.

Thomas, Grant. 1891 (Utah)–1966 (Idaho)
Married: Luella Wall; Nine Mile: ca. 1910; Census 1900: Spanish Fork, Utah County; Census 1910: Nine Mile Canyon; Census 1920: Carey,

Idaho; Census 1930: Paul, Idaho. In 1910, Grant was a nineteen-year-old ranch hand living with and working for William Miles in lower Nine Mile Canyon. He later married and moved on to Idaho.

Thompson, Alma Zerman. Ca. 1873 (Denmark)–1950 (Spanish Fork, Utah County)
Married: Martha Grames; Nine Mile: ca. 1900 to 1920s; Census 1910: Nine Mile Canyon; Census 1920: Nine Mile Canyon. Al Thompson was one of the iconic cowboys of Nine Mile Canyon. He married Martha Grames, but they divorced and Al continued to ranch in Nine Mile Canyon as a single man. In 1920, he had boarders living with him, including Dave Russell, Doyle Barney, and Ed Taylor. There are no vital records of Al after the 1920 census until his death in 1950.

Thompson, Amber M. *See* **Krissman, Amber M. (Thompson)**

Thompson, Crystal Ellen. *See* **Barney, Crystal Ellen (Thompson)**

Thompson, Edmund. Ca. 1916 (Nine Mile Canyon?)–1960 (Duchesne County)
Married: Josephine Fenn; Nine Mile: 1916 to 1920s; Census 1920: Nine Mile Canyon; Census 1930: Bluebell, Duchesne County. Edmund might have been born in Nine Mile Canyon. He was the son of Frank B. and Laura Anderson Thompson. He later moved on to Idaho.

Thompson, Elden. 1899 (Utah)–1968 (Ferron, Emery County)
Nine Mile: ca. 1930; Census 1910: Ferron, Emery County; Census 1920: Hanksville, Wayne County; Census 1930: Nine Mile Canyon. In 1930, Elden was a thirty-year-old ranch hand working for Preston Nutter. He was from Emery County and apparently returned there in later years where he died. There are no marriage records for him. He is listed on the 1930 census for both Ferron and Nine Mile Canyon.

Thompson, Florence. *See* **Russell, Florence (Thompson)**

Thompson, Frank B. 1890 (Utah)–?
Married: Jane Laura; Nine Mile: 1900s to 1920s; Census 1900: Elgin, Grand County; Census 1910: Nine Mile Canyon; Census 1920: Nine Mile Canyon; Census 1930: Bluebell, Duchesne County. In 1910, Frank was an eighteen-year-old boarding with Frank and Nellie Taylor. He was the younger brother of Florence Thompson, who married into the Russell family. By 1920 he had married and started his own family in Nine Mile Canyon.

Thompson, Guy. 1912 (Nine Mile Canyon)–1981 (Roosevelt, Duchesne County)
Nine Mile: ca. 1920; Census 1920: Nine Mile Canyon; Census 1930: Bluebell, Duchesne County. There are no vital records linked to Guy after the 1930 census. He was the son of Frank B. and Laura Anderson Thompson. He was probably born in Nine Mile Canyon.

Thompson, Laura Jane (Anderson). 1894 (Utah)–?
Married: Frank B. Thompson; Nine Mile: 1910s to 1920s; Census 1900: Price, Carbon County; Census 1910: Myton, Duchesne County; Census 1920: Nine Mile Canyon; Census 1930: Bluebell, Duchesne County.

Laura probably married Frank B. Thompson about 1911, when Frank was still in Nine Mile Canyon. Their children might have been born and raised there.

Thompson, Martha E. (Grames). Ca. 1878–?
Married: (?) Hall, Alma Z. Thompson; Nine Mile: ca. 1886 to 1920s; Census 1880: Huntington, Emery County; Census 1910: Nine Mile Canyon; Census 1920: Nine Mile Canyon. Martha Thompson was one of the longest-term residents of the canyon. She arrived with her parents in about 1886, eventually married local rancher Al Thompson, and remained in the canyon with their three daughters after she divorced. She went by Martha Thompson even after her divorce. There are no records of her after the 1920 census. Before marrying Al Thompson, she might have been married to someone named Hall. The 1910 census includes an Earl Hall, listed as stepson to Al Thompson.

Thompson, Morland. 1918 (Nine Mile Canyon)–1995 (Providence, Cache County)
Nine Mile: 1918 to 1920s; Census 1920: Nine Mile Canyon; Census 1930: Bluebell, Duchesne County. Morland (sometimes spelled Marlan) might have been born in Nine Mile Canyon. He was the son of Frank B. and Laura Anderson Thompson. There are no vital records of him after 1930 until his death in 1995.

Thompson, Ruby M. *See* **Powell, Ruby M. (Thompson)**

Thompson, Richard Beamon. Ca. 1843 (England)–1922 (Myton, Duchesne County)

Married: Liberty Brundage (1913); Nine Mile: ca. 1910; Census 1910: Nine Mile Canyon; Census 1920: Myton, Duchesne County (?). In 1910, Richard was a sixty-seven-year-old widower living with and working for Preston Nutter. In 1913, he married Libby Brundage, a widow with deep ties to Nine Mile Canyon, and they lived in Myton until his death in 1923. The database links him to several different Richard Thompsons prior to 1910, and there is uncertainty as to whether or not he is related to any of them.

Thompson, Shelby. 1909 (Utah)–1964 (Carbon County)
Married: Alberta (?); Nine Mile: ca. 1930; Census 1910: Ferron, Emery County; Census 1920: Hiawatha, Carbon County; Census 1930: Nine Mile Canyon. Shelby was born and raised in the Emery and Carbon County areas. In 1930, he was a twenty-one-year-old ranch hand working for and living with Preston Nutter in Nine Mile Canyon. He returned to Carbon County, married, and moved to the Miller Creek area. He does not appear to be related to the other Thompsons in Nine Mile Canyon.

Van Wagoner, Susan. See Hamilton, Susan (Van Wagoner)

Van Wagoner, Minerva. See Hanks, Minerva A. (Van Wagoner)

Wardle, Lella E. (Smith). Ca. 1889 (Utah)–?
Married: Samuel Jed Wardle; Nine Mile: ca. 1893 to ca. 1898; Census 1900: Coyote Creek, Wyoming; Census 1920: Duchesne, Duchesne County; Census 1930: Duchesne, Duchesne County. Lella was a

daughter of Charles M. and Luna Alger Smith, who had a ranch at the mouth of Cow Canyon in the early 1890s. The family sold out after a few years and moved to Wyoming. There are no vital records that link Lella to Nine Mile Canyon, but there are historical accounts. Lella would have been a small child when her family moved to Nine Mile Canyon.

Warren, Alma Z. 1889 (Utah)–?
Married: Erma May Warren; Nine Mile: 1900s to 1920s; Census 1910: Nine Mile Canyon; Census 1920: Nine Mile Canyon; Census 1930: South Ashley, Uintah County. Alma married sometime before 1920, at which time he was listed on the census as a single, widowed man. He remarried after 1920 to Erma May Warren. Warren was perhaps her maiden name. Her parents could have been Amos and Bessie Warren of Neola, Duchesne County. Alma was the oldest son of William Warren and was twenty-one years old when he was listed as the stepson of James H. Blaine in the 1910 census.

Warren, Arthur. 1892 (Utah)–1943 (Carbon County)
Married: Maude Hamilton; Nine Mile: 1900s to 1910s; Census 1900: Price, Carbon County; Census 1910: Nine Mile Canyon; Census 1920: Myton, Duchesne County; Census 1930: Ferron, Emery County. Arthur Warren was a stepson to Parley P. Warren, who married his mother, Sarah, sometime after 1900. The family was living in Nine Mile Canyon in 1910 where Arthur had two new half-siblings. Arthur married Maude Hamilton, daughter of James A. Hamilton, one of the first settlers at the mouth of Minnie Maud Canyon in the 1890s. Their oldest children

might have been born in Nine Mile Canyon.

Warren, Clifford. 1911 (Nine Mile Canyon?)–?
Married: Lula Maude (Warren) Warren; Nine Mile: 1910s; Census 1920: Price, Carbon County; Census 1930: Price, Carbon County. There is no formal documentation that Clifford lived in Nine Mile Canyon, but he was born one year after the 1910 census when his entire family was living there. It is quite possible he was born in Nine Mile Canyon. He was the youngest son of Parley P. and Sarah A. Warren. His wife, Lula Maude, might have been a daughter of his half-brother Arthur and Maude Hamilton.

Warren, Glen. Ca. 1894 (Utah)–?
Married: Theora Jane Cook; Nine Mile: 1930s; Census 1930: Price, Carbon County (1935). Local histories indicate Glen and Theora Warren were living in Nine Mile Canyon in the 1930s, and that Theora was a teacher at the local school. There are few records related to Glen. It appears they moved on to the Uinta Basin. He does not appear to be related to the Parley P. or William Warren families.

Warren, Ida. See Downard, Ida (Warren)

Warren, Joseph G. 1892 (Price, Carbon County)–?
Nine Mile: 1900s to 1910s; Census 1910: Nine Mile Canyon. Joseph joined the military in 1918, presumably to fight in World War I. There are no official records of him after that time. He was the son of William Warren and stepson of James H. Blaine.

Warren, LeRoy. 1902 (Nine Mile Canyon?)–1984 (Duchesne, Duchesne County)
Nine Mile: 1900s to 1910s; Census 1910: Nine Mile Canyon; Census 1920: Blue Bell, Duchesne County; Census 1930: Montello, Nevada. Francis Bowen indicated Roy did not survive World War I, but he would have been only sixteen years old at the time of the war. The 1920 census shows him living in Bluebell, and by 1930 he was a sheepherder in Nevada. There is no record that he married.

Warren, Lorena. *See* **Addley, Lorena (Warren)**

Warren, Mariah (Powell). *See* **Blaine, Mariah (Powell-Warren)**

Warren, Maude (Hamilton). Ca. 1893–1976 (Millard County?)
Married: Arthur Warren; Nine Mile: 1900s; Census 1900: Nine Mile Canyon; Census 1910: Myton, Duchesne County; Census 1920: Myton, Duchesne County; Census 1930: Ogden, Weber County. Maude's husband, Arthur, was a stepson of Parley P. Warren who grew up in Nine Mile Canyon. Maude was the daughter of James A. and Susan Van Wagoner Hamilton, who were among the first settlers at the mouth of Minnie Maud Canyon. She later divorced Arthur and married a man named Stinson. She is buried in Kanosh.

Warren, Norell. 1896 (Price, Carbon County)–1980 (Vernal, Uintah County)
Nine Mile: 1900s to 1930s; Census 1910: Nine Mile Canyon; Census 1920: Price, Carbon County. Norell (or Noral) joined the military in 1917, presumably to fight in World War I.

In 1920, he was living with his sister, Lorena, and brother-in-law, Elmer Addley, in Price. There is no record that he ever married. He was a son of William Warren and a stepson of James H. Blaine. He later proved up on a homestead at the mouth of Argyle Canyon.

Warren, Parley Pratt. 1870 (Utah)–1938 (Carbon County)
Married: Sarah A. Blaine; Nine Mile: 1890s to 1910s; Census 1880: Spanish Fork, Utah County; Census 1900: Nine Mile Canyon; Census 1910: Nine Mile Canyon; Census 1920: Price, Carbon County; Census 1930: Price, Carbon County. Parley P. might have been in Nine Mile Canyon in the 1890s. Dillman indicates he "returned" to the canyon after the Klondike Gold Rush in Alaska. He married Sarah Blaine, who was a sister of James Blaine. James Blaine married Mariah Warren, the widow of his brother. Parley remained in Nine Mile Canyon through the 1910s, eventually moving to Price where he is buried.

Warren, Rex. 1906 (Nine Mile Canyon?)–1994 (Corvallis, Oregon)
Married: Candace (?); Nine Mile: 1900s to 1910s; Census 1910: Nine Mile Canyon; Census 1920: Price, Carbon County; Census 1930: Price, Carbon County. Rex was the second child of Parley P. and Sarah A. Warren. He might have been born in Nine Mile Canyon. By 1940, he had married and was living in Oregon.

Warren, Sarah Amy (Blaine). 1874 (Utah)–1957 (Carbon County)
Married: Parley Pratt Warren; Nine Mile: 1900s to 1910s; Census 1880: Spring City, Sanpete County; Census 1900: Price, Carbon County; Census

1910: Nine Mile Canyon; Census 1920: Price, Carbon County; Census 1930: Price, Carbon County. Sarah was married to Parley Pratt Warren. Sarah was an older sister to James H. Blaine, who had married the widow Mariah Warren and helped raise her children from William Warren. Sarah would have raised her own children in Nine Mile Canyon.

Warren, Theora (Cook). Ca. 1914 (Utah)–1970 (Bluebell)
Married: Glen Warren; Nine Mile: 1930s; Census 1930: Price, Carbon County (1935). Local histories indicate Glen and Theora Warren were living in Nine Mile Canyon in the 1930s, and that Theora was a teacher at the local school. There are few records related to Glen. It appears they moved on to the Uinta Basin.

Warren, William. 1859–before 1910
Married: Mariah Powell; Nine Mile: ca. 1900 to ca. 1903; Census 1870: Spanish Fork, Utah County. William Warren was the older brother to Parley P. Warren and husband of Mariah Powell Warren. He was present in Nine Mile in the early 1900s, if not before, but died prior to the 1910 census. His children were raised by their stepfather, James H. Blaine. There are no historical records related to William Warren other than the 1870 census, when he was an eleven-year-old living in Spanish Fork. He also proved up on a homestead in the Price area before arriving in Nine Mile Canyon.

Warren, William H. 1904 (Nine Mile Canyon?)–1991 (Vernal)
Nine Mile: 1900s to 1910s; Census 1910: Nine Mile Canyon; Census 1920: Bluebell, Duchesne County. It is possible William H. was born in

Nine Mile Canyon. There is no record that he ever married. He was the son of William Warren and Mariah Powell Warren, and he was a stepson to James H. Blaine.

Webb, H. G. ?–?
Nine Mile: 1890s or 1900s. School census records indicate he was a teacher and/or superintendent of the Nine Mile school district. There are no records that are clearly linked to a person of this name.

Whitmore, Frank. Ca. 1891 (Utah)–?
Nine Mile: ca. 1920; Census 1920: Nine Mile Canyon. Frank Whitmore was a twenty-nine-year-old widower when he was living in Nine Mile Canyon in 1920. The census indicated he owned his own place. There are no other vital records cross-referenced to this person, and it is unknown if or how he might be related to the Whitmore family, which was the first to run cattle in Whitmore Park in upper Nine Mile Canyon in the late 1870s.

Wilson, Charles F. 1863 (Utah)–?
Married: Mary (?); Nine Mile: ca. 1900; Census 1900: Nine Mile Canyon; Census 1910: Gunnison, Sanpete County. Charles F. and his wife Mary moved to Nine Mile Canyon sometime before 1900, but by 1910 they might have moved to Sanpete County. Their son Elmer, who was five years old at the time of the 1900 census, later returned to Nine Mile Canyon and was living with Edwin and Josephine Babcock Harmon at the Rock House in 1920. There are very few records of Charles and Mary after the 1910 census. They might have come to Utah by way of Nebraska.

Wilson, Elmer. Ca. 1896 (Nebraska)–?
Nine Mile: ca. 1900 to 1920s; Census 1900: Nine Mile Canyon; Census 1910: Gunnison, Sanpete County (?); Census 1920: Nine Mile Canyon. In 1920, Elmer was listed as a twenty-four-year-old boarder with Edwin and Josephine Babcock Harmon. He was probably the son of Charles and Mary Wilson, who were in Nine Mile Canyon in 1900, and hence Elmer might have grown up in the canyon. His family might have moved on to Sanpete County, where Elmer, his brother James, and their parents are listed, but the census gives a different birthplace for Elmer (Utah instead of Nebraska). There are no clear records of him after the 1920 census. He is mentioned in local histories as "not right" in the head. He was accused of stealing a horse, for which he was dressed down by the sheriff.

Wilson, Ethel. Ca. 1901 (Nine Mile Canyon?)–?
Nine Mile: ca. 1901; Census 1910: Gunnison, Sanpete County. Ethel was the daughter of Charles and Mary Wilson, who were living in Nine Mile Canyon at the time of the 1900 census. Given she was born about a year later she might have been born in the canyon before her family moved to Gunnison. There are no vital records that indicate she lived in Nine Mile Canyon. There are no records of her after the 1910 census.

Wilson, George T. 1895 (Nebraska)–?
Nine Mile: ca. 1900; Census 1900: Nine Mile Canyon. George was the son of Mary and Charles F. Wilson, who were living in Nine Mile Canyon in 1900. Given that George was born in Nebraska in 1895, the Wilson family probably did not arrive before that time. There are no records of George

T. other than his World War I draft registration. He is not listed on the 1910 census when the family could have been living in Gunnison, but there is a "Peter" Wilson who would have been the same age as George. George was born in Nebraska and Peter was born in Utah, and this might not be the same family.

Wilson, Gladys. Ca. 1903 (Utah)–?
Nine Mile: ca. 1920; Census 1920: Nine Mile Canyon. Gladys was listed as a seventeen-year-old single head of household living in a rented house in Nine Mile Canyon in 1920. Her nine-year-old sister, Myrtle, was living with her. From where she came, how she came to be in Nine Mile Canyon, and what became of her cannot be derived from the available records. It is unknown if she was related to the Charles and Mary Wilson family that was here in 1900.

Wilson, James F. Ca. 1899 (Nine Mile Canyon?)–?
Nine Mile: ca. 1899 to after 1900; Census 1900: Nine Mile Canyon; Census 1910: Gunnison, Sanpete County(?). Given that James's older brothers were born in Nebraska and he was born in Utah one year before the 1900 census, he might have been born in Nine Mile Canyon. There are no records of him after the 1910 census when the database links him to his brother Elmer and parents who were living in Gunnison.

Wilson, Mary E. Ca. 1872–?
Married: Charles F. Wilson; Nine Mile: ca. 1900; Census 1900: Nine Mile Canyon; Census 1910: Gunnison, Sanpete County (?). Charles F. and his wife, Mary, moved to Nine Mile Canyon sometime before 1900, but by 1910 they might

have moved to Sanpete County. Their son Elmer, who was five years old at the time of the 1900 census, later returned to Nine Mile Canyon and was living with Edwin and Josephine Babcock Harmon at the Rock House in 1920. There are very few records of Charles and Mary after the 1910 census.

Wilson, Myrtle. Ca. 1911 (Utah)–?
Nine Mile: ca. 1920; Census 1920: Nine Mile Canyon. Myrtle was listed as a nine-year-old living in a rented house in Nine Mile Canyon with her seventeen-year-old sister, Gladys. Who she was, how she came to be in Nine Mile Canyon, and what became of her cannot be derived from the available records. It is unknown if she was related to the Charles and Mary Wilson family that was here in 1900.

Winn, Dennis Alma. 1849 (Utah)–1930 (Carbon County)
Married: Emma Lorena Blair; Nine Mile: 1883 to 1890s; Census 1870: Richmond, Cache County; Census 1880: Franklin, Idaho; Census 1900: Cora, Wyoming; Census 1910: Roosevelt, Duchesne County; Census 1920: North Vernal, Uintah County. There are no vital records to link the Winn family to Nine Mile Canyon, but the historical record indicates they arrived as early as 1883 and constructed the Rock House at the mouth of Harmon Canyon. They had a large number of children living with them at the time. In the 1890s, the Winn family returned to the Uinta Basin. Dennis Winn and his sons were stonecutters and built the Rock House and the saloon/hotel on the John Eagan place. It is uncertain how many of their children were raised in Nine Mile Canyon. Their son John returned in 1896 with his wife, but

they returned to the Uinta Basin in 1898.

Winn, Emma Lorena (Blair). Ca. 1854 (Utah)–1927 (Carbon County)
Married: Dennis Alma Winn; Nine Mile: 1883 to 1890s; Census 1860: Cache County; Census 1870: Richmond, Cache County; Census 1880: Franklin, Idaho; Census 1900: Cora, Wyoming; Census 1910: Roosevelt, Utah; Census 1920: North Vernal, Uintah County. Emma was married to Dennis Alma Winn, one of the early pioneers of the Uinta Basin. They were among the first to settle in Nine Mile Canyon, perhaps as early as 1883. It is unknown how many of their children lived in Nine Mile Canyon.

Winn, Elsie V. 1887 (Nine Mile Canyon?)–?
Nine Mile: 1887 to 1890s; Census 1900: Cora, Wyoming; Census 1910: Vernal, Uintah County; Census 1920: Fremont, Wyoming. Elsie was the daughter of Dennis Alma and Emma Blair Winn, who settled in Nine Mile Canyon as early as 1883. Emma could have been born in Nine Mile Canyon. There are few vital records for her after 1920.

Winn, Fannie Bell (Weeks). 1879 (Caledonia, Vermont)–1968 (Salt Lake County)
Married: John Winn; Nine Mile: 1896 to 1898; Census 1880: Caledonia, Vermont; Census 1900: Vernal, Uintah County; Census 1910: Vernal, Uintah County; Census 1920: Roosevelt, Duchesne County. John and Fannie met as children when the Weeks wagon stopped at the Rock House in Nine Mile Canyon in 1886 as the family was traveling from Price to the Uinta Basin. They returned

to Nine Mile from 1896 to 1898, and their first child was born there.

Winn, Franklin C. 1873 (Idaho)–1930 (Duchesne County)
Married: Effie May Weeks; Nine Mile: 1883 to 1890s; Census 1880: Franklin, Idaho; Census 1900: Cora, Wyoming; Census 1930: Myton, Duchesne County. Franklin C. was the son of Dennis Alma and Emma Blair Winn, who settled in Nine Mile Canyon as early as 1883. He would have been ten years old at the time the family was in Nine Mile Canyon and probably spent his childhood there.

Winn, Hazel V. Ca. 1897 (Nine Mile Canyon)–?
Married: Earl Leroy Allen (1920); Nine Mile: 1897 to 1898; Census 1900: Vernal, Uintah County; Census 1910: Vernal, Uintah County; Census 1920: Roosevelt, Duchesne County; Census 1930: Los Angeles, California. Hazel was the daughter of John and Fannie Weeks Winn. She was born in Nine Mile Canyon, but moved to the Uinta Basin a year later just before her sister Dora was born.

Winn, Jessie. 1892 (Nine Mile Canyon?)–?
Married: Ralph Faler; Nine Mile: ca. 1892; Census 1900: Cora, Wyoming; Census 1910: Roosevelt, Duchesne County. Jessie was the son of Dennis Alma and Emma Blair Winn, who settled in Nine Mile Canyon as early as 1883. He might have been born in Nine Mile Canyon before the family left in the 1890s for the Uinta Basin. There are very few vital records related to him after 1910.

Winn, John. Ca. 1876–1948 (Salt Lake County)

Married: Fannie Weeks; Nine Mile: 1883 to 1898; Census 1880: Franklin, Idaho; Census 1900: Vernal, Uintah County; Census 1910: Vernal, Uintah County; Census 1920: Roosevelt, Duchesne County; Census 1930: Price, Carbon County. John was the son of Dennis Alma and Emma Blair Winn, who settled in Nine Mile Canyon as early as 1883. He would have been seven years old at the time the family was in Nine Mile Canyon, and he probably grew up there. He returned to Nine Mile in 1896 with his wife, Fannie Weeks, and stayed two years before returning to the Uinta Basin. One child, Hazel V., was born there. Their daughter Doris was born just after they returned to Vernal.

Winn, Joseph. 1885 (Nine Mile Canyon?)–1950 (Oregon)
Nine Mile: 1885 to 1890s; Census 1900: Cora, Wyoming. Joseph was a son of Dennis and Emma Blair Winn, who settled in Nine Mile Canyon as early as 1883. Joseph might have been born in Nine Mile Canyon. The family returned to the Uinta Basin a few years after his birth. There are few vital records related to Joseph after the 1900 census.

Winn, William Lafayette. Ca. 1874 (Utah)–1946 (Seattle, Washington)
Married: Susannah Campbell; Nine Mile: 1883 to 1890s; Census 1880: Franklin, Idaho; Census 1900: Cora, Wyoming; Census 1930: Myton, Duchesne County (1935). William L. was the son of Dennis Alma and Emma Blair Winn, who settled in Nine Mile Canyon as early as 1883. He would have been nine years old at the time the family was in Nine Mile Canyon and he probably spent his

childhood there before the family left in the early 1890s.

Wiseman, Emma L. (Hamilton). 1876 (Utah)–?
Married: Frank Wiseman; Nine Mile: 1890s to 1900s; 1880: Gooseberry Valley, Sevier County; Census 1900: Nine Mile Canyon; Census 1910: Myton, Duchesne County; Census 1920: Scofield, Carbon County; Census 1930: Price, Carbon County. Emma was a younger sister of James H. Hamilton and David William Hamilton, who were among the earliest settlers in the 1890s at the mouth of Minnie Maud Canyon. In 1900, Emma's mother, Martha E. Hamilton, was living with the Wiseman family and was listed as a widow at that time.

Wiseman, Eva. 1899 (Nine Mile Canyon?)–?
Nine Mile: 1899 to 1900s; Census 1900: Nine Mile Canyon; Census 1910: Myton, Duchesne County. Eva might have been born in Nine Mile Canyon. There is no record of her after the 1910 census. Her younger sisters Velva and Ella might also have been born in Nine Mile Canyon after 1910, but this is speculative. Eva was the daughter of Frank and Emma Hamilton Wiseman, who had a ranch in the 1890s above the mouth of Minnie Maud Canyon.

Wiseman, Frank Joshua. 1876 (Utah)–1947 (Carbon County)
Married: Emma Hamilton; Nine Mile: 1890s to 1900s; Census 1900: Nine Mile Canyon; Census 1910: Myton, Duchesne County; Census 1920: Scofield, Carbon County; Census 1930: Price, Carbon County. Frank was married to Emma Hamilton, the sister of James and

William Hamilton, who were among the first settlers in Nine Mile Canyon in the 1890s. Frank and Emma might have arrived at the same time as the rest of the Hamilton family. Their ranch was located above the mouth of Minnie Maud Canyon.

Wride, Mary. 1876 (Utah)–1961 (Salt Lake City)
Married: Martin Edwin Andrus; Nine Mile: 1899; Census 1880: Provo, Utah County; Census 1900: Provo, Utah County. School census records indicate Mary Wride was a teacher in Nine Mile Canyon in 1899. This could be Mary Wride who was a daughter of Utah County dairy farmers. She apparently returned to Provo in time for the 1900 census.

Woodruff, George. Ca. 1897 (Colorado)–1976 (Tooele?)
Married: Chloe Cook; Nine Mile: ca. 1930; Census 1910: Loveland, Colorado; Census 1920: Bluebell, Duchesne County; Census 1930: Nine Mile Canyon. In 1930, George is listed as a married head of household living alone in Nine Mile Canyon. His family might have been in the Uinta Basin at the time. The family later moved to Salt Lake and Tooele.

Workman, Ellen. *See* **Mead, Ellen (Workman)**

Yewaya, Alfonso. Ca. 1892 (Spain)–?
Nine Mile: ca. 1920; Census 1920: Nine Mile Canyon. In 1920, Alfonso was a twenty-eight-year-old farm laborer boarding with the Pierre Perry family in Nine Mile Canyon. There are no other records linked to this person to indicate how he came to be in Nine Mile Canyon or what became of him.

Notes

Chapter 1

1. William Miller, "Nine Mile Canyon: New Settlement Patterns in Utah as Seen in the Establishment of a Community in Eastern Utah" (senior thesis, Brigham Young University, 2001): 1–2.
2. Edward A. Geary, "Nine Mile: Eastern Utah's Forgotten Road," *Utah Historical Quarterly* 49, no. 1 (1981): 51.
3. Thursey Jessen Reynolds, comp., *Builders of Uintah: A Centennial History of Uintah County* (Vernal: Uintah County Daughters of the Utah Pioneers, 1947), 260–63.
4. Jerry D. Spangler, *Paradigms and Perspectives Revisited: A Class I Overview of Cultural Resources in the Uinta Basin and Tavaputs Plateau* (Ogden, UT: Uinta Research, 2002). See also Jerry D. Spangler, *Nine Mile Canyon: The Archaeological History of an American Treasure* (Salt Lake City: University of Utah Press, 2012).
5. Little is known of Chief Tavaputs, who posed for famed western photographer John Hillers, presumably in 1871 or 1872. Ute place names are common in the Uinta Basin, but they are extremely rare on the Tavaputs Plateau.
6. Folks living in Duchesne and Uintah County prefer the spelling "Uintah Basin," but the U.S. Geological Survey—the keeper of official place names—spells it Uinta Basin. The spellings are confusing in that there is a Uintah River and a Uintah County, but there are also the Uinta Mountains. We use the official, U.S. government–recognized spelling here as Uinta Basin. We extend our apologies to our friends in the basin who prefer the other spelling.
7. This section is modified and abbreviated from Jerry D. and Donna K. Spangler, *Treasures of the Tavaputs* (Ogden, UT: Colorado Plateau Archaeological Alliance, 2007).
8. John C. Sumner, "J. C. Sumner's Journal," *Utah Historical Quarterly* 25, nos. 1–4 (1947): 108–24, esp. 113–14.
9. Frederick S. Dellenbaugh, *The Romance of the Colorado River* (New York: G. P. Putnam's Sons, 1902), 186.
10. The high plateaus are renowned for their trophy deer and elk. Former President George W. Bush, former Vice President Dick Cheney, and other political heavyweights are frequent guests at a lodge on the high plateau owned by the Hunt Oil Company of Dallas, Texas. Guests rarely leave without bagging an elk.
11. H. Bert Jenson, *The Pioneer Saga of the Nine Mile Road* (Roosevelt, UT: Duchesne County Chamber of Commerce, 1984).
12. Oct. 15, 2013, interview with Ute tribal member Rick Chapoose, who guided the authors on a personal tour of Gate Canyon and the locations where the military reportedly attacked the arch during a training exercise.
13. Newt Stewart, quoted in Jenson, *Pioneer Saga*.
14. John W. Van Cott, *Utah Place Names: A Comprehensive Guide to the Origins of Geographic Names* (Salt Lake City: University of Utah Press, 1990), 274.
15. Geary, "Forgotten Road," 45. William Miles had seven daughters, but only five of them migrated with the family to lower Nine Mile Canyon (see chapter 9).

16. Francis Marion Bishop, "Captain Francis Marion Bishop's Journal," *Utah Historical Quarterly* 25, nos. 1–4 (1947): 189.

17. Bureau of Land Management, "*Nine Mile Canyon*" (2012). http://www.blm.gov/ut/st/en/fo/vernal/recreation_/nine_mile_canyon.html. The correct term is actually "triangulation," not transect. This mapping technique involved identifying three points in a triangle, making a measurement to one location and then using mathematical formulas to calculate the distance to the other points.

18. Bishop was the only member of Powell's expedition to put down roots in Utah. He married into the family of early Mormon apostle Parley P. Pratt, made a name for himself in mining endeavors, taught at the University of Deseret, and was involved in Utah politics. His son would later become one of the early settlers of Duchesne, just north of Nine Mile Canyon.

19. Spangler, *Nine Mile Canyon*, 4–12. See also the citations in Jerry D. Spangler, "Nine Mile, Minnie Maud, and the Mystery of a Place Name," *Utah Historical Quarterly* 79, no. 1 (2011): 42–51.

20. Dale L. Morgan, "The Diary of William H. Ashley (Part 2)," *Bulletin of the Missouri Historical Society* 11, no. 2 (1955). Fred R. Gowans, *Rocky Mountain Rendezvous* (Layton, UT: Peregrine Smith Books, 1985). Melvin T. Smith, "Before Powell: Exploration of the Colorado River," *Utah Historical Quarterly* 55, no. 2 (1987): 109.

21. Warren A. Ferris, *Life in the Rocky Mountains* (Denver: Old West Publishing Company, 1983). Morgan, "Ashley Diary, Part 2," 177. The origins of the name Duchesne are not known, although Dale Morgan speculated there might have been someone named Duchesne in the trapping expedition of Etienne Provost in 1824. A monument erected in Duchesne, Utah, indicates the name could derive from Saint Rose Philippine Duchesne, a pious nun who started free schools in frontier Missouri during the trapper era. According to the monument, she taught the niece of fur trader William Ashley (see chapter 2), and she was the godmother to the daughter of William Clark of Lewis and Clark fame. She was canonized in 1988 by Pope John Paul II. Ferris's reference to the Duchesne River on the 1836 map is the first time the name appears cartographically.

22. John C. Fremont, *The Exploring Expedition to the Rocky Mountains in the Year 1842, and to Oregon and North California in the Years 1843–44* (1845; repr., Washington, DC: Smithsonian Institution Press, 1988). The descriptions of these "forks" offer no convincing clues as to Fremont's exact location, or whether he was anywhere near Nine Mile Canyon. The map on file at the Utah State Historical Society is erroneously dated 1843. Fremont's arrival here occurred in 1844 and the map was published in 1845.

23. Don D. Fowler and Catherine S. Fowler, "Anthropology of the Numa: John Wesley Powell's Manuscripts on the Numic Peoples of Western North America, 1868–1880," *Smithsonian Contributions to Anthropology* 14 (Washington, DC: Smithsonian Institution, 1971): 178.

24. C. Roeser, *General Land Office Map of the Territory of Utah* (Washington, DC: General Land Office, 1876), http://cartweb.geography.ua.edu.

25. John Wesley Powell, *Map of the U.S. Geographical and Geological Survey of the Rocky Mountain Region* (Washington, DC: U.S. Geological Survey, 1878), http://cartweb.geography.ua.edu.

26. John Wesley Powell, *Report on the Lands of the Arid Region of the United States, with a More Detailed Account of the Lands in Utah*, 45th Cong., 2d sess., House Executive Document 73 (Washington, DC, 1879).

27. Ibid., 159–60.

28. Thompson, who was married to Major Powell's sister, Emma, later followed the major to Washington, D.C., becoming chief geographer in the U.S. Geological Survey. He was one of the founding members of the National Geographic Society. One of three boats on the 1871 expedition was named the *Emma Dean* in honor of Mrs. Thompson, as was Emma Park in the extreme upper reaches of Nine Mile Canyon. Thompson is buried in Arlington National Cemetery.

29. This section is an abbreviated version of a more detailed chapter one in Spangler, *Nine Mile Canyon*.

30. Geary, "Forgotten Road," 45.

31. "Minnie and Maud: Canyon named after twin girls," Price *Sun Advocate*, November 5, 1970. Leonard Brown, "History of Minnie & Maud," *Nine Mile Canyon Settlers Association* 1 (January 2005): 1–4.

32. Karen A. Shaffer, interview by Jerry D. Spangler, February 2010.

33. Donald Worster, *A River Running West: The Life of John Wesley Powell* (New York: Oxford University Press, 2001), 548.

34. Karen A. Shaffer and Neva Garner Greenwood, *Maud Powell: Pioneer American Violinist* (Ames: Iowa State University Press, 1988).

35. Roeser, "Territory of Utah."

36. U.S. Geological Survey Relief Map of Utah (Washington, DC: U.S. Geological Survey, 1947). http://cartweb.geography.ua.edu.

37. "Journey to Ashley," *Deseret News*, May 17, 1890.

Chapter 2

1. Mildred Miles Dillman, *Early History of Duchesne County* (Springville, UT: Art City Publishing Company, 1948), 73. The "old fort" is probably Nordell's Fort, which is perched on a high ledge above what was once the Miles Ranch. There was no evidence of these early inscriptions when the site was redocumented in 1989–1990 by Brigham Young University.

2. Ted J. Warner, ed., *The Domínguez-Escalante Journal* (Provo, UT: Brigham Young University Press, 1976). Herbert E. Bolton, *Pageant in the Wilderness* (Salt Lake City: Utah State Historical Society, 1950).

3. Joseph J. Hill, "Spanish and Mexican Exploration and Trade Northwest from New Mexico into the Great Basin," *Utah Historical Quarterly* 3, no. 1 (1930): 16.

4. John R. Alley Jr., "Prelude to Dispossession: The Fur Trade's Significance for the Northern Utes and Southern Paiutes," *Utah Historical Quarterly* 50, no. 2 (1982): 108.

5. Floyd A. O'Neil, "The Old Spanish Trail before 1848" (unpublished manuscript, Special Collections, Marriott Library, University of Utah, 1968).

6. C. Gregory Crampton and Steven K. Madsen, *In Search of the Spanish Trail: Santa Fe to Los Angeles, 1829–1848* (Salt Lake City: Gibbs Smith Publisher, 1994).

7. Gale Ray Rhoades, "Lost Gold of the Uintahs," *Western Treasures* 3, no. 4 (1967): 17.

8. John D. Barton, "Antoine Robidoux and the Fur Trade of the Uinta Basin" (master's thesis, Brigham Young University, 1989): 23.

9. Mexico won its independence from Spain in 1821, and all lands below the forty-second parallel were Mexican territory. American fur trappers forged good relations with the Mexican government in Taos, and those seeking to trap in Utah and Colorado successfully obtained licenses from the Mexican government to do so. North of the forty-second parallel was the "Northwest Territory," an area that by treaty could be jointly occupied by the Americans and British, although the American trappers frequently did not recognize this and conflicts, sometimes violent ones, between British and American trappers were common. The problem facing the trappers was that none of them knew for certain where the forty-second parallel was and there was clearly trespassing on both sides of the line. The trappers themselves probably did not care. There was no government mechanism to prevent encroachment from either side of the line.

10. Polly Schaafsma, "Survey Report of the Rock Art of Utah" (Department of Anthropology, University of Utah, 1970): 85.

11. Barton, "Antoine Robidoux," 34. Leroy R. Hafen, *Mountain Men and Fur Traders of the Far West* (Lincoln: University of Nebraska Press, 1972), 96. Leroy R. Hafen, *Trappers of the Far West* (Lincoln: University of Nebraska Press, 1983), 1–3.

12. Antoine Robidoux, cited in David D. Weber, *The Taos Trappers* (Norman: University of Oklahoma Press, 1970), 74.

13. William Hubbard, cited in Barton, "Antoine Robidoux," 35.

14. Barton, "Antoine Robidoux," 36.

15. James M. Aton, *The River Knows Everything: Desolation Canyon and the Green* (Logan: Utah State University Press, 2009), 67. "William Henry Ashley," *Encyclopedia of World Biography* (2004). Retrieved November 30, 2012, from

Encyclopedia.com: http://www.encyclopedia. com/doc/1G2-3404700299.

16. Morgan, "Ashley Diary, Part 2," 158.

17. William Ashley, cited in ibid., 186. Rufus Wood Leigh, "Naming of the Green, Sevier and Virgin Rivers," *Utah Historical Quarterly* 29, no. 2 (1961): 137–39. William M. Purdy, "An Outline of the History of the Flaming Gorge Area," *University of Utah Anthropological Papers* no. 37 (Salt Lake City: University of Utah, 1959), 3. Leigh asserts the name Green River was not used until 1843, but this is clearly incorrect.

18. David Lavender, *Colorado River Country* (New York: E. P. Dutton, 1982), 35. Dale L. Morgan, ed., "Diary of William H. Ashley, Part 1," *Bulletin of the Missouri Historical Society* 11, no. 1 (1954): 33–34.

19. James P. Beckwourth, *The Life and Adventures of James P. Beckwourth* (Lincoln: University of Nebraska Press, 1972), 57–61. Historians today dismiss Beckwourth's accounts as gross exaggerations and even fabrications, but he was a great storyteller.

20. O. Dock Marston, "The Lost Journal of John Colton Sumner," *Utah Historical Quarterly* 37, no. 2 (1969): 178.

21. Charles Kelly, ed., "Journal of W. C. Powell," *Utah Historical Quarterly* 26–27, nos. 1–4 (1948): 268.

22. Frederick S. Dellenbaugh, *A Canyon Voyage: The Narrative of the Second Powell Expedition Down the Green-Colorado River from Wyoming, and the Explorations on Land, in the Years 1871–1872* (New Haven: Yale University Press, 1908), 28.

23. Morgan, "Ashley Diary, Part 2," 175–77.

24. Ibid., 178–79.

25. Gowans, *Rocky Mountain Rendezvous*, 17. Dale L. Morgan, *The West of William H. Ashley 1822–1838* (Denver: Old West Publishing Company, 1964), 281. Smith, "Before Powell," 109.

26. Barton, "Antoine Robidoux," 37.

27. Aton, *The River Knows Everything*, 68.

28. William H. Ashley, cited in Morgan, "Ashley Journal, Part 2," 182–83. Morgan questions the twenty-four miles and suggests it might have been fourteen.

29. Aton, *The River Knows Everything*, 68–69.

30. Barton, "Antoine Robidoux," 38.

31. Morgan, "Ashley Diary, Part 2," 174.

32. Ibid., 171–72.

33. Ibid., 174. Smith, "Before Powell," 112.

34. Lavender, *Colorado River Country*, 43.

35. Aton, *The River Knows Everything*, 79.

36. Charles Kelly, "The Mysterious D. Julien," *Utah Historical Quarterly* 6, no. 3 (1933): 87.

37. James Knipmeyer, "The Old Trappers Trail through Eastern Utah," *Canyon Legacy* 9 (1991): 14.

38. F. Richard Hauck, "Archaeological Evaluations in the Northern Colorado Plateau Cultural Area: An Investigation of the Seep Ridge, Book Cliffs, Red Wash, Hay Canyon, Whetrock Canyon and Interstate 70–Exit 220 Alternative Highway Routes in Uintah and Grand Counties, Utah," AERC Paper No. 45 (1991): 91–92.

39. James Reed, cited in Gale Ray Rhoades, *Footprints in the Wilderness* (Salt Lake City: Publisher's Press, 1971), 317.

40. Barton, "Antoine Robidoux," 39.

41. Ibid.

42. Ibid., 55.

43. Ibid. Robert Glass Cleland, *The Reckless Breed of Men* (New York: Knopf Publishers, 1950). Charles Kelly, "Antoine Robidoux," *Utah Historical Quarterly* 6, no. 4 (1933): 116. A. Reed Morrill, "The Site of Fort Robidoux," *Utah Historical Quarterly* 9, nos. 1–2 (1941): 2. Albert B. Reagan, "Some Notes on the History of the Uintah Basin, in Northeastern Utah, to 1850," *Utah Academy of Sciences, Arts and Letters* 11 (1934): 56. See also Albert B. Reagan, "Forts Robidoux and Kit Carson in Northeastern Utah," *New Mexican Historical Review* 10 (1935).

44. Leroy R. Hafen, *Old Spanish Trail* (Glendale, CA: Arthur Clark Co., 1954), 102. Dale L. Morgan, *The Great Salt Lake* (Indianapolis: Bobb-Merrill Co., 1947). Paul C. Phillips, *The Fur Trade* (Norman: University of Oklahoma Press, 1961).

45. Kelly, "Antoine Robidoux," 115–16. Charles Kelly, "The Forgotten Bastion, Old Fort Robidoux," *Utah Magazine* (October 1946).

46. Morrill, "Fort Robidoux," 1–11.

47. Barton, "Antoine Robidoux," 103.

48. Ibid., 62–63.

49. As discussed in chapter 1, Ferris's map depicts a river far to the south of the Uintah River in the approximate location of Nine Mile Canyon. He called this stream the Duchesne River.

50. Warren Angus Ferris, cited in J. Cecil Alter, "W. A. Ferris in Utah," *Utah Historical Quarterly* 9, nos. 1–2 (1941): 102.

51. Morrill, "Fort Robidoux," 4.

52. Joseph Williams, cited in Dillman, *Early History of Duchesne County*, 72.

53. Rufus B. Sage, *Rocky Mountain Life* (Boston: Wentworth and Company, 1857), 232.

54. John C. Fremont, *Memoirs of My Life* (New York: Belford, Clarke & Company, 1887), 394.

55. Ibid., 395. *Pinole* is a Spanish word for a coarse-ground corn meal.

56. Sage, *Rocky Mountain Life*, 232.

57. Milo Milton Quaife, ed., *Kit Carson's Autobiography* (Chicago: Lakeside Press, 1935), 34–35.

58. Barton, "Antoine Robidoux," 89.

59. Alter, "W. A. Ferris," 98–99. Nine Mile Canyon is thirty-three river miles to the south of Fort Kit Carson, but probably two-thirds that amount by an overland route.

60. Kelly, "Journal of W. C. Powell," 287.

61. Dillman, *Early History of Duchesne County*, 73.

62. Aton, *The River Knows Everything*, 71.

63. Barton, "Antoine Robidoux," 119.

64. A search of the Ancestry.com database identified a Warren Sulser who was born in 1880 and lived in Duchesne County at the time of the 1920 census.

65. Jerry D. Spangler, *Dust Up: A Baseline Site Condition Assessment and Analysis of Dust Accumulation and Vandalism of Cultural Resources in the Cottonwood Canyon Confluence Area, Nine Mile Canyon, Carbon County, Utah* (Ogden, UT: Colorado Plateau Archaeological Alliance, 2008).

66. Year: 1870; Census Place: Springville, Utah, Utah Territory; Roll: M593_1612; Page: 340B; Image: 677; Family History Library Film: 553111, Ancestry.com database. The database also lists a Stephen Groesbeck who was assigned to Fort Cameron near Cedar City in 1882 and Fort Thornburgh in the Uinta Basin in 1883 (Fort Thornburgh plays into the history of Nine Mile Canyon, see chapter 4). This is probably Stephen Groesbeck's son, Stephen W., who was born in 1857 in Illinois and would have been about twenty-five years old at the time he was assigned to Fort Thornburgh in 1883. By 1885, he was assigned to Fort Douglas. An 1899 article in the *Daily Nevada State Journal* indicates Major Stephen W. Groesbeck was at that time judge advocate of the United States Army. It is unlikely he left the inscription in Nine Mile Canyon as he would have been only about ten years old at the time.

Chapter 3

1. A greatly abbreviated version of this chapter, by the lead author here, appeared in *Outlaw Trail Journal* (Summer 2012): 43–52, under the title "Samuel H. Gilson."

2. Herbert F. Kretchman, *The Story of Gilsonite* (Salt Lake City: American Gilsonite Company, 1957), 28.

3. Jeffrey D. Nichols, "Sam Gilson Did Much More Than Promote Gilsonite," *History Blazer* (1995). Reprinted at http://historytogo.utah.gov.

4. Henry E. Bender Jr., *Uintah Railway: The Gilsonite Route* (Berkeley: Howell-North Books, 1970), 59.

5. Douglas D. Woodard, "The Legend of Sam Gilson" (unpublished manuscript, Utah State Historical Society, 1981), 1–2.

6. Sam Gilson, "Sam Gilson Speaks Out," *Deseret News*, August 9, 1890. Douglas D. Woodard makes the case that Gilson left Illinois in 1850, along with his brother James W. Gilson, to join in the California gold rush. We prefer to accept Gilson's own account that it was in 1853.

7. Bender, *Uintah Railway*, 15. Woodard, "Legend of Gilson," 3.

8. Kretchman, *Gilsonite Story*, 28.

9. Nichols, "More Than Promote."

10. Bender, *Uintah Railway*, 15.

11. Bender believes the 1878 inscription at Horse Canyon was made during Gilson's many trips to move horses to railheads in Wyoming. This is problematic in that Horse Canyon offers an access point into Range Creek Canyon but it does not offer any reasonable access to the Uinta Basin. There are two primary trails from the San

Rafael country of Carbon and Emery Counties to the Uinta Basin, a direct route through Soldier Canyon into Nine Mile Canyon and the other a longer route through the East Tavaputs Plateau beginning near the Colorado-Utah border. Sunnyside Canyon (known as Whitmore Canyon at the time) was also passable but very steep and difficult.

12. Coke is produced by heating coal in ovens to remove impurities. The coke would then burn at higher temperatures necessary to smelt ore. See Ronald G. Watt, *A History of Carbon County* (Salt Lake City: Utah State Historical Society, 1997), 130.

13. Woodard, "Legend of Gilson," 7. Woodard also makes a convoluted case that Gilson could not get his horses up Horse Canyon so he pushed them up Sunnyside Canyon to the north, then south back into Range Creek and then onto the Uinta Basin. This reflects ignorance of the topography of the Tavaputs Plateau in that there is no practical way from Range Creek to the Uinta Basin, and that once at the top of Sunnyside Canyon the route to the Uinta Basin would have been to continue north into Nine Mile Canyon through Dry Canyon or Cottonwood Canyon.

14. Ibid.

15. Sam Gilson, "Gilson Speaks Again," *Deseret News*, August 16, 1890.

16. Ibid.

17. Nichols, "More Than Promote."

18. Stephen Cresswell, "The U.S. Department of Justice in Utah Territory, 1870–90," *Utah Historical Quarterly* 53, no. 3 (1985): 209.

19. Newspaper accounts invariably refer to him as Marshal Gilson, Marshal Samuel Gilson, Marshal Sam Gilson, or Marshal S. H. Gilson, the latter being the most common moniker. His formal title was Deputy U.S. Marshal.

20. "Character of the Means Employed," *Deseret News*, February 11, 1885.

21. "Sam Gillson Arrested," *Deseret News*, May 8, 1872.

22. William A. Hickman, cited by Woodard, "Legend of Gilson," 6.

23. Nichols, "More Than Promote."

24. "Samuel H. Gilson, Widely Known in West, Is Dead," *Deseret News*, December 3, 1913.

25. Woodard, "Legend of Gilson," 6. The two ranches have continued to be operated together by a succession of owners through the present day. The Oak Spring Ranch south of Emery is located in what is still called Gilson Valley.

26. Glynn Bennion, "A Pioneer Cattle Venture of the Bennion Family," *Utah Historical Quarterly* 34, no. 4 (1966): 319–20.

27. Ibid.

28. The Bennion family was running large herds in Castle Valley in 1875, but they did not establish a permanent ranch there. Rather, younger family members were left there to tend the herds. See Bennion, "Pioneer Cattle Venture." It was quite common for early ranchers to leave their families in more established communities, especially during winter months. This practice persisted in Nine Mile Canyon through the 1930s where ranchers would have their place in the canyon and a second home in Price, Wellington, or Sunnyside. See chapter 9.

29. Year: 1880; Census Place: Gooseberry Valley, Sevier, Utah; Roll: 1338; Family History Film: 1255338; Page: 488C; Enumeration District: 069. Several families living in the Gooseberry Valley Precinct (Salina Canyon) in 1880 later moved on to settle Nine Mile Canyon. It is certainly possible they learned of Nine Mile Canyon from Sam Gilson.

30. Cresswell, "Justice in Utah," 209.

31. "Another Hunt: S. H. Gilson and Marshal Dyer Ransack Buildings," *Deseret News*, Feb. 23, 1887. "Another Raid in Salt Lake," *The Daily Enquirer*, February 22, 1887.

32. "Another Hunt," *Deseret News*.

33. Ibid.

34. "Means Employed," *Deseret* News.

35. "A Corroborative Statement," *Deseret News*, February 18, 1885. For the *Deseret News* to even hint at a profanity itself reflects the Mormon community's outrage toward Gilson. As late as the 2000s, the *Deseret News* had a policy of never using even mild profanities unless specifically approved by the editor-in-chief, which rarely ever happened.

36. Cresswell, "Justice in Utah," 214.

37. "A Poor Widow Defrauded by a Deputy Marshal," *Deseret News*, Feb. 18, 1885. "Corroborative Statement," *Deseret News*.

38. "Premature Petitions," *Deseret News*, March 2, 1889.

39. "Some Pointed Questions and Suggestions," *Deseret News*, January 29, 1885.

40. Ibid.

41. "Another Hunt," *Deseret News*.

42. Gilson, "Speaks Out," *Deseret News*.

43. Actually, there was one prominent polygamist hiding right under the government's nose in Price. John Ammon Powell, who is credited with guiding the U.S. military in 1886 to identify a freight route through Nine Mile Canyon, had three wives and 31 children. He lived for a time in Nine Mile Canyon in about 1900 with his third wife, Rosealtha, but he also maintained households in Price and Salt Lake City. See "A Life Sketch of John Ammon Powell Which He Dictated," http://michael3900.blogspot.com/2011/04/life-sketch-of-john-ammon-powell-which.html.

44. Kretchman, *Gilsonite Story*, 27.

45. Woodard, "Legend of Gilson," 7.

46. Nichols, "More Than Promote."

47. Bender, *Uintah Railway*, 14.

48. F. M. Endlich, *United States Geological and Geographical Survey of the Territories, 10th Annual Report* (Washington, DC: U.S. Government Printing Office, 1878), 85–86. See also A. C. Peale, same publication, 175.

49. Bender, *Uintah Railway*, 15.

50. William P. Blake, "Uintahite—A New Variety of Asphaltum from the Uintah Mountains, Utah," *The Engineering and Mining Journal* 40, no. 26 (December 26, 1885): 431.

51. E. W. Harmer, "Gilsonite Mining in Utah Expands," *The Mining Journal (Arizona)* 23, no. 7 (1939): 6, cited by Bender, *Uintah Railway*, 15.

52. Bender, *Uintah Railway*, 15–16. See Bender citations for the patent numbers.

53. Kretchman, *Gilsonite Story*, 27.

54. Bryce T. Tripp, "Gilsonite: An Unusual Utah Resource," *Utah Geological Survey Notes* 36 (July 2004): 1–2. Karine Walker, "Uinta Basin's Black Gold," *Outlaw Trail Journal* (Summer 2005): 2–3.

55. Tripp, "Gilsonite," 31.

56. Bender, *Uintah Railway*, 16.

57. The first seven claims were actually filed under the names of individuals other than Gilson or his business partner Bert Seaboldt, but all of whom were unmistakably associated with them. The date on the claims suggests that the Gilson-Seaboldt partnership and any investigation of the Carbon Vein actually occurred in 1885.

58. Bender, *Uintah Railway*, 16.

59. Robert Athearn, *The Denver and Rio Grande Western Railroad: Rebel of the Rockies* (Lincoln: University of Nebraska Press, 1962).

60. Bender, *Uintah Railway*, 16.

61. Ibid.

62. The removal of the White River and Uncompahgre bands from Colorado to the Uinta Basin did not set well with the Uintah Utes already residing there. The Uintah Utes had played no role in the Meeker War that had precipitated the removal of the Colorado Utes, but their government allocations were withheld by the local administrator as punishment for the events in Colorado.

63. Cresswell, "Justice in Utah." Cresswell indicates that U.S. Justice Department attorneys at the time earned $250 per year, plus expenses. It can be assumed that the deputy U.S. marshals working for them made even less.

64. Kretchman, *Gilsonite Story*, 28. Charles O. Baxter later became a primary mover behind the Uintah Railway, which itself spelled the demise of Nine Mile Canyon as a freight route (see chapter 8). Baxter Pass in the Douglas Creek area of northwest Colorado is named after Charles and/or his brother.

65. Letter from Seaboldt to A. L. Crawford dated May 20, 1946, cited in Bender, *Uinta Railway*, 16. Congress has a long-running history of disenfranchising Indian tribes whenever valuable economic resources are discovered on tribal lands.

66. Bender, *Uintah Railway*, 17.

67. The Strip was located at the western extreme of Uintah County and far beyond the reach of local lawmen. In no short order, a mining town had sprung up, also called The Strip, that boasted four saloons and at least as many "hog ranches," the frontier vernacular for houses of ill repute, which catered to miners, freighters, and soldiers.

The town was renowned for its violence and law-lessness. The military tried to prohibit soldiers from visiting The Strip, even posting guards at a bridge to catch soldiers sneaking back to their posts. It became standard practice for soldiers to consume all their whiskey before swimming the river. They disposed of the empty bottles in a ravine—called Bottle Hollow today—at the east edge of The Strip. See John D. Barton, *A History of Duchesne County* (Salt Lake City: Utah State Historical Society, 1998), 72.

68. Bender, *Uintah Railway*, 16–17. Kretchman, *Gilsonite Story*, 26.

69. Bender, *Uintah Railway*, 17.

70. Kretchman, *Gilsonite Story*, 37.

71. Cresswell, "Justice in Utah," 206–7.

72. Kretchman, *Gilsonite Story*, 32.

73. Bender, *Uintah Railway*, 19.

74. Ibid.

75. Ibid.

76. Ibid., 17. Kretchman, *Gilsonite Story*, 30.

77. Woodard, "Legend of Gilson," 6.

78. "Gilson's New Discovery," *Salt Lake Herald*, April 5, 1900.

79. Given his U.S. marshal's duties and his dabbling in Gilsonite speculation, it would seem unlikely he would have found the time to make the required improvements to gain a land patent. Under terms of the law, Gilson would have had three years to bring into cultivation at least one-eighth of the 320 acres granted under the patent. These improvements were probably made by his brother James on his behalf.

80. "Sam Gilson Is Under Arrest," *Salt Lake Herald*, April 26, 1904.

81. "Mr. Gilson Talks," *Eastern Utah Advocate*, March 26, 1903.

82. "Sam Gilson's Statement," *Salt Lake Herald*, April 26, 1904.

83. "Sam Gilson's Explanation," *Ogden Standard*, May 27, 1894.

84. Ibid.

85. Kretchman, *Gilsonite Story*, 28. "Samuel H. Gilson, Widely Known in West, Is Dead," *Deseret News*, December 3, 1913.

86. Woodard, "Legend of Gilson," 9.

87. Jerry D. Spangler, *The Upper Fringe: Archaeological Inventory in Upper Nine Mile Canyon, Carbon County, Utah* (Ogden, UT: Colorado Plateau Archaeological Alliance, 2011), 13. Gilson must have been pretty spry for a seventy-four-year-old. The inscription is located on a cliff face where he would have had to crawl out on a very narrow ledge with a forty-foot sheer drop if he had made one misstep.

88. Births, Marriages and Deaths, from the *Carbon Advocate*, 1892–1893, http://freepages.genealogy.rootsweb.ancestry.com.

Chapter 4

1. The Union Pacific Railroad had a long-standing monopoly on rail freight into Utah since its arrival in 1869, something that evoked repeated complaints of price gouging. Utahns were generally resentful of the Union Pacific. The arrival of the Denver and Rio Grande Railroad in 1883 resulted in higher competition and lower prices, and Utahns looked on this railroad far more favorably, and in some cases as an economic "savior." In 1883, the military was paying three dollars per hundred pounds to ship freight from Union Pacific railheads at Fort Bridger to Fort Thornburg in the Uinta Basin. In 1887, it was paying one dollar per hundred pounds to ship freight from Denver and Rio Grande railheads in Price to Fort Duchesne. See Athearn, *Rebel of the Rockies*, and Leonard Arrington, *Great Basin Kingdom: Economic History of the Latter-Day Saints, 1830–1900* (Lincoln: University of Nebraska Press, 1958).

2. Thomas Alexander and Leonard Arrington, "The Utah Military Frontier, 1872–1912: Forts Cameron, Thornburgh, and Duchesne," *Utah Historical Quarterly* 32, no. 4 (1964): 342–43. Byron Loosle, ed., *Carter Military Road Project: 2004–2007* (Vernal, UT: Ashley National Forest, U.S. Department of Agriculture, 2011).

3. Henry Fiack, "Fort Duchesne's Beginnings," *Utah Historical Quarterly* 2, no. 1 (1929): 32. Gary Weicks, "Frontier Soldiering in Nine Mile Canyon," *Outlaw Trail Journal* (Summer 2011): 7.

4. Leland Powell, cited by Geary, "Forgotten Road," 47.

5. Gary Weicks, "Fort Duchesne Twilight Years: Countdown to Shutdown of a Frontier Army Post," *Outlaw Trail Journal* (Summer 2012): 25.

6. Jody Patterson, email communication with the lead author, February 20, 2014. It is not known if the same army protocols were in effect in 1886.

7. Miller, "New Settlement Patterns," 1–2.

8. Fanny Weeks Winn family history, cited in Norma Dalton, "Nine Mile Canyon Builders," *Nine Mile Canyon Settlers Association* 2 (2012): 3.

9. Ranchers began to arrive in Nine Mile Canyon in 1877, working on what appears to have been only seasonal ranches, perhaps little more than temporary shelters for cowboys who could have hauled in needed supplies with pack horses. Once families began to arrive, there would have been a greater need for a wagon road, not just for transporting food and household items but for farming supplies, blacksmithing equipment, construction materials, and firewood.

10. Weicks, "Frontier Soldiering," 7. Fanny Weeks Winn also indicates she traveled the road in the fall of 1886 and stayed at the Winn house on her way to the Uinta Basin with her family.

11. Fort Duchesne general orders, September 10, 1886, cited by Weicks, "Frontier Soldiering," 7. Rural Utahns have long been noted for their unusual vernacular, but it is puzzling why the army would assign an interpreter to the reconnaissance.

12. Fort Douglas general orders, September 16, cited by Weicks, "Frontier Soldiering," 7. "In Military Circles," *Salt Lake Tribune*, September 18, 1886.

13. Untitled, *Salt Lake Tribune*, October 8, 1886.

14. "Military Circles," *Salt Lake Tribune*.

15. Fort Duchesne general orders, November 9, 1886, cited in Weicks, "Frontier Soldiering," 9.

16. Weicks, "Frontier Soldiering," 9–11.

17. Bruce Hawkins, "Archaeological Survey Conducted at the Site of Fort Thornburgh No. 2 (42Un788), Utah, 1882–1883" (unpublished manuscript, Utah Division of State History, 1981).

18. Alexander and Arrington, "Military Frontier," 340–41.

19. Weicks, "Frontier Soldiering," 3–4. The soldiers traveled to the Uinta Basin by way of a rough wagon road from Park City that is today U.S. Highway 40.

20. Alexander and Arrington, "Military Frontier," 340–41.

21. Ibid., 341.

22. Major E. G. Bush, who commanded Fort Thornburgh at the time of its abandonment, was the same Major Edward Bush who was ordered in 1886 to examine the suitability of a supply route through Nine Mile Canyon.

23. Alexander and Arrington, "Military Frontier," 341–43.

24. Derek A. Stertz, "Carter Road History," in *Carter Military Road Project: 2004–2007*, ed. Byron Loosle (Vernal, UT: Ashley National Forest, U.S. Department of Agriculture, 2011), 3–7. Michael W. Johnson, Robert E. Parson, and Daniel A. Stebbins, *A History of Daggett County: A Modern Frontier* (Salt Lake City: Utah State Historical Society, 1998), 51.

25. Stertz, "Carter Road History," 5. "Carter Military Road History," U.S. Forest Service, http://www.fs.usda.gov/detail/ashley/learning/history-culture/?cid=fsm9_002401.

26. The road built by Judge Carter must not have been very functional, at least for military purposes, as both Weicks ("Frontier Soldiering," 4) and Alexander and Arrington ("Military Frontier," 342) credit U.S. Army troops with the road construction in 1882.

27. Stertz, "Carter Road History," 5. William and Willie Carter might have been middle men, taking their cut of the trade without actually freighting supplies. Alexander and Arrington indicate the military's freight contracts were let in 1882 and 1883 to John H. Arnold, Merrill L. Hoyt, and Joseph Hatch at $3.10 and $3.00 per hundred pounds. See Alexander and Arrington, "Military Frontier," 342.

28. Alexander and Arrington, "Military Frontier," 341–42.

29. Ibid.

30. A. R. Standing, "Through the Uintas: History of the Carter Road," *Utah Historical Quarterly* 35, no. 3 (1967): 260. Doris Karen Burton, *A History of Uintah County: Scratching the Surface* (Salt Lake City: Utah State Historical Society, 1996), 194.

31. Kretchman, *Gilsonite Story*, 37.

32. Jeffrey Rust, email communication, December 10, 2012. Gary Weicks, email communication, December 10, 2012.

33. The soldiers traveled by Union Pacific train to Carter Station and then marched overland on the Carter Road over the Uinta Mountains.

34. Ronald G. Coleman, "The Buffalo Soldiers: Guardians of the Uintah Frontier, 1886–1901," *Utah Historical Quarterly* 47 (1979): 421–39. Weicks, "Frontier Soldiering," 6.

35. Sources disagree on how the name "buffalo soldiers" began. According to the Buffalo Soldiers National Museum, the name originated with the Cheyenne warriors in the winter of 1877, the actual Cheyenne translation being "wild buffalo." However, writer Walter Hill documented the account of Colonel Benjamin Grierson, who founded the Tenth Cavalry regiment, recalling an 1871 campaign against Comanches. Some sources assert that the nickname was given out of respect for the fierce fighting ability of the Tenth Cavalry. Other sources assert that Native Americans called the black cavalry troops "buffalo soldiers" because of their dark curly hair, which resembled a buffalo's coat. Still other sources point to a combination of both legends. The term *buffalo soldiers* became a generic term for all African American soldiers.

36. "The Ninth Cavalry." http://www.buffalosoldiers-lawtonftsill.org/9-cav.htm.

37. Will Bagley, "Buffalo Soldiers Served with Distinction in Utah," *Utah History to Go*, http://historytogo.utah.gov/salt_lake_tribune/history_matters/081901.

38. Harold Schindler, "Frederick Benteen and Fort Damn Shame," *Utah Historical Quarterly* 66, no. 3 (1998): 267.

39. Ibid.

40. Untitled, *Salt Lake Tribune*, July 10, 1887. Weicks cites an account of James William Nixon, who made several trips with a two-horse team and wagon to haul freight between Price, Fort Duchesne and Vernal in the summer and fall of 1886; see "Frontier Soldiering," 9.

41. Weicks, "Frontier Soldiering," 7.

42. Schindler, "Fort Damn Shame," 267.

43. Weicks, "Frontier Soldiering," 10.

44. Schindler, "Fort Damn Shame," 267–68.

45. Military report, cited in Schindler, *Fort Damn Shame*, 268.

46. Schindler, "Fort Damn Shame," 270. Weicks, "Frontier Soldiering," 12.

47. Watt, *A History of Carbon County*, 32.

48. Weicks, "Frontier Soldiering," 12.

49. Coleman, "The Buffalo Soldiers," 438.

50. Stephen Perry Jocelyn letter, October 1886, cited by Weicks, "Frontier Soldiering," 11.

51. Weicks, "Frontier Soldiering," 12–13.

52. Remnants of the telegraph relay station at the Nutter Ranch near the mouth of Gate Canyon are still visible next to the road. The location of a second relay station is not known with certainty, but local tradition holds that it was at the Edwin Lee Ranch just above Argyle Canyon.

53. Weicks, "Frontier Soldering," 13.

54. Fiack, "Fort Duchesne's Beginnings," 32.

55. Weicks, "Frontier Soldiering," 18.

56. Ibid., 13–14.

57. Ibid., 14–15.

58. "One of the Boys," *Salt Lake Tribune*, September 23, 1887. The reference to "different mines" is interesting. If this is a reference to the Gilsonite mines, it would indicate Sam Gilson and Bert Seaboldt were illegally mining the ore a year before Congress removed the Gilsonite deposits from the Ute Reservation.

59. Geary, "Forgotten Road," 53.

60. Dillman, *Early History of Duchesne County*, 256.

61. Weicks, "Frontier Soldiering," 15.

62. Ibid., 17.

63. Inflation Calculator, http://www.davemanuel.com/inflation-calculator.php.

64. See Cresswell, "Justice in Utah," 212.

65. Bender, *Uintah Railway*, 16. Bender's assertion that Seaboldt remained with the Denver and Rio Grande Railroad through 1890 could explain Seaboldt's determination that the ores be shipped to his employer's railhead at Price. When Gilson and Seaboldt sold out to the Gilson Asphaltum Company in 1889, Seaboldt went to work for the new company as superintendent of mines.

66. Weicks, "Frontier Soldiering," 17.

67. Inflation Calculator, http://www.davemanuel.com/inflation-calculator.php.

68. Kretchman, *Gilsonite Story*, 37.

69. Bender, *Uinta Railway*, 16. Once Congress had opened the reservation to Gilsonite miners, Ute

approval was still needed. Seaboldt is reported to have secured that approval by providing free whiskey to tribal members in exchange for their signatures. See Burton, *A History of Uintah County.*

70. "One of the Boys," *Salt Lake Tribune.*
71. Weicks, "Frontier Soldiering," 20.
72. Ibid., 21.

Chapter 5

1. Dillman, *Early History of Duchesne County*, 256.
2. Jerry D. Spangler and Donna K. Spangler, *Horned Snakes and Axle Grease: A Roadside Guide to the Archaeology, History, and Rock Art of Nine Mile Canyon* (Salt Lake City: Uinta Publishing, 2003).
3. Jerry D. Spangler, *Fremont, Freighters, and Flagpoles: An Archaeological Inventory of the North Side of Nine Mile Canyon Between Gate Canyon and Pete's Canyon* (Ogden, UT: Colorado Plateau Archaeological Alliance, 2012), 66–75.
4. Spangler, *Paradigms and Perspectives Revisited.*
5. Geary, "Forgotten Road," 46.
6. Dillman, *Early History of Duchesne County*, 253.
7. Geary, "Forgotten Road," 46. Edward Geary, "History Written on the Land in Emery County," *Utah Historical Quarterly* 66, no. 3 (1998): 212. Geary calls this trail the Midland Trail, although other historians of western cattle ranching do not mention that name for a trail in Utah and it does not appear on Old West cattle trail maps of Utah. One map indicates the presence of an unnamed trail from Santa Fe, New Mexico, that trends north and then follows the base of the Book Cliffs to the Wasatch Front and then on to Fort Hall, Idaho. The military might also have used this trail in 1860. No other Utah trails are illustrated. See Terry G. Jordan, *North American Cattle-Ranching Frontiers* (Albuquerque: University of New Mexico Press, 1992), 268. Today, this trail is recognized as U.S. Highway 6, which passes within ten miles of Soldier Creek, a major access point to upper Nine Mile Canyon.
8. B. A. M. Froiseth, *Froiseth's New Sectional & Mineral Map of Utah compiled from the latest U.S. Government Surveys and other authentic sources* (B. A. M. Froiseth, 1878).

9. Thomas Rhoades and his son Caleb remain legendary among "lost treasures" aficionados for what has become known as the Lost Rhoades Mine. Legend has it that Thomas Rhoades discovered vast quantities of gold ore, cached Spanish gold bars, Ute gold, and/or Aztec artifacts at an undisclosed location in the Uinta Basin foothills. The gold was retrieved by Thomas and Caleb Rhoades and given to LDS Church President Brigham Young, who purportedly used it to fund church operations, including the gilding of the Angel Moroni on the Salt Lake Temple. Treasure hunters have been looking for the lost mine ever since. See Gregory Thompson, *Faded Footprints: The Lost Rhoades Gold Mines and Other Hidden Treasures of the Uintas* (Salt Lake City: Dream Garden Press, 2006).
10. Watt, *A History of Carbon County*, 22.
11. Miller, "New Settlement Patterns," 3.
12. Powell, *Report on the Lands of the Arid Region*, 159–60. The original document was drafted in 1877 and released in 1878, but it was corrected and rereleased in 1879 as the document available to researchers today.
13. General Land Office map by Augustus Ferron of parts of Township 12 South, Range 13 East, cited by Miller, "New Settlement Patterns." This map was not identified during the course of our research.
14. Historical accounts all list his name as Alford Lunt, but LDS Church immigration records list his name as Alfred Lunt, son of Edward and Harriet Lunt, who sailed from Liverpool, England, in 1857. Alfred was ten years old at the time. See http://lib.byu.edu/mormonmigration/person.php?id=25811&q=Shadrach%20Lunt.
15. "Sunnyside, Utah." http://en.wikipedia.org/wiki/Sunnyside,_Utah.
16. The Whitmores were wealthy in their own right. Ancestry.com also links the genealogy of the Lunt family to the wealthy McCune family at that time.
17. Pearl Wilson, *A History of Juab County* (Salt Lake City: Utah State Historical Society, 1999), 97.
18. Family Group Record: Ancestral File Number 1QC-HC, cited by Miller, "New Settlement Patterns," 5.

19. General Land Office Historical Index, Salt Lake Meridian Township 12 South, Range 13 East, U.S. Federal Census 1900. Enumeration district 86, Sheet 11, cited by Miller, "New Settlement Patterns," 5.

20. Various historic records list his name as "Shedrach" Lunt, but LDS Church immigration records list his name as Shadrach Lunt, son of Edward and Harriet Lunt, who sailed from Liverpool, England, in 1857. See http://lib.byu.edu/mormonmigration/person.php?id=25811&q=Shadrach%20Lunt.

21. Dillman, *Early History of Duchesne County*, 258.

22. See 1880 and 1900 census records for Nephi, Juab, Utah.

23. Mormon Migration: http://lib.byu.edu/mormon-migration/person.php?id=25811&q=Shadrach%20Lunt. Family records posted on Ancestry.com indicate the Lunt family arrived as handcart pioneers.

24. Aton, *The River Knows Everything*, 112.

25. Myrna Rasmussen, "Alfred and Shadrach Lunt" (unpublished family biography, no date).

26. Dillman, *Early History of Duchesne County*, 25.

27. Aton, *The River Knows Everything*, 112–13.

28. Dillman, *Early History of Duchesne County*, 258.

29. Rasmussen, "Alfred and Shadrach," 1.

30. Aton, *The River Knows Everything*, 112–13.

31. Jerry D. Spangler, *Of Owls and Cranes: A Cultural Resource Inventory in Middle Nine Mile Canyon* (Ogden, UT: Colorado Plateau Archaeological Alliance, 2011), 64.

32. National Park Service, "Journey Through Time" (no date), http://www.nature.nps.gov/views/sites/para/HTML/ET_04_Journey.htm. See also National Park Service, "The Mormon Militia and Pipe Springs" (no date), http://www.nps.gov/pisp/photosmultimedia/the-mormon-militia-and-pipe-springs.htm.

33. Ibid.

34. Pearl Baker, *The Wild Bunch at Robbers Roost* (1971; repr., Lincoln: University of Nebraska Press, 1989), 67.

35. U.S. Census, 1860; Census Place: Great Salt Lake City Ward 15, Salt Lake, Utah Territory ; Roll: M653_1313; Page: 217; Image: 223; Family History Library Film: 805313, Ancestry.com database.

36. Ancestry.com. *Texas Marriage Collection, 1814–1909 and 1966–2002* [database on-line]. Provo, UT: Ancestry.com Operations Inc., 2005.

37. Daughters of the Utah Pioneers, *Pioneer Women of Faith and Fortitude*, Vol. 4 (Salt Lake City: Daughters of the Utah Pioneers, 1998), 3349–50.

38. Ibid.

39. "Mormon Pioneer Overland Travel, 1847–1866," http://www.lds.org/churchhistory/library.

40. Daughters of the Utah Pioneers, *Pioneer Women*, 3349.

41. National Park Service, "Pipe Springs," http://www.nps.gov/pisp/planyourvisit/sevents.htm. The Arizona Strip is that portion of northern Arizona separated from the rest of the state by the Colorado River and the impassable Grand Canyon. Its culture and history are closely tied to the Mormon settlement of southern Utah.

42. National Park Service, "National Register of Historic Places Nomination, George Carter Whitmore Mansion" (1978).

43. James H. Beckstead, *Cowboying: A Tough Job in a Hard Land* (Salt Lake City: University of Utah Press, 1991), 56–57.

44. Daughters of the Utah Pioneers, *Pioneer Women*, 3350.

45. Ibid.

46. Ibid.

47. National Park Service, "Whitmore Mansion National Register."

48. Baker, *The Wild Bunch*, 50.

49. Beckstead, *Cowboying*, 57.

50. National Park Service, "Whitmore Mansion National Register."

51. Maude A. Bellows, "History of Hyrum Argyle Sr.," unpublished family history in the possession of Norma Dalton, dated February 21, 2013.

52. Steven L. Gerber and James M. Aton, "Empires and Homesteads: Making a Living in Range Creek," *Utah Historical Quarterly* 79, no. 1 (2011): 23–25.

53. Beckstead, *Cowboying*, 57.

54. Clarence Pilling, cited by Beckstead, *Cowboying*, 58.

55. Beckstead, *Cowboying*, 58.

56. Geary, *Forgotten Road*, 49.

57. Ibid., 47–48.

58. Ibid., 48.

59. Kretchman, *Gilsonite Story*, 37.
60. Some estimates place the amount of weight hauled on a single trip at nine tons on one extreme and three tons on the other. Geary's estimate, based on his grandfather's personal recollections, seems to be a fair middle ground. Some freighters would have operated double wagons, whereas others were small, single-wagon affairs that could have hauled only a fraction of the weight.
61. Inflation Calculator, http://www.davemanuel.com/inflation-calculator.php.
62. Geary, *Forgotten Road*, 49.
63. Kretchman, *Gilsonite Story*, 37.
64. Watt, *A History of Carbon County*, 34. The Gilson Manufacturing Company was established in 1888 and was purchased the following year by the Gilson Asphaltum Company. If Watt's sources are correct that it was indeed 1887, it would discredit the popular account of how the latter company got its name (that Gilson in 1889 paid one dollar if they would keep his name on the new company). It would also lend credence to the suspicions discussed in chapter 4 that Gilsonite ores were being shipped as early as 1887, or a year before the carbon veins had been removed from the reservation, and that Sam Gilson and Bert Seaboldt were acting as front men for the Gilson Asphaltum Company.
65. Weicks, "Frontier Soldiering," 17.
66. Cited in ibid., 9.
67. Watt, *A History of Carbon County*, 26.
68. Ibid., 32.
69. Ibid., 31.
70. Arthur E. Gibson, cited in Geary, *Forgotten Road*, 49.
71. Prostitution was a thriving and openly practiced enterprise throughout Utah, especially in Price, at this time and it would have been unusual if it had not extended to the rough-and-tumble culture of freighting along the Nine Mile Road.
72. "Brock, Who Killed Foote to Trial at Provo for Manslaughter on Account of It," *Salt Lake Tribune*, September 24, 1890.
73. Weicks, "Frontier Soldiering," 14.
74. "Cattle Stealing," *Daily Enquirer*, November 15, 1887.
75. Ibid.

76. Ibid. The newspaper account lists testimony of William Turner, followed immediately by the testimony of Sheriff J. W. Turner. It is not known if this was the same individual or different persons with nearly identical names.
77. Ibid.
78. Weicks, "Frontier Soldiering," 14.
79. Geary, *Forgotten Road*, 46.
80. Bureau of Land Management, Desert Land Act, http://www.blm.gov/ut/st/en/res/utah_public_room/desert_land_entries.html.
81. Miller, "New Settlement Patterns," 5.
82. Geary, *Forgotten Road*, 51.
83. "Frank Foote Killed by a Saloon Keeper in Emery County," *The Daily Enquirer*, November 12, 1889.
84. Fort Duchesne General Orders, July 5, 1887, cited in Weicks, "Frontier Soldiering," 13.
85. P. J. Bolton, *Salt Lake Tribune*, January 30, 1888.
86. Dianne Brock, email communication, March 6, 2014.
87. "The Foote Tragedy, Brock Examined Before Commissioner Hills," *Daily Enquirer*, November 22, 1889.
88. The Alger name is well entrenched in the history of Nine Mile Canyon, but this particular John Alger is unknown to descendants. Rather, the Nine Mile region was home to Frank Alger and his brothers Alonzo (Lon) and Gerrett (Gett), all of whom came to this country by way of St. George, Orangeville, and Sunnyside. Their father was named John, but there is no family record that the father was ever in Nine Mile Canyon or anywhere else in eastern Utah, and the father was estranged from his sons. See Dalton, "Nine Mile Canyon Builders," 19–21.
89. "The Foote Tragedy," *Daily Enquirer*.
90. Ibid.
91. Ibid.
92. Ibid.
93. "Foote's Murder," *Ogden Standard Examiner*, November 20, 1889.
94. "Frank Foote Killed," *Daily Enquirer*.
95. "The Foote Tragedy," *Daily Enquirer*.
96. William Brock, quoted in "The Foote Murder, Brock Brought to Provo and Landed in Jail," *Daily Enquirer*, November 19, 1889.

97. "Brock, Who Killed Foote, A Trial at Provo for Manslaughter on Account of It," *Salt Lake Tribune*, September 24, 1890. "Brock Murder Case: The Regular Panel of Jurors Is Exhausted," *Daily Enquirer*, September 23, 1890.

98. "Brock Not Guilty," *Salt Lake Herald*, September 25, 1890. "Brock Not Guilty of Manslaughter—So Says the Jury in the Case," *Daily Enquirer*, September 26, 1890.

99. "The Foote Murder," *Daily Enquirer*.

100. Telephone interview with Diane Brock by Jerry D. Spangler, January 23, 2012.

101. Ibid.

102. Untitled, *Daily Enquirer*, April 12, 1897.

103. Baker, *The Wild Bunch*, 216.

104. Aton, *The River Knows Everything*, 106.

105. "Journey to Ashley," *Deseret News*, May 17, 1890. See also Weicks, "Frontier Soldiering," 16.

106. It retained the name Brock or Brock's Place after he sold out to Pete Francis because that was the name of the post office there. The place name Brock appears on Utah maps throughout the 1890s.

107. "The Experience of an Officer in a Wild Country," *Daily Inquirer*, July 1, 1897.

108. Ibid.

109. Ibid.

110. "Dave Russell Shoots and Kills Peter Francis," *Eastern Utah Advocate*, October 10, 1901.

111. Geary, *Forgotten Road*, 51.

112. "Famous Utah Outlaw Dead," *Salt Lake Herald*, October 26, 1901.

113. "Pete Francis Killed, Shot Twice by Dave Russell at Brock's Road House," *Vernal Express*, October 12, 1901.

114. "Dave Russell Shoots," *Eastern Utah Advocate*.

115. "Two Bullets in the Forehead," *Deseret News*, October 8, 1901.

116. "Dave Russell Shoots," *Eastern Utah Advocate*. Hank Stewart was not mentioned as a witness. The George Stewart mentioned in the newspaper accounts was Hank's brother and business partner in various mining and ferry ventures.

117. "Dave Russell Held for the Murder of Pete Francis," *Deseret News*, October 16, 1901.

118. "District Court in February," *Deseret News*, January 15, 1902.

119. "Russell Not Guilty," *Eastern Utah Advocate*, February 20, 1902.

120. Norma Dalton, email correspondence with Jerry D. Spangler, December 3, 2012.

121. "Dave Russell Shoots," *Eastern Utah Advocate*.

122. "Francis' Remains Brought to Price," *Salt Lake Herald*, October 10, 1901.

123. "Orangeville," *Emery County Progress*, November 16, 1901.

124. Dillman, *Early History of Duchesne County*, 258.

125. Geary, *Forgotten Road*, 52.

126. Spangler, *Owls and Cranes*, 29.

127. It is uncertain what constituted legal and illegal sales of alcohol. There are references at that time to illegal "whiskey ranches" that sold bootleg liquor. But saloons seemed to operate with impunity, and they were more than prevalent throughout the region, at both ends of the Nine Mile Road and in between.

128. "Post Office Changes," *Deseret News*, January 24, 1900. Erma Armstrong indicates that Pete Francis lost the post office contract in 1899 after growing suspicion that Francis had been part of C. L. "Gunplay" Maxwell's gang since 1896, and that he used the position to provide information on payroll shipments to the robbers. Erma Armstrong, "Aunt Ada and the Outlaws," *Outlaw Trail Journal* (Winter 1997): 14–15.

129. Geary, *Forgotten Road*, 53.

Chapter 6

1. Pearl Baker, *The Wild Bunch at Robbers Roost* (1971; repr., Lincoln: University of Nebraska Press, 1989). Charles Kelly, *The Outlaw Trail: A History of Butch Cassidy and His Wild Bunch* (1938; repr., Lincoln: University of Nebraska Press, 1996). Richard Patterson, *Butch Cassidy: A Biography* (Lincoln: University of Nebraska Press, 1998).

2. Patterson, *Butch Cassidy*, 106. "Bold Outlaws Get $7,000 in Gold," *Eastern Utah Advocate*, April 22, 1897.

3. Kelly, *The Outlaw Trail*, 139.

4. "Famous Utah Outlaw Dead," *Salt Lake Herald*, October 26, 1901.

5. Historian Edward Geary recalled an interview with Howard Price Jr., the son-in-law of Preston Nutter, who said the old-timers told stories of

herds of horses being driven through the canyon in the dead of night, presumably by outlaws.

6. Kelly, *Outlaw Trail*, 6.

7. Ibid., 146.

8. Patterson, *Butch Cassidy*, 71–78.

9. Bill Betenson, "Bub Meeks: The Unfortunate Outlaw," *Outlaw Trail Journal* (Summer 2003): 2.

10. Matt Warner, *The Last of the Bandit Riders . . . Revisited* (Salt Lake City: Big Moon Traders, 2000), 43.

11. Baker, *The Wild Bunch*, 66–67.

12. James is sometimes referred to in historical accounts as Tobe or Tobey.

13. Kelly, *Outlaw Trail*, 171.

14. Baker, *The Wild Bunch*, 71.

15. Ibid., 67.

16. Kelly, *Outlaw Trail*, 172.

17. Baker, *The Wild Bunch*, 72–73.

18. Patterson, *Butch Cassidy*, 105. Baker, *The Wild Bunch*, 76.

19. Patterson, *Butch Cassidy*, 139. Kelly, *Outlaw Trail*, 177.

20. Baker, *The Wild Bunch*, 77.

21. Joel Frandsen, "The Posse Shootout—The Slaying of Jack Watson," *Outlaw Trail Journal* (Winter 2000): 13–15.

22. Kelly, *Outlaw Trail*, 176.

23. Baker, *The Wild Bunch*, 80–81.

24. Kelly, *Outlaw Trail*, 178.

25. Lula Parker Betenson, cited in Patterson, *Butch Cassidy*, 139.

26. Telephone interview with Dianne Brock, March 4, 2014.

27. Patterson, *Butch Cassidy*, 140.

28. Armstrong, "Aunt Ada," 13.

29. Ibid., 23.

30. Ibid., 14. "Gunplay Maxwell is Dead," *Davis County Clipper*, August 27, 1909. Erma Armstrong indicates his name in prison was William Johnson, but this name does not appear anywhere else and Wyoming Archives lists his prison name as Richard Carr.

31. Patterson, *Butch Cassidy*, 74. Erma Armstrong indicates his father's name was Alphonso Bliss of Eddyville, Middleboro, Massachusetts. See "Aunt Ada," 17.

32. "Gun-Play Maxwell is Demonstrative," *Inter Mountain Republican*, February 26, 1908.

33. "Gunplay Man Under Arrest," *Salt Lake Herald*, June 17, 1908.

34. Kelly, *Outlaw Trail*, 184.

35. "Lone Women Weep at Bad Man's Bier," *Salt Lake Telegram*, August 25, 1909.

36. Patterson, *Butch Cassidy*, 74.

37. "Why Gunplay Maxwell Was Finally Betrayed," *Deseret News*, August 27, 1909.

38. "New Stories About Maxwell," *Salt Lake Herald*, August 30, 1909. "When He Was in the Butcher Business," *Carbon County News*, September 3, 1909.

39. C. L. Maxwell application to the Board of Pardons for commutation of sentence, August 18, 1902, Utah State Archives, http://images. archives.utah.gov/cdm/compoundobject/ collection/328/id/56339/rec/1.

40. "Lone Women Weep," *Salt Lake Telegram*.

41. Kelly, *Outlaw Trail*, 180.

42. Armstrong, "Aunt Ada," 15.

43. A year later, when Gunplay Maxwell was jailed in Provo for the botched robbery of a Springville Bank, Ren Wilkins was the lawman who thwarted an escape attempt wherein Gunplay had constructed a facsimile of a pistol. See Ellen S. Kiever, "Rejected by Many: Gunplay Maxwell," *Outlaw Trail Journal* (Winter 2011): 10.

44. "The Experience of an Officer in a Wild Country," *Daily Inquirer*, July 1, 1897.

45. Armstrong, "Aunt Ada," 15.

46. Local legend has it there were numerous attempts to rob military payrolls as they passed through Gate Canyon. One account, related in the minutes of the Nine Mile Canyon Settlers Association meetings, credits Gett Alger with foiling a robbery attempt when he was driving the stage to Myton. Another account, related by descendants of the Lee Lisonbee family, claims Lee was driving the stage when it was held up by the Wild Bunch. Lee's wife, a passenger, hid the payroll under her baby's soiled diapers, and the loot and passengers all made it safely to Fort Duchesne.

47. A. E. L. Carpenter, cited in Armstrong, "Aunt Ada," 15–16. Kiever, "Rejected by Many," 4–5.

48. Coleman, "The Buffalo Soldiers," 431.

49. Commission Minutes, cited by Baker, *The Wild Bunch*, 49. Historian Joel Frandsen indicated that Donant made the request of the commission to hire Maxwell on April 4 and again on April 16, and was denied on both occasions. Donant wasn't fired from his job until June or July, which would explain why he was still sheriff at the time of Butch Cassidy's holdup of the Pleasant Valley payroll in late April.

50. Ibid.

51. Patterson, *Butch Cassidy*, 105.

52. Baker, *The Wild Bunch*, 50.

53. Kelly, *Outlaw Trail*, 137.

54. Patterson, *Butch Cassidy*, 104.

55. Kelly, *Outlaw Trail*, 151. Jack Cottrell later became a deputy sheriff in Emery County. It was common in that day for outlaws to switch sides. The most famous outlaw-turned-lawman in eastern Utah was Matt Warner, long-time friend of Butch Cassidy.

56. Ibid., 180.

57. "New Stories About Maxwell," *Salt Lake Herald*. "Butcher Business," *Carbon County News*.

58. Lamont Johnson, cited in Armstrong, "Aunt Ada," 18.

59. "Gunplay Maxwell," unpublished and undated manuscript on file with the Utah State Historical Society.

60. Kelly, *Outlaw Trail*, 180–81.

61. Baker, *The Wild Bunch*, 46–47.

62. Kelly, *Outlaw Trail*, 181–82.

63. Baker and Kelly both give the name of the accomplice as Porter, although Maxwell refused to identify who the dead man was. Years later, it was reported in the *Carbon County News* in September 1909 that the man was Billy Pearson, a Maxwell accomplice from his cattle rustling days in Thermopolis, Wyoming (see "Butcher Business"). In 1902, Maxwell applied for commutation of his sentence. He listed his accomplice's name as William Carter. The dead man was carrying guns etched with the name Pete Nelson, a Robbers Roost outlaw also known as Pete Logan, but Logan lived well beyond this incident and it certainly wasn't him.

64. Kelly, *Outlaw Trail*, 182. Historian Joel Frandsen said the outlaw with the relay horses was Pete Logan, who was waiting for Maxwell in Provo

Canyon. It seems he had not been told that the original plan to rob a bank in Provo had been changed to a bank in Springville. Logan later married Maxwell's widow, Ada Slaugh, under his real name, Pete Nelson.

65. Armstrong, "Aunt Ada," 19. There is some question whether Ada and C. L. Maxwell were ever legally married.

66. "Gunplay Maxwell Is Dead," *Carbon County News*, August 27, 1909.

67. Kiever, "Rejected by Many," 9.

68. Lamont Johnson and Joel Frandsen, "Edward B. Johnstone: The Man who Killed C. L. 'Gunplay' Maxwell," *Outlaw Trail Journal* (Winter 2011): 23.

69. "Bandit's Life in Prison," *Salt Lake Herald*, August 28, 1909.

70. "Gunplay Maxwell Is Dead," *Davis County Clipper*, August 27, 1909.

71. Armstrong, "Aunt Ada," 19.

72. "Gunplay Maxwell Badly Wounded," *Deseret News*, September 23, 1907. "Famous Bad Man Refuses to Talk," *Salt Lake Herald*, September 26, 1907.

73. "Famous Bad Man," *Salt Lake Herald*.

74. "Dime Novel Hero Attracts Crowds," *Inter Mountain Republican*, September 28, 1907.

75. "Famous Bad Man," *Salt Lake Herald*.

76. Ibid.

77. "New Role for Maxwell," *Deseret News*, February 17, 1908.

78. "Maxwell Is Demonstrative," *Inter Mountain Republican*. "Sues Republican for $50,000," *Inter Mountain Republican*, March 11, 1908.

79. "Maxwell Is Demonstrative," *Intermountain Republican*.

80. "Finally Betrayed," *Deseret News*. Richard Shaw, "Gunplay Maxwell draws his gun—and his last breath," *Sun Advocate*, November 29, 2012. Some newspaper accounts indicate Johnstone was at times a deputy sheriff, while others refer to him as a special officer who worked for the mining companies. A biographical sketch indicates he had been a deputy U.S. marshal since 1901, at age sixteen, and that he was called in to handle difficult cases. He certainly had history with Maxwell. He investigated Gunplay Maxwell for a stage robbery in Goldfield, Nevada, in

1907. See Johnson and Frandsen, "Edward B. Johnstone," 22–23.

81. Johnson and Frandsen, "Edward B. Johnstone," 26.

82. Ibid., 27.

83. "Maxwell Killing Justifiable," *Inter Mountain Republican*, August 25, 1909.

84. Kiever, "Rejected by Many," 18.

85. Ibid.

86. "Banker Wants Revolver," *Inter Mountain Republican*, August 31, 1909.

87. Johnson and Frandsen, "Edward B. Johnstone," 22.

88. "Lone Women Weep," *Salt Lake Telegram*.

89. Ibid.

90. Johnson and Frandsen, "Edward B. Johnstone," 31.

91. Ibid., 35.

92. Interview with Joel Frandsen, February 27, 2014.

93. Joel Frandsen, draft copy of "The Noted C. L. 'Gunplay' Maxwell and His Burial," provided to the authors on March 13, 2014.

94. Norma R. Dalton, "The Outlaw Cabin Below Flat Iron Mountain," *Outlaw Trail Journal* (Summer 2011): 24.

95. Norma R. Dalton, "Mystery of the Cowboy Bench Rock House," *Outlaw Trail Journal* (Summer 2011): 32.

96. "Minutes of the Nine Mile Canyon Settlers Association Board Meeting" (September 27, 2008), 2.

97. Virginia N. Price and John T. Darby, "Preston Nutter: Utah Cattleman, 1886–1936," *Utah Historical Quarterly* 32, no. 3 (1964): 241.

98. Interview with George Fasselin, August 13, 2011.

99. Price and Darby, "Preston Nutter," 241.

100. Patterson, *Butch Cassidy*, 141–43.

101. Baker, *The Wild Bunch*, 96. Historian Joel Frandsen believed Pearl Baker was wrong in her identification of George Curry as the man involved in the cow theft. He found Wayne County court records that indicate the person involved was actually Pete Logan, also known as Pete Nelson, who worked for Nutter in the early 1900s (see chapter 7).

Chapter 7

1. "Masonic Funeral Scheduled for Last Great Cattle King," *Salt Lake Telegram*, January 28, 1936.

2. Beckstead, *Cowboying*, 58.

3. Ibid.

4. Roy Webb, *Register of the Records of the Preston Nutter Corporation (1876–1981)*, Manuscript Collection, Special Collections, University of Utah Library (1987), 11.

5. Preston Nutter's journals reveal little about his thoughts or impressions of the cowboy life. Rather they are mostly daily comments about business transactions, individuals encountered, expenses, and catalogs.

6. Webb, *Register of the Records*, 11.

7. Janet Taylor, "A Tough Cattleman in a Tough Land: Preston Nutter," *The Outlaw Trail Journal* (Summer 2001): 37.

8. Webb, *Register of the Records*, 11.

9. Price and Darby, "Preston Nutter," 234.

10. Ibid.

11. Webb, *Register of the Records*, 11.

12. Packer was born "Alfred" Packer in Pennsylvania in 1842, but by the time he enlisted in the U.S. Army during the Civil War he had become known as "Alferd" Packer.

13. Price and Darby, "Preston Nutter," 235.

14. Ann Oldham, *Alferd G. Packer, Soldier Prospector and Cannibal* (Pagosa Springs, CO: self-published, 2005), 41.

15. The harrowing experiences of this party have been largely forgotten and remain untold due to the aftermath and notoriety of the Alferd Packer incident.

16. The student cafeteria at the University of Colorado is named after Alferd Packer.

17. Price and Darby, "Preston Nutter," 235.

18. Oldham, *Alferd G. Packer*, 41–45.

19. Ibid.

20. Ibid.

21. Ibid., 133. The legends that have grown up around the Alferd Packer story have resulted in a sizeable contingent of folks, including many historical scholars, who believe Alferd was innocent of killing his five companions, and had he been tried anywhere else but in Lake City, Colorado, he would have been acquitted. Rather he was a victim of sensationalist media attention,

witnesses who held back important facts, and a judicial system determined to make an example of the "man eater." If he was indeed innocent, then Preston Nutter helped put him in prison.

22. Price and Darby, "Preston Nutter," 235.
23. Webb, *Register of the Records*, 12.
24. Ibid.
25. Ibid.
26. Price and Darby, "Preston Nutter," 236.
27. Beckstead indicates Nutter traveled the Mormon settlements in Utah buying up cattle from poor farmers, probably at bargain prices. Cash was a rare commodity in rural Utah, which was primarily a barter economy at that time, often through LDS Church cooperatives. Accounts vary as to what cattle prices were in the 1880s, but the prices seem to have ranged from about $2.50 to $12.50 per head.
28. Price and Darby, "Preston Nutter," 236. Webb, *Register of the Records*, 12; Beckstead, *Cowboying*, 59.
29. The so-called Meeker War involving the White River Utes provided a convenient excuse for government officials to also dispossess the Uncompahgre Utes, whose reservation included Colorado lands coveted by homesteaders at that time. The Uncompahgre Utes resented their forced removal to the Uinta Basin, and bad blood between them and their White River Ute cousins persisted for years.
30. Price and Darby, "Preston Nutter," 236.
31. Ibid.
32. "District Court Judgments," *Salt Lake Tribune*, July 15, 1894.
33. Price and Darby, "Preston Nutter," 238.
34. Webb, *Register of the Records*, 12; Taylor, "A Tough Cattleman," 39.
35. Taylor, "A Tough Cattleman," 39. Beckstead, *Cowboying*, 59–60.
36. Beckstead, *Cowboying*, 59–60.
37. Preston Nutter Journal (1886–87), the Preston Nutter Corporation Collection, Special Collections, Marriott Library, University of Utah. It should be noted that this journal is incorrectly located in a file labeled as 1949.
38. Ibid.
39. Price and Darby, "Preston Nutter," 241.
40. Betensen, "Bub Meeks," 2.

41. Baker, *The Wild Bunch*, 96.
42. "Last Great Cattle King," *Salt Lake Telegram*.
43. Lee Sage, *The Last Rustler: The Autobiography of Lee Sage* (New York: Little, Brown and Company, 1930).
44. "After Cattle Thieves," *American Eagle*, September 4, 1897.
45. "John A. 'Jack' Watson—Soldier, Blacksmith, Texas Ranger, Outlaw, Lawman, Private Investigator and Friend to Cyrus 'Doc' Shores—A Man to Cross Rivers With," http://freepages.genealogy.rootsweb.ancestry.com/~hookersbend/bio_john_a_watson.htm.
46. Doc Shores is a notable historical character in his own right. He worked from time to time for the Pinkerton Detective Agency, including one stint where his partner was famed assassin Tom Horn. In 1904 Shores was in charge of Utah Fuel Company's team of "special deputies" assigned to protect the company during a violent coal strike. One of his deputies was C. L. "Gunplay" Maxwell (see chapter 6). He later became chief of police in Salt Lake City.
47. "A Man to Cross Rivers With," 2. "Jack Watson Killed," *Salt Lake Tribune*, July 24, 1898. "From Monday's Daily July 25," *Deseret News*, July 30, 1898.
48. Frandsen, "Posse Shootout," 24–26.
49. "A Man to Cross Rivers With," 3.
50. Frandsen, "Posse Shootout," 26.
51. Ibid.
52. Ibid., 19–20.
53. Joel Frandsen, "In Search of Lee Sage, Pete Logan's Son," *Outlaw Trail Journal* (Winter 2008): 36–55.
54. Ibid., 47.
55. Ibid., 48.
56. "Last Great Cattle King," *Salt Lake Telegram*. Even though the LDS Church had renounced polygamy in 1890, church assets had been seized by the federal government as part of its campaign against polygamy. But the church had remained owner of the largest cattle operation in southern Utah and northern Arizona throughout the 1880s, using unindicted surrogates, like Ivins. Today, the LDS Church owns one of the nation's largest cattle operations, the Deseret Land and Livestock Company, which was started in 1891.

57. Price and Darby, "Preston Nutter," 244.

58. Jerry D. Spangler, *Vermillion Dreamers and Sagebrush Schemers: An Overview of Human Occupation in the House Rock Valley and Eastern Arizona Strip* (Ogden, UT: Colorado Plateau Archaeological Alliance, 2007). Nutter always had cordial business relations with the Mormon Church, although not always with individual Mormon ranchers.

59. Price and Darby, "Preston Nutter," 244.

60. Preston Nutter, Letter from Preston Nutter to J. N. Darling, on file with the Utah State Historical Society.

61. Juanita Brooks, "The Arizona Strip," *The Pacific Spectator* 3 (1949): 297.

62. The Arizona Strip Oral History Project (98-012), Dixie Pioneers (1998), 9. Oral histories are on file with the Utah Historical Society.

63. Price and Darby, "Preston Nutter," 244.

64. Webb, *Register of the Records*, 12.

65. "Reservation Cattle," *Salt Lake Tribune*, August 7, 1894.

66. Price and Darby, "Preston Nutter," 243.

67. "Grand Jury Report," *Daily Enquirer*, October 17, 1893.

68. Price and Darby, "Preston Nutter," 245.

69. "Flockmasters Get Uintah Lands," *Salt Lake Herald*, March 15, 1900. Local lore has it that Nutter's original Strawberry Valley deal was exploitive of the Utes, who came to resent him for it. The disparity between what Nutter paid for the leases in 1893 and what they sold for in 1900 hints that Nutter's original lease was greatly undervalued. No historical record was found to suggest the original lease was rigged in Nutter's favor, nor were there any accusations at the time that Nutter acquired it through nefarious means. It is just as likely the favorable terms resulted from his long-standing friendship with Chipeta and other Ute leaders.

70. Price and Darby, "Preston Nutter," 246.

71. The Pete Francis establishment was commonly referred to as Brock's Place even after Francis ran the joint. This was probably due to the fact the post office had been named after Brock. It was not until the post office was moved to Edwin Lee's place in the late 1890s that the name of the post office was then changed to Harper.

72. Gerber and Aton, "Empires and Homesteads," 31.

73. Beckstead, *Cowboying*, 61.

74. Price and Darby, "Preston Nutter," 246.

75. "Ninemile Scenery Rivals the Famous Bryce Canyon," *Duchesne County Newspapers*, June 15, 1923. The account is certainly an exaggeration on one point. The seventy-five-mile gorge Nutter referred to is clearly Desolation Canyon, but there are several side canyons to Desolation, such as Rock Creek, Steer Ridge and Flat Canyon, where horse and rider can make it out of the gorge on cow trails that Nutter's hands knew very well. Those trails are still used by cowboys today.

76. "Last of the West's Cattle Queens Dies Saturday," *Vernal Express*, July 22, 1965. Price and Darby, "Preston Nutter," 247. Taylor, "A Tough Cattleman," 41. The cabin built by Katherine Fenton has since been moved to the Nutter Ranch in Nine Mile Canyon, where the current owner, Hunt Oil of Dallas, Texas, has stabilized it.

77. "Preston Nutter Weds Miss Fenton," *Eastern Utah Advocate*, December 17, 1908.

78. "Preston Nutter Ranch at Nine Mile Burns," *Vernal Express*, June 30, 1955.

79. Year: 1910; Census Place: Salt Lake City Ward 5, Salt Lake, Utah; Roll: T624_1607; Page: 16B; Enumeration District: 0141; FHL microfilm: 1375620, Ancestry.com database.

80. Year: 1920; Census Place: Harper, Duchesne, Utah; Roll: T625_1862; Page: 1A; Enumeration District: 173; Image: 506. Year: 1930; Census Place: Harper, Duchesne, Utah; Roll: 2415; Page: 1A; Enumeration District: 40; Image: 1118.0; FHL microfilm: 2342149. Ancestry.com database.

81. Ed. F. Harmston, "Diary and Report of Ed. F. Harmston, Engineer, on Feasibility of Line for Railroad from Green River on Denver & Rio Grande R.R. to Roosevelt in Uintah Basin, State of Utah" (Unpublished manuscript, copy in the possession of James M. Aton, Cedar City, Utah), 2.

82. Jerry D. Spangler, "Site Distribution and Settlement Patterns in Lower Nine Mile Canyon: The Brigham Young University Surveys

of 1989–91" (master's thesis, Brigham Young University, 1993).

83. "Nutter Buys Another Bunch of Steers," *Emery County Progress*, May 1, 1909.

84. "Local and Personal," *Carbon County News*, September 10, 1909.

85. "Wellington Notes," *Carbon County News*, January 28, 1910.

86. "Preston Nutter," *Myton Free Press*, February 14, 1918.

87. "Death of Pioneer," *Carbon County News*, June 25, 1915. Price and Darby, "Preston Nutter," 247–48.

88. "Pioneer Cattleman of Greenriver Observes his 82nd Birth Date," *Times Independent*, March 9, 1950. Gerber and Aton indicate Milton managed the Range Creek component of the Nutter operation.

89. Preston Nutter Diary (1919). Preston Nutter Collection. This could be the same Billy McGuire who was working for the Whitmore brothers when he was beaten by outlaw Joe Walker (see chapter 6).

90. Beckstead, *Cowboying*, 61.

91. Preston Nutter Diary, September 10, 1918.

92. Price and Darby, "Preston Nutter," 247.

93. Preston Nutter Diary, September 30, 1919.

94. "District Court," *Duchesne County Newspapers*, September 7, 1923.

95. "Salt Lake Wants Livestock Meeting," *Salt Lake Telegram*, January 11, 1926.

96. "Delinquent Tax List," *Carbon County News*, December 2, 1910.

97. "New Trial Carbon County vs. Nutter," *Myton Free Press*, March 24, 1921.

98. "Big Cattle Owner," *Vernal Express*, February 7, 1913.

99. "Cattle Prices Enrich Nutter," *Myton Free Press*, November 30, 1916.

100. Price and Darby, "Preston Nutter," 245.

101. "Short Orders," *Salt Lake Tribune*, July 15, 1894. "District Court Orders," *Salt Lake Tribune*, September 25, 1894.

102. No attempt was made to identify all of the Preston Nutter court cases, but rather those that were mentioned in Utah newspapers of the day. It is quite possible that Nutter was very successful in court, but these cases were never reported in newspapers.

103. "Says He's Harassed," *Salt Lake Herald*, May 13, 1900.

104. "Nutter Wins Suit," *Duchesne County Newspapers*, March 19, 1926.

105. "Verdict Against Nutter," *Salt Lake Tribune*, April 9, 1885.

106. "Battle Over Water Is Ended," *Salt Lake Herald*, December 7, 1916. "Nutter Loses in Big Land Contest," *Myton Free Press*, December 14, 1916.

107. Gerber and Aton, "Empires and Homesteads," 34.

108. *John D. Niles v. Preston Nutter*, Preston Nutter Collection.

109. Gerber and Aton, "Empires and Homesteads," 34.

110. Ibid., 35.

111. Ibid., 36.

112. Aton, *The River Knows Everything*, 123.

113. Gerber and Aton, "Empires and Homesteads," 38. Preston Nutter Diary, entry for August 28, 1920.

114. Gerber and Aton, "Empires and Homesteads," 38.

115. "Slip One Over on the Cattle Man," *Myton Free Press*, February 15, 1917.

116. Gerber and Aton, "Empires and Homesteads," 39.

117. "Herd of Cattle Brings $200,000," *Salt Lake Telegram*, October 29, 1928.

118. Price and Darby, "Preston Nutter," 250.

119. Utah congressman Don Colton was a major architect of the Taylor Grazing Act. Colton was a former resident of Vernal, and Nutter was probably well acquainted with him.

120. "Preston Nutter Suffers Broken Hip," *Duchesne County Newspapers*, August 26, 1927.

121. Howard Price Jr. was the son of the former commander of Fort Douglas, and himself a career soldier. Local residents recall with some disdain that he always insisted on being addressed as "Colonel." Preston's heirs, his granddaughters, received nothing from the estate.

122. Webb, *Register of the Records*, 16. The Nutter holdings were later acquired by Hunt Oil of Dallas, Texas, which has restored the name "Preston Nutter Ranch" to all of its holdings in

the Nine Mile area and on the West Tavaputs Plateau. Hunt Oil manages the Nutter lands for wildlife conservation and limited livestock grazing. The Range Creek holdings are now owned by the state of Utah, held in trust for the University of Utah as a scientific research station.

Chapter 8

1. Weicks, "Frontier Soldiering," 13–21.
2. Weicks, "Fort Duchesne Twilight Years," 26–30.
3. Schindler, "Frederick Benteen and Fort Damn Shame."
4. Untitled, *Eastern Utah Advocate*, May 14, 1891.
5. Bert Jenson, "Smith Wells, Stagecoach Inn on the Nine Mile Canyon Road," *Utah Historical Quarterly* 61, no. 2 (1993): 185.
6. A "water witch" is an individual who claims to be able to find underground water through use of a divining rod—a Y-shaped stick made of willow, peach, or witch hazel that will point to the water source when held by the diviner. Water witches are sometimes referred to as "dowsers." The practice has been around for hundreds of years, and was brought to the United States by English and German immigrants. There is no scientific evidence that water witching works, and scientists point out that "success stories" are suspect because water is found just below the earth's surface almost everywhere, and it would not be surprising to find it with or without the witch. But the Smith Wells case appears to be an exception because the water was found at 180 feet below the surface. See http://ga.water.usgs.gov/edu/dowsing.
7. Jenson, "Smith Wells," 185.
8. Dogs could drink for free.
9. Jenson, "Smith Wells," 186–88.
10. Ibid., 189.
11. Weicks, "Twilight Years," 26–27.
12. Watt, *A History of Carbon County*, 32.
13. Ibid.
14. Bender, *Uintah Railway*, 23–24.
15. Ibid., 56.
16. Weicks, "Twilight Years," 29.
17. Bender, *Uintah Railway*, 56.
18. Ibid., 57.
19. Ibid., 59.

20. "Uinta Not What Was Represented," *Deseret News* (September 25, 1861).
21. Daughters of the Utah Pioneers, *Builders of Uintah: A Centennial History of Uintah County, 1872 to 1947* (Springville, UT: Art City Publishing, 1947), 15–16.
22. "The Indians' Lands Are Wanted," *Deseret News*, May 9, 1888. The flattering accounts of a balmy climate must have evoked guffaws from the soldiers and settlers living in the Uinta Basin, where winter temperatures frequently drop to minus 30 degrees Fahrenheit.
23. Ibid.
24. Abraham O. Woodruff, cited in Craig Woods Fuller, "Land Rush in Zion: Opening of the Uncompahgre and Uintah Indian Reservation" (PhD dissertation, Brigham Young University, Provo, 1990): 138–39.
25. Fuller, "Land Rush," 226.
26. Ibid., 215–16.
27. William B. Smart, *Mormonism's Last Colonizer: The Life and Times of William H. Smart* (Logan: Utah State University Press, 2008). The Mormon Church must have been at least moderately successful in its efforts to stack the lottery with faithful members and to buy up homestead claims from non-Mormons. The early "centennial" histories of Duchesne County and Uintah County, published in 1948 and 1947, respectively, contain numerous interviews with many first arrivals, the vast majority of whom were Mormon. The histories of the local Mormon wards and the first Mormon leaders of the communities figure quite prominently, whereas non-Mormons are given only passing references. Of course, this could be biased by those who wrote the histories. Most Uinta Basin communities today are predominantly Mormon.
28. John D. Barton, "The Dawes Act and the Northern Utes," *Outlaw Trail Journal* (Summer 2011): 34. One of the greatest cultural disconnects in American history has been the issue of land ownership. Euro-Americans have a long history of laws that define individual land ownership through titles, deeds, and patents. Many, if not most, Native American groups view land in terms of collective ownership or rights of use,

and individual ownership of land was a concept largely foreign to them.

29. Ibid., 35.
30. Ibid.
31. Weicks, "Twilight Years," 28.
32. Ibid., 30.
33. Fuller, "Land Rush," 211–49.
34. Ibid., 243–45. Barton, *A History of Duchesne County*, 113–14.
35. The Uinta Basin land rush was the last of its kind in the West, and it was seen by many as a "last chance" to acquire government land at minimal cost. Few had any experience with desert farming and most were undercapitalized, and the failure rate would be expected to be high even without droughts.
36. George Stewart, cited by Barton, *Duchesne History*, 116.
37. Dillman, *Early History of Duchesne County*.
38. Watt, *Carbon County History*. Barton, *Duchesne History*.
39. Barton, *Duchesne History*, 113.
40. Ibid., 221.
41. Ibid., 280.
42. Ibid., 221.

Chapter 9

1. Miller, "New Settlement Patterns."
2. John Alton Peterson, *Utah's Black Hawk War* (Salt Lake City: University of Utah Press, 1999).
3. Ronald Watt indicates that Emery County was discovered by Warren Snow and his command of one hundred militiamen from the Sevier and Sanpete Valleys who traveled by way of Salina Canyon, and by Reddick Allred and his command of eighty militiamen who at the same time marched across the Wasatch Plateau, probably by way of Cottonwood and Huntington Creeks, probably in 1865 or 1866. They met up on the Price River, but there is no indication they ventured any farther to the northeast where they could have discovered Nine Mile Canyon. See Watt, *Carbon County History*, 20.
4. Utah State Archives and Records Service. *Utah Index to Indian War Service Affidavits, 1909–19* [database online]. Provo, UT: Ancestry.com Operations Inc., 2003.
5. Blanch Anderson Johnstun, "A Summary of George Carlos (Don) Johnstun." Photocopied manuscript in the possession of Norma Dalton (original source is unknown).
6. Mormon Pioneer Overland Travel Database. http://www.lds.org/churchhistory/library/pioneercompanysearchresults/1,15792,4017-1-392,00.html.
7. National Archives and Records Administration. *U.S., Civil War Pension Index: General Index to Pension Files, 1861–1934* [database online]. Provo, UT: Ancestry.com Operations Inc., 2000.
8. Utah State Historical Society, comp., *Utah Cemetery Inventory* [database online]. Provo, UT: Ancestry.com Operations Inc., 2000.
9. Miller, "New Settlement Patterns," 3.
10. There never was a branch of the Mormon Church or a dedicated church building in Nine Mile Canyon, and there were certainly different levels of adherence to the faith, given it was an area spatially detached from Mormon wards in Price or Vernal. There are multiple references in the local histories to families getting together for church functions and rites of passage among the children. There are just as many references to smoking, drinking, and gambling among the Mormon residents here. The latter vices were common regardless of religious affiliation.
11. Mormon Pioneer Overland Travel Database, online at http://history.lds.org/overlandtravels/pioneerDetail?lang=eng&pioneerId=43326.
12. Year: 1870; Census Place: Richmond, Cache, Utah Territory; Roll: M593_1610; Page: 174B; Image: 353; Family History Library Film: 553109. Year: 1880; Census Place: Franklin, Oneida, Idaho; Roll: 173; Family History Film: 1254173; Page: 293A; Enumeration District: 025; Image: 0606.
13. Dalton, "Nine Mile Canyon Builders," 1–4.
14. Miller, "New Settlement Patterns," 5–6.
15. Year: 1910; Census Place: Harper, Carbon, Utah; Roll: T624_1603; Page: 24A; Enumeration District: 0034; FHL microfilm: 1375616.
16. Year: 1920; Census Place: Harper, Duchesne, Utah; Roll: T625_1862; Page: 1A; Enumeration District: 173; Image: 506.
17. Johnstun, "George Carlos Johnstun," 35.
18. Brown, "History of Minnie & Maud," 2.

19. Dillman, *Early History of Duchesne County*, 256.

20. "Quarantine Regulations," *Deseret News*, February 27, 1903.

21. National Archives and Records Administration. *U.S., Civil War Pension Index: General Index to Pension Files, 1861–1934* [database online]. Provo, UT, USA: Ancestry.com Operations Inc., 2000. Ancestry.com. *U.S. Army, Register of Enlistments, 1798–1914* [database online]. Provo, UT, USA: Ancestry.com Operations Inc., 2007.

22. "Commissioners Appoint Election Judges," *Duchesne County Newspapers*, October 5, 1928.

23. Year: 1930; Census Place: Myton, Duchesne, Utah; Roll: 2415; Page: 2A; Enumeration District: 8; Image: 974.0; FHL microfilm: 2342149.

24. Ben Mead, "From Kiz to Nine Mile—from Nine Mile Canyon to White Rocks and Back Again," *Nine Mile Canyon Settlers Association* 1 (2005): 13–14.

25. Kent Wimmer, "Ralph Gibboney," *Nine Mile Canyon Settlers Association* 1 (2006): 32.

26. "The Nine Mile Canyon School," *Nine Mile Canyon Settlers Association Newsletter* (Fall and Winter 2010): 4. Kent Wimmer, "My School Days in Nine Mile Canyon," *Nine Mile Canyon Settlers Association Newsletter* (Fall and Winter 2010): 18.

27. Dillman, *Early History of Duchesne County*, 255.

28. Norma Dalton, email communication with the lead author, December 11, 2012.

29. Ibid.

30. Year: 1880; Census Place: Gooseberry Valley, Sevier, Utah; Roll: 1338; Family History Film: 1255338; Page: 487B; Enumeration District: 069.

31. Year: 1900; Census Place: Minnie Maude, Carbon, Utah; Roll: 1682; Page: 12A; Enumeration District: 0086; FHL microfilm: 1241682.

32. Year: 1910; Census Place: Myton, Wasatch, Utah; Roll: T624_1610; Page: 5A; Enumeration District: 0207; FHL microfilm: 1375623. Year: 1920; Census Place: Myton, Duchesne, Utah; Roll: T625_1862; Page: 8A; Enumeration District: 64; Image: 502. Year: 1930; Census Place: Myton, Duchesne, Utah; Roll: 2415; Page: 1B; Enumeration District: 8; Image: 973.0; FHL microfilm: 2342149.

33. Year: 1880; Census Place: Harrisburg, Washington, Utah; Roll: 1339; Family History Film: 1255339; Page: 388D; Enumeration District: 094. Year: 1900; Census Place: Minnie Maude, Carbon, Utah; Roll: 1682; Page: 11B; Enumeration District: 0086; FHL microfilm: 1241682.

34. Year: 1910; Census Place: Myton, Wasatch, Utah; Roll: T624_1610; Page: 3A; Enumeration District: 0207; ; FHL microfilm: 1375623. Year: 1920; Census Place: Antelope, Duchesne, Utah; Roll: T625_1862; Page: 6B; Enumeration District: 58; Image: 390.

35. Year: 1900; Census Place: Minnie Maude, Carbon, Utah; Roll: 1682; Page: 11B; Enumeration District: 0086; FHL microfilm: 1241682.

36. Dillman, *Early History of Duchesne County*, 255.

37. Dalton, email correspondence with Jerry D. Spangler, December 11, 2012. Norma Dalton is the niece of Thelma "Babe" Russell, a daughter of Harrison Russell.

38. Mormon Pioneer Overland Travel Database, http://www.lds.org/churchhistory/library/pioneercompanysearchresults/1,15792,4017-1-343,00.

39. Year: 1860; Census Place: Payson, Utah, Utah Territory; Roll: M653_1314; Page: 872; Image: 343; Family History Library Film: 805314.

40. Yates Publishing. *U.S. and International Marriage Records, 1560–1900* [database online]. Provo, UT: Ancestry.com Operations Inc., 2004.

41. Mormon Pioneer Overland Travel Database, http://www.lds.org/churchhistory/library/pioneerdetails/1,15791,4018-1-57299,00.

42. Year: 1860; Census Place: Spanish Fork, Utah, Utah Territory; Roll: M653_1314; Page: 971; Image: 443; Family History Library Film: 805314.

43. Year: 1880; Census Place: Gooseberry Valley, Sevier, Utah; Roll: 1338; Family History Film: 1255338; Page: 487B; Enumeration District: 069.

44. Year: 1900; Census Place: Minnie Maude, Carbon, Utah; Roll: 1682; Page: 11B; Enumeration District: 0086; FHL microfilm: 1241682.

45. Yates Publishing, *U.S. and International Marriage Records, 1560–1900* (online database).

46. Carbon County deed (Entry 5398), dated May 12, 1902, transferring water rights to Nine Mile Creek to the Minnie Maud Reservoir and Irrigation Company, photocopy reproduced in *Nine Mile Canyon Settlers Association* 1, no. 2 (2005): 6–7.

47. Year: 1920; Census Place: Harper, Carbon, Utah; Roll: T625_1862; Page: 23A; Enumeration District: 40; Image: 132.

48. Year: 1910; Census Place: Harper, Carbon, Utah; Roll: T624_1603; Page: 25A; Enumeration District: 0034; FHL microfilm: 1375616.

49. Year: 1930; Census Place: Harper, Carbon, Utah; Roll: 2415; Page: 1A; Enumeration District: 31; Image: 345.0; FHL microfilm: 2342149.

50. Brown, "History of Minnie & Maud," 2.

51. Minnie Hall, quoted in unnamed newspaper account from November 1970, cited by Brown, "History of Minnie and Maud," 4.

52. Utah State Historical Society, comp. *Utah Cemetery Inventory* [database online]. Provo, UT, USA: Ancestry.com Operations Inc., 2000.

53. General Land Office maps for Township 11 South, Ranges 14, 15, and 17 East and Township 12 South Ranges 13, 14, 15, 16, and 17 East Salt Lake Meridian, cited by Miller, "New Settlement Patterns," 6.

54. Not all areas of Nine Mile Canyon are well suited to farm and pasture lands. Rather, the best agricultural lands are those near the mouths of the numerous side canyons that enter on both the north and south sides of Nine Mile Canyon. Flooding from these side canyons deposited more nutrient-rich soils onto the Nine Mile Canyon floodplain. It would be expected that "prime" agricultural lands would be located at the mouths of these side canyons, and there would be fewer, if any, ranches in the narrower, less arable areas of the canyon. The same pattern appears to hold true for prehistoric farmers in the canyon, where evidence of prehistoric farming is much more prevalent at the mouths of the side canyons.

55. Mormon Pioneer Overland Travel Database, http://www.lds.org/churchhistory/library/pioneercompanysearchresults/1,15792,4017-1-163,00.

56. Year: 1880; Census Place: Greenwich, Piute, Utah; Roll: 1336; Family History Film: 1255336; Page: 544C; Enumeration District: 037.

57. Edmund West, comp. *Family Data Collection - Individual Records* [database online]. Provo, UT, USA: Ancestry.com Operations Inc., 2000.

58. Year: 1910; Census Place: Harper, Carbon, Utah; Roll: T624_1603; Page: 24A; Enumeration District: 0034; FHL microfilm: 1375616.

59. Year: 1920; Census Place: Harper, Duchesne, Utah; Roll: T625_1862; Page: 1A; Enumeration District: 173; Image: 506.

60. Ancestry.com. *Web: Utah, Find A Grave Index, 1850-2011* [database online]. Provo, UT, USA: Ancestry.com Operations, Inc., 2012.

61. Year: 1910; Census Place: Harper, Carbon, Utah; Roll: T624_1603; Page: 24A; Enumeration District: 0034; FHL microfilm: 1375616.

62. Norma Dalton, "Nine Mile Canyon Dwellers," *Nine Mile Canyon Settlers Association Newsletter* (Spring 2011): 1–2. Dalton, "Canyon Builders," 21–22.

63. http://www.lds.org/churchhistory/library/pioneercompanysearchresults/1,15792,4017-1-99,00.

64. *Passenger Lists of Vessels Arriving at New Orleans, Louisiana, 1820–1902*; Series: M259; Roll #: 37, LDS Family History Center.

65. Year: 1880; Census Place: Castledale, Emery, Utah; Roll: 1336; Family History Film: 1255336; Page: 325A; Enumeration District: 018.

66. Year: 1900; Census Place: Minnie Maude, Carbon, Utah; Roll: 1682; Page: 11B; Enumeration District: 0086; FHL microfilm: 1241682.

67. Craig Houskeeper, "Theodore Frelizing Houskeeper Homestead Cabin," *Nine Mile Canyon Settlers Association* 1 (2004).

68. Ibid.

69. Year: 1920; Census Place: Wellington, Carbon, Utah; Roll: T625_1862; Page: 31B; Enumeration District: 44; Image: 327. Family histories indicate Jane Alger split her time between the homes of her daughters, Clarissa Houskeeper and Luna Smith, and her bachelor son Frank.

70. Year: 1930; Census Place: Harper, Duchesne, Utah; Roll: 2415; Page: 1A; Enumeration District: 40; Image: 1118.0; FHL microfilm: 2342149.

71. Ancestry.com. *Web: Utah, Find A Grave Index, 1850-2011* [database online]. Provo, UT, USA: Ancestry.com Operations, Inc., 2012.

72. Spangler, *The Upper Fringe*, 84.

73. Dalton, "Canyon Builders," 20.

74. Ibid., 21.

75. Ibid., 22.

76. Ibid.

77. "Minutes of the NMCSA Board Meeting" (September 27, 2008): 2.

78. Ibid.

79. Dalton, "Mystery of the Cowboy Bench Rock House," 3–5.

80. Year: 1900; Census Place: Coyote Creek, Sweetwater, Wyoming; Roll: 1827; Page: 1B; Enumeration District: 0056; FHL microfilm: 1241827.

81. Year: 1900; Census Place: Election District 18, Carbon, Wyoming; Roll: 1826; Page: 5A; Enumeration District: 0018; FHL microfilm: 1241826.

82. Year: 1910; Census Place: Harper, Carbon, Utah; Roll: T624_1603; Page: 24A; Enumeration District: 0034; FHL microfilm: 1375616.

83. Year: 1920; Census Place: Lusk, Niobrara, Wyoming; Roll: T625_2028; Page: 16A; Enumeration District: 86; Image: 356. Ancestry.com. South Dakota Marriages, 1905-1949 [database online]. Provo, UT, USA: Ancestry.com Operations Inc., 2005.

84. Ancestry.com. U.S. City Directories, 1821-1989 (Beta) [database online]. Provo, UT, USA: Ancestry.com Operations, Inc., 2011. The database lists the year as 1907, but this is incorrect as they were not married until 1920. It was probably the year 1927.

85. Utah State Archives and Records Service; Salt Lake City, UT; Utah State Archives and Records Service; File Number #: 1949003648.

86. Year: 1920; Census Place: Hill Creek, Uintah, Utah; Roll: T625_1868; Page: 9A; Enumeration District: 130; Image: 48.

87. Utah State Archives and Records Service; Salt Lake City, UT; Utah State Archives and Records Service; File Number #: 1913001331.

88. Brown, "History of Minnie and Maud," 2.

89. Year: 1910; Census Place: Price, Carbon, Utah; Roll: T624_1603; Page: 1B; Enumeration District: 0238; FHL microfilm: 1375616.

90. Dillman, Early History of Duchesne County, 254–55.

91. Year: 1870; Census Place: Payson, Utah, Utah Territory; Roll: M593_1612; Page: 239B; Image: 475; Family History Library Film: 553111.

92. Watt, Carbon County History, 23.

93. Year: 1880; Census Place: Huntington, Emery, Utah; Roll: 1336; Family History Film: 1255336; Page: 323A; Enumeration District: 018.

94. Watt, Carbon County History, 47. See also: http://trees.ancestry.com/tree/491422/person/-2076105361/story/f92abc64-b0ca-4add-8f6f-f5908ad25e5d?src=search.

95. Watt, Carbon County History, 33.

96. Ibid., 34.

97. Utah State Historical Society, comp. Utah Cemetery Inventory [database online]. Provo, UT, USA: Ancestry.com Operations Inc., 2000.

98. Year: 1910; Census Place: Harper, Carbon, Utah; Roll: T624_1603; Page: 24A; Enumeration District: 0034; FHL microfilm: 1375616. Year: 1920; Census Place: Harper, Carbon, Utah; Roll: T625_1862; Page: 23A; Enumeration District: 40; Image: 132.

99. Year: 1910; Census Place: Harper, Carbon, Utah; Roll: T624_1603; Page: 24A; Enumeration District: 0034; FHL microfilm: 1375616.

100. Al Thompson had a reputation as a crotchety rancher but one who was respected and admired by other ranch families in the canyon. Local legend has it that his divorce from Martha Grames "was not his fault."

101. Year: 1940; Census Place: Altonah, Duchesne, Utah; Roll: T627_4212; Page: 7B; Enumeration District: 7-11. See also: Barton, A History of Duchesne County, 124.

102. Dillman, Early History of Duchesne County, 256.

103. Year: 1910; Census Place: Harper, Carbon, Utah; Roll: T624_1603; Page: 25A; Enumeration District: 0034; FHL microfilm: 1375616.

104. Year: 1920; Census Place: Blue Bell, Duchesne, Utah; Roll: T625_1862; Page: 3A; Enumeration District: 57; Image: 357.

105. Year: 1880; Census Place: Salem, Utah, Utah; Roll: 1338; Family History Film: 1255338; Page: 241D; Enumeration District: 086.

106. Year: 1880; Census Place: Salem, Utah, Utah; Roll: 1338; Family History Film: 1255338; Page: 241D; Enumeration District: 086.

107. Year: 1880; Census Place: Spring, Sanpete, Utah; Roll: 1338; Family History Film: 1255338; Page: 434C; Enumeration District: 066.

108. Year: 1910; Census Place: Harper, Carbon, Utah; Roll: T624_1603; Page: 24B; Enumeration District: 0034; FHL microfilm: 1375616.

109. Ancestry.com. *Web: Utah, Find A Grave Index, 1850-2011* [database online]. Provo, UT, USA: Ancestry.com Operations, Inc., 2012. The only historical record to Parley's older brother William is the 1870 Census and a homestead patent for land in Price that predates his arrival in Nine Mile Canyon.

110. Utah State Archives and Records Service; Salt Lake City, Utah; *World War I Service Questionnaires, 1914–1918*; Creating Agency: *State Historical Society*; Series: *85298*; Reel: *23*.

111. Year: 1930; Census Place: South Ashley, Uintah, Utah; Roll: 2424; Page: 3B; Enumeration District: 16; Image: 118.0; FHL microfilm: 2342158.

112. Homestead Act Records, General Land Office Database. http://www.glorecords.blm.gov/details/patent/default.aspx?accession=1103829&docClass=SER&sid=cxha5dd1.3tr

113. Francis Bowen, "Big Blow Up," *Nine Mile Canyon Settlers Association* 1 (2005): 21.

114. Year: 1930; Census Place: Montello, Elko, Nevada; Roll: 1296; Page: 1B; Enumeration District: 46; Image: 496.0; FHL microfilm: 2341031.

115. Local histories refer to the family as the Johnsons, but all census records indicate it was Johnston. A history of Don Johnston prepared by a family member spells the name Johnstun. We retain the Johnston spelling here.

116. Dillman, *Early History of Duchesne County*, 256.

117. Year: 1910; Census Place: Harper, Carbon, Utah; Roll: T624_1603; Page: 24A; Enumeration District: 0034; FHL microfilm: 1375616.

118. Year: 1920; Census Place: Harper, Carbon, Utah; Roll: T625_1862; Page: 23A; Enumeration District: 40; Image: 132. The census database misspells the family name as Johnstone, but it is clearly the same George C. Johnston family.

119. The buying and selling of Indian children was common in early Utah history. The "purchase" of captive Indian children was frowned upon by the Mormon Church, but there were several incidents when the captives were executed in front of the horrified settlers when they refused to make the purchase. This resulted in an informal policy where families would pay the ransom and adopt the Indian children into their families.

120. Johnstun, "George Carlos Johnstun," 36.

121. Year: 1930; Census Place: Price, Carbon, Utah; Roll: 2415; Page: 2B; Enumeration District: 20; Image: 215.0; FHL microfilm: 2342149.

122. Year: 1870; Census Place: Manti Ward 4, Sanpete, Utah Territory; Roll: M593_1612; Page: 50B; Image: 105; Family History Library Film: 553111.

123. Bill Lines acquired the Whitmore cabin after the Whitmore family lost it in a tax sale. The Whitmore family later reacquired the cabin and continued to use it as a camp for their cowboys.

124. Johnstun, "George Carlos Johnstun," 34–35.

125. Ibid. Miller, "New Settlement Patterns," 5.

126. Dillman, *Early History of Duchesne County*, 256.

127. *Passenger Lists of Vessels Arriving at New Orleans, Louisiana, 1820–1902*; Series: *M259*; Roll #: *39*.

128. Year: 1880; Census Place: Springville, Utah, Utah; Roll: 1338; Family History Film: 1255338; Page: 162A; Enumeration District: 082.

129. A Depression era mural in the Price City Hall identifies A. J. Lee as the Price agent for the Gilson Asphaltum Company.

130. Dillman, *Early History of Duchesne County*, 260.

131. Ibid., 256.

132. Utah State Archives and Records Service; Salt Lake City, UT; *Utah State Archives and Records Service*; File Number #: *1949002207*.

133. Utah State Historical Society, comp., *Utah Cemetery Inventory* [database online]. Provo, UT, USA: Ancestry.com Operations Inc., 2000.

134. "Minutes of the NMCSA Board Meeting" (September 27, 2008): 2.

135. Ibid., 24.

136. Dalton, "Canyon Dwellers," 1–2. Dalton, "Canyon Builders," 24–25.

137. Dalton, "Canyon Builders," 28.

138. Dillman, *Early History of Duchesne County*, 256–60.

139. Dalton, "Canyon Builders," 25. Some histories indicate the community center of Harper was the Frank Alger place, but in actuality Harper was the Edwin Lee ranch, which was a voting precinct, stage stop, post office, and hotel.

140. Dillman, *Early History of Duchesne County*, 256–58.

141. Spangler, *Of Owls and Cranes*, 29.

142. Dillman, *Early History of Duchesne County*, 258.

143. Year: 1870; Census Place: Centre, Union, Indiana; Roll: M593_363; Page: 17A; Image: 343; Family History Library Film: 545862. Year: 1880; Census Place: Center, Union, Indiana; Roll: 316; Family History Film: 1254316; Page: 43A; Enumeration District: 049; Image: 0088.

144. Year: 1910; Census Place: Harper, Carbon, Utah; Roll: T624_1603; Page: 24B; Enumeration District: 0034; FHL microfilm: 1375616.

145. Ancestry.com. *Indiana Deaths, 1882-1920* [database online]. Provo, UT, USA: Ancestry.com Operations Inc., 2004.

146. Year: 1930; Census Place: San Francisco, San Francisco, California; Roll: 199; Page: 11A; Enumeration District: 140; Image: 968.0; FHL microfilm: 2339934.

147. "Carbon County Woman Dies of Bullet Wound, Succumbs to Accidental Injury at Ranch Near Price," *Salt Lake Telegram*, June 18, 1929.

148. Aton, *The River Knows Everything*, 79–80.

149. Ibid., 127.

150. Ibid., 130–32.

151. Year: 1880; Census Place: Gooseberry Valley, Sevier, Utah; Roll: 1338; Family History Film: 1255338; Page: 487B; Enumeration District: 069.

152. Aton, *The River Knows Everything*, 130–32.

153. Year: 1920; Census Place: Roosevelt, Duchesne, Utah; Roll: T625_1862; Page: 8A; Enumeration District: 65; Image: 522.

154. Dillman, *Early History of Duchesne County*, 281.

155. Ibid., 256.

156. Year: 1880; Census Place: Bellevue, Kane, Utah; Roll: 1336; Family History Film: 1255336; Page: 429A; Enumeration District: 028.

157. Dillman, *Early History of Duchesne County*, 280.

158. Utah State Historical Society, comp., *Utah Cemetery Inventory* [database online]. Provo, UT, USA: Ancestry.com Operations Inc., 2000. As beloved as Neal Hanks was, Minerva Hanks had a reputation among canyon residents as a somewhat difficult woman to be around.

159. Aton, *The River Knows Everything*, 133–34.

160. William Miller, "New Settlement Patterns," 7.

161. Ibid., 8.

162. 1900 Federal Census Enumeration District 86, Sheet 11 and 12, 1910 Federal Census Enumeration District 44 Sheet 10 and 11, and General Land Office Historical Index for Township 11 South Ranges 14, 15, and 17 East and Township 12 South Ranges 13, 14, 15, 16, and 17 East Salt Lake Meridian.

163. William Miller, "New Settlement Patterns," 8.

164. Desert Land Act Patent, General Land Office Database. http://www.glorecords.blm.gov/details/patent/default.aspx?accession=UTUTAA%20018724&docClass=SER&sid=wgetnwzi.dou.

165. Desert Land Act Patent, General Land Office Database. http://www.glorecords.blm.gov/details/patent/default.aspx?accession=UTUTAA%20018636&docClass=SER&sid=yxodndgc.nkc.

166. Desert Land Act Patent, General Land Office Database. http://www.glorecords.blm.gov/details/patent/default.aspx?accession=UTUTAA%20018635&docClass=SER&sid=yxodndgc.nkc.

167. Desert Land Act Patent, General Land Office Database. http://www.glorecords.blm.gov/details/patent/default.aspx?accession=UTUTAA%20018637&docClass=SER&sid=yxodndgc.nkc.

168. General Land Office Database. http://www.glorecords.blm.gov/details/patent/default.aspx?accession=UTUTAA%20018617&docClass=SER&sid=yxodndgc.nkc.

169. General Land Office Database. http://www.glorecords.blm.gov/details/patent/default.aspx?accession=UTUTAA%20018722&docClass=SER&sid=yxodndgc.nkc.

170. General Land Office Database. http://www.glorecords.blm.gov/details/patent/default.aspx?accession=UTUTAA%20018795&docClass=SER&sid=yxodndgc.nkc. http://www.glorecords.blm.gov/details/patent/default.aspx?accession=UTUTAA%20018723&docClass=SER&sid=yxodndgc.nkc.

171. The canyon residents, when asked their occupation, used the words "rancher" and "farmer" interchangeably. For example, Edwin Lee and Preston Nutter listed themselves as farmers when, in fact, they were large cattle ranchers.

We also use farming and ranching interchangeably here. It should also be noted that several early residents listed their occupations as
"freighter," and they probably were, in addition
to their farming.

172. Bert Jenson, "History of the Minnie Maud
School District," *Nine Mile Settlers Association
Newsletter* (Fall and Winter 2010): 26.

173. Dillman, *Early History of Duchesne County*, 260.

174. Ibid. Preston Nutter might have made attempts
to buy out his neighbors to the east, but he was
apparently unsuccessful except for one forty-acre
parcel near Franks Canyon that is still part of
the Nutter Ranch.

175. Year: 1900; Census Place: Minnie Maude,
Carbon, Utah; Roll: 1682; Page: 11A;
Enumeration District: 0086; FHL microfilm:
1241682.

176. Mormon Pioneer Overland Travel
Database. http://www.lds.org/churchhis-
tory/library/pioneercompanysearchresu
lts/1,15792,4017-1-234,00.

177. Spangler, *The Upper Fringe*, 84.

178. Norma Dalton, "History of Thorald C. Rich,"
Nine Mile Settlers Association, no. 3 (2005): 3.

179. Year: 1930; Census Place: Harper, Carbon, Utah;
Roll: 2415; Page: 1A; Enumeration District: 31;
Image: 345.0; FHL microfilm: 2342149.

180. Year: 1930; Census Place: Sunnyside, Carbon,
Utah; Roll: 2415; Page: 1A; Enumeration
District: 29; Image: 322.0; FHL microfilm:
2342149. Note: Thorald is listed on the 1930
Census records for both Sunnyside and Nine
Mile Canyon.

181. Norma Dalton, email communication with the
lead author, March 25, 2014.

182. Dalton, "Thorald C. Rich," 4.

183. Year: 1920; Census Place: Harper, Carbon,
Utah; Roll: T625_1862; Page: 23A; Enumeration
District: 40; Image: 132.

184. Norma R. Dalton, "Clarence Adelbert Barney"
(unpublished manuscript in the possession of the
author, who derived the information through
interviews with the Jennie V. Barney family,
2013).

185. Ibid.

186. Dillman, *Early History of Duchesne County*, 260.

187. Dalton, email correspondence, December 11,
2012.

188. Dillman, *Early History of Duchesne County*, 260.

189. Dalton, email correspondence, December 11,
2012.

190. Spangler, *Nine Mile Canyon*.

191. Dillman, *Early History of Duchesne County*, 260.

192. Norma Dalton and Jerrold Dalton, "Land and
Water," *Nine Mile Canyon Settlers Association
Newsletter* (Summer 2010): 3.

193. Dillman, *Early History of Duchesne County*, 260.

194. The electronic census database does not list
the family in the 1900 Census for Nine Mile
Canyon, but the handwritten ledger of names
for Nine Mile Canyon (Minnie Maud Precinct)
clearly lists all four individuals.

195. Year: 1900; Census Place: Pleasant Grove,
Utah, Utah; Roll: 1687; Page: 17A; Enumeration
District: 0162; FHL microfilm: 1241687.

196. Dillman, *Early History of Duchesne County*, 260.

197. Year: 1900; Census Place: Salt Lake City
Ward 2, Salt Lake, Utah; Roll: 1684; Page: 1A;
Enumeration District: 0023; FHL microfilm:
1241684. The 1900 Census incorrectly lists his age
at that time as fifty, although all other records
indicate he was born in Missouri in about 1860,
making him forty years old at the time.

198. Year: 1880; Census Place: Payson, Utah, Utah;
Roll: 1338; Family History Film: 1255338; Page:
210A; Enumeration District: 084.

199. Utah State Archives and Records Service; Salt
Lake City, UT; *Utah State Archives and Records
Service*; File Number #: *1923001818*.

200. Dillman, *Early History of Duchesne County*, 256.

201. Year: 1910; Census Place: Price, Carbon, Utah;
Roll: T624_1603; Page: 2B; Enumeration
District: 0031; FHL microfilm: 1375616. Year:
1920; Census Place: Price, Carbon, Utah; Roll:
T625_1862; Page: 22B; Enumeration District: 44;
Image: 309

202. Year: 1930; Census Place: Harper, Duchesne,
Utah; Roll: 2415; Page: 1A; Enumeration
District: 40; Image: 1118.0; FHL microfilm:
2342149. Year: 1930; Census Place: Price, Carbon,
Utah; Roll: 2415; Page: 10B; Enumeration
District: 22; Image: 273.0; FHL microfilm:
2342149.

203. This perch was still there in 1989 when the lead author was involved in archaeological surveys around the ranch. Norma Dalton attributes the perch to Dave Nordell, who constructed it as an amusement for visitors.

204. Spangler, *Nine Mile Canyon*. It is interesting that Harvard University chose to use the Pace Ranch instead of the Nutter Ranch. Mildred Dillman states that Nutter's daughter, Virginia, had studied archaeology under famed southwestern archaeologist Byron Cummings (probably at the University of Arizona), and that she assisted many universities in their studies of Nine Mile Canyon archaeology.

205. Utah State Archives and Records Service; Salt Lake City, UT; *Utah State Archives and Records Service*; File Number #: *1937000245*. The stories told about the Pace suicide are suspiciously similar to an account of a Nine Mile rancher named "Ollie," who slit his own throat. It is possible the Pace suicide, if it ever happened, got confused through time with the suicide of another rancher named "Ollie." See Norma Dalton, "Oliver Rasmussen and Bill Gweythers," *Nine Mile Canyon Settlers Association Newsletter* (Spring 2011).

206. Dave Nordell was a notorious spinner of tall tales that he claimed to be fact. Norma Dalton indicates he perpetuated the story of lassoing the cougar, but in reality the cougar was killed by government trapper Willis Butolph. The carcass had frozen stiff in the winter weather, which made it easy for Nordell to use it to stage the photos of the now-legendary event.

207. Jenny Christensen, "Scary Wild Animal Stories," *Nine Mile Canyon Settlers Association Newsletter* (Spring 2010): 5.

208. Norma R. Dalton, "Caleb Gibbons Edwards" (unpublished document in the possession of Norma Dalton, derived from an interview with Francis Edwards Bowen, a granddaughter of Caleb Elisha Edwards, 2013).

209. Year: 1910; Census Place: Harper, Carbon, Utah; Roll: T624_1603; Page: 24A; Enumeration District: 0034; FHL microfilm: 1375616.

210. Dalton, "Caleb Gibbons Edwards."

211. Ibid.

212. *Year: 1920; Census Place: Wellington, Carbon, Utah; Roll: T625_1862; Page: 34B; Enumeration District: 44; Image: 333. Year: 1930; Census Place: Harper, Carbon, Utah; Roll: 2415; Page: 1A; Enumeration District: 31; Image: 345.0; FHL microfilm: 2342149. Year: 1940; Census Place: Northeast Price, Carbon, Utah; Roll: T627_4211; Page: 1A; Enumeration District: 4-36.*

213. Norma Dalton, email communication with Jerry D. Spangler, December 22, 2012.

214. Year: 1930; Census Place: Columbia, Carbon, Utah; Roll: 2415; Page: 5B; Enumeration District: 36; Image: 390.0; FHL microfilm: 2342149.

215. Edmund West, comp. *Family Data Collection - Individual Records* [database online]. Provo, UT, USA: Ancestry.com Operations Inc., 2000.

Bibliography

Alexander, Thomas, and Leonard Arrington. "The Utah Military Frontier, 1872–1912: Forts Cameron, Thornburgh, and Duchesne." *Utah Historical Quarterly* 32, no. 4 (1964): 330–54.

Alley, John R., Jr. "Prelude to Dispossession: The Fur Trade's Significance for the Northern Utes and Southern Paiutes." *Utah Historical Quarterly* 50, no. 2 (1982): 104–23.

Alter, J. Cecil. "W. A. Ferris in Utah." *Utah Historical Quarterly* 9, nos. 1–2 (1941): 81–108.

Anonymous. "William Henry Ashley." *Encyclopedia of World Biography*, 2004. http://www.encyclopedia.com/doc/1G2-3404700299.html. Last accessed February 19, 2015.

Armstrong, Erma. "Aunt Ada and the Outlaws." *Outlaw Trail Journal* (Winter 1997): 13–23.

Arrington, Leonard J. *Great Basin Kingdom: Economic History of the Latter-Day Saints, 1830–1900.* Lincoln: University of Nebraska Press, 1958.

Athearn, Robert. *The Denver and Rio Grande Western Railroad: Rebel of the Rockies.* Lincoln: University of Nebraska Press, 1962.

Aton, James M. *The River Knows Everything: Desolation Canyon and the Green.* Logan: Utah State University Press, 2009.

Bagley, Will. "Buffalo Soldiers Served with Distinction in Utah," *Utah History to Go.* http://historytogo.utah.gov/salt_lake_tribune/history_matters/081901. Last accessed February 18, 2015.

Baker, Pearl. *The Wild Bunch at Robbers Roost.* 1971; reprint, Lincoln: University of Nebraska Press, 1989.

Barton, John D. "Antoine Robidoux and the Fur Trade of the Uinta Basin." Master's thesis, Brigham Young University, 1989.

———. "The Dawes Act and the Northern Utes." *Outlaw Trail Journal* (Summer 2011): 33–40.

———. *A History of Duchesne County.* Salt Lake City: Utah State Historical Society, 1998.

Beckstead, James H. *Cowboying: A Tough Job in a Hard Land.* Salt Lake City: University of Utah Press, 1991.

Beckwourth, James P. *The Life and Adventures of James P. Beckwourth.* Lincoln: University of Nebraska Press, 1972.

Bellows, Maude A. "History of Hyrum Argyle Sr." Unpublished manuscript dated February 21, 2013, in the possession of Norma Dalton.

Bender, Henry E., Jr. *Uintah Railway: The Gilsonite Route.* Berkeley: Howell-North Books, 1970.

Bennion, Glynn. "A Pioneer Cattle Venture of the Bennion Family," *Utah Historical Quarterly* 34, no. 4 (1966): 315–25.

Betensen, Bill. "Bub Meeks: The Unfortunate Outlaw." *Outlaw Trail Journal* (Summer 2003): 2–14.

Bishop, Francis Marion. "Captain Francis Marion Bishop's Journal." *Utah Historical Quarterly* 25, nos. 1–4 (1947): 153–254.

Blake, William P. "Uintahite—A New Variety of Asphaltum from the Uintah Mountains, Utah." *The Engineering and Mining Journal*, no. 26 (December 26, 1885): 431.

Bolton, Herbert E. *Pageant in the Wilderness.* Salt Lake City: Utah State Historical Society, 1950.

Bowen, Francis. "Big Blow Up." *Nine Mile Canyon Settlers Association Newsletter* 1 (2005).

Brooks, Juanita. "The Arizona Strip." *The Pacific Spectator* 3 (1949): 290–301.

Brown, Leonard. "History of Minnie & Maud." *Nine Mile Canyon Settlers Association*, no. 1 (January 2005): 1–4.

Bureau of Land Management. Desert Land Act. http://www.blm.gov/ut/st/en/res/utah_public_room/desert_land_entries.html.

———. "Nine Mile Canyon." U.S. Department of Interior online publication (2012): http://www.blm.gov/ut/st/en/fo/vernal/recreation/nine_mile_canyon.html. Last accessed February 18, 2015.

Burton, Doris Karen. *A History of Uintah County: Scratching the Surface*. Salt Lake City: Utah State Historical Society, 1996.

Christensen, Jenny. "Scary Wild Animal Stories." *Nine Mile Canyon Settlers Association Newsletter* (Spring 2010).

Cleland, Robert Glass. *The Reckless Breed of Men*. New York: Knopf Publishers, 1950.

Coleman, Ronald G. "The Buffalo Soldiers: Guardians of the Uintah Frontier, 1886–1901." *Utah Historical Quarterly* 47, no. 1 (1979): 421–39.

Crampton, C. Gregory, and Steven K. Madsen. *In Search of the Spanish Trail: Santa Fe to Los Angeles, 1829–1848*. Salt Lake City: Gibbs Smith Publisher, 1994.

Cresswell, Stephen. "The U.S. Department of Justice in Utah Territory, 1870–90." *Utah Historical Quarterly* 53, no. 3 (1985): 204–22.

Dalton, Norma R. "Caleb Gibbons Edwards." Unpublished manuscript in the possession of Norma Dalton, 2013.

———. "Clarence Adelbert Barney." Unpublished manuscript in the possession of Norma Dalton, 2013.

———. "History of Thorald C. Rich." *Nine Mile Canyon Settlers Association Newsletter*, no. 3 (2005).

———. "Mystery of the Cowboy Bench Rock House." *Outlaw Trail Journal* (Summer 2011): 28–32.

———. "Nine Mile Canyon Builders." *Nine Mile Canyon Settlers Association Newsletter* 2, nos. 1–2 (2012): 1–54.

———. "Nine Mile Canyon Dwellers," *Nine Mile Canyon Settlers Association Newsletter* (Spring 2011): 1–2.

———. "Oliver Rasmussen and Bill Gweythers." *Nine Mile Canyon Settlers Association Newsletter* (Spring 2011).

———. "The Outlaw Cabin Below Flat Iron Mountain," *Outlaw Trail Journal* (Summer 2011): 23–27.

Dalton, Norma, and Jerrold Dalton. "Land and Water." *Nine Mile Canyon Settlers Association Newsletter* (Summer 2010).

Daughters of the Utah Pioneers. *Builders of Uintah: A Centennial History of Uintah County, 1872 to 1947*. Springville, UT: Art City Publishing, 1947.

———. *Pioneer Women of Faith and Fortitude*. Vol. 4. Salt Lake City: Daughters of the Utah Pioneers, 1998.

Dellenbaugh, Frederick S. *A Canyon Voyage: The Narrative of the Second Powell Expedition Down the Green-Colorado River from Wyoming, and the Explorations on Land, in the Years 1871–1872*. New Haven: Yale University Press, 1908.

———. *The Romance of the Colorado River*. New York: G. P. Putnam's Sons, 1902.

Dillman, Mildred Miles. *Early History of Duchesne County*. Springville, UT: Art City Publishing Company, 1948.

Endlich, F. M. *United States Geological and Geographical Survey of the Territories, 10th Annual Report*. Washington, DC: U.S. Government Printing Office, 1878.

Ferris, Warren A. *Life in the Rocky Mountains*, edited by LeRoy Hafen. Denver: Old West Publishing Company, 1983.

Fiack, Henry. "Fort Duchesne's Beginnings." *Utah Historical Quarterly* 2, no. 1 (1929): 31–32.

Fowler, Don D., and Catherine S. Fowler. "Anthropology of the Numa: John Wesley Powell's Manuscripts on the Numic Peoples of Western North America, 1868–1880." *Smithsonian Contributions to Anthropology* 14 (1971). Washington, DC: Smithsonian Institution.

Frandsen, Joel. "The Posse Shootout—The Slaying of Jack Watson." *Outlaw Trail Journal* (Winter 2000): 13–28.

———. "In Search of Lee Sage, Pete Logan's Son." *Outlaw Trail Journal* (Winter 2008): 36–55.

Fremont, John C. *The Exploring Expedition to the Rocky Mountains in the Year 1842, and to Oregon and North California in the Years 1843–44*.

1845. Reprint, Washington, DC: Smithsonian Institution Press, 1988.

———. *Memoirs of My Life*. New York: Belford, Clarke & Company, 1887.

Froiseth, B. A. M. *Froiseth's New Sectional & Mineral Map of Utah compiled from the latest U.S. Government Surveys and other authentic sources*, 1878. Special Collections, Marriott Library, University of Utah.

Fuller, Craig Woods. "Land Rush in Zion: Opening of the Uncompahgre and Uintah Indian Reservation." PhD dissertation, Brigham Young University, Provo, Utah, 1990.

Geary, Edward A. "History Written on the Land in Emery County." *Utah Historical Quarterly* 66, no. 3 (1998): 196–224.

———. "Nine Mile: Eastern Utah's Forgotten Road." *Utah Historical Quarterly* 49, no. 1 (1981): 42–55.

Gerber, Steven L., and James M. Aton. "Empires and Homesteads: Making a Living in Range Creek." *Utah Historical Quarterly* 79, no. 1 (2011): 20–41.

Gowans, Fred R. *Rocky Mountain Rendezvous*. Layton, UT: Peregrine Smith Books, 1985.

Hafen, Leroy R. *Mountain Men and Fur Traders of the Far West*. Lincoln: University of Nebraska Press, 1972.

———. *Old Spanish Trail*. Glendale, CA: Arthur Clark Co., 1954.

———. *Trappers of the Far West*. Lincoln: University of Nebraska Press, 1983.

Harmer, E. W. "Gilsonite Mining in Utah Expands." *The Mining Journal (Arizona)* 23, no. 7 (August 30, 1939).

Harmston, Ed. F. "Diary and Report of Ed. F. Harmston, Engineer, on Feasibility of Line for Railroad from Green River on Denver & Rio Grande R.R. to Roosevelt in Uintah Basin, State of Utah." Unpublished manuscript, copy in the possession of James M. Aton, Cedar City, Utah.

Hauck, F. Richard. "Archaeological Evaluations in the Northern Colorado Plateau Cultural Area: An Investigation of the Seep Ridge, Book Cliffs, Red Wash, Hay Canyon, Whetrock Canyon and Interstate 70–Exit 220 Alternative Highway Routes in Uintah and Grand Counties, Utah." *AERC Paper* No. 45 (1991).

Hawkins, Bruce. "Archaeological Survey Conducted at the Site of Fort Thornburgh No. 2 (42Un788),

Utah, 1882–1883." Unpublished manuscript, Utah Division of State History, 1981.

Hill, Joseph J. "Spanish and Mexican Exploration and Trade Northwest from New Mexico into the Great Basin." *Utah Historical Quarterly* 3, No. 1 (1930): 2–23.

Houskeeper, Craig. "Theodore Frelizing Houskeeper Homestead Cabin." *Nine Mile Canyon Settlers Association Newsletter* 1 (2004).

Jenson, H. Bert. "History of the Minnie Maud School District." *Nine Mile Settlers Association Newsletter* (Fall and Winter 2010).

———. *The Pioneer Saga of the Nine Mile Road*. Roosevelt, UT: Duchesne County Chamber of Commerce, 1984.

———. "Smith Wells, Stagecoach Inn on the Nine Mile Canyon Road." *Utah Historical Quarterly* 61, no. 2 (1993): 182–97.

Johnson, Lamont, and Joel Frandsen. "Edward B. Johnstone: The Man who Killed C. L. 'Gunplay' Maxwell." *Outlaw Trail Journal* (Winter 2011): 20–37.

Johnson, Michael W., Robert E. Parson, and Daniel A. Stebbins. *A History of Daggett County: A Modern Frontier*. Salt Lake City: Utah State Historical Society, 1998.

Johnstun, Blanch Anderson. "A Summary of George Carlos (Don) Johnstun." Unknown source and unknown date, 34–38. Photocopy in the possession of Norma Dalton.

Jordan, Terry G. *North American Cattle-Ranching Frontiers*. Albuquerque: University of New Mexico Press, 1993.

Kelly, Charles. "Antoine Robidoux." *Utah Historical Quarterly* 6, no. 4 (1933): 114–16.

———. "The Forgotten Bastion, Old Fort Robidoux." *Utah Magazine* (October 1946).

———, ed. "Journal of W. C. Powell." *Utah Historical Quarterly* 26–27, nos. 1–4 (1948): 252–490.

———. "The Mysterious D. Julien." *Utah Historical Quarterly* 6, no. 3 (1933): 83–88.

———. *The Outlaw Trail: A History of Butch Cassidy and His Wild Bunch*: 1938. Reprint, Lincoln: University of Nebraska Press, 1996.

Kiever, Ellen S. "Rejected by Many: Gunplay Maxwell." *Outlaw Trail Journal* (Winter 2011): 2–19.

Knipmeyer, James. "The Old Trappers Trail through Eastern Utah." *Canyon Legacy* 9 (1991): 10–15.

Kretchman, Herbert F. *The Story of Gilsonite*. Salt Lake City: American Gilsonite Company, 1957.

Lavender, David. *Colorado River Country*. New York: E. P. Dutton, 1982.

Leigh, Rufus Wood. "Naming of the Green, Sevier and Virgin Rivers." *Utah Historical Quarterly* 29, no. 2 (1961): 136–47.

Loosle, Byron, ed. *Carter Military Road Project: 2004–2007*. Vernal, UT: Ashley National Forest, U.S. Department of Agriculture, 2011.

Marston, O. Dock. "The Lost Journal of John Colton Sumner." *Utah Historical Quarterly* 37, no. 2 (1969): 173–89.

Mead, Ben. "From Kiz to Nine Mile—from Nine Mile Canyon to White Rocks and Back Again." *Nine Mile Canyon Settlers Association Newsletter* 1 (2005).

Miller, William. "Nine Mile Canyon: New Settlement Patterns in Utah as Seen in the Establishment of a Community in Eastern Utah." Senior Thesis, Brigham Young University, 2001.

Morgan, Dale L., ed. "The Diary of William H. Ashley (Part 1)." *Bulletin of the Missouri Historical Society* 11, no. 1 (1954): 9–40.

———, ed. "The Diary of William H. Ashley (Part 2)." *Bulletin of the Missouri Historical Society Bulletin* 11, no. 2 (1955): 158–86.

———, ed. "The Diary of William H. Ashley (Part 3)." *Bulletin of the Missouri Historical Society* Bulletin 11, no. 3 (1955): 279–302. St. Louis.

———. *The Great Salt Lake*. Indianapolis: Bobb-Merrill Co., 1947.

———. *The West of William H. Ashley 1822–1838*. Denver: Old West Publishing Company, 1964.

Morrill, A. Reed. "The Site of Fort Robidoux." *Utah Historical Quarterly* 9, nos. 1–2 (1941): 1–11.

National Park Service. "Journey through Time." http://www.nature.nps.gov/views/sites/para/HTML/ET_04_Journey.htm. Last accessed February 18, 2015.

———. "The Mormon Militia and Pipe Springs." http://www.nps.gov/pisp/photosmultimedia/the-mormon-militia-and-pipe-springs.htm.

———. "Pipe Springs." http://www.nps.gov/pisp/planyourvisit/sevents.htm. Last accessed February 19, 2015.

———. "Whitmore Mansion National Register Nomination." Unpublished manuscript, Utah Division of State History National Register files, 1978.

Nichols, Jeffrey D. "Sam Gilson Did Much More Than Promote Gilsonite." *History Blazer* (1995). Reprinted at http://historytogo.utah.gov/utah_chapters/mining_and_railroads/samgilson-didmuchmorethanpromotegilsonite.html. Last accessed February 19, 2015.

"Nine Mile Canyon School." *Nine Mile Canyon Settlers Association Newsletter* (Fall and Winter 2010): 4.

Nutter, Preston. Diary, 1919. Preston Nutter Collection.

Oldham, Ann. *Alferd G. Packer, Soldier Prospector and Cannibal*. Pagosa Springs, CO: self-published, 2005.

O'Neil, Floyd A. "The Old Spanish Trail before 1848." Unpublished manuscript, Special Collections, Marriott Library, University of Utah (1968).

Passenger Lists of Vessels Arriving at New Orleans, Louisiana, 1820–1902; Series: *M259*; Roll #: *37*. LDS Family History Center.

Patterson, Richard. *Butch Cassidy: A Biography*. Lincoln: University of Nebraska Press, 1998.

Peterson, John Alton. *Utah's Black Hawk War*. Salt Lake City: University of Utah Press, 1999.

Phillips, Paul C. *The Fur Trade*. Norman: University of Oklahoma Press, 1961.

Powell, John Wesley. *Map of the U.S. Geographical and Geological Survey of the Rocky Mountain Region*. Washington, DC: U.S. Government, 1878.

———. *Report on the Lands of the Arid Region of the United States, with a More Detailed Account of the Lands in Utah*. 45th Congress, 2nd Session. H.R. Exec. Doc. 73, Washington, DC (1879).

Price, Virginia N., and John T. Darby. "Preston Nutter: Utah Cattleman, 1886–1936." *Utah Historical Quarterly* 32, no. 3 (1964): 232–51.

Purdy, William M. "An Outline of the History of the Flaming Gorge Area." *University of Utah Anthropological Papers*, no. 37. Salt Lake City: University of Utah, 1959.

Quaife, Milo Milton, ed. *Kit Carson's Autobiography.* Chicago: Lakeside Press, 1935.

Rasmussen, Myrna. "Alfred and Shadrach Lunt." Unpublished family biography, no date.

Reagan, Albert B. "Forts Robidoux and Kit Carson in Northeastern Utah." *New Mexican Historical Review* 10 (1935).

———. "Some Notes on the History of the Uintah Basin, in Northeastern Utah, to 1850." *Utah Academy of Sciences, Arts and Letters* 11 (1934): 55–64.

Reynolds, Thurssey Jesson, comp. *Builders of Uintah: A Centennial History of Uintah County.* Vernal: Uintah County Daughters of the Utah Pioneers, 1947.

Rhoades, Gale Ray. *Footprints in the Wilderness.* Salt Lake City: Publisher's Press, 1971.

———. "Lost Gold of the Uintahs." *Western Treasures* 3, no. 4 (1967): 14–19.

Roeser, C. *General Land Office Map of the Territory of Utah.* Washington, DC: General Land Office, 1876.

Sage, Lee. *The Last Rustler: The Autobiography of Lee Sage.* New York: Little, Brown and Company, 1930.

Sage, Rufus B. *Rocky Mountain Life.* Boston: Wentworth and Company, 1857.

Schaafsma, Polly. "Survey Report of the Rock Art of Utah." Unpublished manuscript, Department of Anthropology, University of Utah, 1970.

Schindler, Harold. "Frederick Benteen and Fort Damn Shame," *Utah Historical Quarterly* 66, no. 3 (1998): 264–70.

Shaffer, Karen A., and Neva Garner Greenwood. *Maud Powell: Pioneer American Violinist.* Ames: Iowa State University Press, 1988.

Smart, William B. *Mormonism's Last Colonizer: The Life and Times of William H. Smart.* Logan: Utah State University Press, 2008.

Smith, Melvin T. "Before Powell: Exploration of the Colorado River." *Utah Historical Quarterly* 55, no. 2 (1987): 105–19.

Spangler, Jerry D. *Dust Up: A Baseline Site Condition Assessment and Analysis of Dust Accumulation and Vandalism of Cultural Resources in the Cottonwood Canyon Confluence Area, Nine Mile Canyon, Carbon County, Utah.* Ogden, UT: Colorado Plateau Archaeological Alliance, 2008.

———. *Fremont, Freighters, and Flagpoles: An Archaeological Inventory of the North Side of Nine Mile Canyon Between Gate Canyon and Pete's Canyon.* Ogden, UT: Colorado Plateau Archaeological Alliance, 2012.

———. *Nine Mile Canyon: The Archaeological History of an American Treasure.* Salt Lake City: University of Utah Press, 2012.

———. "Nine Mile, Minnie Maud, and the Mystery of a Place Name." *Utah Historical Quarterly* 79, no. 1 (2011): 42–51.

———. *Of Owls and Cranes: A Cultural Resource Inventory in Middle Nine Mile Canyon.* Ogden, UT: Colorado Plateau Archaeological Alliance, 2011.

———. *Paradigms and Perspectives Revisited: A Class I Overview of Cultural Resources in the Uinta Basin and Tavaputs Plateau.* Ogden, UT: Uinta Research, 2002.

———. *The Pete's Canyon Complex: Formal Site Documentation and Analysis of Visitor Impacts in Nine Mile Canyon, Duchesne County, Utah.* Ogden, UT: Colorado Plateau Archaeological Alliance, 2011.

———. "Samuel H. Gilson." *Outlaw Trail Journal* (Summer 2012): 43–52.

———. "Site Distribution and Settlement Patterns in Lower Nine Mile Canyon: The Brigham Young University Surveys of 1989–91." Master's thesis, Brigham Young University, 1993.

———. *The Upper Fringe: Archaeological Inventory in Upper Nine Mile Canyon, Carbon County, Utah.* Ogden: Colorado Plateau Archaeological Alliance, 2011.

———. *Vermillion Dreamers and Sagebrush Schemers: An Overview of Human Occupation in the House Rock Valley and Eastern Arizona Strip.* Ogden, UT: Colorado Plateau Archaeological Alliance, 2007.

Spangler, Jerry D., and Donna K. Spangler. *Horned Snakes and Axle Grease: A Roadside Guide to the Archaeology, History, and Rock Art of Nine Mile Canyon.* Salt Lake City: Uinta Publishing, 2003.

———. *Treasures of the Tavaputs.* Ogden, UT: Colorado Plateau Archaeological Alliance, 2007.

Standing, A. R. "Through the Uintas: History of the Carter Road." *Utah Historical Quarterly* 35, no. 3 (1967): 256–67.

Stertz, Derek A. "Carter Road History." In *Carter Military Road Project: 2004–2007*, edited by Byron Loosle. Vernal, UT: Ashley National Forest, U.S. Department of Agriculture, 2011.

Sumner, John C. "J. C. Sumner's Journal." *Utah Historical Quarterly* 25, nos. 1–4 (1947): 108–24.

Taylor, Janet. "A Tough Cattleman in a Tough Land: Preston Nutter," *The Outlaw Trail Journal* (Summer 2001): 37–44.

Thompson, Gregory. *Faded Footprints: The Lost Rhoades Gold Mines and Other Hidden Treasures of the Uintas.* Salt Lake City: Dream Garden Press, 2006.

Tripp, Bryce T. "Gilsonite: An Unusual Utah Resource." *Utah Geological Survey Notes* 36, no. 3 (2004): 1–7.

U.S. Forest Service. "Carter Military Road History." http://www.fs.usda.gov/detail/ashley/learning/history-culture/?cid=fsm9_002401. Last accessed February 18, 2015.

U.S. Geological Survey. *Relief Map of Utah.* Washington, DC: U.S. Geological Survey, 1947.

Van Cott, John W. *Utah Place Names: A Comprehensive Guide to the Origins of Geographic Names.* Salt Lake City: University of Utah Press, 1990.

Walker, Karine. "Uinta Basin's Black Gold." *Outlaw Trail Journal* (Summer 2005): 2–32.

Warner, Matt. *The Last of the Bandit Riders… Revisited.* Salt Lake City: Big Moon Traders, 2000.

Warner, Ted J., ed. *The Dominguez-Escalante Journal.* Translated by Fray Angelico Chavez. Provo: Brigham Young University Press, 1976.

Watt, Ronald G. *A History of Carbon County.* Salt Lake City: Utah State Historical Society, 1997.

Webb, Roy. *Register of the Records of the Preston Nutter Corporation (1876–1981).* Manuscript Collection, Special Collections, University of Utah Library, 1987.

Weber, David D. *The Taos Trappers.* Norman: University of Oklahoma Press, 1970.

Weicks, Gary. "Fort Duchesne Twilight Years: Countdown to Shutdown of a Frontier Army Post." *Outlaw Trail Journal* (Summer 2012): 23–34.

———. "Frontier Soldiering in Nine Mile Canyon." *Outlaw Trail Journal* (Summer 2011): 2–21.

Wilson, Pearl. *A History of Juab County.* Salt Lake City: Utah State Historical Society, 1999.

Wimmer, Kent. "My School Days in Nine Mile Canyon." *Nine Mile Canyon Settlers Association Newsletter* (Fall and Winter 2010).

———. "Ralph Gibboney." *Nine Mile Canyon Settlers Association Newsletter* 1 (2006).

Woodard, Douglas D. "The Legend of Sam Gilson." Unpublished manuscript, Utah State Historical Society, 1981.

Worster, Donald. *A River Running West: The Life of John Wesley Powell.* New York: Oxford University Press, 2001.

Yates Publishing, *U.S. and International Marriage Records, 1560–1900* (online database). Provo, UT: Ancestry.com Operations Inc., 2004. Source number: 120.000; Source type: Electronic Database; Number of Pages: 1; Submitter Code: GRG.

Index

Numbers in *italics* refer to images.

Lee, Thesrilda, 300
Lee, Veloy, 300
Lee, Walter Scott, 300
legends, of outlaws in American West, 129–30
Liddell, Charlotte, 300
Liddell, Mary L. (Brundage), 300
Lines, Amy Catherine, 245
Lines, Bill, 240, 245
Lisonbee, Alva Leonidas "Lee," 148, 300, 339n46
Lisonbee, Elva (Christiansen), 301
Lisonbee, Shelby, 301
Little Bighorn, Battle of (1876), 75–76
Lloyd, Jessie Myrtle (Hall), 301
Logan, Harvey, *129*
Logan, Pete, 137, 147, 165, 167, 340n63–64, 341n101
Long, George, 183
Longabaugh, Harry A. "Sundance Kid," *129*
Lost Rhoades Mine, 22, 335n9
lottery, and homesteading in Uintah Basin, 207–8
Lovejoy, A. L., 35
Lunt, Alfred, 95, 301, 335n14
Lunt, Ann (Pitt), 96
Lunt, Shadrach, 95–97, 116, 232, 301, 336n20; home in Nephi, *97*
Lyman, Chester, 301
Lyman, Claude E., 301
Lyman, Edna C., 301
Lyman, Elizabeth A., 302, 263–64
Lyman, George, 302
Lyman, Ira D., 263–64, 302

Mack, Paddy, 144
Madson, Christian, 303
mail service, 84
Mair, Ellen Pearl (Hamilton), 303
marriage, and interconnectedness of families in Nine Mile Canyon, 233–37, 265. *See also* divorces
Marriott Library (University of Utah), 156
Masonic Lodge, 161
Mathis, Reed, 170
Maxwell, Ada (Slaugh), 120, 137, 138, 143, 144, 146, 147, 165, 340n64
Maxwell, Clarence Lewis "Gunplay," 118–19, 133, 134, 136–47, *138*, *140*, *144*, *145*, 148, 150, 164, 167, 270, 339n30, 339n43, 340n63, 340n80, 342n46
Maxwell, Myrtle Bliss, 137
McClain, Isaac, 302
McCourt, Rhoda B. (Brundage), 302
McCoy, Fred M., 302

McCoy, Julia Amy, 302
McCoy, Linn H., 302
McCoy, William Walter, 176, 177–78, 302–3
McGuire, Billy, 134–35, 344n89
McGuire, W. G., 178
McIntire, John O., 303
McIntyre, Robert, 98
McKee, Almira, 303
McPherson, Jim, 148, *149*, 150, 167
Mead, Ben, 222, 266
Mead, Ellen (Workman), 222–23, 303
Mead, Meril E., 222–23, 303
Meeker, Nathaniel, 161
Meeker War (1879), 71, 331n62, 342n29
Meeks, Henry Rhodes (Bub), Jr., 132, 164
Mexico, and forty-second parallel, 327n9
Milburn, Chub, *140*
Miles, Lorenea (or Lorenzo), 303
Miles, Lucretia (Wightman), 250, 258–59, 303–4
Miles, Ruby V., 304
Miles, William Allen, 258–59, 265–66, 304, 325n15; ranch, *260*
Miller, William, 68, 94, 95, 113, 216–17, 219, 221, 224, 227–28, 233, 247–48, 249
Millett, Matthew F., 304
Mills, Jerald, 304
Milton, L. H., 178
mining industry. *See* coal workers; Gilsonite
Minnie Maud Canyon, 227
Minnie Maud Creek, 16, 18, 227
Mitchell, Thomas, 114, 115, 116, 304
Mojave Cattle Company, 169
Montana Bob, *222*, 223
Morgan, Dale, 14, 30–31, 326n21, 328n28
Morgan, Ellen Gertrude (Smithson), 304
Morgan, Fern (Casady), 304
Mormon Migration database, 216
Mormon Pioneer Overland Database, 216
Mormons: and Black Hawk War, 94; and cattle ranching, 342n56; Samuel Gilson as U.S. Marshal and federal campaign against polygamy, 45–51; settlement of in Nine Mile Canyon, 219–23, 272; shift in attitudes toward settlement in Uintah Basin, 201–3, 345n27; and uniqueness of history of Nine Mile Canyon due to settlement outside patterns established by, 3
Morris, Charles E., 304
Mott, Julia Ann, 225
Mountain Meadows Massacre, 46, *47*

mules, and Preston Nutter, 155
Murray, Bernard, 304–5
Myton, H. P., 171, 181

Nagel, Charles, 58
Native Americans: and buffalo soldiers, 334n35; changes in federal Indian policy and economic decline of Nine Mile Canyon, 201–13; and early history of Nine Mile Canyon, 3–4; and Gilsonite, 51, *52*; and purchase of Indian scrip by Preston Nutter, 169, 170; and slavery in early Utah history, 350n119; and views of land ownership, 345n28. *See also* Arapaho; Sioux; Utes
Nelson, Pete. *See* Logan, Pete
Nelson, William, 46
Niles, John, 182–83
Nine Mile Canyon: cattle ranching and early history of, 94–106; date of first Euro-American presence in, 92; economic decline and decrease of population after 1910, 189–213; family histories on life in, 214–66; freighting and history of, *64*, 65–88, 106–25; fur trappers and discovery of, 20–39; Gilsonite and mining industry in, 40–63; history of in context of Old West, 267–72; and industrialization in 2000s, 89; Native Americans and history of, 3–4, 91–92; origins of name, 13–19; and outlaw era of 1890 to 1909, 127–52; present status of, 4, 266, 267; Preston Nutter and cattle ranching in, 153–87; remnants of historical structures in, 91; and settlement patterns established by Mormon Church, 3; as transportation corridor in prehistoric period, 91–92
Nine Mile Canyon Settlers Association, 216
Nine Mile Creek, *10*: beaver population of, 24; earliest references to, 13; importance of as water source, 9; naming of, 18–19
Nine Mile Road: demise of as major economic thoroughfare, 189–91; and history of Nine Mile Canyon, 65–88; homesteading and increase in use of, 208–9; impact of Uintah Railway on, 201; and northern fringe of Nine Mile Canyon, 261
Nordell, Dave, 259, 260, 352n203, 353n206
Northwest Territory, and forty-second parallel, 327n9
Nutter, Catherine, 175, *175*, 176, 187
Nutter, Christopher and Catherine Pugh, 157
Nutter, Cleveland, 176
Nutter, Grace (Gordon), 176, 305
Nutter, Harold Stanley, 176, 305
Nutter, Jasper, 176, 305

Nutter, Katherine (daughter of Katherine Fenton Nutter), 305
Nutter, Katherine (Fenton), 174–76, *175*, 180, 186–87, 209, 305
Nutter, Preston, 96, 106, 122, 123, 148, 150–52, 153–87, *153*, *155*, *179*, *186*, 246, 256, 265–66, 268, 269, 271, 305, 341n5, 341n21, 342n27, 343n58, 343n69, 344n102, 351n171, 352n174
Nutter, Talmage Cleveland, 305
Nutter Corporation, 172, 178, 187

Odekirk, I. W., 195
O'Fallon, Mabel (Lyman), 305–6
Ogden Standard, 61
Old Spanish Trail, 22
Olsen, Blaine, 306
Olsen, Byron L., 306
Olsen, E. K., 181
Olsen, Frank H., 306
Olsen, John Henry, 252, 306
Olsen, Marian, 306
Olsen, Olive, 252, 306
Olen Canyon, 252
O'Neil, Floyd, 21
oral history, and family histories of life in Nine Mile Canyon, 214–66
Ouray, Chief (Ute), 158, *159*
Ouray Agency, 71
"Outlaw Cabin," 148
outlaws: and cattle ranching in Nine Mile Canyon, 164–67; and Nine Mile Canyon in era of 1890 to 1909, 127–52, 269–70, 272, 340n55
Outlaw Trail, The (Kelly), 127
Outlaw Trail Journal (Taylor), 156

Pace, Carlyle, 260, *261*
Pace, John Albert, 259–60, 306, 353n105; ranch, *260*
Pace, Ada (Cottam), 259–60
Packer, Alferd G., *158*, 158–60, 341n12, 341n15–16, 341n21
Panic of 1893, 132
Park City Road, *67*, 73, 74
Parker, Lt. J. C., 69
Parker, Robert Leroy, *129*
Patrick, M. T., 46
Patterson, Jody, 68
Patterson, Richard, 127
Paulk, Hyrum, 111–12
Peabody Museum (Harvard University), 25